MEMORY DISORDERS
IN CLINICAL PRACTICE

Dedicated to my parents
Phulan Rani and Dwarka Nath Kapur

Memory Disorders in Clinical Practice

Narinder Kapur

Wessex Neurological Centre,
Southampton, UK

 LAWRENCE ERLBAUM ASSOCIATES, PUBLISHERS
Hove (UK)   Hillsdale (USA)

Copyright © 1994 by Lawrence Erlbaum Associates Ltd.
    All rights reserved. No part of this book may be reproduced in any
    form, by photostat, microform, retrieval system, or any other
    means without the prior written permission of the publisher.

First published by Butterworth & Co. (Publishers) Ltd, 1988

This edition published by:
Lawrence Erlbaum Associates Ltd., Publishers
27 Palmeira Mansions
Church Road
Hove
East Sussex, BN3 2FA
U.K.

British Library Cataloguing in Publication Data
A catalogue record for this title is available from the British Library

ISBN 0-86377-357-5

Printed and bound in the United Kingdom by Page Bros, Norwich, Norfolk.

Preface

'My purpose in this work is to provide a psychological monograph upon the diseases of memory . . . The phenomena of memory have often been investigated, but never from a pathological viewpoint', thus wrote Ribot (1885) approximately 100 years ago. The study of memory disorders has advanced considerably since Ribot's contribution. However, although numerous articles and several books have been published in recent years in this area, there remain two serious limitations in this body of literature. First, Ribot's original aspiration appears in part to have remained unfulfilled. Thus, there has been relatively limited discussion of memory disorders from the perspective of clinical pathology. The pioneering volume of Lishman (1978) has highlighted the importance of considering neuropsychiatric abnormalities in terms of specific cerebral diseases, but there has been, until very recently, an absence of any such approach to the study of neuropsychological conditions such as memory disorders. Second, in the area of memory disorders there has been, in my opinion, an excessive preoccupation with the amnesic syndrome, and comparatively little attention to other memory disorders, which may often be less severe and less pure than those seen in amnesia, but which occur much more frequently in routine neurological practice and may be more pressing from the standpoint of practical management. I hope, therefore, that this book will help to redress the balance in respect of these two deficiencies.

Although I have tried to be as comprehensive as possible in my coverage of previous research, a certain degree of selectivity is inevitable in an enterprise of this type. First, while the framework of the book is clinical, my primary focus has been on objective studies of memory disorder rather than simple clinical descriptions of memory impairment, and my coverage of the latter has therefore been relatively limited. Second, this book is principally concerned with acquired neurological disorders, and so most congenital and psychiatric conditions are not covered in depth, although I occasionally refer to them where they relate to particular neurological problems. Third, I have made limited reference to articles where a group of neurological patients has consisted of a mixture of aetiologies – this is not to decry the contribution made by such studies, but such evidence is obviously difficult to interpret in the context of the approach adopted in this book.

Narinder Kapur
March 1987

Acknowledgements

'It is not our patient who is dependent on us, but we who are dependent on him. By serving him, we are not obliging him; rather, by giving us the privilege to serve him, he is obliging us.'

Mahatma Gandhi

It is a pleasure to be able to record the assistance of those who have helped me in this venture, although shortage of space limits the scope of my acknowledgements. My secretary, Judy Moody, has shared almost every part of this work from its beginnings to the point of publication. Her dedication and kindness throughout this period have been invaluable. An exercise such as that entailed in producing this book can benefit considerably if a colleague has the time and expertise to read through the manuscript line-by-line and to help in bibliographic tasks. I am fortunate to have such an able colleague in Sandra Horn, and her numerous efforts in this regard are warmly appreciated. I am grateful to an anonymous reviewer for her helpful reading of the manuscript, and to Nick Leng for his comments on Chapter 8. I am also fortunate in having available the expertise in clinical neuroscience which is provided by my colleagues in the Wessex Neurological Centre. I thank in particular, Jason Brice, Lee Illis, Philip Kennedy and John Pickard for providing comments on certain chapters, and for the support and encouragement which they, together with the Amandus Club of the Neurological Centre, have given me over the years. I am also grateful to the staff of the Neuroradiology Department, especially Dr E. Burrows, Dr P. Cook and Miss P. Kimber, for making available the specialist resources of their department. I have made extensive use of microcomputers while preparing this book, and I thank Chris Colbourn of the University of Southampton for his advice, on this and related matters. The Wessex Medical Library staff have proved an excellent resource over the years, and Jackie Welch has been more than generous with her time and her expertise in on-line literature searches. The help given to me by the staff of our Department of Teaching Media is also gratefully appreciated. Charles Fry and the editorial staff Butterworths have helped to make the transition from manuscript to publication a smooth and pleasant one. I thank the various authors and publishers who kindly gave me permission to reproduce illustrations and figures.

Space does not permit me to mention all my mentors and those researchers who have influenced my thinking. I feel, however, that I would be amiss if I did not express my debt to a few individuals: John Graham-White and the staff of the neurosurgical unit at the Royal Victoria Hospital, Belfast for introducing me to clinical neuropsychology; Nelson Butters and his former colleagues at the Boston VA Hospital for helping me develop my interest in memory disorders; Tim Crow, Chris Frith and the staff of the Division of Psychiatry at the Clinical Research Centre, Harrow for their stimulation and encouragement.

Writing a book is a task which inevitably intrudes onto one's private life. 'A stable marriage and tolerant children are perhaps the most important prerequisites', advises Cook (1985) in his delightful article on writing a single-author book. It is a joy to be able to record the domestic bliss which my wife Ritu has provided through her love and understanding. To her, and to my daughter Sarina, I owe more than words can say.

Terminology used in text

Anterograde memory deficits/anterograde amnesia Impairment in retaining everyday information, considered to be severe if the term 'amnesia' is used. These terms correspond to memory difficulties as they are usually understood and as they are offered by most patients who offer memory symptoms.

Brown–Peterson paradigm This memory test paradigm is often used for the assessment of short-term memory. It typically consists of the presentation of a set of items, usually around three items, followed in most cases by asking the patient to engage in some distracting activity (e.g. counting backwards from a three digit number) for a predetermined time interval, usually between a range of 2 and 30 seconds; this is followed by a retention test trial for the material. A number of such presentation and test trials are administered, usually between 10 and 20 trials.

Explicit memory tests Memory tests which require conscious recall/recognition of specific information which has recently been presented. Memory instructions are usually given at the time of presentation and time of retention testing to indicate clearly the nature of the task. These tests correspond to most traditional forms of memory tests.

Implicit memory tests Memory tests where retention is implicit in test performance but not explicitly requested. The test is usually administered as a test of some function other than memory (e.g. reading, skill learning), and memory is assessed indirectly from changes in performance on the task in question. Instructions at time of initial presentation of the material and at time of test trials usually avoid any indication that the task is being used to assess memory.

Post-ictal amnesia Memory loss for events following a non-traumatic insult to the brain. The duration of this memory loss may be as long as several months. In cases of severe, permanent memory disorder this period may be difficult to distinguish from *anterograde amnesia*.

Post-traumatic amnesia Memory loss for events following a head injury, up to a period of several months. As in *post-ictal amnesia,* this period may merge with the period of *anterograde amnesia* if the patient is left with a severe memory disorder.

Pre-ictal amnesia Memory loss for events prior to a sudden, non-traumatic insult to the brain. As used here, the term refers to memory loss which lasts, in a continuous or discontinuous form, up to approximately one month prior to the insult. For periods of time beyond this, the term *retrograde amnesia* is used.

Pre-traumatic amnesia   Memory loss for events prior to a head injury. As in the case of pre-ictal amnesia, the term is mainly used to indicate memory loss for events up to approximately one month prior to the injury. For periods of time beyond this, the term *retrograde amnesia* is used.

Proactive interference   This term is usually used to refer to impaired performance on a memory test trial, where the impairment is due to interference from earlier trials of the same memory test, or from earlier memory tests or other cognitive tests. In some cases, where the category of the material-to-be-retained is changed after a number of trials, memory performance subsequently improves – this is usually termed *release from proactive interference*.

Retrograde memory deficits/remote memory loss   Impaired memory for informa-tion which has been acquired in a normal fashion prior to the onset of the patient's illness. The terms *pre-ictal amnesia* and *pre-traumatic amnesia* (*see above*) are used for relatively short periods of pre-illness memory loss when there has been a sudden insult to the brain. For conditions with a gradual onset, such as most forms of dementia, the term *retrograde amnesia/remote memory loss* is used to cover all periods prior to the estimated onset of the condition.

Contents

Chapter 1

Assessment of memory functioning

Webster's dictionary (1966) defines memory as the 'conscious or unconscious evocation of things past'. As such, the term 'memory' can refer to a variety of learned behaviours, and it could be argued that many aspects of perception and language involve the use of certain memory systems. A number of authors have alluded to the range of possible human memory systems (e.g. Allport, 1985; Tulving, 1985; Warrington, 1986), but in the present context I will mainly be concerned with the more customary use of the term; i.e. the retention of specific information which has been acquired in the recent past. It is this aspect of memory which forms the basis of most of the memory symptoms reported by brain damaged patients (Kapur and Pearson, 1983), and which is the main focus of subsequent chapters. Difficulties at the level of identification of overlearned material, as occur in the various types of agnosia and as are found in some language disorders, will therefore be given relatively limited coverage.

Impaired memory functioning represents one of the most common cognitive symptoms and neuropsychological deficits found in neurological disease. In conditions with an insidious onset, memory difficulties are frequently one of the earliest features of cognitive deterioration; impaired memory functioning is also one of the most common residual deficits which form part of a patient's permanent neurological disability. The early development of memory test procedures has been outlined elsewhere (Erickson and Scott, 1977). Many of the earlier tests of memory functioning were somewhat poorly designed, or were developed without any reference to experimental or theoretical insights into normal human memory. In recent years, this limitation has been partly rectified, with a greater interchange between research workers in the area of normal and abnormal memory function, and also between clinicians involved in the neuropsychological assessment of memory dysfunction and neuropsychologists who carry out research on memory disorders. Some of the most promising findings in recent research on memory disorders have been based on procedures originally developed by experimental psychologists. For a more detailed account of such procedures, the reader is referred to sources which have described research methods used to study normal memory (Puff, 1982; Underwood, 1983). Further sources which may be of use in selecting materials for memory test construction are indicated in Appendix 1.

Memory assessment in specific clinical conditions

Memory assessment in clinical practice may often be directed towards distinguishing between various forms of cerebral pathology, or between various sites in the brain which may be affected by a known pathology. The approach to such a clinical problem should, ideally, be framed in terms of the various diagnostic hypotheses which are tenable, and in terms of the features of memory functioning which may help to reject or confirm such hypotheses. The reader is referred to later chapters for information relating to distinctive features of memory functioning which may help in the diagnosis of specific clinical aetiologies, but for illustrative purposes I have designed a flowchart to exemplify this 'hypothesis generation and testing' approach (*see* Wood, 1984). This flowchart is shown in *Figure 1.1* and represents, in a preliminary form, the prototype of a possible 'expert system' which could act as an aid to a clinician in the diagnosis of neurological conditions that may be accompanied by memory disorder. The following sections consider in more detail some of the common clinical conditions where memory assessment may be important for diagnostic purposes.

Distinguishing psychiatric from neurologically-based memory impairment

Symptoms of everyday memory difficulty and impaired performance on memory tests may be present in psychiatric patients in whom evidence of specific cerebral pathology cannot be established, and in this section I wil briefly review some of the features of memory disorders in psychiatric conditions which may distinguish such disorders from neurologically-based memory loss. The distinction between a 'functional' and an 'organic' disorder has in recent years become somewhat blurred, especially in view of the introduction of advanced imaging procedures which may indicate the presence of subtle cerebral metabolic or structural abnormalities in patients with psychiatric disorder (Gur, 1985). This overlap between psychiatric and neurological mechanisms for memory dysfunction is occasionally evident in patients with frontal lobe pathology, some of whom may show affective and volitional changes which contribute towards impaired performance on certain memory tasks. For most diagnostic purposes, any distinction between a psychiatric and a neurological basis to impaired memory should rely on a number of observations, preferably gathered over a period of time, since inconsistencies between sets of observations and across repeat assessments tend to occur more frequently in psychiatric conditions (*see* Zangwill, 1943). In the following sections, I will review some of the main psychiatric conditions in which memory symptoms may occur, and where evidence is available on similarities or differences with memory disorder in cerebral disease. The following sections will of necessity be tentative, since there are few 'hard' data available, and since many comparative studies of neuropsychological functioning in psychiatric and neurological patients have used heterogeneous or poorly defined groups for one or both sets of subjects (Heaton, Baade and Johnson, 1978).

Depression/marked anxiety

A significant proportion of patients with depression may include memory difficulties as part of their psychological symptomatology. In an individual case, it is important to be clear as to the specific differential diagnosis under consideration.

The presence of depression itself is seldom at issue, but where this needs to be ascertained, then it may be useful to document symptoms such as weight loss, sleep disturbance, loss of libido, etc. Where memory deficits are not apparent over a range of memory tasks, especially difficult tasks which have, for example, a delayed recall or paired-associate learning component, then the question of further differentiation seldom arises, and it may be possible to indicate that depression/anxiety is likely to underlie the memory symptoms.

Where memory deficits are apparent, then the differential diagnosis may be one between memory impairment due to depression and that due to a specific cerebral pathology. In such cases, one can consider a number of features: Zangwill (1943) referred to inconsistencies in memory performance which may be evident across repeat assessments; inconsistencies between memory tests also support a psychiatric basis to any memory symptoms, especially where the two tests tend to be performed at an equivalent level by neurological patients with the condition which forms part of the differential diagnosis in question, or where the relative test scores are in the reverse direction to that which might be expected in a neurological condition. In addition, it may be useful to ask a patient, after he has performed at an average or above average level on a certain memory task, how well he feels he has done. If the patient thinks he has performed very poorly and could have done much better, this may often be an indication that high anxiety levels play a part in the patient's complaint of everyday memory difficulties.

A further form of differentiation may relate to a patient with an established neurological condition, and where there is undoubted evidence of depression. The question may then be phrased in terms of evaluating the relative contribution of both aetiologies in determining the extent of any memory deficits. This type of clinical diagnosis is perhaps the most difficult of all, and it may be useful simply to list those features of memory symptoms and performance which tend to be associated with the particular neurological condition in question, and then to assess the extent to which they are present in the results of the memory assessment.

At the clinical level, features of the patient's psychiatric history (e.g. past history of depression) and present condition (e.g. reports of depressed mood or anxiety) may help to distinguish patients whose memory impairment is secondary to depression (Rabins, Merchant and Nestadt, 1984). It is also important to gather information both on the general chronological occurrence of affective and memory symptoms, and the sequence of specific symptoms at a particular time (it may be useful to obtain information on this from a close observer of the patient, if one is available). Where the onset of memory difficulty has occurred some time after the onset of depression or some stressful life event, or where specific memory symptoms appear to occur only after a depressed mood state, then this is more likely to indicate a psychiatric rather than neurological basis to the patient's memory difficulties. The number, recency, and unilateral versus bilateral nature of electroconvulsive therapy (ECT) should be taken into account, as should any possible side-effects of antidepressant medication on memory functioning.

The number and duration of memory symptoms may also, in some cases, help to identify memory disorder based mainly on anxiety or depression. If the patient admits to a large number of memory symptoms, in the context of only mild or moderate memory test impairment, or if the symptom duration is more than several years, in the context of few other cognitive or physical symptoms, then a psychiatric basis to the memory difficulties may be more likely (Kahn et al., 1975). Further, where the patient complains of marked memory difficulties, yet is able to give a

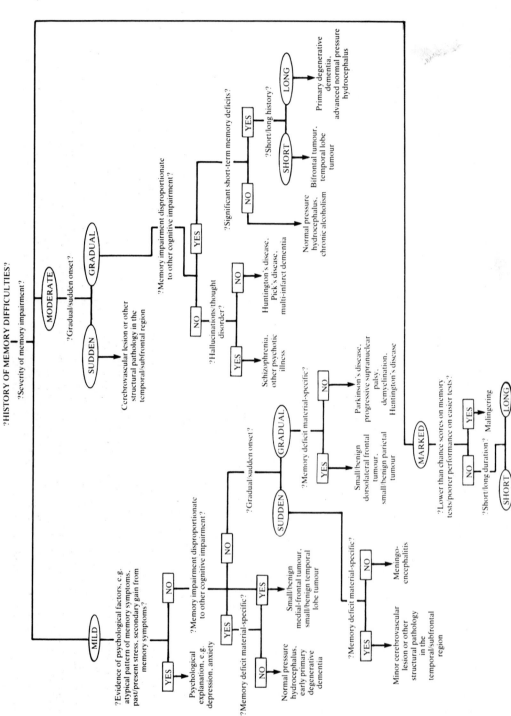

'HISTORY OF MEMORY DIFFICULTIES'?

'Severity of memory impairment'?

MILD

'Evidence of psychological factors, e.g. atypical pattern of memory symptoms, past/present stress, secondary gain from memory symptoms'?

YES — Psychological explanation, e.g. depression, anxiety

NO — 'Memory impairment disproportionate to other cognitive impairment'?

'Memory deficit material-specific'?

NO — Normal pressure hydrocephalus, early primary degenerative dementia

YES — Small/benign medial-frontal tumour, small/benign temporal lobe tumour

'Gradual/sudden onset'?

GRADUAL — 'Memory deficit material-specific'?

YES — Small/benign dorsolateral frontal tumour, small/benign parietal tumour

NO — Parkinson's disease, progressive supranuclear palsy, demyelination, Huntington's disease

SUDDEN — 'Memory deficit material-specific'?

YES — Minor cerebrovascular lesion or other structural pathology in the temporal/subfrontal region

NO — Meningo-encephalitis

MODERATE

'Gradual/sudden onset'?

SUDDEN — Cerebrovascular lesion or other structural pathology in the temporal/subfrontal region

GRADUAL — 'Memory impairment disproportionate to other cognitive impairment'?

NO — 'Hallucinations/thought disorder'?

YES — Schizophrenia, other psychotic illness

NO — Huntington's disease, Pick's disease, multi-infarct dementia

YES — 'Significant short-term memory deficits'?

NO — Normal pressure hydrocephalus, chronic alcoholism

YES — 'Short/long history'?

SHORT — Bifrontal tumour, temporal lobe tumour

LONG — Primary degenerative dementia, advanced normal pressure hydrocephalus

MARKED

'Lower than chance scores on memory tests/poorer performance on easier tests'?

YES — Malingering

NO — 'Short/long duration'?

SHORT

LONG

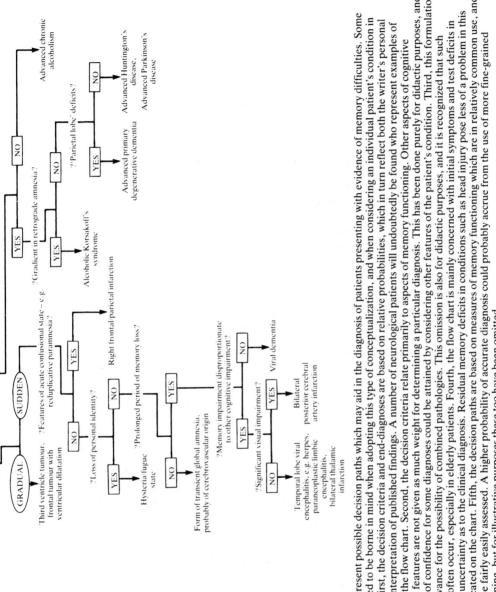

Figure 1.1 Flow chart to represent possible decision paths which may aid in the diagnosis of patients presenting with evidence of memory difficulties. Some important qualifications need to be borne in mind when adopting this type of conceptualization, and when considering an individual patient's condition in relation to the flow chart. First, the decision criteria and end-diagnoses are based on relative probabilities, which in turn reflect both the writer's personal clinical experience and his interpretation of published findings. A number of neurological patients will undoubtedly be found who represent examples of 'mis-matches' in relation to the flow chart. Second, the decision criteria relate primarily to aspects of memory functioning. Other aspects of cognitive functioning or other clinical features are not given as much weight for determining a particular diagnosis. This has been done purely for didactic purposes, and it is likely that higher levels of confidence for some diagnoses could be attained by considering other features of the patient's condition. Third, this formulation does not make explicit allowance for the possibility of combined pathologies. This omission is also for didactic purposes, and it is recognized that such combined pathologies may often occur, especially in elderly patients. Fourth, the flow chart is mainly concerned with initial symptoms and test deficits in conditions in which there is uncertainty as to the clinical diagnosis. Residual memory deficits in conditions such as head injury pose less of a problem in this respect, and so are not indicated on the chart. Fifth, the decision paths are based on measures of memory functioning which are in relatively common use, and in most instances they can be fairly easily assessed. A higher probability of accurate diagnosis could probably accrue from the use of more fine-grained analyses of memory functioning, but for illustrative purposes these too have been omitted.

detailed account of his everyday memory symptoms and of their chronological development, then this may also be a pointer towards a non-organic basis to the symptoms. Behaviour during memory testing tends to be a less certain indicator of the basis of impaired memory functioning, although there is a tendency for depressed patients to give up more easily and to offer 'don't know' responses rather than intrusion errors on particular test items.

Several studies have compared memory functioning in patients with depression and those with neurologically-based memory disorders. Cutting (1979) found that patients with 'psychotic or retarded depression' were impaired on a verbal paired-associate learning task and a visual pattern recognition memory test. From the group mean scores provided by Cutting, depressed patients performed better on the verbal learning task than patients with alcoholic Korsakoff's syndrome and patients with primary degenerative dementia (although this latter group was diagnosed only on the basis of atrophy shown by pneumoencephalography). They performed worse on this task than patients with focal right hemisphere lesions. However, only the differences with respect to patients with Korsakoff's syndrome and those with right hemisphere damage reached statistical significance. In the case of the pattern recognition memory test, depressed patients performed better than patients with right hemisphere lesions, with the first two of these differences reaching statistical significance. In terms of false-positive responses on the pattern memory task, depressed patients made more errors of this type than patients with dementia, Korsakoff's syndrome or left hemisphere lesions, but none of these differences reached statistical significance. Taylor *et al.* (1986) observed impaired short-term memory performance in a group of patients with endogenous depression, and found that their test scores were significantly higher than those of a group of patients with Parkinson's disease, some of whom also showed a significant degree of depression.

Using a group of patients with milder depression than those studied by Cutting (1979) or Taylor *et al.* (1986), Coughlan and Hollows (1984) also compared memory performance in depressed patients with that of neurological patients. The latter group was, however, somewhat heterogeneous, mainly comprising patients with severe head injury, but also including other cerebral pathologies. Depressed patients were psychiatric inpatients or day patients, and all were diagnosed by a psychiatrist as suffering from depression. Neurological patients performed worse than depressed patients on most verbal and non-verbal memory tests which were administered (*see* p. 43 for more information on these tests), and the most marked inferiority emerged on a forced-choice faces-recognition memory test (Warrington, 1984). Impaired performance on at least one memory test of each type (verbal/non-verbal) also distinguished depressed from neurological patients with a high level of confidence. A notable finding from the study by Coughlan and Hollows was that little relationship emerged between memory performance and self-rated depression in the group of psychiatric patients.

Schizophrenia

While several authors have commented on impaired memory functioning in schizophrenia (e.g. Cutting, 1985b; Kolakowska *et al.*, 1985; Robertson and Taylor, 1985), few comparisons have been made of memory performance between such patients and those with specific neurological conditions. In most clinical settings, any memory difficulties present in schizophrenic patients will seldom represent an isolated deficit, and other features of the psychiatric condition will usually be more informative in any differential diagnosis relative to a possible neurological condition. In any such comparisons, it is important to take into account variables such as the chronic versus acute nature of the schizophrenic illness, and also the duration of medication, since both neuroleptic drugs (Famuyiwa *et al.*, 1979), and anticholinergic medication used to treat the side-effects of such drugs (Tune *et al.*, 1982), have been associated with impaired memory in schizophrenic patients.

Cutting (1985b) has referred to distinct patterns of memory deficits in acute and chronic schizophrenia. Acute schizophrenics tend to show more subtle memory deficits, evident in their use of mnemonic strategies and in their memory for certain material with an emotional content. On the other hand, chronic schizophrenics more commonly display marked memory impairment similar to that found in degenerative dementia. Cutting has argued that the memory deficits in acute schizophrenia 'are consistent with a diminution of the right hemisphere's contribution to memory' (1985b), but he has not presented strong evidence in favour of such a hypothesis.

In the study by Cutting (1979), the memory performance of both acute and chronic schizophrenics was compared to that of neurological patients. On a verbal paired-associate learning test, chronic schizophrenics showed impaired performance compared to normal control subjects and to patients with right hemisphere lesions. Their level of impairment was similar to that shown by patients with dementia, and slightly better than those with Korsakoff's syndrome. On the visual pattern memory task, they were impaired relative to control subjects and patients with left hemisphere lesions, but performed better than patients with Korsakoff's syndrome or patients with dementia. In the case of patients with acute schizophrenia, Cutting found that they were impaired relative to control subjects only on the verbal paired-associate learning task, performing significantly better on this test than patients with Korsakoff's syndrome. On the test of visual pattern memory, they performed better than patients with dementia, Korsakoff's syndrome or right hemisphere lesions. Both acute and chronic schizophrenics made more false positive responses than patients with Korsakoff's syndrome or dementia on the pattern memory task, and chronic schizophrenic patients also made significantly more false positive errors than patients with left hemisphere lesions.

Hysterical and fugue states

In 1961, Lewis observed that 'there is nothing in the known psychopathology of hysterical amnesia which has not been observed in the organic cerebral syndrome'. A number of reviews of fugue states and hysterical memory loss are available (Pratt, 1977; Zangwill, 1983), and the reader is referred to these for more detailed documentation of relevant studies. Pratt (1977) has described the wandering away from normal surroundings which characterizes the initial stages of fugue state, followed either by recovery of identity and an amnesic gap for the episode or by loss of personal identity and extensive retrograde amnesia. Loss of personal identity and other personal information, together with retrograde amnesia disproportionate to anterograde memory functioning, are usually the two main features which help in distinguishing hysterical memory loss from neurologically-based amnesia (although it should be remembered that relatively isolated retrograde amnesia can occur in neurological conditions such as transient global amnesia – e.g. Roman-Campos, Poser and Wood, 1980). Other factors include the abrupt termination of the amnesia found in hysterical memory loss compared to the more gradual return of normal memory in conditions such as transient global amnesia, and the hysterical patient's relative indifference to his memory disorder compared to the perplexed state usually associated with transient global amnesia (Croft, Heathfield and Swash, 1973). Furthermore, the hysterical patient may seek help from organizations such as the police rather than medical agencies.

It is also worth bearing in mind that sudden psychogenic memory loss may often be related to stressful events in the patient's personal life. In addition, some form of secondary gain may exist, perhaps only at an unconscious level, for the initiation and persistence of the hysterical patient's memory disorder, and it is usually prudent to explore this possibility. In the case of criminal offences, hysterical amnesia has been well documented; it is particularly likely to occur where a crime of violence has been committed, and may often be accompanied by other conditions such as alcohol abuse, schizophrenia or depression (Taylor and Kopelman, 1984). The possibility should also be borne in mind of the co-occurrence of a hysterical and cerebral aetiology, and Zangwill (1967, 1983) has discussed this possibility with respect to a celebrated case where a patient initially suffered carbon monoxide poisoning, made a good recovery from this, but 5 weeks later developed marked memory symptoms which were unusually severe and were later accompanied by a reluctance by the patient to be examined any further. It is possible that in this case psychiatric factors may have helped to perpetuate and perhaps exacerbate an originally mild condition based on a specific cerebral pathology. A further instance of possible dual aetiology relates to the occurrence of wandering behaviour, with subsequent amnesia for such episodes, which has been reported as a specific condition in some epileptic patients. Mayeux et al. (1979) described three patients with this condition, termed 'poriomania', and in all three patients there was evidence both of temporal lobe EEG abnormality and some degree of psychiatric disability. All three patients showed amelioration of the condition after adjustment of their anticonvulsant medication.

Few formal comparisons of hysterical and neurologically-based memory loss have been carried out. Schacter et al. (1982) pointed to the lack of temporal gradient, whereby memories for the recent past are more impaired than those from the distant past, in the functional retrograde amnesia of their patient who entered a fugue state after the death of his grandfather; they contrasted this with the temporal gradient which is usually observed in retrograde amnesia based on cerebral pathology. They also observed that in their patient 'islands' of intact memory in the period of retrograde amnesia were those which had a strong affective component, rather than those which were related to any particular temporal sequence.

Memory loss for events surrounding a physical insult to the brain is a well-established phenomenon which may accompany a range of neurological conditions (Alexander, 1982). However, such memory loss may also occur following psychological trauma. Many instances of physical trauma incorporate some degree of psychological trauma, and it is therefore possible that in some cases both may interact to produce the resultant loss of memory. No studies appear to have reported on a systematic comparison of sudden memory loss due to a physical insult to the brain and that due to a stressful event. One study has, however, offered some evidence which may be of value in distinguishing the two forms of memory loss. Loftus and Burns (1982) were able to show that if subjects viewed a film with a sudden shocking incident, information presented prior to the incident was poorly retained, both on recall and recognition testing. While this memory loss bears some resemblance to the pre-traumatic/pre-ictal amnesia found in some neurological conditions, contrary to what is found in organic amnesia, subjects were able to offer a clear memory for the traumatic event itself which induced the pre-traumatic memory loss.

In the 'Ganser' state, which has sometimes been associated with hysterical conditions and sometimes with malingering, the patient typically offers 'approximate' answers to questions from the examiner. Few systematic studies of memory functioning in such a condition appear to have been carried out (*see* Lishman (1987) for a detailed discussion of clinical aspects of this condition). In my experience, the condition may be manifest on relatively simple memory tests such as forward digit span. For example, on hearing the sequence '5983' the patient may respond with '5982', and may continue to offer this pattern of responses.

Malingering

In general, patients who malinger will show a pattern of memory test scores quite contrary to that shown by neurological patients, e.g. they may have a low forward digit span in the absence of any dysphasia, but perform normally on more difficult memory tasks, or they may show more marked impairment on immediate than delayed recall tasks or on recognition than recall tasks. They may also be susceptible to suggestions by the examiner that a specific test is particularly difficult, and it may be useful to explore this possibility with a task where most neurological patients score well (e.g. forward digit span, short-term verbal recognition memory). It may also be useful to see if the patient admits to memory symptoms which are seldom offered by neurological patients, such as memory loss for childhood events, impaired recognition of familiar faces, etc.

True malingering may be evident in other, more specific, ways. Some psychological tests relevant to the detection of malingering are discussed by Lezak (1983). Benton and Spreen (1961) asked a group of normal subjects to imagine they had incurred a head injury 3 months earlier, and that they suffered memory impairment as a consequence; they were instructed to simulate what they thought would be their poor memory performance on a design recall task. Compared to a group of brain-damaged patients, the simulated group performed at a significantly lower level. In addition, they tended to make more distortion errors than brain-damaged patients (e.g. recalling a square instead of a circle, two small triangles instead of one large triangle, etc.), and also made slightly fewer omission and perseverative errors. Unusually poor performance in simulated forgetting may also be apparent in other ways. Brandt, Rubinsky and Lassen (1985) have described a patient who claimed amnesia for the alleged murder of his wife; he scored at less than chance level on a short-term verbal memory test, a pattern of scores which uld very rarely be found in neurological patients. Similarly, Binder and Pankratz (1987) reported a patient, who complained of poor memory and was being assessed in respect of a claim for social security benefit, and who was presented with a task where a black or yellow pencil was shown, then removed while she counted up to 20. She was then asked to indicate which of the two items had been shown. Over 100 such trials, their patient performed at lower than chance level. Schacter (1986) has been able to show that while simulated and genuine forgetting (in normal student subjects) was similar in many respects, subjects who simulated poor memory tended to express lower confidence than 'genuine' subjects regarding the extent to which their memory would be improved by cues or by a recognition testing format.

Transient memory disturbance

Transient loss of memory can occur in a variety of neurological conditions, most commonly those with a traumatic, vascular or epileptic basis. Few opportunities may occur to examine a patient during or shortly after an episode of transient memory loss. Where this is possible, it is important to assess both current or 'anterograde' memory functioning, which will usually be markedly impaired, and memory loss for events in the recent and distance past. This is because some studies (Gordon and Marin, 1979; Caffarra et al., 1981) have found evidence of extensive retrograde amnesia during a transient amnesic episode, although other studies have found this to be more limited (Wilson, Koller and Kelly, 1980). Immediate memory span and non-memory cognitive functions are usually intact in such conditions, and it may be useful to confirm this with a brief assessment (Donaldson, 1985; Gallassi, Lorusso and Stracciari, 1986). The assessment of memory functioning should be repeated within the following few days, to assess recovery of memory deficits evident during the episode and to document memory loss for the episode itself (Regard and Landis, 1984). It may also be useful to carry out a longer-term follow-up at least several months later to establish the presence or otherwise of any residual memory difficulties, since these have been reported by some researchers (Mazzucchi et al., 1980; Caffarra et al., 1981). In the case of patients who have incurred a mild, concussional head injury, repeat testing in the minutes following the injury may demonstrate delayed onset of memory loss for the event (Lynch and Yarnell, 1973). The assessment of pre-traumatic and post-traumatic memory loss is discussed in more detail in Chapter 5, and ictal amnesia which has a vascular or epileptic basis is discussed in Chapters 2 and 9 respectively.

Post-traumatic and post-ictal amnesia are usually interpreted as the period of time from the point of injury for which the patient does not have continuous memory. In a number of instances, it may not be possible to determine accurately the duration of post-ictal or post-traumatic amnesia, and one may often have to rely on particular landmarks in the patient's treatment such as his admission to hospital, events during his hospital stay, discharge from hospital and events during the first few weeks at home. Similarly, pre-ictal and pre-traumatic amnesia may be difficult to assess validly, especially if the patient in question was accustomed to a fairly routine daily schedule. In the case of both pre-ictal and pre-traumatic amnesia, it is probably better to express these as a minimum and maximum range rather than an absolute time period, since patients may have patchy memories for some events during a period of amnesia. Attempts to assess learning capacity during the post-traumatic 'confusional state' have been made (Levin, O'Donnell and Grossman, 1979; Fortuny et al., 1980). The duration of any post-illness amnesic period will depend on the sensitivity of the test procedures used, and any repeat testing needs to take into consideration practice-effects and appropriate data from control subjects.

The amnesic patient

Some patients with amnesia, more especially those with an alcoholic Korsakoff's syndrome, may lack any insight into their everyday memory impairment, and may deny any such difficulties. In some cases of amnesia, severe memory impairment may be the sole cognitive impairment which a particular patient displays, but in a significant proportion of cases additional cognitive deficits will be present. It is therefore important, in the initial assessment of an amnesic patient, to obtain some information with regard to non-memory functions. In most instances, this will consist of administration of tests such as the Wechsler Adult Intelligence Scale (WAIS), but it may also be useful to complement this with an assessment of frontal lobe functioning, since some aspects of frontal lobe dysfunction appear to be present in certain amnesic populations. In comparing an amnesic patient with others reported in the literature, the presence of such coexisting cognitive deficits together with the severity of amnesia (which will be discussed later), are more likely than most other variables to influence the pattern of observed memory deficits.

The presence of marked everyday memory impairment can usually be detected in the initial conversation one has with an amnesic patient. In the case of inpatients with an amnesic syndrome, ward staff will frequently report an inability of the patient to find his or her way around the ward and a tendency to ask the same questions repeatedly, forget information which he or she had been told, etc. The initial conversation with an amnesic patient can be used to ascertain the presence or absence of marked everyday memory impairment. This, for example, could include questions such as asking the patient whether or not he has met the examiner before. Where the patient answers in the affirmative, in the absence of any previous meetings, or in the negative where there have been a large number of recent encounters, this will usually indicate the presence of significant memory impairment. Asking the patient about current news events, what he did earlier in the day or in the previous days or weeks, will also provide evidence of the presence or absence of severe memory impairment. In some cases it may be useful to frame some of those questions around specific activities, e.g. sports, in which the patient has had a keen interest.

Most memory testing procedures used in the assessment of amnesic patients are not specific to the amnesic syndrome, and are reviewed in sections dealing with the assessment of various components of memory functioning. Squire and Shimamura (1986) have discussed the application of some of the more commonly used memory tests in the assessment of the amnesic patient. Some research workers and clinicians have used differences between intelligence (IQ) and memory quotients as operational criteria to assist in the diagnosis of an amnesic syndrome. For example, Butters and Cermak (1980) have adopted a difference of 20–30 points between the WAIS IQ and Wechsler memory quotient as representing the 'psychometric hallmark' of the amnesic syndrome. The limitations of the Wechsler memory quotient will be discussed later (*see* p. 39). As Mair, Warrington and Weiskrantz (1979) have pointed out, the scale has deficiencies when applied to amnesic patients; e.g. the inclusion of non-memory items, the lack of a delayed component to the memory tests, the limited assessment of visual non-verbal memory, etc. The net result of most of these limitations is that a patient's memory quotient would tend to result in an underestimate of his amnesia, but another feature is that patients selected on the basis of a low Wechsler memory quotient would be more likely to have impaired short-term memory, since this is the bias of most of the memory tests in the battery.

In my own clinical and research work, I would classify patients as amnesic only if they perform at least two standard deviations below the mean of control subjects on delayed (at least 5 minutes) recall of both verbal and non-verbal material, and if they showed some degree of disorientation for time (year, month or day of the week). Most patients who are significantly disorientated for a time will also be impaired on delayed recall tests, and so this in itself could be used as a brief clinical screening criterion for excluding those patients with insufficiently severe memory impairment to be classified as suffering from an amnesic syndrome. The assessment of features such as confabulation, retrograde amnesia and preserved learning are discussed in more detail in later sections of this chapter, and the reader is referred to these sections for discussion of these aspects of memory functioning in the amnesic patient.

The dysphasic patient

Dysphasic patients may show evidence of memory impairment ranging from repetition difficulty as part of a 'conduction dysphasia' to the presence of an amnesic syndrome, as in the later stages of a primary degenerative dementia. Impairments in language functioning, together with a variable degree of motor weakness in the right hand, combine to make assessment of memory functioning of dysphasic patients somewhat difficult. It is important, therefore, to obtain as accurate and comprehensive a picture as possible of the pattern and severity of language impairment so that appropriate qualifications can be made when interpreting the significance of particular test deficits. Ideally, one should administer memory tests where there is minimum interference from any aspects of the patient's dysphasia, and from any motor deficits, but in practice this may prove impossible.

For the assessment of the presence of everyday memory symptoms, it may be useful, in the case of dysphasic patients, to specify a number of examples of everyday memory difficulty, since word-finding difficulties will invariably be present and may be confused with memory deficits. Tests of current awareness which assess orientation for time, place, age, etc., may often be correctly performed by dysphasic patients since they tend to require only a single word response. However, an error made by a dysphasic patient should always be treated with some caution, more especially if the patient shows evidence of word-finding difficulty when attempting to make a response on a test of orientation, and particularly if they interchange items from different categories, such as for example offering a month in the year when asked the day of the week. In such situations where significant dysphasia is suspected, it may be useful to ask the patient to recite the items in sequence (e.g. days of the week), if this is applicable, to ensure that the items themselves can be retrieved normally. In addition, a recognition format may be adopted, and the patient asked to point to one of a set of items, e.g. days of the week, months of the year, etc. Where an error is made on such recognition test paradigms it may also be important to assess for simple recognition reading, using similar testing formats, to exclude the possibility that dyslexia may be contributing towards test deficits.

Turning to tests which require a minimal verbal output and minimal speech comprehension, picture memory tests, where patients have to select target pictures among a number of distractors, are particularly suited for administration to dysphasic patients (e.g. Locke and Deck, 1978; Rothi and Hutchinson, 1981). In addition, spatial pointing tasks, where pointing span or supraspan learning are assessed (Goodglass, Gleason and Hyde, 1970; Milner, 1971), should also be within the repertoire of most dysphasic patients. Free or forced-choice recognition memory tests are particularly suited to assessing memory function in dysphasic patients. These may take the form of verbal recurrent recognition tasks such as that used by Kimura (1963), or recurrent recognition tests where patients have to indicate whether an item, either identical or having similar features to a previous item, has occurred before (Cermak and Moreines, 1976), or two-choice forced-alternative verbal recognition tests such as that described by Warrington (1984). The latter test is the only one where detailed normative and validational data have been gathered, and is particularly useful since it allows for a comparison of verbal and non-verbal recognition memory and can be performed by patients with significant speech or motor disability. However, if the dysphasic patient in question is also dyslexic, this will obviously affect performance on visually presented verbal memory tests such as the one described by Warrington (1984).

Assessment of specific memory deficits

Since memory is not a unitary ability, it is unlikely that any single memory test will do justice to the intactness or otherwise of memory functioning in a given individual. A number of 'memory batteries' have been developed which include assessment of different aspects of memory functioning. Lezak (1983) has described many of these in some detail, and in the present section I will review the more commonly-used tests which have been published and which are relatively easily available. The major emphasis of this section is on memory assessment procedures for adult neurological patients. The reader is referred to other sources (e.g. Wilson, 1986) for information on memory test procedures for use with school and pre-school children. In addition to the procedures described by Wilson, it is worth noting the British Ability Scales (Elliot, Murray and Pearson, 1983) which have been standardized for use in the UK. This scale includes a test of forward digit span, a test of immediate and delayed picture recall, short-term recognition of visual patterns and short term recall of visual designs. Some memory tests used with adult subjects have also been standardized for use with children, e.g. the Benton Visual Retention Test (Benton, 1974; see p. 29) and recall of the Rey-Osterreith figure (Waber and Holmes, 1986).

The development of memory test procedures for neuropsychological assessment needs to take into account a number of factors in addition to the general issues of reliability and validity (Professional Affairs Board, 1980) which apply to any psychological test instrument. A 'battery' of memory tests should sample as many different, non-overlapping aspects of memory as possible, ensuring that material-specific memory deficits are detectable, that both recall and recognition processes are sampled and that some of the tests tap memory processes which can be related, at least in part, to common everyday memory symptoms. Many everyday memory situations involve 'incidental' rather than 'intentional' learning, and it may therefore be useful to have, within a battery of tests, at least one memory task where the subject is not forewarned of a subsequent retention test.

Individual memory tests should be applicable to a variety of disease aetiologies; they should also be sensitive to differing stages within a specific aetiology, and in this respect care should be taken that floor and ceiling effects are minimal. Ideally, a test should be unaffected by factors such as mood state, medication, etc., or by more general variables such as age and educational level. However, this will seldom be the case, and it will usually be necessary to gather normative data in respect of such variables. Estimated premorbid level of memory functioning may often be determined by the patient's age and educational level, and it may be useful to gather data from a test of vocabulary or an adult reading test, since performance on such tests often correlates highly with memory test performance. However, it is important to bear in mind that the effects of age and educational/vocabulary level may vary with the particular test or set of tests under consideration; it is also useful to take heed of a patient's occupational background, in case he has particular skills or knowledge which would affect any estimate of his premorbid level of performance on a particular memory task. Where a battery consists of a number of memory tests, clinicians may tend to administer only a subset of these, perhaps due to time limitations or because others are superfluous to the clinical problem at hand. It is, therefore, useful if standardization data include evidence on the performance of individual subtests administered in isolation, as well as a complete battery, so that any differences in normative scores may be evident.

An overall 'memory quotient' may be of use, especially where this relates to performance on a range of memory test procedures, but allowance should also be made for a 'test profile' to be drawn to cater for cases where there is significant variability between performance on different subtests, since the absence of change in a memory quotient from one testing to another may mask marked changes in individual subtest scores without any change in overall performance. Memory tests should be appealing to the patient, and should not place excessive demands on sensory or motor systems (e.g. vision, manual dexterity) which may be impaired in some neurological conditions.

Administration of the test should be relatively easy to learn, with minimal scope for variability in procedure between examiners. The test should ideally be designed such that 'qualitative' aspects of performance, in addition to level of impairment, may be documented. Thus, for example, it should be possible to gather evidence on the effects of stimulus factors (e.g. related versus unrelated words in verbal list learning) or of particular response features (e.g. intrusions or perseverations over repeated test trials). Where possible, there should be a delayed retention testing component in the task; this will depend on the type of material – for some types of verbal and non-verbal material 5 minutes will suffice, whereas for picture stimuli 24 hours delayed testing may be more appropriate. A delayed retention test component is critical since some memory deficits may only be apparent on delayed rather than immediate testing, and since delayed testing comprises a more significant 'memory factor' than immediate retention testing (Larrabee *et al.*, 1985). The intervening activities before delayed testing must be clearly specified. Where other memory tasks intervene they should not include materials which overlap with those in the test in question, unless this is itself a feature of the memory assessment, in which case the extent of the similarity should be systematically formulated, as in the case of some aspects of Luria's memory assessment procedures (Luria, 1976). The design of a memory test should permit the development of equivalent parallel forms, with minimal practice/interference effects on repeat testing, so that possible changes in memory function can be monitored reliably.

When gathering data for purposes of validation of a memory test or set of memory test procedures, it is usually worth keeping in mind at least four sets of validational data. First, the test should be able to discriminate patients with differing sites of cerebral pathology, both between and within cerebral hemispheres, and between cortical and subcortical sites. Second, the test should be able to distinguish diagnostic groups which may share similar clinical features, e.g. depression versus degenerative dementia. Third, the test should be able to reflect severity of brain damage, e.g. there should be a high correlation between performance on the memory test and duration of post-traumatic amnesia in patients with blunt head injury. Fourth, the test should correlate with well-validated memory tests. This aspect of validation may be somewhat complicated by the fact that there are few well-validated memory tests currently available, and the absence of any correlation with other memory tests may also simply reflect the fact that the two sets of memory test procedures tap different memory processes. The test should, if possible, be amenable to automated administration; however, where this is the case separate norms need to be gathered for manual and automated versions, if both are available.

Automated testing has its own merits and limitations, and these may be briefly reviewed. In addition to facilitating reliable, timed presentation of test stimuli, automated testing has several other advantages. It enables complex stimulus parameters to be generated and easily presented; response accuracy and latency can be accurately and rapidly processed; and, in many cases, the test procedure is rendered more attractive both for the patient and for the examiner. However, relatively few automated memory tests with detailed normative data are available for clinical use. An automated test battery which includes some memory tests has been published by Acker and Acker (1982). This includes two memory tests; a verbal recognition memory task, and a non-verbal recognition memory test. The verbal memory task entails presentation of a list of words followed by two-alternative forced-choice recognition. The non-verbal memory task resembles a Brown-Peterson paradigm, with presentation of a complex pattern followed by an unfilled delay of up to 10 seconds, followed by a three-choice recognition test. These particular tests include the advantages indicated above relating to automated test administration. In addition, the distractor stimuli for retention testing in the case of the non-verbal memory test bear a systematic relationship to the presentation stimuli. The tests do, however, have significant limitations, in that both seem to suffer from ceiling effects. For example, in the initial validation study, it is only at the 10 second interval that differences between alcoholic and control subjects reached significance. In addition, there is no distractor activity in the non-verbal memory task between presentation and retention testing, thus allowing for considerable individual variation in strategies used to perform a task. Detailed information on the performance of neurological patients other than chronic alcoholics has not been reported, and the test may well have limited applicability outside the original sample for which it was developed.

A few general limitations accompany microcomputer-based automated testing. These include the visuoperceptual demands of most tests where stimuli are displayed on a computer monitor. The legibility and size of graphic display need to be carefully designed, so that patients with reduction in visual acuity secondary to their pathology (e.g. patients with cerebral tumours which are pressing on the optic pathways) are not disproportionately handicapped. Factors such as unilateral neglect also need to be borne in mind, and alternative items in a forced-choice display should therefore be presented in a vertical rather than a horizontal array.

Test batteries exclusively based on microcomputer administration tend to neglect auditory-verbal presentation modes and verbal-retrieval/motor-retrieval response modes, and the test user needs to consider his particular test application to ensure that he is sampling a sufficiently wide range of test behaviours for valid conclusions to be drawn. In addition, general limitations of computerized testing include the cost, both in time and money, of developing procedures to display certain items such as complex pictorial stimuli. Slide-based procedures may in some cases be more suitable in this respect, and slide projectors with programmable slide presentation intervals are, in my experience, well-suited to some memory testing paradigms.

Everyday memory symptoms

The presence or absence of insight into memory impairment, the extent of this insight, and the presence of symptoms of everyday memory difficulty where none is apparent on formal testing, may each offer valuable information in the initial assessment of memory functioning in a patient with suspected or established cerebral pathology. The extent of insight may vary with the patient's premorbid intellectual level, how significant any memory difficulties are for the patient's everyday adjustment, and the extent to which a patient's memory deficits affect the ability to record and to recall specific lapses of memory. The way in which the presence of insight into memory impairment is elicited may sometimes have bearing on the patient's response. Therefore, while it may be appropriate to ask a patient a general question such as 'Do you have any difficulty with your memory these days?', it may be more appropriate in some cases to rephrase the question in terms of specific comparisons the patient can make, for example in asking the patient to compare his memory now to how it was prior to his illness or injury. A few patients with left hemisphere lesions may admit to everyday memory difficulty on initial questioning, but on more detailed probing this may turn out to be a difficulty in 'remembering' the right word to describe what it is that the patient wants to say. Such a deficit in 'semantic memory' must be clearly delineated from other 'episodic memory' symptoms.

In some cases, where the patient is unsure of the significance of memory symptoms and cannot make a temporal comparison, it may be useful to ask how he would rate his memory compared to someone of similar age and educational background (e.g. the patient's spouse). If the patient indicates the presence of some everyday memory difficulty, then it is often useful to ask for at least three further sets of information; the duration of the memory impairment, whether the onset was gradual or sudden, and the extent of any perceived deterioration or improvement in memory since the onset.

A patient's report of everyday memory difficulty is of particular significance when considered in relation to level of memory test performance. Thus, as Zangwill (1977) has pointed out, patients with alcoholic Korsakoff's syndrome may often report the absence of any memory difficulties, while showing a considerable degree of impairment on formal testing. Patients with frontal lobe pathology may also lack some degree of insight into their memory impairment, but since the level of memory impairment in patients with frontal lobe lesions tends to be somewhat variable, and seldom approaches that of an amnesic patient (Stuss and Benson, 1984), the absence of memory symptoms in patients with frontal lobe lesions is usually without any immediate significance. In my experience, most patients with primary degenerative dementia, especially in the earlier stages of their illness, will report some degree of everyday memory difficulty, and in the case of two patients with similar memory test performance, this observation in itself may help to distinguish a degenerative from a frontal neoplastic pathology. The onset, duration and presence of any change in memory functioning over the previous few months and years may offer additional information of value, but usually such information correlates with that related to physical symptoms, and as such is seldom of unique significance. The duration of memory symptoms tends, in my experience, to be longer in patients with primary degenerative dementia than in patients with cerebral tumours. In the former case, this will usually not be more than a few years in duration, and where a patient presents symptoms of memory impairment longer than this, and there appear to be few additional neuropsychological or physical signs, this may lend support to a 'functional' rather than neurological basis for the symptoms.

Perceived progression of memory difficulty, however, tends to be variable, and while it may often be present in degenerative and neoplastic pathology, in some cases no significant change in memory functioning may be reported, perhaps partly due to the emergence of more noticeable and more immediately distressing physical symptoms. In the case of head-injury patients, memory symptoms may not be apparent in the early stages of recovery but may be more prominent later, simply due to the relatively sheltered life which may be led by patients shortly after the injury, such that they are not exposed to situations which may tax memory to a significant degree.

Information regarding the presence or absence of memory impairment should also, where possible, be corroborated by an independent observer who has been in relatively close contact with the patient. Where such information indicates the presence of memory symptoms and is considered to be reliable, then the reported absence of memory symptoms by a patient suspected of a neurological disease may lend support to a diagnosis of frontal lobe pathology, or in a few cases may reflect an advanced stage of degenerative dementia. Where patients complain of everyday memory difficulty in the absence of significant memory test deficits, this often reflects the presence of psychiatric factors such as anxiety or depression. However, such a conclusion should always be made with care, since the absence of memory test deficits may simply reflect lack of sensitivity of the particular tests used, or possibly the patient's high premorbid intellectual level, and/or his use of strategies to perform well on memory tasks. At the diagnostic level, more specific information regarding the occurrence of everyday memory symptoms may be of additional value. For example, in the case of a patient where emotional factors may possibly play a part in the development of cognitive symptoms, it may be useful to ask the patient whether memory symptoms tend to post-date any period of change in affect, or whether change in affect has followed on from frustration due to everyday memory difficulties. In addition, in those patients who are taking medication which may affect cognitive functioning, it may sometimes be valuable to ascertain whether any changes in amount or type of medication seem to coincide with changes in severity of memory symptoms.

Having obtained information as to the presence or absence of memory symptoms, it may in some cases be useful to obtain more detailed information with regard to the types of memory symptoms which form the basis of the patient's complaint. This information does, however, become even more dependent on the type and severity of cerebral dysfunction underlying the patient's condition, and the value of such information may be limited to certain neurological populations. Patients with amnesia or dementia, for example, will usually be unable to offer detailed and accurate information about everyday memory symptoms. For those clinicians or research workers who wish to obtain more specific information on everyday memory symptoms, a number of questionnaires/inventories are available, most of which have been reviewed by Hermann (1982). The majority of these procedures, such as the one used by Bennett-Levy, Polkey and Powell (1980), list a series of everyday memory activities which a patient or observer has to rate on a scale ranging from 'very bad' to 'very good'. In general, such questionnaires are only of value if they are completed by an independent observer in addition to any ratings obtained from the patient. The patient's memory may be faulty with regard to the recollection of the presence and severity of particular symptoms, and in such instances the ratings obtained from an observer tend to be somewhat more reliable estimates of everyday memory difficulty.

In general, ratings of everyday memory difficulties have been found to show a low correlation with memory test performance (Kapur and Pearson, 1983), and in some cases the presence of correlation may be specific to certain subgroups of patients, e.g. head injury patients assessed several years after their injury (Sunderland, Harris and Baddeley, 1983), or alcoholic inpatients with fairly marked memory impairment (Knight and Godfery, 1985). A number of research workers (e.g. Sunderland, Harris and Baddeley, 1983) have asked patients to use questionnaires to record memory lapses as they occur in daily activities. Such information is obviously of greater validity than retrospective assessments of memory symptoms, but it can suffer from a number of possible artefacts; for example, the act of recording symptoms may make patients more aware of their everyday symptoms, and perhaps help to reduce the number of memory lapses. In a few instances, patients may display memory symptoms which correlate closely with their memory test performance. For example, Newcombe (1969) reported symptoms relating to verbal memory and spatial orientation in some patients with left and right hemisphere cerebral missile wounds.

The degree of correlation between memory test performance and memory symptoms will obviously vary with the procedure used. Thus, face-name learning performance and symptoms with regard to remembering people's names may show a high correlation, and patients with marked verbal memory deficits will usually admit to symptoms such as difficulties in remembering what someone has just told them. On the other hand, patients with significant non-verbal memory test deficits may report analogous everyday memory symptoms less frequently, possibly due to the use of verbal mediators in everyday situations to help overcome a non-verbal memory deficit. Thus, while difficulty in remembering peoples' names represents one of the most common memory symptoms reported by neurological patients (Kapur and Pearson, 1983), difficulty in recognizing familiar faces or in remembering that one has seen a face several days earlier seldom occurs as a symptom in neurological disease. Similarly, patients will rarely report any memory impairment for events which have occurred in their childhood. In instances where one suspects malingering or significant exaggeration of memory difficulties on the part of the patient, additional support for such a diagnosis may be gained if the patient readily admits to such rarely-offered memory symptoms. In general, patients who have retrograde amnesia will rarely offer memory loss for past events as a symptom simply because it seldom impinges on everyday memory activities. However, an independent observer may confirm the presence of retrograde amnesia which is evident on formal memory testing, and this may take the form of a patient forgetting significant events such as holidays, changes in occupation, etc. which have occurred in the preceding 10–20 years. When documenting retrograde memory functioning in this way, it is important to note both the sample of specific events which are used in assessing the patient and also temporal parameters (e.g. duration, chronological sequence, etc.), since the latter information is generally a particularly sensitive indicator of remote memory loss and may indicate a deficit where memory for the events themselves seems relatively intact.

Disorientation

The term disorientation tends to be used in at least two separate ways. First, it may refer to an inability to find one's way around a familiar or unfamiliar route; second, it may denote impaired memory for basic current information such as awareness of time and place. It is this latter aspect of orientation which I will be considering in more detail in this section. A number of 'mental state' batteries include assessment of orientation for time and place, and similar items are also incorporated in memory scales such as the Wechsler Memory Scale.

Benton *et al.* (1983) have described a scale for the assessment of temporal orientation which is based on a large pool of normative data and incorporates a scoring system for degrees of disorientation. Disorientation for time is the most frequently impaired aspect of orientation. In my experience, it is usually only informative to obtain responses with regard to year, month and day of the week, since some non-brain-damaged patients may not know the specific date. Disorientation for time is more commonly found in bilateral than unilateral pathology (Benton, Van Allen and Fogel, 1964), although it may also be evident as part of a more general disorientation in patients with acute confusional states following right parietal infarction (Mesulam *et al.*, 1976).

Assessment of orientation for place should ideally include both orientation for the type of building in which the patient thinks he is at present, and awareness of the particular town or city in which the interview is taking place. Patients may sometimes be aware of the former but not of the latter, whereas if they show impairment for a type of building, it often follows that they may also not know the area in which they are. The phenomenon of 'reduplicative paramnesia', where patients think that there are two forms of the place in which they are located, is discussed in a later section (*see* p. 21). In some instances where disorientation for place is elicited, it may be useful to probe further the patient's account of where he is at present, and where he might have been recently.

Disorientation for age would seem, at least on the surface, to be a somewhat different form of disorientation from that for time and place; in my experience, where significant disorientation for age (at least 2 years' deviation from the patient's chronological age) occurs, it reflects the presence of marked neuropsychological impairment, either as part of an amnesic syndrome (Zangwill, 1953) or as an indication of generalized cognitive dysfunction (Liddle and Crow, 1984). Where the patient does show disorientation for age, it may be useful to explore this further by ascertaining whether he/she is aware of his date of birth and the current year, so as to shed more light on the nature of the age disorientation.

With regard to awareness of the current head of state, while most normal and many brain-damaged patients without amnesia will be aware of the current head of state, in a few instances this may simply reflect a lack of interest in politics. In addition, knowledge of the head of state can occur in the presence of a significant degree of dementia (Deary, Wessely and Farrell, 1985), and so the absence of this deficit is of limited value. Disorientation for person is rarely found in cerebral disease, usually only in the acute stages of an illness, or in the advanced stage of a progressive disease, where patients have significant retrograde amnesia and may describe themselves by their maiden name, or name by a previous marriage (e.g. Glees and Griffith, 1952). Disorientation for person, when it is combined with marked loss of memory of past events, may reflect hysterical memory loss if it occurs in the context of intact performance on standard memory tasks and the absence of more common everyday memory symptoms (Williams, 1977).

Confabulation

In a few patients with disorientation, features of a confabulatory state may be evident, although confabulation can occur without evidence of any disorientation. 'Confabulation' itself is a somewhat loosely defined term, and from the point of view of neuropsychological assessment, no standardized procedures are readily available. Mercer et al. (1977) have, however, presented a systematic attempt to assess confabulation in certain neurological patients. They used a set of 41 questions covering remote memory (e.g. patient's birth place), recent memory (e.g. orientation for time and place), questions based on current environmental cues (e.g. the weather) and general knowledge questions which frequently draw a 'don't know' response from control subjects. Confabulation was elicited on all types of items, but was particularly evident on questions relating to recent memory. A further study (Shapiro et al., 1981) found that this set of items helped to distinguish neurological patients with mild and severe forms of confabulation.

At the clinical level, patients may be asked whether they have seen the examiner before, and if so when and where, how they arrived in the setting where they now find themselves, etc. They may also be asked about their particular symptoms and their work activities, and how they have spent the current day or previous days. In cases of severe confabulation, the patient's fabrications may be spontaneous, bear little relationship to real or plausible events, and be offered by the patient without any particular prompts from the clinician. At the other extreme, the confabulation may simply represent temporal or spatial distortion of real events; it may also be quite plausible, and may only be manifest after specific questions have been asked of the patient. If a specific set of questions is to be asked, then it may be useful to score answers to such items along three dimensions; whether the confabulation is offered spontaneously or only elicited after direct questioning, whether it is related to a real past event, and whether the confabulation is plausible or implausible. In some instances, it will not be possible to verify the actual responses made by a patient, or they may be verifiable only by exhaustive enquiry from a close relative. A significant degree of confabulation is usually associated with marked frontal lobe dysfunction, together with a variable degree of memory impairment, and so it is useful in the assessment of confabulation to include some screening for the extent of frontal lobe damage. In addition, some forms of confabulation may reflect a primary disturbance of language functioning (Sandson, Albert and Alexander, 1986), and it is therefore also important to assess this aspect of the patient's neuropsychological functioning.

A form of confabulation, where the patient's erroneous behaviour includes a partial duplication of his memory for a place or person, comes under the term 'reduplicative paramnesia'. Although this form of paramnesia may be manifest in a number of ways (Weinstein, 1969), it occurs most commonly as a form of environmental reduplication. The patient may, for example, be able to name the hospital he is in, but he may give the wrong city as its location and indicate that there are two such hospitals of the same name, or he may say that the hospital is a branch of an identical hospital in another place. Often this 'other place' will be somewhere of significance in the patient's past. Since this form of confabulation is manifest by the patient's verbal report rather than by formal memory test scores, and since patients may become aware of inconsistencies during an interchange with the clinician and may therefore offer varying responses during a session or between sessions, it is often useful to tape-record and later transcribe a patient's actual verbal reports. Florid confabulation such as reduplicative paramnesia is usually a temporary phenomenon, and it is therefore useful to carry out repeat interviews with the patient at regular intervals during his hospital stay to document any inconsistencies in response or other examples of reduplication, and to establish the point of recovery from the episode of paramnesia. Both right hemisphere pathology (Vighetto, Aimard and Confavreux, 1980; Ruff and Volpe, 1981; Fisher, 1982b) and bilateral frontal disturbance (Benson, Gardner and Meadows, 1976) have been implicated in reduplicative paramnesia. It is, therefore, important to assess in some detail visuospatial and frontal lobe functioning as well as carrying out a detailed analysis of memory performance.

A specific type of reduplicative paramnesia, where the patient believes that some members of his family have been replaced by imposters who have similar physical appearance and behaviour, is termed the 'Capgras syndrome'. It may sometimes be found in conjunction with reduplicative paramnesia for place, but usually occurs in isolation. Although the Capgras syndrome has generally been associated with 'functional' psychiatric disorders, it has also been well-documented in neurological conditions (Cummings, 1985), and generally occurs in association with the presence of both right hemisphere and bifrontal pathology (Alexander, Stuss and Benson, 1979; Staton, Brumback and Wilson, 1982). In any patients who are considered to be candidates for the Capgras syndrome, it is important to exclude purely psychological explanations for the clinical features and to interview relevant family members. From the neuropsychological point of view, the assessment should be similar to that outlined above in respect of reduplicative paramnesia for place, although it would also be prudent to include an assessment of the patient's face perception and his ability to identify famous faces from the past. It may also be of interest to explore the patient's misidentification of his family members by examining family photographs with the patient, especially those in which he is included in the picture.

Verbal memory deficits

Digit retention

Tests of 'memory span' frequently make use of digit sequences, and such tests are often incorporated into intelligence test batteries. Tests of forward digit span tend to reflect attention rather than memory factors, and are relatively insensitive to the presence of cerebral pathology. For example, most amnesic patients, and many patients in the early stages of dementia, tend to have normal forward digit span scores. Forward digit span is mainly of use in documenting a limited span which may be present in dysphasic conditions. Test batteries which sample forward digit span include the WAIS and the Wechsler Memory Scale. These batteries score forward digit span as the number of items correctly repeated on two successive trials, although the more recent version of the WAIS (Wechsler, 1981) allows for a more sensitive scoring procedure. For some purposes, examiners may find it more useful to carry out a more fine-grained scoring procedure, such as computing the number of pairs of digits correctly reproduced, e.g. the sequence '371849' which a patient repeated as '371284' would be scored as three out of a possible score of five. Backward digit span is usually more difficult for patients, and performance may depend on coding or visualization strategies used by the patient, in addition to serial digit retention (Larrabee and Kane, 1986). It encompasses a greater memory component than the corresponding forward digit span, and thus may be a more sensitive index of neurological dysfunction than the forward span score.

Since simple forward digit span scores in themselves seldom detect cerebral pathology, some researchers have extended the test to assess 'supraspan' learning. Zangwill (1943) was one of the first to suggest that asking patients to learn a sequence of digits greater than the forward digit span might be useful in detecting memory deficits. While several studies have shown that supraspan digit learning may be sensitive to the presence of neurological dysfunction (Drachman and Arbit, 1966; Drachman and Hughes, 1971), the major normative and validational studies of supraspan digit learning are those reported by Hamsher, Benton and colleagues (Hamsher, Benton and Digre, 1980; Benton et al., 1983). They described two forms of a supraspan digit learning task. One version, comprising eight digits, is intended for subjects aged 65 years or more, and those under 65 who had less than 12 years of education. The second version, comprising nine digits, is usually only given to subjects under the age of 65 who have had 12 or more years of education, although it may also be given to other subjects, e.g. older subjects who are graduates, or subjects who have a normal digit span of seven or more. Patients are given up to 12 trials to learn the supraspan sequence, and the test is discontinued after two successive correct trials. Two points are given for each correct repetition, and one point is given for a 'near-correct response', i.e. where only one digit is omitted, substituted or interchanged with an adjacent digit. The maximum possible score is 24, and if subjects reach criterion before trial twelve, they are given maximum points for the remaining trials.

Benton et al. (1983) reported that age and educational level both had a significant effect on test performance. They suggested that scores at or below the seventh percentile represented impaired performance with scores from the fourth to seventh percentile indicating a mild deficit, scores in the second and third percentiles being interpreted as moderately defective and scores below the second percentile being classified as severely defective. In their clinical population (patients with unilateral or bilateral cerebral pathology), 36% of patients with unilateral left hemisphere lesions showed defective performance, 25% of patients with right hemisphere pathology had impaired scores, and 60% of those with bilateral pathology scored in the impaired range. However, somewhat disappointing findings, in terms of differentiation of neurological from psychiatric patients' memory performance, have been reported by Kopelman (1986b) in respect of supraspan digit learning. He found that this test did not allow ready discrimination between the performance of patients with alcoholic Korsakoff's syndrome and those primary degenerative dementia, or between the scores of these combined groups and the combined scores of normal control and depressed patients.

Other digit learning tests have been used in experimental studies, although in such cases the normative and clinical data would be of limited value in routine assessment of memory functioning. In Hebb's recurring digits test (Milner, 1970), subjects are asked to recall a list of digits one greater than the immediate memory span. Different lists of supraspan digits are presented on each trial, but on each third trial the same list is repeated. Milner (1970) found that performance on this repeated list improved over successive trials in normal subjects, but not in those with left temporal lobectomy; the severity of this deficit varied with the extent of hippocampal removal.

Retention of letters and syllables

As in the case of digit span, letter span is seldom sensitive enough to prove of use in detecting memory impairment in neurological patients, and is of limited localizing value except in patients with dysphasia following focal left hemisphere damage (Newcombe, 1969). In her study, Newcombe also assessed memory of nonsense syllables (consonant-vowel-consonant trigrams) by presenting a list of eight syllables for 3 minutes, and asking for recall both immediately and after 5 minutes. She found immediate and delayed recall of such syllables to be impaired in patients with left hemisphere lesions, but not in those with right hemisphere damage. Using a similar paradigm, Talland (1965) also reported impaired memory for nonsense syllables in patients with alcoholic Korsakoff's syndrome.

A frequently used paradigm for testing memory for nonsense syllables is the Brown–Peterson paradigm (Brown, 1958; Peterson and Peterson, 1959). A large number of studies of patients with alcoholic Korsakoff's syndrome (e.g. *see* Butters and Cermak, 1980) have assessed memory of trigrams, usually consonant trigrams, by presenting a stimulus set visually or aurally, asking the patient to count backwards for a period of up to 20–30 seconds, and then asking for recall of the trigrams. A number of such trials, with varying distraction intervals, are usually administered. The findings of these and similar studies are outlined elsewhere (*see* p. 160). Few of the studies, however, have detailed normative or clinical data which would be of other than limited use to clinicians in routine assessment.

Several points are worth making in relation to the use of nonsense syllables in memory testing; first, it is important to control for factors such as association value of the sets of nonsense syllables used (*see* Brown, 1976 for relevant norms in respect of material such as nonsense syllables). Second, it is usually necessary to ask for a written response, or to ask the patient to spell his response, in order to score the patient's recall reliably. Third, tests which use nonsense syllables are of limited use in assessing the role of intra-list or extra-list intrusions, since these are more likely to occur in respect of more meaningful material such as words or sentences.

Retention of single words and word lists

Tests which assess memory for words fall into two main types – those which use a Brown–Peterson paradigm and assess memory for subspan material after a filled distraction interval, and those which assess memory for word lists, where the list of words usually exceeds the patient's memory span.

Considering the first type of paradigm, this does not as yet form part of any clinically established test of memory function, but it has been fairly widely used in research studies. For example, Butters and Cermak (1980) have described applications of the technique to the assessment of memory functioning in patients with alcoholic Korsakoff's syndrome. In the typical test setting, three or four words are presented to the patient, some form of distraction task is then performed to prevent rehearsal of the items, and after an interval of up to 20–30 seconds recall is assessed. Proactive interference, in the form of deterioration in performance over a series of trials, usually builds up, especially where the category of material is the same over trials. Indeed, this variation of the test is useful for detecting prior intrusion errors and perseverative responses in short-term memory (Kapur, 1985). Improvement in memory test scores ('release from proactive interference') usually occurs in normal subjects when the category of the words is changed on the final trial. Other advantages of this technique for assessing short-term memory are that in the case of some verbal items, the test is similar to everyday memory situations where patients may complain that they cannot remember something they have just heard; and the test is sensitive to a variety of forms of neurologically-based memory impairment (Samuels et al., 1971; Kopelman, 1985).

The main disadvantages of the task are that it may be difficult to prevent some patients from rehearsing items, either prior to the onset of distracting activity or during the distracting activity (see Butters and Cermak, 1974; Butters and Grady, 1977); there may be some variability between patients in the ease with which they can perform the distracting activity, so that this may have to differ slightly between patients; a large number of trials (usually at least 10) often have to be administered before any meaningful amount of data can be gathered; and, where patients are performing badly on the test, some may find it rather distressing after a few trials have been administered. Finally, the verbal recall version, which is the most frequently adopted paradigm, cannot meaningfully be given to dysphasic patients.

Turning to word-list recall, this has been used in a wider range of neurological studies than the Brown–Peterson task, and more clinically relevant data have been gathered regarding the performance of neurological patients. In the prototypical situation, a list of 10–15 words is read by the examiner at a rate of one word every 2 seconds, the patient is then asked for immediate recall of the words in any order ('free recall'). Usually, several such presentation and recall trials are administered, and in some test settings a delayed recall trial, usually around 30 minutes later, is also given. Word-list recall forms part of the Adult Memory and Information Processing Battery described later (see p. 43). Two individual word-list recall tasks which have achieved some degree of clinical acceptability are the Rey auditory verbal learning test (RAVLT) and the Buschke word-list learning test.

The RAVLT (Rey, 1964; see Lezak, 1983 for details of administration) requires the immediate, free recall of a list of 15 common nouns (list A) which have been spoken by the examiner at a one-per second rate. Five such presentation and recall trials are administered, and recall on trial five is followed by administration of a second list of 15 nouns (list B). Presentation and recall instructions for this list are identical to those for list A, but only one presentation-recall sequence is followed. Following the recall trial, the patient is asked for a further recall of list A. Lezak (1983) has described a recognition memory test which may follow this recall of list A. This comprises 50 words, the 30 items in lists A and B, and 20 new, 'distractor' words. Rey (1964) has provided some limited norms for performance on trials one to five for list A, and Lezak has also provided some normative and clinical data from a research study for trials 5 and 6 for list A (based on the performance of 26 control subjects and 17 head-injured patients). Although Lezak (1983) indicated the possibility of administering a delayed (30 minute) recall trial, little clinical or control data have been reported for such a procedure. Rosenberg, Ryan and Prifitera (1984) have indicated that the RAVLT can distinguish between patients classified as impaired or unimpaired according to their scores on the Wechsler Memory Scale (their group included both neurological and psychiatric patients). Query and Megran (1983) have published more detailed normative data on the RAVLT, presenting recall and recognition data from subjects with an age range of 19–81 years (although the recognition data relate to memory for list A items, and not for both lists as in the procedure described by Lezak (1983)). They indicated that none of these control subjects was 'severely brain-damaged', although they did not indicate whether mild or moderate degrees of cerebral pathology were excluded in the screening process. In addition, subjects in the young age groups scored close to ceiling levels on the recognition part of the test, and it is possible that this portion of the task may not detect minor degrees of memory impairment. In most situations where subjects are asked for free recall of word-list material, they will offer the last items first, followed by items from the beginning of the list, and then items from the middle of the list. In such cases, items from the end of the list would be repeated by the subject from an 'echoic' memory similar to that used in digit span memory tests; it would seem wise to eliminate or somehow control for this portion of free recall, especially since this 'short-term memory' component is relatively insensitive in detecting memory deficits in a number of neurological conditions (e.g. Brooks, 1975).

Buschke has described two word-list learning paradigms – the selective reminding test and the restricted reminding test (Buschke 1973; Buschke and Fuld, 1974). In the selective reminding test, free recall of a spoken word-list is assessed in the usual way on the first recall trial. On subsequent trials, however, only those words are presented which have not been recalled in the preceding recall trial. This is continued until perfect recall is attained by the subject. In the restricted reminding version of the task, subsequent presentation trials only include those words which have not been recalled on any of the preceding recall trials, and recall is terminated when all the words from the list have been recalled at least once. Buschke has argued that by detailed analysis of recall performance on the selective reminding test it is possible to distinguish various aspects of storage and retrieval processes in the individual patient. Some research workers have outlined a theoretical framework for the test along these lines (Kraemer *et al.*, 1983). However, the terms 'storage' and 'retrieval' have such varied connotations, and are probably both material-specific and specific to retention testing paradigms (e.g. the temporal parameters of the storage in question), so that their use in word-list learning contexts must of necessity be somewhat arbitrary and specific to the paradigm in question. Lezak (1983) has also criticized the use of words from a single category in some of Buschke's early studies, since this may be conducive to guessing responses which are difficult to distinguish from true recall. A number of researchers have provided clinical and some normative data with regard to the performance of a wide range of patients, including those with head injury (Levin, Benton and Grossman, 1982), primary degenerative dementia (Fuld, 1982) and alcoholic Korsakoff's syndrome (Buschke and Fuld, 1974). Hannay and Levin (1985) have gathered a large amount of normative data on parallel forms of the selective reminding test.

Recurrent recognition testing paradigms such as those used by Kimura (1963) may also be useful in assessing memory for word-list material. A version of such a task might be where patients are presented with a list of items, some of which recur, and the patient simply indicates whether an item has been seen previously. This type of task has proved to be useful in the assessment of patients with focal cortical lesions and patients with amnesia (Milner and Teuber, 1968). The advantages of such a task are that it is less taxing for patients to perform than free recall tests, and it is easy to vary the number of items between presentation and testing. The procedure may also usefully pick up false-positive responses, especially where there are similarities between repeating items and non-repeating items. In addition, such a paradigm is easily amenable to the construction of analogous verbal and non-verbal forms. The main disadvantages of the test are that it may not be so sensitive a test of short-term memory as one which employs a recall paradigm, and perhaps does not relate as closely to some everyday memory symptoms as certain recall tasks.

Verbal paired-associate learning

Verbal paired-associate learning tasks have long been used as a means for assessing learning ability in patients with suspected or established neurological disease. Paired-associate learning represents one of the most sensitive measures of memory impairment in both neurological and psychiatric populations, and verbal paired-associate learning has been found to correlate highly with more naturalistic measures of memory impairment (Wilson, Cockburn and Baddeley, 1985). Inglis (1959) and Isaacs and Walkey (1964) have described short paired-associate learning tests, together with data from psychiatric and heterogeneous groups of brain-damaged patients. However, some researchers (e.g. Priest, Tarighati and Shariatmadri, 1969) have noted diagnostic misclassifications which accompanied the use of cut-off scores from the tests, these errors mainly reflecting the poor performance of patients with psychiatric disorder. The Wechsler Memory Scale includes a verbal paired-associate learning test which varies in the degree of association between items. Such variation has proved to be a potent determinant of the memory performance of patients with alcoholic Korsakoff's syndrome. For example, Winocur and Weiskrantz (1976) found that pairs which were semantically (e.g. table–chair) or phonetically (e.g. table–cable) associated were easily learned by amnesic patients, in contrast to their poor performance on unrelated pairs of words. They also noted that perseveration of prior paired-associate learning could be assessed by linking the original stimulus words to other response words (e.g. table–desk). Desrosiers and Ivison (1986) have presented normative data relating to the performance of 500 subjects on the 'easy' and 'hard' items in the Wechsler Memory Scale paired-associate learning subtest.

The main advantages of such paired-associate learning tests are that they are relatively sensitive indicators of the presence of memory impairment, although it is useful if a delay component can be included (i.e. recall and relearning of the items after at least 20 minutes), since in some instances delayed retention may be more sensitive in detecting deficits on paired-associated learning tasks (Milner, 1962). They also allow for administration using a variety of test materials, and in the case of tasks such as face-name learning they may closely reflect everyday memory symptoms. The main disadvantages of paired-associate learning tasks are that for some types of verbal tests the task may appear somewhat artificial to the patient. In addition, manual administration of paired-associate learning tests requires some degree of practice to ensure that accurate and consistent time intervals are allowed for presentation and testing of items, and for gaps between trials. A similar form of learning to that which occurs in paired-associate learning tasks has been assessed by asking patients to learn definitions of words with which they are unfamiliar. Such 'new word learning' has ranged from learning the definitions of unfamiliar words (Meyer and Yates, 1955; Walton and Black, 1957) to learning to associate words to neologisms (Hetherington, 1967).

Sentence and paragraph retention

In general, immediate memory span for sentence material will usually be slightly longer than that for other verbal items such as digits or single words. This may be due to the meaningful nature of sentence material which helps to provide semantic and grammatical cues to assist recall, and it may also reflect that fact that sentences tend to be spoken at a faster rate than that used for presenting discrete items. For example, Williams (1965) has indicated that the average adult sentence span is around 25 syllables; in contrast, forward digit span scores tend to be around 'seven plus or minus two' (Miller, 1956). However, the actual length of sentence span will depend on a number of factors, including the semantic and grammatical complexity of the sentence, and whether it contains parts of speech with 'high probability' value (e.g. the phrase 'on the other hand'). The use of sentence and paragraph material will, therefore, have the benefit of providing scope for a wider variation in number of items recalled, and they may also be of use where the examiner is specifically interested in exploring semantic/grammatical variables in a patient's memory functioning.

Although memory for sentence material may be impaired in patients with focal left hemisphere pathology, regardless of the presence of dysphasia (Newcombe and Marshall, 1967), memory for short sentences tends to be mainly impaired in patients with dysphasia (Caramazza, Zurif and Gardner, 1978). One of the major sources for such material, therefore, lies in procedures for the assessment of dysphasia. Dysphasia batteries, such as the Multilingual Aphasia Examination (Benton and Hamsher, 1978) and the Boston Diagnostic Aphasia Examination (Goodglass and Kaplan, 1983), provide lists of short phrases/sentences which can be used to assess repetition performance. Items in such tests vary in terms of parameters such as sentence length, probability value (e.g. 'down to earth' is of high probability of occurrence in everyday speech, whereas 'limes are sour' is of relatively low probability value).

With regard to supraspan memory tasks which incorporate single sentence items, Babcock (1930) has published a number of single sentences of varying length, some of which tend to be slightly longer than the normal sentence span. One of the most celebrated of these is the sentence: 'One thing a nation must have to become rich and great is a large, secure supply of wood'. Newcombe (1969) reported that anomalous sentences were particularly poorly recalled by her group of patients with left hemisphere pathology. Lishman (1987) has indicated that a patient of average intelligence should be able to achieve perfect reproduction after three attempts at learning the above 'Babcock sentence', but Warburton (1963) found that the sentence could only be reliably well learned by normal subjects under 40 years, and that some older subjects could learn the sentence normally if they were of high intelligence. However, little in the way of detailed standardization data appears to have been gathered on anomalous sentences, and one study (Kopelman, 1986b) found that learning scores for the 'Babcock sentence' were rather poor at distinguishing between patients with alcoholic Korsakoff's syndrome and those with primary degenerative dementia (except when performance over all 10 learning trials was considered), and at distinguishing between the combined performance of these groups and that non-neurological subjects (depressed and normal control subjects).

In the case of paragraph material, this has formed one of the most commonly used means of assessing verbal memory functions in neurological patients, and in some patients such as those with blunt head injury, memory performance correlates well with everyday memory symptoms (Sunderland, Harris and Baddeley, 1983). Memory for short paragraphs forms part of a number of memory test batteries, such as the Wechsler Memory Scale and the Adult Memory and Information Processing Battery, which are reviewed later. Talland (1965) assessed memory for paragraphs in some detail in his studies of patients with alcoholic Korsakoff's syndrome, and his monograph includes a number of sample stories, together with data relating to the performance of patients with alcoholic Korsakoff's syndrome and matched control subjects.One of the inherent difficulties in using story material lies in the difficulty of constructing items along precise parameters. This in turn leads to complexities in matters such as the construction of parallel forms of stories, scoring of recall, etc. Voss, Tyler and Bisanz (1982) have described methodological aspects of memory test procedures which involve the use of prose material.

In my experience, two aspects of memory for paragraph material are particularly worth bearing in mind. First, a further, delayed recall for the story material will usually offer a more sensitive measure of memory functioning than simply using immediate recall performance. In fact, it may be preferable to administer story recall in such a way that only delayed recall is tested. I have used such a modification in some of my studies (Kapur, 1987c), and the procedure I use requires subjects to make a semantic judgement on the story (e.g. is the story realistic?), and to administer an unexpected recall test after a delay of 30 minutes. A limitation of this method of memory testing is that it is mainly of use in a 'one-off' assessment with repeat testing, many subjects will obviously be aware that delayed recall will be assessed and may rehearse material in the intervening period. Second, the role of interference in a patient's memory performance may be conveniently assessed by asking for recall of two or more stories in succession (e.g. Butters, 1985). Although some proactive interference may be evident in immediate recall of the two stories, one after the other (with items from the first story intruding into recall of the second story), both retroactive and proactive interference will be more likely to occur on delayed recall testing. Lezak (1983) has described some preliminary sets of material and data which relate to the assessment of such interference, and Ivson (1986) has presented normative data for relative performance on the two stories used in the Wechsler Memory Scale.

Non-verbal memory deficits

Design recall and recognition

Design recall tasks represent one of the most common forms of 'non-verbal' memory tasks. While they have proven to be popular among clinical neuropsychologists they do suffer from a number of limitations. These include the potential for verbal mediation which is present to a variable degree in such tasks, individual differences in copying skill which may contribute to memory performance, limitations in administering the task to patients with loss of manual power or dexterity, and difficulties in constructing parallel forms for such tests. In addition, for some design recall tests there is limited control of factors such as duration of presentation of the design to be tested for recall, and scoring of a subject's recall may be both time-consuming and rather arbitrary.

Design recall tasks fall into two main types: those which ask for a copy and later recall of a single, complex design, and those which require, over a number of trials, recall of a simpler design, without an intervening copy. In the case of the first type of design recall task, the most celebrated is the Rey-Osterreith recall task*. Several variants of administration of this task have evolved over the years, but the task usually involves an initial copy of a complex figure, followed in some administrations by immediate recall and/or delayed recall; this delay has varied from 3 to 45 minutes across the various administrations. Lezak (1983) has presented Osterreith's norms for the copy and 3-minute recall trials, and a number of research studies which have used the test have provided some further, limited normative data together with findings related to specific clinical populations (e.g. Brooks, 1972; Taylor, 1979; Wood, Ebert and Kinsbourne, 1982). In addition, Bennet-Levy (1984) has published norms for copying and for 40-minute delayed recall of the figure (without any intervening immediate recall), which take into account subjects' strategies for copying the task, and he has derived a regression equation for predicting delayed recall from a subject's age and copying strategies. Most of the normative and clinical data which have been published on memory performance for the Rey-Osterreith figure are, however, somewhat sparse, both in terms of number of subjects and age-groups sampled, and in terms of allowance for educational level. The study of Bennet-Levy (1984), which is among the most thorough of all the relevant studies reporting normative data, did consider the role of general intellectual level, although his study does suffer from the relatively young age (mean = 29 years) of the population sampled. A number of other complex-design recall task have been reported or published. Taylor (1979) has described a design recall tasks using a figure of similar complexity to the Rey-Osterreith figure. Coughlan and Hollows (1985) have reported a design recall task, with two parallel forms, as part of the cognitive battery described later (*see* p. 43).

In the case of multitrial design recall tasks, a number of these have been published. These include the Benton Visual Retention Test† (Benton, 1974) and the Memory-for-designs test‡ (Graham and Kendall, 1960). In addition, a number of the memory scales and general cognitive batteries described later have included multitrial design recall tasks, e.g. the Wechsler Memory Scale (Wechsler, 1945) and the British Abilities Scales (Elliot, Murray and Pearson, 1983). The Benton Visual Retention Test (BVRT) is the most widely used of this type of design recall task (Benton, 1974), and has three alternative procedures for administration as a memory task – 10 seconds' exposure of the design followed by immediate recall, 5 seconds' exposure followed by immediate recall, and 10 seconds' exposure

---

* A version of this test has been published by Visser (1980) and is available from Swets Publishing Service, Heereweg 347, 2161 Ca Lisse, The Netherlands.
† This test is available from a number of sources – e.g. The Psychological Corporation Ltd., Foots Cray High Street, Sidcup, Kent DA14 5HP, UK; The Psychological Corporation Inc., 555 Academic Court, San Antonio, USA.
‡ This test is available from NFER-Nelson, Darville House, 2 Oxford Road East, Windsor, Berkshire SL4 1DF, UK.

followed by a 15 seconds' unfilled delay which is then followed by recall. Allowing for the limitations in design recall tasks noted above, the BVRT has a number of virtues, such as the availability of three parallel forms and the inclusion of norms which allow for variation both in age and educational level.

Design recognition memory tests, using materials similar to those used in multitrial design recall tests, have also been incorporated in some memory test procedures. The British Ability Scales (Elliot, Murray and Pearson, 1983) include a multi-choice memory for designs test. Kimura (1963) employed a somewhat different form of design recognition memory test, using a recurring recognition format*. An initial presentation of 20 stimuli is followed by 140 test trials, some of which contain a subset of the original stimuli and some of which comprise new, 'distractor' designs. Since the subset of the original 20 stimuli is repeated a number of times during the set of test trials, the test incorporates both a memory and learning component. Published normative and clinical data for this test mainly relate to small groups of patients, e.g. those with temporal or frontal lobectomy (Kimura, 1963; Milner, 1970), those with cerebral missile wounds (Newcombe, 1969) or those who have suffered a blunt head injury (Brooks, 1974b). Short-term recognition memory for non-verbal material, using the Brown–Peterson or similar paradigm, has been assessed, and has included materials such as chequered-squares (Warrington and James, 1967), computer-generated designs (Acker and Acker, 1982) and Vanderplas-Garvin random shapes (Vanderplas and Garvin 1959; Butters and Cermak, 1980). Unlike the retention of verbal material, performance on non-verbal short-term memory tasks does not appear to be as critically dependent on the presence and type of intervening activity (DeLuca, Cermak and Butters, 1975).

Other non-verbal memory tests

While a wide variety of non-verbal memory test procedures other than design retention tasks has been used in research studies of memory disordered patients, few have been published or well-standardized. Thus, memory-for-faces tests have been frequently used in clinical memory research (e.g. Milner and Teuber, 1968; Yin, 1970), but only one such task has been published – the non-verbal part of the Recognition Memory Test described later (see p. 41). The block tapping test devised by Corsi, and described by Milner (1971) has been used in a number of studies of non-verbal memory functioning. In this task, the subject is required to repeat a sequence of taps demonstrated by the examiner, and where this sequence exceeds the patient's immediate memory span it may usefully elicit specific memory deficits in neurological populations (e.g. De Renzi, Faglioni and Villa, 1977; De Renzi et al., 1984).

A similar type of non-verbal memory task is described by Barbizet and Cany (1968), and in a somewhat different form by Rao et al. (1984). In the latter version of the test, subjects are shown an array of seven chips randomly displayed on a 6 × 4 matrix of squares, and then asked to reproduce the display using the chips and an empty matrix. Five such trials are administered, followed by a sixth trial using a new array, followed by a seventh trial in which the subject is again asked to reproduce the original matrix used on the five learning trials; Rao et al. (1984) also administered a 30-minutes delayed recall trial for the original matrix.

* This test, and its equivalent verbal version, are available from DK Consultants, 412 Dufferin Ave., London, Ontario N68 IZ6, Canada.

Maze-learning tasks have long been a favoured means of testing non-verbal memory (e.g. Newcombe, 1969; De Renzi, Faglioni and Villa, 1977), and a task similar to that used by Newcombe is shown in *Figure 1.2*. The performance of a group of penetrating head injury patients on this task is described in Chapter 4.

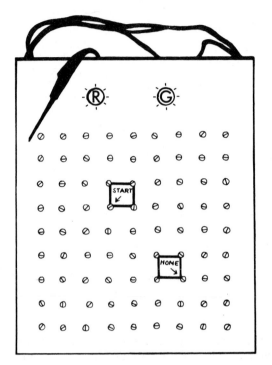

Figure 1.2 Maze-learning task, in which the subject has to learn the path from START to HOME after it has been briefly demonstrated by the examiner. When an incorrect choice-point is crossed, the red light is illuminated, and a click is heard, When the subject reaches HOME, the green light is illuminated. Performance is assessed over a number of learning trials, usually around 20–25 (see Ch. 4 for a discussion of performance of brain damaged patients on this task)

The various non-verbal memory tests described so far have been similar to analogous verbal tasks which have employed list learning or Brown–Peterson paradigms. In the case of paired-associated learning tests, relatively few non-verbal learning tasks have been described in which minimal verbal mediation is possible. Face-name learning tasks have often been used in studies of memory dysfunction (e.g. Becker *et al.*, 1983a), as have symbol–digit paired-associate learning tests (e.g. Kapur and Butters, 1977). However, the verbal retrieval component of such tasks clearly limits their usefulness to being general memory test procedures rather than material-specific techniques which may be useful for detecting focal cerebral pathology. Milner (1982) has described a paired-associate learning task where subjects had to associate one of six plain cards, in a horizontal array, with one of a number of randomly located lights. However, even this task does not completely exclude the possibility of verbal mediation playing a part in memory test performance.

Other aspects of memory assessment

Picture/object memory tasks

Picture and object memory tasks have been less frequently used by clinicians and researchers than other types of memory tests, and this may be due to the relative lack of hemispheric specificity of impaired performance (Milner, 1980). Memory for pictures is assessed in two memory test batteries discussed later – the Williams Memory Scale and the British Ability Scales. Memory for objects and memory for complex scenes have been studied by a number of researchers (e.g. Fowler, 1969; Fuld, 1980; Butters *et al.*, 1983). Few of these studies have gathered detailed normative or clinical data other than that related to the specific aims of the study, although the object learning task described by Fuld (1980), which assesses retention of objects presented in the tactile modality, has been published with extensive norms for the 70–90 years age group, and is available in two parallel forms*. One task, for which more detailed standardization data have been gathered, tests recall of line drawings of objects as part of a more general cognitive assessment of the elderly (Kendrick, 1985). Recognition memory for pictures of objects tends to be at a high level in the normal population (Standing, Conezio and Haber, 1980), and so the use of such tests with clinical populations needs to take into account the possibility of ceiling effects. They may, therefore, be of greater benefit for testing more severely impaired neurological patients, e.g. elderly patients with dementia, rather than young patients with mild head injury. They may also be particularly useful in assessing long-term forgetting over periods of days or weeks. The extent of long-term forgetting of material probably bears a close relationship, at least in some cases, to how well the information has been learned in the first instance (Slamecka and McElree, 1983), although the interpretation of such evidence is a matter of some debate (Loftus, 1985a,b; Slamecka, 1985).

Accurate assessment of 'rate of forgetting' is fraught with methodological difficulties, and any generalizations from such data with regard to 'storage mechanisms' must be tentative. Some authors (e.g. Huppert and Piercy, 1978b) have attempted to equate the initial level of learning between control and neurological patients by varying the number of exposures of pictorial stimuli. The advantage of this technique is that there is, at the surface, some degree of equivalence between initial levels of learning, with which one might compare subsequent test performance hours or days later. There are several limitations to this method: first, if different items are tested for retention at the various testing intervals, one is not dealing directly with decay of information of a specific set of items over a period of time, but with an overall level of performance which may relate to performance on target items, distractor items, or differing combined distributions of both, although in the study by Huppert and Piercy (1978b), the relative scores for these parameters remained remarkably constant over the various retention intervals. Second, at least in the case of patients with alcoholic Korsakoff's syndrome, there is considerable individual variability in the pattern of forgetting rates, and this may depend on the type of statistic used to compute recognition accuracy (Kopelman, 1985). In addition, a similar level of performance at initial memory testing may not necessarily reflect equivalent degrees of learning (*see* Martone, Butters and Trauner, 1986). Third, somewhat different findings

* This test is available from NFER-NELSON, Darville House, 2 Oxford Road East, Windsor, Berkshire, SL4 IDF, UK.

seem to occur from the use of yes-no or two-alternative forced-choice recognition testing situations (Freed, Corkin and Cohen, 1984). Finally, the picture memory test described by Huppert and Piercy (1978b) is quite time-consuming and somewhat impractical in many clinical assessment settings.

In addition to testing recall/recognition memory for pictures or objects, a further form of memory testing procedures is one where memory for the spatial location of objects is assessed. Such a test is included in the Rivermead Behavioural Memory Test reviewed later (*see* p. 41), and also in some 'mental status' examinations (Strub and Black, 1977). Such a task usually involves hiding each of several objects in various places in the room where the patient is being examined, and after an interval (usually around 10–20 minutes later) asking for recall of their location. This type of memory test is notoriously difficult to standardize, if only because individual clinicians' rooms must vary considerably in the type and number of cues which they provide to the patient!

'Implicit memory' tasks

Neurological patients who display marked everyday memory impairment may, nonetheless, show evidence of some residual memory functioning in certain test situations. This is often particularly evident in learning situations where the patient's familiarity with the perceptual/perceptual-motor features of an event is assessed, usually by paradigms where memory may be secondary to actual task performance. At the anecdotal level, such evidence is available in the literature, e.g. the description by Claparede (1911) referred to elsewhere (*see* p. 166) where a patient with alcoholic Korsakoff's syndrome displayed avoidance learning in a simple conditioning setting. However, such anecdotes need to be interpreted with some degree of caution, especially since somewhat conflicting observations have also been reported (Barbizet, 1970).

At the clinical level, it may be possible to detect such learning by asking a patient to read words which are outside his vocabulary, and which cannot easily be read simply from their spelling, e.g. the word 'meringue', or by providing incomplete spelling of the word, e.g. T-B-E for table. (It is obviously important, in the selection of words, to control for guessing responses by subjects, and to obtain relevant normative data.) Providing a set of learning trials, and/or asking a patient to read these words again on a later occasion, should provide some evidence of residual learning at the linguistic level, even though the patient may not recall having read the words previously. When using this type of paradigm, it is important in the test instructions to avoid presenting the test as a memory task, so that on test trials the patient sees the task more as a guessing game rather than a test of recall (Graf, Squire and Mandler, 1984). A large variety of test situations has been used to establish evidence for residual memory function in memory-impaired, or more commonly amnesic patients, and some of these studies are reviewed elsewhere (Parkin, 1982; Moscovitch, 1984).

At the perceptual level, tasks such as naming pictures on the basis of reducing visual cues, and reading of mirror-reversed words, may yield evidence of residual memory functioning over successive learning trials. Perceptual-motor tasks such as learning a simple maze, pursuit rotor learning, and learning to assemble a jigsaw puzzle may also indicate evidence of memory in situations where the patient may in fact forget having performed the task before. Of these various tasks, in my

Figure 1.3 Pursuit rotor task (Forth Instruments, Livingston, Scotland) used to assess perceptual-motor learning. The subject has to follow the moving light by holding the stylus tip over the light source. A tone is emitted while the stylus is over the target. The speed of the target can be controlled, and time-on-target for each trial is indicated on the display panel. Such a task is often performed well by neurological patients who otherwise have marked impairment on more traditional memory tests

experience, pursuit rotor learning (*Figure 1.3*) is one of the most sensitive and reliable for detecting residual learning ability in patients with marked memory disorder, and a number of studies (e.g. Corkin, 1968) have highlighted the usefulness of this task in detecting residual learning ability. In the case of such perceptual and perceptual-motor tasks, it is obviously important to exclude the presence of any perceptual-motor deficits. In patients with a pure amnesic syndrome, such tests can readily be given without any need to bear such qualifications in mind, but in patients where amnesia coexists with other cognitive deficits, such tasks may not be applicable. It is also important to ensure that normal control data are gathered with respect to learning curves and delayed retention/relearning, and also that the normative data do not show any ceiling effects.

In recent years, a number of more sophisticated perceptual learning situations have been adopted to assess for residual memory in amnesic patients. These include 'priming' tasks, where patients are initially exposed to a set of words and then, sometime later, are asked to identify or make some other response to a subset of these words intermingled with words which they have not seen before (Schacter and Graf, 1986; Shimamura, 1986). The response required on the second occasion may consist of generating free associations to the words, word identification where the presentation exposure is very brief, etc. In one situation (Jacoby and Witherspoon, 1982), patients were asked to respond to lower-frequency forms of a set of homophones, and were later asked to spell the homophones. In spite of poor recognition memory for the words, they were as likely as control subjects to offer the lower frequency versions which had been primed earlier. However, Cermak, O'Connor and Talbot (1986) and Kapur (1987b) have found less striking effects using a similar paradigm. Classical conditioning paradigms, such as eye-blink conditioning, have also been used by a few research workers (Weiskrantz and Warrington, 1979), although most of these may not be immediately applicable in clinical settings.

Retrograde amnesia tests

Although retrograde amnesia has been a relatively neglected aspect of memory assessment, in recent years there has been an upsurge of interest relating to assessment of memory for events prior to the onset of an illness or injury. Memory loss for events immediately preceding an acute neurological illness or injury is discussed elsewhere (*see* p. 98). Little attention has been paid to the extent to which such pre-ictal or pre-traumatic amnesia is different from more general retrograde amnesia, and the extent to which the two may be continuous or discontinuous. Any assessment of remote memory functioning must be related to the age of the patient, and should also bear in mind the learning capacity of the patient during the years which are being sampled by the particular test.

At the clinical level, it may often be possible to ask the patient about public events which have happened in the years prior to the onset of his illness, or about specific events in his life in the recent or distant past (e.g. schools attended, holidays, names of teachers or best friends, etc.). In the case of personal topics, it is important to gather corroborative evidence from a close relative, and to be aware that recall of personal life events may sometimes be faulty in normal subjects (Jenkins, Hurst and Rose, 1979; Bradburn, Rips and Shevell, 1987). It may be useful to obtain this type of information beforehand and then confront the patient with some questions relating specifically to the personal episodes in question. Barbizet (1970) has described some of the events, which may be usefully sampled in this way. In addition to being unable to recall specific episodes or events which have occurred in the past, patients may perform poorly when they are presented with the information in question, as in a recognition testing format. In such situations, there are three main levels at which remote memory loss may be evident: failure to recognize an item as familiar, inability to indicate why the item is distinctive, and poor temporal positioning or temporal sequencing of the item in memory. For example, such assessment may take the following format: 'Does the name xxxxx ring a bell? Do you know why the name is famous? Can you tell me when he or she was famous? Can you tell me when the event occurred?'

In general, questions relating to specific features of items or to sequencing of items will be more sensitive than simple familiarity recognition in detecting remote memory loss. Other simple means for assessing retrograde amnesia include asking the patient to list the names of heads of state since the Second World War. While a high level of performance on such a task may exclude a marked retrograde amnesia, impaired performance may not be a particularly sensitive indicator of cerebral pathology, and it may be more preferable to present patients with a list of names in random order and to ask for them to be arranged in chronological order (Hamsher and Roberts, 1985). At the non-verbal level, presenting the patient with photographs of faces of heads of state or other personalities who have been famous over the past few decades, and asking for the three types of information outlined above, may also give an indication of the extent of any retrograde amnesia. More general questions which may uncover evidence of retrograde memory loss include asking patients to indicate the price of certain everyday items (e.g. an average family saloon car, a pint of beer, etc.), and in some instances they may offer a price which is a number of years out of date. Where the patient's anterograde amnesia has been present for a number of years, such errors may, however, represent the combined effects of anterograde and retrograde amnesia.

More formal means of assessing retrograde amnesia have been developed in recent years, and these have been reviewed in a number of articles (Butters and Albert, 1982; Squire and Cohen, 1982). Some methodological aspects of constructing retrograde amnesia tests are described by Sanders (1972) and by Bahrick and Karis (1982). Test items may range from questions about events which have occurred in previous decades (Sanders and Warrington, 1971), the recognition of famous voices (Meudell *et al.*, 1980), and the identification of famous faces or items relating to television programmes which have been broadcast at certain dates. A further procedure which has been used to probe the extent of retrograde amnesia is to ask the patient to describe a particular past experience in response to a set stimulus, for example the word 'flag'. Although such a procedure has often been used to assess 'autobiographical memory' in neurological patients (*see* Rubin (1986) for a discussion of studies which have examined this aspect of memory), this type of information may sometimes be rather ambiguous and difficult to verify, and it is often useful to retest the patient with the same question several days/weeks later to see if there is some consistency of response and to help exclude mere confabulations. Use of certain items such as television programmes is obviously culture-specific and limited to certain socio-economic levels.

At the time of test construction, pilot studies are needed to equate for difficulty level of items across time periods, and to validate the restriction of items to a specific time period (asking younger subjects to respond to items sampled from earlier decades can be a useful indicator as to whether such items simply reflect general knowledge or are specific to a time period in the past). It is also useful to control for the level of general knowledge of the patient, and I have found that the information subtest of the Wechsler Adult Intelligence Scale (Wechsler, 1955, 1981) is sometimes helpful in this respect. As indicated earlier, patients may often be more impaired in allocating temporal information to the items in question; for example, indicating the decade in which an item was famous compared to offering information about the item in question (*see* Hirst and Volpe, 1982). It is also useful to try to incorporate both recognition and recall testing. Some researchers have distinguished free recall from cued recall in their assessment of remote memory loss (e.g. Albert, Butters and Brandt, 1981a)*, although there is as yet limited evidence for any particular neurological patients who are differentially aided by alphabetic/semantic cues.

Assessment of change in memory functioning

Many of the published memory test procedures currently available were developed primarily for diagnostic purposes, for which a single assessment often sufficed,

---

* The Boston remote memory test battery is available from Dr M. Albert, Department of Psychiatry, Harvard Medical School, Massachusetts General Hospital, Fruit Street, Boston, Massachusetts 2114, USA

rather than for monitoring change in memory function over time. Their initial design and supporting standardization data tended, therefore, not to address issues relating to the assessment of change in memory function. In recent years, however, more attention has been given to the need for tests to assess recovery and deterioration in memory. Drug trials for conditions such as degenerative dementia require the selection of tests which may be sensitive to changes in memory functioning (*see* Brinkman and Gershon, 1983). Several criteria need to be met before memory tests can be reliably used in such situations; tasks need to have at least two parallel forms, which are equivalent in difficulty level and in the pattern of errors which subjects are likely to make; and evidence needs to be gathered on any changes which occur when the alternate forms are administered over various intervening time periods.

In memory testing situations where repeat testing is carried out for the same set of items, as for example in a free recall paradigm, some allowance has to be made for the possible differential effects of test trials on memory performance, since it is well established that test trials can function as training or presentation trials, in terms of their effects on subsequent memory performance (e.g. Darley and Murdock, 1971). I will now review memory tests for which parallel forms have been developed, and consider their suitability for monitoring change in memory functioning.

Two forms are available for the Wechsler Memory Scale, although relatively little normative data are available for form II compared with form I. As a number of authors have pointed out (e.g. Prigatano, 1978), the two forms do not appear to be equivalent in difficulty level, with the visual reproduction and paired-associate learning subtests showing the most marked discrepancies (Bloom, 1959). In addition, little data appear to have been gathered on practice-effects associated with repeat administration of one scale, or alternate administration of both scales.

The Rivermead Behavioural Memory Test (*see* p. 41) has the virtue of having as one of its original aims the assessment of change in memory function. Four parallel forms are available, and the items for these forms appear to be equivalent in difficulty level. Performance of matched groups of control subjects on the different forms has not yet been reported, but test–retest reliability data have been found to be relatively high ($r \geqslant 0.8$). One of the limitations of the test battery is the relatively small range of tests scores which is possible on individual subtests; thus, changes in specific areas of memory function may be underestimated by the limited scope of large variations in test scores. The overall screening score also has a relatively small range (0 to 12), and since this is a score summed from individual subtest scores, it runs the risk, if used in isolation, of not reflecting significant changes in individual areas of memory function in situations where there is a large degree of intertest variability in performance. It should, however, be possible to develop an overall score with a larger range, and to construct a profile of performance on individual subtests. Such information should become available in later developments of the battery. A final limitation of the use of this battery in repeat testing is that for two subtests (delayed retention of a route, and delayed recall of a story), no forewarning is given to the patient. In any repeat assessments, some patients may anticipate a further test of their memory for such items, thus reducing the comparability of the first and subsequent testing situations.

The Adult Memory and Information Processing Battery (AMIPB) (*see* p. 43) has two parallel forms, with separate norms for each form. The normative data indicate a similar level of difficulty for the two forms in the case of the 18–30 years and the

31–45 years age groups. However, in the case of the 46–60 years and the 61–75 years age groups, immediate and delayed story recall levels for form 2 are somewhat lower than those for form 1, and this may be related to the relatively small numbers of subjects for social class 1 in the standardization group for form 2 compared to the population used for form 1. Test–retest reliability coefficients (with an intervening period of median 2.8 days) were obtained by testing on one form and retesting on the alternative form. These correlations were generally high, although there was some variability between correlations for individual subtests.

Williams (1968) described a series of memory tests, for which three parallel forms were developed, and also included some data on their equivalence and test–retest characteristics. The series of tests includes digit span, learning the meaning of unfamiliar words, delayed recall of a set of pictures, learning the position of a peg on a board, and some questions relating to remote memory. Performance on the three versions of the test did not differ significantly in the case of the normal control sample of 50 subjects. Repeat testing at intervals of 2–4 days resulted in some improvement on the digit span, and deterioration on the picture recall task. White, Merrick and Harbison (1969) administered parallel forms of the test, usually after a one-month interval, to patients with suspected cerebral pathology, and found a higher test–retest reliability for verbal memory items than for the peg-board or picture memory tests. Although they reported a significant correlation between different forms of the scale, they concluded that 'for no test is the correlation so high that one set can be regarded as interchangeable with another for our population'. One of the tests which White, Merrick and Harbison found to be most useful in the assessment of memory dysfunction – a delayed picture recall task – has some limitations. The pictures are rather small, and some of them may be misnamed by a patient with perceptual difficulties; no specific time period is indicated for stimuli presentation; and cued recall performance may be compounded with subsequent recognition testing since some patients may recognize items on the basis of the cues just provided, rather than from their memory for the original presentation trial.

Turning to individual memory tests for which parallel forms are available, the Benton Visual Retention Test (Benton, 1974) has three parallel forms which were constructed to be similar in difficulty level. Riddel (1962) found evidence that in a group of elderly psychiatric patients form D was slightly more difficult than form C. Lezak (1983) has reported that repeat testing of normal control subjects after 6 and then 12 months yielded similar scores on the three forms of the test. Hannay and Levin (1985) have described four parallel forms of the selective reminding test (Buschke and Fuld, 1974). Even though items in the various lists were matched for word frequency, the first form yielded lower scores than the remaining three forms. Improvement was evident on repeat testing from week one to week two, but not on the two following repeat assessments. However, their data were derived from college students, and it remains to be seen if the normative data described in their paper generalizes to clinical populations. The Rey Auditory Verbal Learning Test is another list-learning task for which alternative forms have been constructed. Ryan et al. (1986) found a high correlation between the administration of alternative forms, with an average test–retest interval of 140 minutes. However, the clinical sample was somewhat heterogeneous, comprising several neurological and psychiatric groups.

Memory test batteries

Wechsler Memory Scale*

Detailed reviews of the Wechsler Memory Scale (Wechsler, 1945) have been published elsewhere (Erickson and Scott, 1977; Prigatano, 1978; Lezak, 1983). The scale includes tests of orientation for time and place, story recall, digit span, recall of visual designs, and verbal paired-associate learning. Overall memory performance can be expressed in terms of a 'memory quotient'. The main advantages of the Wechsler Memory Scale are its brevity of administration, and the large amount of data which have been collected on performance relating to a variety of neurological conditions. Its main limitations are the inclusion of non-memory items such as reciting the alphabet; an over-emphasis on verbal memory, so that it is relatively insensitive to some forms of right hemisphere pathology, e.g. Rao and Bieliauskas (1983) have reported a patient with a right temporal lobectomy who had a Wechsler memory quotient of 140; an over-emphasis on immediate/short-term retention with no facility for delayed retention testing; there is some degree of ambiguity (from the patient's point of view) of test instructions and procedure for the verbal paired-associate learning task, where some neurologically impaired subjects may be led to believe that it is a free-association task rather than a memory test; and the questionable use of both 'easy' and 'hard' paired-associate items within a single test (*see* Wilson *et al.*, 1982b). Some of these limitations have been borne out by factor analytical studies of the Wechsler Memory Scale (*see* Skilbeck and Woods (1980) for a review of such studies).

Modified versions of the Wechsler Memory Scale have been developed to try to overcome some of these and other limitations (Loring and Papanicolaou, 1987). Russell (1975) introduced a set of tests based on delayed (30 minutes) recall of the subtests dealing with retention of stories and visual designs. Such a modification was welcome, since, as Russell (1982) has pointed out, some patients may perform well on immediate recall, yet be unable to offer any memory for items on delayed recall. A further modification introduced by Russell was the provision of cues to prompt subjects who cannot recall for any of the stories or designs. Norms for these modified subtests have been provided by Russell, although separate norms for cued and uncued delayed recall are not given. Russell's (1975) data refer to the performance of 30 control subjects with a mean age of 36 years, and his clinical data included findings from patients with unilateral cerebral lesions of varying pathology.

Logue and Wryick (1979) have reported further data relating to Russell's modified form of the Wechsler Memory Scale. In their study, data from two groups of 29 elderly subjects (range 55–85 years) are reported, a normal control group and a 'dementia' group, although the precise pathology of the latter subjects is not indicated. Haaland *et al.* (1983) have also provided normative data from an elderly population (from a mean of 67–83 years). It is worth noting, however, that the subjects in their study were of above average educational level. McCarty *et al.* (1980) have provided some data relating to alternate-form reliability of the two forms of the Wechsler Memory Scale when administered using Russell's revised procedure; these data were also from an elderly sample of subjects, ranging from 71

* This test is available from a number of sources – e.g. The Psychological Corporation Ltd., Foots Cray High Street, Sidcup, Kent DA14 5HP, UK; The Psychological Corporation Inc., 555 Academic Court, San Antonio, USA.

to 93 years. One of the findings from this latter study was that the percentage of immediate recall items retained at the time of delayed recall was not highly correlated between the two forms of the test. Keesler *et al.* (1984) have pointed to differences in figure and story recall between performance on Russell's revision of form I of the Wechsler Memory Scale and on form II of the scale. A further set of data on Russell's revised Wechsler Memory Scale, from normal control subjects and patients with primary degenerative dementia, has been reported by Brinkman *et al.* (1983).

Milberg *et al.* (1986) have described more detailed modifications to the Wechsler memory scale. These included the addition of a third paragraph to the 'logical memory' subtest. This paragraph is read aloud and then recalled by the patient. Retention of all three paragraphs is retested after 20 minutes. In the case of the paired-associate learning subtest, a fourth test trial has been added, in which patients are presented with the second (response) item in each pair and asked to recall the first (stimulus) item. A delayed (20 minutes) uncued recall trial for all the pairs is also administered, followed by a standard recall trial. For the visual designs subtest, the patient is asked to copy the items following the immediate recall trial, and 20 minutes later is asked for a further recall of the designs. Although most of these modifications would appear to address some of the limitations of the Wechsler Memory Scale outlined above, no detailed normative or clinical data were reported by Milberg *et al.* (1986) with respect to the modifications.

Williams Memory Battery*

Williams (1968) has described a memory scale comprising a range of memory tests, and developed three parallel forms for these. The tests include digit span, peg-board position learning, word-definition learning, delayed (7–10 minutes) recall of pictures (followed by cued recall and recognition testing, depending on the subject's level of performance), and a brief assessment of past personal events (e.g. 'describe your first school'). Williams reported data from 50 normal control subjects (aged between 17 and 50 years), who were administered each form of the scale at intervals of 2–4 days. The three forms were found to be equivalent in terms of difficulty level; with repeat testing there was a tendency for digit span to improve and for delayed picture recall to deteriorate between test sessions. Four clinical groups were also tested on the memory scale, and these included neurotic patients, depressed patients, alcoholic patients and an 'organic' group. Unfortunately, no further diagnostic information was reported on the latter patients. Williams found that delayed picture recall was one of the best measures of distinguishing the 'organic' group from 'non-organic' and control subjects.

Although most of the tests are attractive both to the patient and to the clinician, the scale suffers from a number of limitations. First, the data reported by Williams (1968) were quite restricted both in the age ranges of normal control subjects and in the neurological patients sampled, and although some follow-up studies have been reported (White, Merrick and Harbison, 1969), the overall level of standardization of the battery is somewhat unsatisfactory. Second, the delayed picture recall test, which both Williams (1968) and White, Merrick and Harbison (1969) found to be particularly useful in memory testing, does itself have a number of limitations. These include lack of guidance as to the exposure period for the set of pictures,

* This test is described in detail in the appendix to the article by Williams (1968).

absence of control data to see if subjects might recall the pictures by simply guessing from the cues alone, and some degree of confounding between the recall and recognition trials–the patient may recognize a picture on the basis of the set of cues given in the previous cued recall trial rather than from his memory of the initial presentation trial.

Recognition Memory Test*

The Recognition Memory Test (Warrington, 1984) consists of two tests; one comprising immediate, forced-choice, recognition memory for 50 words, and a corresponding test using faces materials. Its main advantages are that detailed normative data have been gathered, together with 'discrepancy scores' relating to differences between performance on the two tests; data have been gathered on performance of patients with focal cerebral lesions; earlier published data are available on the performance of amnesic patients (Warrington, 1974); the faces-recognition memory test appears to be useful in distinguishing neurological patients from those with depression (Coughlan and Hollows, 1984); and the use of a recognition testing format renders the test particularly applicable to patients with manual or speech expression deficits.

The main disadvantages of the test are ceiling effects (especially for younger subjects) in the case of the verbal recognition test (Sunderland, Harris and Baddeley, 1983); some of the initial standardization data indicate that the faces-recognition test may not be highly specific for right hemisphere pathology, since the overall group mean scores of patients with left-hemisphere lesions were impaired relative to control subjects. This may perhaps have been related to some limitation in the particular stimuli used in the faces-memory test, since these include some pieces of clothing. Although distractor stimuli have a similar composition, in the writer's experience a few patients may 'latch' onto these and thus introduce a verbal mediation element into task performance. Tests of faces-recognition memory which have minimized such cues have been useful in detecting focal memory deficits (e.g. Yin, 1970). In general, recognition memory testing is less sensitive in detecting memory deficits than tests which require a retrieval response, and the normal performance of certain patients on the recognition memory test, e.g. patients with Parkinson's disease (Lees and Smith, 1983), may not necessarily indicate the absence of memory deficits in such a population. Finally, one of the groups used by Warrington to validate the test was a neurological group with cerebral atrophy (no other information on the group was provided). While most of those patients may well have been suffering from some degree of primary degenerative dementia, the lack of equivalence between atrophy and dementia (Freedman et al., 1984a) suggests caution in the interpretation of this particular set of data.

Rivermead Behavioural Memory Test†

This test (Wilson, Cockburn and Baddeley, 1985) comprises a series of memory tasks, the overall aims of which are to '(1) predict which people will experience everyday memory problems, (2) describe the nature of those problems, (3) identify

* This test is available from NFER-Nelson, Darville House, 2 Oxford Road East, Windsor, Berkshire SL4 1DF, UK.
† This test is available from the Thames Valley Test Company, 22 Bulmershe Road, Reading, Berkshire RG1 5KJ, UK.

areas for treatment, and (4) monitor change over time'. The test includes an assessment of retention (approximately 25 minutes) of the name associated with a face, remembering after a similar period to ask for an item and remembering where it was hidden; remembering after 20 minutes to ask a question of the examiner; recognition testing of 10 pictures after a few minutes; immediate and delayed (20 minutes) recall of a short story; recognition memory testing of five faces after about 5 minutes; immediate and delayed (20 minutes) retention of a short route; remembering to do something during both parts of the latter test; and a current awareness test covering orientation for items such as time, place, etc.

Detailed standardization and related test data are still being gathered for this test. So far, normative data have been collected (Wilson, Cockburn and Baddeley, 1987) from 137 normal control subjects aged between 16 and 75 years. The mean 'screening score' (maximum = 12) of control subjects on the Rivermead Behavioural Memory Test was 10.34, with a range from 7 to 12. In addition, the test has been administered to a separate population of two groups of normal elderly subjects, aged 50–69 years and 70–90 years respectively. Certain items from the test (remembering to ask for a belonging, remembering an appointment, and remembering to deliver a message) have been found to differentiate significantly between the two groups, with the older group performing less well than younger subjects. Data from 175 brain-damaged patients, aged between 16 and 69 years, have also been collected. These patients included those with left and right hemisphere cerebrovascular disease, patients with blunt head injury, and patients from several other diagnostic groups (e.g. anoxia, encephalitis). Repeat administration of parallel forms of the test to 118 neurological patients has indicated relatively high test–retest reliability coefficients ($r \geqslant 0.8$).

Randt, Brown and Osborne Memory Scale*

Randt, Brown and Osborne (1983) have described a memory test battery, composed of a series of memory tests, which are available in five parallel forms. The tests include general information (e.g. orientation for time and place), forward and backward digit span, learning and long-term retention (over a number of intervals) of a set of five words, learning a set of six verbal paired-associate items, recall of a short story, and retention of a set of 15 pictures. Long-term retention is assessed by memory testing after an intervening memory test and also after 24 hours. A further feature of the battery is the inclusion of a memory task in which subjects are given an unexpected recall test for the names of the six tests which have been administered. Randt, Brown and Osborne have described normative data from subjects aged between 20 and 79 years, and also reported data from a relatively ill-defined group of subjects over the age of 60 years who complained of memory loss and had some cognitive impairment, but who did not show any evidence of focal neurological deficits nor any features such as depression or anorexia. These subjects presumably suffered from a primary degenerative dementia, although it is not clear if attempts were made to distinguish between aetiologies such as degenerative and cerebrovascular disease. Although the test battery has positive features such as delayed retention testing and a wide age-range for the normative data base, it also has a number of limitations. These include the

---

* This test is described in detail in the article by Randt, Brown and Osborne (1983). Test forms are available from Dr C. T. Randt, Department of Neurology, New York University Medical Center, New York, New York 10016, USA.

absence of non-verbal memory tests, the absence of validation data from patients with specific neurological disease, the lack of data relating to test–retest reliability, and the absence of data on the effects of educational level on memory test performance.

Adult Memory and Information Processing Battery*

This battery of tests (Coughlan and Hollows, 1985) includes two verbal memory tests – immediate and delayed recall of a short story, and word-list learning – and two non-verbal memory tests – immediate and delayed recall of a complex figure, and learning of a design outlined on a 4 × 4 dot array. Administration and scoring of all the memory tests take around 45–60 minutes. Since this battery of tests has only recently been published, only a limited evaluation is possible, although some positive features and limitations may be noted. The battery of tests has the advantage of providing a comprehensive assessment of various aspects of memory functioning, including delayed recall and learning ability, with detailed normative data for both forms of the test. Some useful data from a group of depressed patients have also been gathered, although the battery has, however, only been validated against a group of neurological patients of mixed aetiology (Coughlan and Hollows, 1984), and its emphasis on recall and reproduction response measures may limit its use to certain neurological populations. The specific order of presentation of the tests in the standardization study is unfortunately not indicated. It is likely that the presence or absence of the design learning test before delayed recall of the complex figure might have some influence on the accuracy of delayed recall. As in the case of other complex figure recall tests, the test employed in this battery is of limited validity when used with patients who have copying difficulties and score less than perfectly on the copying trial (most control subjects obtained perfect scores on the copying trial). In addition, in my experience, 30 minutes delayed recall of a complex figure is quite difficult for a large number of neurological patients; it is of note that in the case of the complex figure used in this test, the normative data indicate that at least one control subject performed at zero level on the delayed recall portion of the task.

Neuropsychological test batteries

The Luria-Nebraska set of tests† (Golden, Hammeke and Purisch, 1980) includes an assessment of memory functioning. This comprises a series of relatively brief memory tasks encompassing a variety of materials and modalities, including the short-term recall of words, recall of visual designs, pairing words with pictures, repeating a rhythm and reproducing hand postures. Performance on the memory subtests of the Luria-Nebraska neuropsychological battery has been shown to be positively correlated with performance on some of the subtests of the Wechsler Memory Scale (*see* Kane, 1986 for a review of relevant studies). The positive features of this battery of memory tests include its brevity, the sensitivity of some of the tests to interference effects in memory, and the inclusion, in one of the verbal memory tasks, of a difference score which compares a patient's actual recall with

* This test is available from Dr A. K. Coughlan, Psychology Department, St James's University Hospital, Beckett Street, Leeds LS9 7TF, UK.
† This test is available from a number of sources – e.g. NFER-Nelson, Darville House, 2 Oxford Road East, Windsor, Berkshire SL4 1DF, UK.

his predicted recall (Luria (1976) has suggested that marked discrepancy in the two measures may reflect frontal lobe dysfunction). The battery of tests does, however, have significant limitations; there is sole emphasis on short-term memory tasks, with verbal materials predominating; there is limited scope for a wide range of scores within a particular subtest; and the neurological standardization data relate to a 'mixed' group of patients from a variety of aetiologies, with no subclassification according to pathology or anatomical locus. In addition, the tests do not have parallel forms to enable repeat testing to be carried out.

Babcock (1930) described several memory tests within a more general cognitive test battery. These tests included immediate and delayed recall of a short story, digit span, verbal paired-associate learning, repetition of a sequence of taps, a picture recognition memory test, repetition of sentences of varying length, immediate recall of designs and a verbal recognition memory test. While this set of tests would provide a comprehensive and useful assessment of memory functioning, the limited clinical data reported by Babcock and the necessity for more up-to-date norms significantly hinder the usefulness of the tests for routine clinical use.

The Halstead-Reitan battery (see Reitan and Davison, 1974) does not offer a detailed assessment of memory functioning. It does, however, include a test of tactile memory. Subjects are first asked to allocate, with their eyes blindfolded, geometric forms onto their spaces on a form board. The form board is then concealed, and subjects asked to draw the board from memory, indicating both the shapes and their positions relative to each other. Two scores are computed; the number of shapes correctly reproduced, and the number of shapes placed in their correct relative position. While considerable normative, clinical and research data have been collected using this test, some of this is contradictory (see Lezak, 1983 for a summary of this work). In my view, the test has little logical rationale and is probably of greater value if used as a test of tactile form perception, for which it was originally designed. It is obviously important, when using the test, to take into account any primary sensory abnormalities which may be present.

Chapter 2

Cerebrovascular disease

While vascular diseases of the brain are among the most common sources of cerebral dysfunction, the amount of systematic neuropsychological research on memory problems related to cerebrovascular disease (CVD) has, until recent years, been somewhat limited. Textbooks which include sections on memory disorders in brain-damaged patients (e.g. Squire and Butters, 1984) seldom make specific reference to disorders resulting from cerebrovascular lesions, and textbooks on cerebrovascular disease (e.g. Russell, 1983) have tended to make only a passing reference to memory disorders. More recently, some degree of cross-fertilization between the study of cerebrovascular disease and the study of memory has taken place (Baird *et al.*, 1985; Ljunggren *et al.*, 1985), but this has not yet tapped the enormous potential of clinical and theoretical knowledge which remains to be exploited.

When considering the effects of cerebrovascular disease on memory functioning, a number of factors need to be taken into account. These include the site of lesion, and the realization that the site of, e.g. an aneurysm, may be some distance from the site of the main cerebral pathology; the size/depth of the lesion, and an awareness of the remote pathophysiological effects of some cerebrovascular lesions (Lavy, Melamed and Portinoy, 1975; Powers and Raichle, 1985). The stage of recovery/ progression at which the patient with cerebrovascular disease is assessed also needs to borne in mind; some allowance should be made for individual differences in cerebrovascular topography; finally, the type of disease needs to be considered – the two main forms consist of cerebral infarction, either from thrombosis of an artery or from an embolus which has blocked an artery, and cerebral haemorrhage, in which bleeding may occur into brain tissue and/or into the subarachnoid space and hence into the cerebrospinal fluid. While no detailed comparison has been reported of the relative effects of these two forms of cerebrovascular disease on memory functioning, it would be prudent to assume that their effects may not be similar, and to make appropriate allowance for this in any study which includes both types of patients.

In this chapter, I will be considering memory disorders in cerebrovascular disease from four standpoints. First, I will review memory disorders related to cerebrovascular disease which has been classified in terms of a particular arterial system in the brain. Second, I will consider memory disorders associated with vascular lesions which have been defined in terms of damage to specific anatomical structures. Third, I will assess evidence relating to memory functioning in episodic cerebrovascular disturbance. Fourth, I will examine studies which have attempted to improve memory functioning in patients with cerebrovascular disease.

Arterially-defined lesions

Anterior cerebral artery

The anterior cerebral artery and its branches (*Figure 2.1; see Plate 1*) supply areas which are either directly involved in memory functioning, or are adjacent to such structures (Crowell and Morawetz 1977; Berman, Hayman and Hinck, 1980). It is not surprising therefore that disturbances of the anterior cerebral artery have been associated with significant memory disorder.

Most studies of memory disorder associated with disturbance of the anterior cerebral artery have focused on the anterior communicating artery; a few studies have been reported of memory dysfunction associated with disease of the anterior cerebral artery, whether or not this has been specific to the anterior communicating artery. One of the few systematic studies in this respect was that by Logue *et al.* (1968) who found evidence of memory impairment in a number of patients several years after the original haemorrhage. Several aspects of memory functioning were reported by Logue *et al.*, including memory loss for events preceding and following the haemorrhage, everyday memory symptoms, the presence of confusion (assessed retrospectively from the case notes) in the postoperative period, and the extent of deficit on a number of memory tasks. Pre-haemorrhage and post-haemorrhage amnesia of more than one week's duration were present in 9% and 52% of patients respectively. Confabulation at some point in the postoperative period was noted in 18 of the 79 patients, but the presence of such confabulation did not correlate with confabulatory responses on memory testing at time of subsequent follow-up. No memory test data from control subjects were gathered, but nevertheless some informative group differences emerged. For example, patients with left-sided aneurysms tended to forget prose material at a faster rate than patients with right-sided aneurysms, even though immediate recall was the same in both groups. Apart from this study by Logue *et al.* and a few clinical reports (e.g. Critchley 1930; Walton 1953; Brion *et al.*, 1969; Storey 1970), there has been little in the way of systematic neuropsychological investigation of memory disorders from disturbances of the anterior cerebral artery alone.

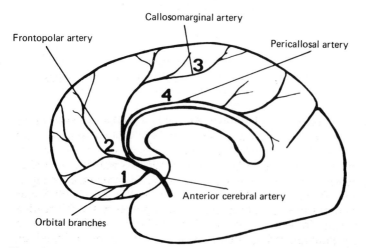

Figure 2.1 Anterior cerebral artery and its branches (from Walsh, 1978. Reproduced by permission of Churchill Livingstone)

Studies which have focused on vascular lesions in the territory of the anterior communicating artery (*Figure 2.2*) have been much more numerous, and in recent years have been one of the main sources of neuropsychological data regarding memory dysfunction after cerebrovascular disease, due in part to the proximity of limbic system structures to branches of this artery (Perlmutter and Rhoton, 1976; Gade 1982).

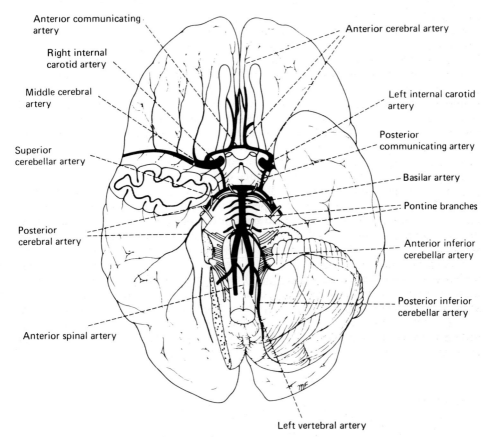

Figure 2.2 Arteries at the base of the brain (from Snell, 1987. Reproduced by permission of Little, Brown and Company)

Among the types of memory disorder which have been studied in relation to disturbance of the anterior communicating artery, the topic of confabulation has arisen in a number of studies. Both milder, 'momentary' and more severe, 'fantastic' confabulation (Berlyne, 1972) have been noted in a number of studies which included patients with anterior communicating artery disease in their sample, (e.g. Sweet, Talland and Ballantyne, 1966; Luria 1976; Stuss *et al.*, 1978; Kapur and Coughlan 1980), and in some cases they may blend together in the fabrication offered by patients (Damasio *et al.*, 1985a). Most studies of confabulation in patients with anterior communicating artery aneurysms have been based on observations made in the post-surgical period. Studies such as those by Stuss *et al.* (1978), Kapur and Coughlan (1980) and Vilkki (1985) have implicated frontal lobe dysfunction in the aetiology of the confabulation observed in their clinical sample. It seems likely that the greater the degree of frontal lobe dysfunction, the more severe the confabulation, and the more closely it resembles Berlyne's second form of confabulation i.e. 'fantastic' confabulation. It is important to note that confabulation is rarely a permanent sequel of disturbance in the anterior communicating artery, and that when it occurs in its more florid forms, it is often associated with changes in insight and affect (Talland, Sweet and Ballantyne, 1967).

A number of studies have reported amnesia in relation to anterior communicating artery disturbance (e.g. Lindquist and Norlen, 1966; Talland, Sweet and Ballentyne, 1967; Gade 1982; Alexander and Freedman 1984), although few detailed comparisons have yet been carried out of any differences in the severity or pattern of memory impairment in patients with this disturbance and amnesic patients of other aetiologies. A number of studies have, however, identified particular anatomical structures around the area of the anterior communicating artery which may underlie the amnesic syndrome in patients with vascular lesions in this region. Volpe, Herscovitsch and Raichle (1984) implicated the medial temporal lobes on the basis of positron emission tomography. Damasio *et al.* (1985a), in their study of patients with mainly anterior cerebral/anterior communicating artery disturbance, proposed that the common anatomical lesion in their group involved 'the posterior aspect of the ventromedial sector of the frontal lobe'. They suggested that damage to basal forebrain structures such as the septal nuclei, nucleus accumbens, substantia innominata and related pathways may be critical to the occurrence of memory disorder by causing interference with hippocampal function. Alexander and Freedman (1984) also hypothesized that septal–hippocampal damage may underlie the amnesia in patients with disturbance in the anterior communicating artery. In general, amnesia as a residual sequel of such disturbance is usually a transitory feature, and those patients who are left with a global amnesic syndrome are relatively few. In addition, patients with anterior communicating artery aneurysm who do have residual amnesia have been found to be less impaired on memory tasks than amnesic patients of other aetiologies (Corkin *et al.*, 1985). This may be due in part to advances in neurosurgical techniques. Gade (1982) noted differences in the incidence of amnesic syndrome associated with differing surgical procedures; trapping of an aneurysm, which may disrupt blood supply to branches of the anterior communicating artery, was more likely to result in an amnesic syndrome than ligation of the neck of the aneurysm (*Figure 2.3*).

Occlusion of the neck of the aneurysm was the procedure used by Sengupta, Chui and Brierly (1975) in their study of patients who had rupture of an anterior communicating artery aneurysm. They reported a temporary confusional state in a few patients shortly after surgery but, at longer term follow-up (between 4 and 33 months later), normal memory performance was found on the Wechsler Memory Scale. In a recent survey of patients with aneurysm of the anterior communicating artery, Teisser du Cros and Lhermitte (1984) also found relatively good recovery in their series of 32 patients who were examined between 12 and 15 months after surgery. They noticed that memory impairment was more likely to be present if the gyrus rectus had been resected at the time of operation. Unfortunately, the possible connection between resection and memory difficulty was clouded by the fact that eight out of the 12 patients were described as having an 'average or poor' level of memory functioning prior to surgery.

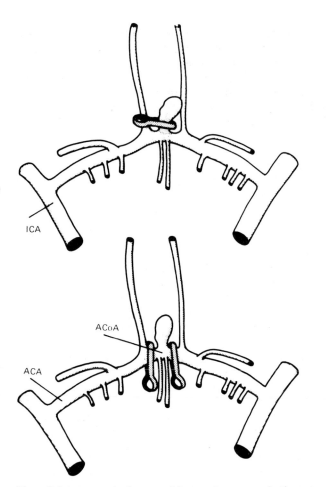

Figure 2.3 Aneurysm in the area of the anterior communicating artery (ACoA). Both drawings show the internal carotid arteries (ICA), and the anterior cerebral arteries (ACA). In the upper picture, ligation of the neck of the aneurysm has been performed, sparing perforating branches from the ACoA. The lower picture shows trapping of the aneurysm and of the perforating branches from the ACoA. Nine out of 11 patients operated upon by trapping developed the amnesic syndrome (from Gade, 1982. Reproduced by permission of Elsevier Science Publishing Company)

A few studies have shed light on the nature of the memory disorder underlying amnesia following disturbance of the anterior communicating artery. Volpe and Hirst (1983a) found poor recall of word-list material, with less marked impairment on recognition performance for both verbal and non-verbal stimuli. They found that patients with aneurysms of the anterior communicating artery were helped by semantic cues more than control patients, and the former patients also showed a greater susceptibility to proactive interference on a word-list recall task. Damasio *et al.* (1985a) found that cueing helped reduce both the severity of retrograde amnesia and the confabulatory responses offered by patients. Vilkki (1985) also found that cues helped memory performance in some patients with aneurysms of the anterior communicating artery who showed marked memory impairment, but that this was restricted to those patients with evidence of frontal lobe damage. Luria (1976) has pointed to a number of features of the memory disturbance of patients with aneurysms of the anterior communicating artery. In one set of observations, based on the performance of such patients in the first few months after operation, he found evidence of significant interference effects on memory tasks, and also noted confabulation, both in conversational behaviour and in memory test performance. He further pointed to a dissociation between 'involuntary imprinted connections and their active recall'. This dissociation is, in fact, now a well-documented feature of amnesic patients' memory performance, and resembles the distinction between, for example, intact conditioned learning responses and impaired recall of specific events (Weiskrantz and Warrington, 1979).

In a second set of observations, relating to patients with anterior communicating artery aneurysms studied at longer term follow-up (usually at least one year after surgery), Luria also found interference effects in memory tasks, and reported test deficits which were both modality-non-specific and material-non-specific. There was also evidence of impairment in memory for temporal order of stimuli. Luria suggested that in patients with anterior communicating artery aneurysms who are left with marked memory impairment, there may initially have been significant haemorrhage spreading to the region of the floor of the third ventricle, with resultant damage in the hypothalamothalamic region. Two of the features noted by Luria – susceptibility to interference and impaired temporal discrimination – were reported by Parkin *et al.* (1987) to be present in the memory performance of a patient who suffered rupture of an aneurysm of the anterior communicating artery.

Middle cerebral artery

Although the middle cerebral artery (*Figure 2.4; see Plate 2*) is the largest single source of blood supply to the cerebral hemispheres, surprisingly little work has been published on memory functioning as a specific result of impaired flow in this artery. Mesulam *et al.* (1976) reported acute confusional states associated with right middle cerebral artery infarctions, and suggested that the main deficit was one of

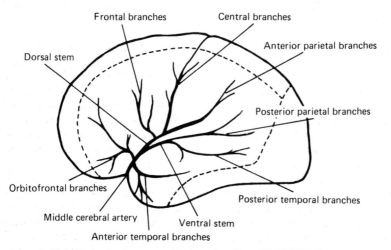

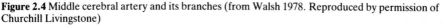

Figure 2.4 Middle cerebral artery and its branches (from Walsh 1978. Reproduced by permission of Churchill Livingstone)

selective attention. Several years later, Mullalay *et al.* (1982) indicated the presence of chronic confusional states in patients with right middle cerebral artery occlusion, and proposed that some conditions of apparent dementia may in fact be due to focal vascular disease rather than a generalized degenerative disorder. Schmidley and Messing (1984) demonstrated that two out of 46 patients with right middle cerebral artery infarction had an agitated confusional state. They reported that these two patients had a mild hemiparesis, compared to the marked motor deficits in the remaining patients with right middle cerebral artery infarcts but without evidence of an acute confusional state.

One of the difficulties relating to some of these studies has been the lack of an operational definition of acute confusional state and consequently the absence of any standard procedure for assessing the presence and severity of 'confused' behaviour. In addition, studies of patients with acute confusional states following right middle cerebral artery infarction have seldom reported detailed memory testing. Descriptions from the paper by Schmidley and Messing (1984) paper do, however, illustrate some of the main clinical features of acute confusional states. One patient was described as being 'alert, agitated and disoriented in all spheres, with auditory and visual hallucinations. She spoke rapidly with confabulation, and continuously picked at the bed sheets and examiner's clothes.' The second patient was described as 'agitated, easily distracted, uncooperative, and oriented only to person. Her speech was fluent but with perseveration and inappropriate, flippant content. Insight was poor. She seemed unable to produce a coherent sequence of thoughts or actions.' It is worth noting that acute confusional states are not synonymous with amnesia, and that some of the 44 patients who were described by Schmidley and Messing as not having the agitated confusional state were, nevertheless, disorientated for time and place. In addition, Ahmed (1978) has reported a case of transient global amnesia after bilateral middle cerebral artery infarction, without any evidence of a confusional state of the type described above. It is also worth pointing to the wide distribution of lesion localization which may accompany middle cerebral artery pathology. This has varied from posterior parietal and frontal lesion sites in the study by Mesulam *et al.* (1976), to hydrocephalus combined with anterior cerebral pathology in a case of paramnesia following haemorrhage from a right middle cerebral artery aneurysm (Bouckoms *et al.*, 1986).

Memory deficits, apart from acute confusional states, have seldom been documented in detail for patients with middle cerebral artery pathology. Exceptions to this include the report by Kapur and Dunkley (1984) of a right-handed patient with dysphasia following a right middle cerebral artery infarction. This patient showed memory impairment on both verbal and non-verbal recognition memory tests, and it is of note that post-mortem investigations indicated marked shrinkage of the right mamillary body and also, to a lesser extent, of the right thalamus. Wood, Ebert and Kinsbourne (1982) reported that patients with left middle cerebral artery infarction differed in the pattern of memory performance on a complex figure recall task compared to patients with right middle cerebral artery infarction. The former patients tended to preserve the overall organization of the figure but to omit details, whereas the latter patients showed the reverse pattern of performance. Wood, Ebert and Kinsbourne also commented that there was relatively little change in test scores from immediate to delayed (30 minutes) recall performance in either group, although they did not report actual test scores.

Posterior cerebral and vertebrobasilar arteries

There have been a number of reports of persistent memory deficits associated with disturbance of the posterior cerebral artery (*Figure 2.5; see Plate 3*), with the deficits ranging from relatively mild focal memory impairment to significant anterograde and retrograde amnesia (Victor *et al.*, 1961; Geschwind and Fusillo, 1966; Brion *et al.*, 1968; Mohr *et al.*, 1971; Benson, Marsden and Meadows, 1974; Ross, 1980a). Transient episodes of memory loss have also been associated with

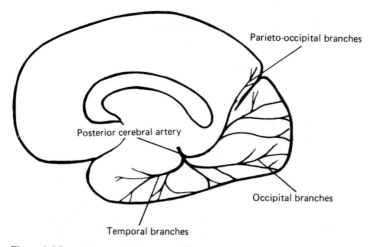

Figure 2.5 Posterior cerebral artery and its branches (from Walsh 1978. Reproduced by permission of Churchill Livingstone)

disturbance of the posterior and vertebrobasilar arteries, and these are discussed in more detail in a later section. Focal memory deficits may be present after unilateral posterior cerebral artery infarction. For example, short-term memory impairment for colour information (Davidoff and Ostergaard, 1984) may follow left posterior cerebral artery infarction, and impaired recognition of unknown or unfamiliar faces may be present after pathology implicating the right posterior cerebral artery (De Renzi, 1986). However, some debate remains as to whether a unilateral lesion associated with posterior cerebral artery infarction can result in amnesia. This discussion has to some extent been hampered by the lack of detailed testing covering various aspects of memory. While some authors (e.g. Brion *et al.*, 1968) have contended that bilateral lesions are necessary for amnesia to be present, others (e.g. Benson, 1982) have argued that a unilateral (left-sided) infarction of the posterior cerebral artery will suffice.

Victor *et al.* (1961) assessed autobiographical retrograde amnesia in some detail in a patient who had bilateral posterior cerebral artery occlusion, and found that he had an incomplete retrograde amnesia of around 2 years. Benson, Marsden and Meadows (1974) followed up the single-case study of Victor *et al.* (1961) by documenting the existence of an amnesic syndrome associated with occlusion of the posterior cerebral artery. They reviewed 10 patients who suffered an acute onset of amnesia with unilateral or bilateral occlusion of the posterior cerebral artery. They found four cases of unilateral (left-sided) infarction accompanied by amnesia. However, in two of the cases long-term follow-up was not carried out to establish

Anterior cerebral territory in axial

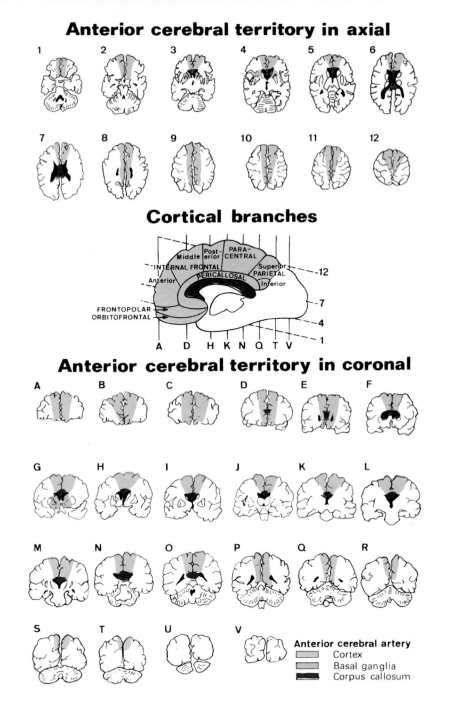

Cortical branches

Anterior cerebral territory in coronal

Anterior cerebral artery
Cortex
Basal ganglia
Corpus callosum

Plate 1 Cortical branches of the anterior cerebral artery, shown in the form of anatomical territories which are supplied by these branches. Axial and coronal computerized tomography cuts which correspond to these territories are also shown (Taken in part from Berman, Hayman and Hinck, 1980. Reproduced by permission of Williams and Wilkins Company).
Anatomical regions corresponding to axial slices: 1 – Inferior part of the medial surface of the frontal lobes; 2 – Central part of the medial surface of the frontal lobes; 3 – Medial frontal lobes, basal ganglia and corpus callosum; 4 – Frontal lobes, basal ganglia and corpus callosum; 5 – Medial frontal lobes, corpus callosum and septum pellucidum; 6 – Medial frontal lobes, corpus callosum and splenium of corpus callosum; 7 – Medial frontal lobes, body and splenium of corpus callosum; 8–10 – Medial surface of hemispheres; 11–12 – Superior part of medial surface of hemispheres

Middle cerebral territory in axial

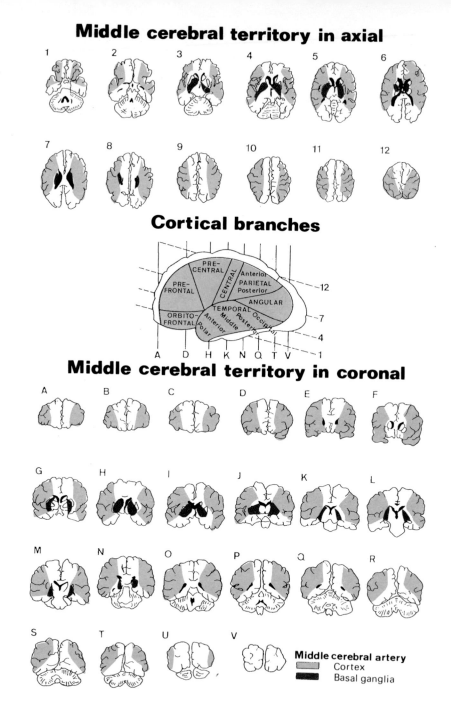

Cortical branches

Middle cerebral territory in coronal

Middle cerebral artery
- Cortex
- Basal ganglia

Plate 2 Cortical branches of the middle cerebral artery, shown in the form of territories which are supplied by these branches. Axial and coronal computerized tomography cuts which correspond to these territories are also shown (Taken in part from Berman, Hayman and Hinck, 1980. Reproduced by permission of Williams and Wilkins Company). Anatomical regions corresponding to axial slices: 1 – Lateral surface of frontal lobes and anterior tip of temporal lobes; 2 – Lateral frontal lobes and anterior third of temporal lobes; 3 – Lateral frontal lobes, anterior two thirds of temporal lobes, and basal ganglia; 4 – Frontal and temporal opercula and basal ganglia; 5–8 – Frontal and parietal lobes and basal ganglia; 9–12 – Lateral part of parietal lobes

Posterior cerebral territory in axial

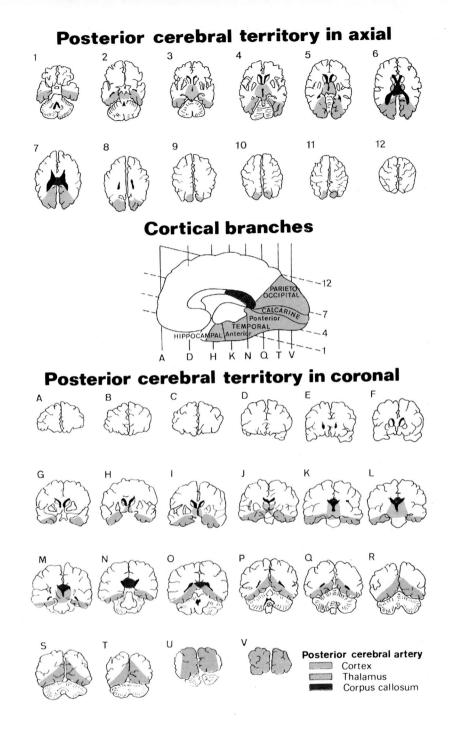

Cortical branches

Posterior cerebral territory in coronal

Posterior cerebral artery
- Cortex
- Thalamus
- Corpus callosum

Plate 3 Cortical branches of the posterior cerebral artery, shown in the form of territories which are supplied by these branches. Axial and coronal computerized tomography cuts which correspond to these territories are also shown (taken in part from Hayman *et al.*, 1981. Reproduced by permission of Williams and Wilkins Company). Anatomical regions corresponding to axial slices: 1 – Inferomedial portion of temporal lobes; 2 – Inferomedial portion of temporal lobes and brainstem; 3 – Parietomedial portion of temporal lobes and brainstem; 4 – Occipital lobes, thalamus and posterior part of internal capsule; 5–6 – Occipital lobes and thalamus; 7 – Occipital lobes and splenium of corpus callosum; 8 – Occipital lobes; 9–12 – Tips of occipital lobes

whether the amnesia was persistent or transient. The third patient had a history of memory difficulty which predated the infarction. The remaining patient did appear to display persistent amnesia after unilateral vascular pathology, and had a low Wechsler memory quotient 18 months after the stroke. Benson, Marsden and Meadows implicated vascular supply from the posterior cerebral artery to medial temporal lobe and hippocampal structures as underlying the memory deficits displayed by their patients. All of their patients had visual field defects in addition to memory impairment, and some patients also had dyslexia. They reported that the patients displayed some degree of retrograde amnesia, but this was not quantified in terms of actual test performance. They also noted that difficulties in colour identification and word-finding deficits were associated with the clinical picture, and they questioned whether vascular abnormalities ever produce a permanent amnesia in the absence of other clinical deficits.

There are two limitations to the study by Benson, Marsden and Meadows. One is the lack of detailed memory test data reported in the paper. This is all the more important since amnesia which is assessed clinically, or on the basis of tests such as the Wechsler Memory Scale, may be biased toward verbal memory deficits, and this may partly explain their observation of a higher incidence of amnesia associated with left posterior cerebral artery infarction. A second limitation is that the study was performed prior to the introduction of CT scanning, and therefore it is impossible to exclude the possibility that, in some of their cases of amnesia after apparent unilateral vascular pathology, there was a 'clinically silent' lesion in the right hemisphere. For example, in the case reported by Caplan and Hedley-Whyte (1974), the main infarction was in the area of the left posterior cerebral artery, but at post-mortem other areas of infarction were found in the right parietal and occipital lobes. A further two cases of posterior cerebral artery infarction in conjunction with marked memory disorder were subsequently reported by Brindley and Janota (1975). Both these cases had cortical blindness, and post-mortem verification of the lesion sites was obtained in the second case. In the first patient, marked memory impairment lasted for one month, and angiography showed partial occlusion of the left posterior cerebral artery and 'irregularity of calibre of the right vertebral artery'. In the second case, the memory loss lasted up to the patient's death 6 years later. At post-mortem, both posterior cerebral arteries were extremely narrow, and infarction was present in the medial aspects of the occipital lobes and also involved the hippocampus and the inferior part of the corpus callosum. In both cases, however, the memory disturbance was not documented by formal memory testing. On the basis of these various studies, it would appear that it is possible for a temporary amnesia to be brought about by unilateral posterior cerebral artery infarction, but that for anterograde and retrograde amnesia to persist, bilateral dysfunction is necessary.

Patients with disease of the vertebrobasilar arteries have also been found to display persistent impairment in the learning of new material (e.g. Lunsford, Maroon and Vega, 1977). Donnan, Walsh and Bladin (1978) reported depressed performance on the Wechsler Memory Scale in their groups of patients with vertebrobasilar disturbance. However, Baird et al. (1984) did not find deficits on subtests of the Wechsler Memory Scale in their group of patients with vertebrobasilar arterial occlusive disease, although they used published norms rather than data from control subjects for purposes of comparison. Only one of their 11 patients had a Wechsler memory quotient which was markedly below the corresponding full scale IQ score. Similarly, Perez et al. (1975) reported a mean

Wechsler memory quotient of 96.8 in their group of patients with vertebrobasilar insufficiency, although no control subjects were specifically tested for comparison. In a more extensive investigation, Ponsford, Donnan and Walsh (1980) administered a range of memory tests to patients with symptoms of vertebrobasilar disease and noted impaired performance on a number of tests, including recall and recognition of visual designs, word-list learning and paired-associate learning. They noted that severity of memory impairment correlated with several aspects of their patients' neurological condition, especially the temporal proximity of the last episode of vertebrobasilar insufficiency.

Anatomically-defined lesions

Focal cortical lesions

Relatively few studies have examined the effects of focal cortical lesions on memory where the pathology has been limited to the cerebrovascular system. In most studies of the effects of localized brain damage on memory functioning, several aetiological groups have been included, and it has therefore been difficult to ascertain any specific effects due to vascular pathology. In some studies where the aetiology has been limited to vascular disease (e.g. Reitan and Fitzhugh, 1971), memory testing has often been limited or absent.

Sudden loss of memory, with or without the presence of delusional or confabulatory behaviour, has been noted in a number of studies of patients with focal vascular lesions. In cases of transient global amnesia, a few patients may show focal vascular lesions on computerized tomography, with the most common sites being the temporal and occipital lobes (Ahmed, 1978; Ladurner, Skuarc and Sager, 1982; Landi, Giusti and Guidotti, 1982). Temporal lobe EEG abnormalities have also been noted in such patients (e.g. Lou, 1968; Fogelholm, Kivalo and Bergstrom, 1975; Rowan and Protass, 1979; Cattaino et al., 1984). Crowell et al. (1984) have reported parietal and temporal lobe abnormalities in cerebral blood flow patterns in a study of 12 patients with transient global amnesia.

A number of studies have reported disorientation for place in patients with acute right parietal (Cummings, Landis and Benson, 1983) or parieto-occipital (Fisher, 1982b) vascular lesions. This work to some extent overlaps with that covered in the section relating to the middle cerebral artery, although it is worth noting that some of the cases reported by Fisher (1982b) had lesions resulting from disturbance in arteries other than the middle cerebral artery. A more extreme form of disorientation has been noted by Levine and Grek (1984) who reported evidence of delusion in a series of patients with right hemisphere vascular disease. They observed that their group of patients invariably had some degree of cerebral atrophy in addition to the vascular lesion. The content of patients' delusions included disorientation for time and place, fabrication of events which may have occurred in the past, and misidentification of familiar people. No particular right hemisphere site was associated with the presence of delusions, and no evidence was presented with respect to the involvement of particular arteries. In some patients, delusions were transient and disorganized, but in others they tended to be more persistent and coherent.

An equally severe, but rather more specific, form of disorientation was noted by Patterson and Mack (1985). Their patient had persistent reduplicative paramnesia following a right hemisphere cerebrovascular accident (no further localization of the lesion was reported). This disorientation for place included the duplication of other hospitals in the neighbouring region, such that the patient thought he was residing in these hospitals. Their patient was aware of the inconsistencies in some of his statements, and on formal testing showed retention deficits which were most marked on non-verbal memory tasks. Where disorientation for place is characterized by florid confabulation such as reduplicative paramnesia, some degree of frontal lobe pathology is usually present. A patient with reduplicative paramnesia recently studied by the author incurred a focal right frontal haemorrhage which is shown in *Figure 2.6*. His reduplicative paramnesia included an inability to recognize his home as his own, claiming that there were two identical places with the same street name, and a belief that several hospitals existed, all with the same name.

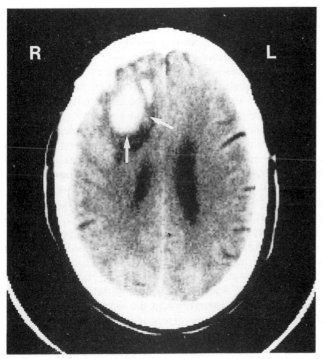

Figure 2.6 Right frontal haemorrhage in a 71-year-old man with memory disturbance characterized by reduplicative paramnesia

More specific topographical disorientation after cerebrovascular pathology, usually restricted to the posterior right hemisphere, and involving an inability to find one's way about, has been reported by a number of researchers (e.g. Assal, 1969; De Renzi, Faglioni and Villa, 1977; Hecaen, Tzortzis and Rondot, 1980; Vighetto *et al.*, 1980; Aimard *et al.*, 1981). In most of these studies the disorientation was evident both clinically and on formal testing. The patient reported by De Renzi, Faglioni and Villa (1977), whose lesion was presumed to be in the right temporoparietal region, had difficulty in finding her way around the ward, and in finding her way around the garden outside the clinic. On a visual maze-learning test which required the patient to learn a series of 23 choice points, she showed marked impairment. This patient performed normally on tests of 'space perception', including tests of copying, reproducing the orientation in space of a rod, and a tactile shape discrimination task, and she had no difficulty on other tests of verbal and non-verbal memory. Hecaen, Tzortzis and Rondot (1980) found that their patient, who had a right occipital lesion, showed deficits in both everyday topographical memory tasks and in performing a maze-learning test. Their patient also had great difficulty in learning the verbal paired-associate subtest of the Wechsler Memory Scale, and in learning non-verbal paired-associate items. In contrast to the series of single-case studies of patients with *right* posterior cerebrovascular lesions, relatively few investigations have been reported on memory disturbance in patients with *left* posterior vascular pathology, and any reports of such patients have tended to show minimal preoperative memory impairment (Conley, Moses and Helle, 1980). This may be due in part to the prominence of dysphasia in some patients' clinical presentation, which may detract from significant memory deficits, or to the possibility that marked memory disorders of the type seen in right posterior pathology are simply less likely to occur after corresponding left hemisphere damage.

Several studies have pointed out the presence of marked memory deficits, which may be accompanied by behavioural disturbance and confabulation, in patients with lesions to cortical structures in the limbic system, especially the hippocampus and hippocampal gyri (e.g. Horenstein, Chamberlain and Conomy, 1967; Van Buren and Borke, 1972). Medina, Rubino and Ross (1974) found that post-mortem evidence in the case of their memory disordered patient showed infarctions in the area of the hippocampus, fusiform and lingual gyri, and the pulvinar. Bilateral lesions in the hippocampus were considered critical in a clinicopathological study by Woods, Schoene and Kneisley (1982), where the patient had amnesia together with some language and drawing impairment. De Jong, Itabashi and Olson (1969) have described a case of amnesia (although minimal test data were reported), where there was evidence of bilateral vascular lesions affecting the hippocampus. They noted that the distribution of the hippocampal lesions was consistent with infarcts in the territories of the perforating branches of the posterior cerebral arteries. They pointed out that structures such as the mamillary bodies and the anterior and dorsal medial nuclei of the thalamus were intact in their patient, but it is worth noting that their patient also had infarctions in the occipital lobes.

Relatively few group studies have examined the effects of cerebrovascular lesions on laboratory tests of memory, as opposed to clinically obvious memory dysfunction. Studies of memory function in dysphasic patients with left hemisphere vascular lesions have found predictable deficits on tests such as Brown–Peterson short-term verbal memory tasks (Rothi and Hutchinson, 1981). In some cases, auditory-verbal short-term memory deficits may be present without any accompanying dysphasia or long-term memory impairment (Basso *et al.*, 1982). In one study (Oxbury, Campbell and Oxbury, 1974), where patients with significant dysphasia were excluded from the data analysis, delayed recall of a short story was at similar levels, and within normal limits, after right and left hemisphere cerebrovascular lesions. Grober (1984) was unable to find any impairment on a verbal recognition memory test (indicating the frequency of repetition of words on a visually-presented list) or on a spatial memory task, in patients with dysphasia following cerebrovascular disease. The presence of normal verbal memory in this study is somewhat surprising, and may partly have been related to the recognition testing format and to the possibility that, judging from the reported mean scores, some neurological and control subjects may have obtained perfect scores on the task and contributed to a slight ceiling effect. The mechanisms of impaired verbal memory after left hemisphere cerebrovascular disease remain unresolved, although some neuropsychological evidence (Moore, 1986) has suggested the participation of right hemisphere structures in mediating some aspects of verbal memory functioning.

A number of group studies such as these have tended to use functional (e.g. fluent versus non-fluent dysphasia) rather than anatomical within-group distinctions, although there are a few exceptions to this trend. Capitani et al. (1980) failed to discover any effects of hemisphere side or intra-hemispheric site of vascular lesion on performance in a test of memory for spatial position. A more unusual form of memory deficit, short-term memory impairment for tactile information, has been noted in patients with unilateral temporal lobe vascular lesions (Ross, 1980b), with the loss demonstrated in the hand contralateral to the lesion. Zaidel (1986) found impaired memory for pictorial material in patients with left or right posterior vascular lesions, but not in patients with left anterior vascular lesions (patients with right anterior lesions were not assessed). Zaidel also observed that patients with left posterior vascular lesions were selectively impaired on memory for scenes comprising novel, relatively unorganized material as opposed to more familiar, organized pictures. For the former type of material, patients with right posterior lesions were poorer than those with left posterior lesions on memory for details in the pictures, but this relationship between the two groups was reversed in the case of memory for whole scenes. None of the cerebrovascular lesion groups was impaired on a recognition version of the Benton Visual Retention Test.

Focal subcortical lesions

Patients with focal subcortical vascular lesions, whether they be due to infarction or haemorrhage, have formed the basis of a number of reports of significant memory disorder (e.g. Mills and Swanson, 1978; Castaigne et al., 1981; Destee et al., 1985). Although patients with thalamic haemorrhage have been a source of observations on amnesia (Choi et al., 1983), the main body of work with respect to memory functioning after focal subcortical vascular lesions has come from studies of patients with unilateral or bilateral infarction of thalamic nuclei.

Patients with unilateral thalamic infarction often show focal memory deficits, although there have been differing patterns of findings between studies. This may be due in part to variation in the type and range of memory tests administered, and also to the fact that there are a large number of nuclei within the thalamus, with the likelihood that different nuclei may be selectively damaged across studies, and may contribute in distinctive ways to impairments of memory functioning. In a single-case study of infarction of the right thalamus, Speedie and Heilman (1983) found evidence for focal visuospatial memory deficits. They could not elicit any remote memory impairment on a verbal test of retrograde amnesia. Graff-Radford et al. (1984) carried out detailed assessment of memory functioning in five patients with focal infarction in the area of the thalamus. Three of the patients had left tuberothalamic infarcts, one had a right tuberothalamic infarct, and the fifth patient had a deep interpeduncular vascular lesion. In the three patients with left tuberothalamic infarcts, and the single patient with a deep interpenduncular vascular lesion, both verbal and non-verbal memory were impaired. In the remaining patient with a right tuberothalamic infarct, only non-verbal memory was impaired. Somewhat surprisingly, patients with left thalamic lesions were impaired on non-verbal memory tests, including a test of remote memory for famous faces. A similar lack of material-specificity of memory deficit after left thalamic infarction has also been reported by other researchers (Abbruzzese *et al.*, 1986; Rousseaux *et al.*, 1986).

In contrast, Speedie and Heilman (1982) found that in a patient with an infarct in the left dorsomedial nucleus of the thalamus, there was anterograde amnesia for verbal material but not for non-verbal stimuli. Remote memory testing was limited to a questionnaire-based procedure, and on this test the patient performed normally. A similar pattern of anterograde and retrograde memory performance was reported by Michel *et al.* (1982) in a patient with a left paramedian thalamic infarct. Further evidence for material-specific anterograde memory deficits after left thalamic lesions comes from a study by Goldenberg, Wimmer and Maly (1983). They described a patient with amnesia after occlusion of the central branch of the left middle cerebral artery, with hyperaemia of the anterior thalamic area supplied by the thalamostriate perforating arteries. Computerized tomographic scans initially and after 2 months showed a hypodense area in the left anterior nuclei of the thalamus. The memory deficit was restricted to anterograde verbal memory tasks (retrograde amnesia was only informally assessed). This deficit partly resolved over a 7-month period. Wallesch *et al.* (1983) reported Wechsler Adult Intelligence Scale digit span, Benton Visual Retention Test performance and 'sequential learning' (learning the sequence of six colours in a series of 72 cards) in patients with unilateral vascular thalamic lesions, some of which were ischaemic and some haemorrhagic. Impairment on the Benton memory test showed a slight relationship with the rostral-caudal (anterior-posterior) dimension of the thalamic region, defined in relation to the massa intermedia or 'waist' of the third ventricle. Caudal lesions were more likely to result in low scores on this test, and rostral lesions tended to be associated with low scores on the Wechsler Adult Intelligence Scale digit span and sequence learning test.

Patients with bilateral thalamic infarction inevitably have marked memory deficits over a range of tasks, and their marked memory disorder contrasts with the more limited disorder seen after unilateral thalamic infarction (Rousseaux *et al.*, 1986). Some patients, especially in the early stages of their illness may, in addition, show signs of dementia (Schott *et al.*, 1980) and also display eye-movement disorders (e.g. Petit *et al.*, 1981; Vighetto *et al.*, 1986), although in a case reported by Barbizet *et al.* (1981) no eye-movement disorder was apparent on clinical examination. The focal lesions which follow such infarcts may be clearly distinguishable on CT and NMR scanning (Karabelas *et al.*, 1985; Swanson and Schmidley, 1985), and they afford an excellent opportunity for studying brain-behaviour relationships (*Figure 2.7*). In a series of patients with thalamic infarction, reported by Von Cramon, Hebel and Schuri (1985), three patients with bilateral thalamic lesions were described as amnesic, although generalized anterograde and retrograde memory deficits were only evident in the neuropsychological performance of one of them. The authors concluded, on the basis of their anatomical findings, that the mamillothalamic tract and the ventral portion of the lamina medullaris played a key role in amnesia following pathology in this region.

Guberman and Stuss (1983) reviewed earlier studies and presented further clinical material of their own in relation to the syndrome of bilateral anterior paramedian thalamic infarction, resulting from occlusion of a bilaterally distributed thalamosubthalamic paramedian artery. Of the two patients discussed in their

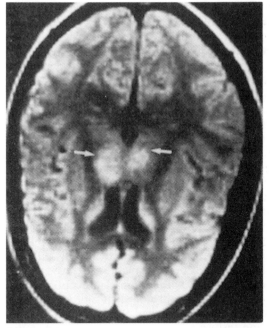

(a)

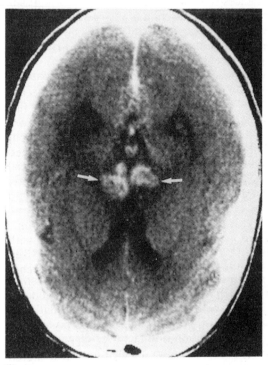

(b)

Figure 2.7 Bithalamic lesions in an amnesic patient. (*a*) NMR scan 24 hours after ictus, revealing increased signal density from both medial thalamic nuclei. (*b*) Contrast CT scan at 8 days showing infarction in similar region (from Swanson and Schmidley, 1985. Reproduced by permission of the American Heart Association Inc.)

paper, one patient had, in the initial stages, hypersomnia and vertical gaze disturbance, in addition to amnesia. In the second patient, where the thalamic lesion was mainly right-sided, eye-movement problems and memory deficits were also present initially, but showed good recovery. In both patients there was also evidence of visuospatial deficits, both initially and at follow-up, and in the first patient, the authors reported the presence of 'subcortical dementia', with impairment on language and attention tasks in addition to the visuospatial deficits. This dementia partly resolved on follow-up. They attributed the initial hypersomnia to bilateral lesions in the intralaminar nuclei, which are part of the rostral extension of the midbrain reticular formation. They reported retrograde amnesia in both patients, but did not indicate how this was assessed.

In a large-scale study of non-haemorrhagic thalamic infarcts, Graff-Radford et al. (1985) provided evidence of marked anterograde and retrograde amnesia in the two patients with bilateral medial thalamic infarction. They found additional cognitive deficits in both patients, although long-term (18 months) follow-up of one patient did reveal a relatively pure amnesic syndrome. They were unable to discern any temporal 'gradient' in the pattern of remote memory loss. Winocur et al. (1984) carried out a detailed neuropsychological analysis of their patient with bilateral medial thalamic infarction, and noted impaired performance on delayed recall, recognition and cued learning tasks, together with minimal susceptibility to interference in short-term memory tasks. They could not elicit any evidence of significant retrograde amnesia, although the small number of tests given, and the fact that one of these was a recognition task, may have partly contributed to this finding.

Caplan (1980) has reviewed disturbances of memory and other behavioural and neurological abnormalities that may accompany infarction of the rostral brainstem, and the posterior regions of the cerebral hemispheres fed by the distal basilar artery. He noted that sleepiness, apathy and impaired attention may result from infarction of the rostral medial reticular formation due to occlusion of the mesencephalic artery or some of its branches. He further observed that patients with rostral brainstem infarction may show a marked degree of confabulation, and this may be accompanied by misuse of environmental cues. Caplan pointed out that this type of 'extraordinary confabulation' is usually associated with disturbances of wakefulness. Few group studies of memory functioning in patients with brainstem vascular lesions have been reported, apart from one investigation (Oxbury, Campbell and Oxbury, 1974) which found normal delayed recall of a short story by patients with brainstem infarction who were assessed 3–4 weeks after onset of the illness (more detailed localization of lesion was not indicated).

Generalized cerebrovascular disease

Although the concepts of 'multi-infarct dementia' and 'arteriosclerotic dementia' have been the subject of much discussion (Brust, 1983b; Pearce, 1983), there have been relatively few systematic studies of memory functioning in patients classified under these conditions. It is likely that such patients form quite a heterogeneous population of dementing conditions, if only because the particular constellation of vascular lesions is unlikely to be identical in any two patients. It is also possible, as some have argued (Brust, 1983a), that the condition is in fact over-diagnosed, and that some patients with vascular dementia may suffer from other neurological conditions (e.g. cerebral degnerative disease) more critical to their dementia than

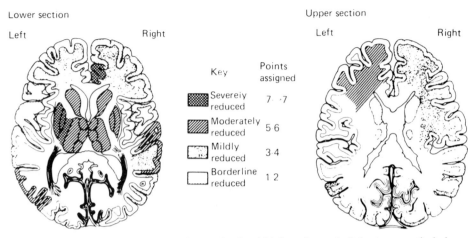

Figure 2.8 Areas of infarction as evident in a study of multi-infarct dementia. Infarcts are particularly evident in the thalamus bilaterally, both basal ganglia, both temporal cortices plus the left internal capsule and the right cingulate cortex (from Kitagawa *et al.*, 1984. Reproduced by permission of the American Heart Association Inc.)

specific areas of infarction. A cerebrovascular disturbance has frequently been postulated as underlying transient global amnesia, and it is possible that cerebral atrophy reported in the CT scans of some patients (e.g. Cattaino *et al.*, 1984) represents diffuse cerebrovascular disease. One of the CT scans in the study by Cattaino *et al.* did in fact show evidence of multiple cortical vascular lesions.

Eslinger *et al.* (1984) obtained quantitative indices of cerebral atrophy and ventricular dilatation in a group of patients with dementia related to generalized cerebrovascular disease. From a correlation matrix of four such measures with

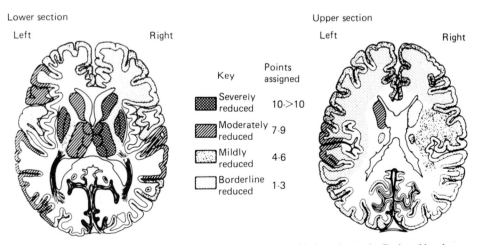

Figure 2.9 Areas of reduced cerebral blood flow in a study of multi-infarct dementia. Reduced levels are evident in the thalamus bilaterally, both basal ganglia, both temporal cortices, the left inferior frontal cortex and the left parietal cortex (from Kitagawa *et al.*, 1984. Reproduced by permission of the American Heart Association Inc.)

seven memory test scores, only two correlations proved to be statistically significant – retention of visual designs with dilatation of the frontal horns, and story recall with width of the interhemispheric fissure. Perez *et al.* (1977) observed that the memory impairment in patients with vascular dementia did not correlate with reduction of cerebral blood flow. Kitagawa *et al.* (1984) did, however, find some evidence for such a correlation in their study of patients with multi-infarct dementia. The most common sites of cerebral infarction and reduced cerebral blood flow included regions, such as the thalamus and temporal lobes, which have been considered to play an important role in memory function (*Figures 2.8* and *2.9*). Reduced cerebral blood flow in the left mid-temporal region correlated with low verbal memory scores (non-verbal memory was not tested), and disorientation for time and place was associated with reduced flow in the left or right frontal cortex, and also in the right cingulate cortex.

Episodic cerebrovascular disturbance and related disorders

Transient global amnesia

Although transient episodes of memory loss may arise from a variety of aetiologies, one of the most common sources is some form of cerebrovascular disturbance. The condition known as transient global amnesia has been a major focus of attention by research workers interested in cerebrovascular disease, and the condition has been extensively reviewed by Markowitsch (1983) and Caplan (1985). In the present section, I will be mainly concerned with those instances where a specific cerebrovascular aetiology has been implicated in the memory disturbance. Aspects of the assessment of patients with transient global amnesia are discussed in Chapter 1 (p. 10).

Instances of transient global amnesia have often been associated with disturbance in the vertebrobasilar arterial system (e.g. Shuttleworth and Wise, 1973; Longridge, Hachinski and Barber, 1979; Ponsford and Donnan, 1980), and a history of vertebrobasilar ischaemia appears to be a significant predisposing risk factor for the occurrence of transient global amnesia (Kushner and Hauser, 1985). One study, however, has reported a case of transient global amnesia in association with bilateral middle cerebral artery disturbance (Ahmed, 1978). Patients with a diagnosis of transient global amnesia are mostly over 50 years of age and usually experience one attack, although a few patients may suffer from recurrent attacks. Attacks start suddenly and generally involve:

(1) An inability to form new memories of events experienced during the episode. This memory deficit is usually quite generalized, with some degree of disorientation for time and place. However, more limited, partial forms of memory loss have also been reported (Damasio and Graff-Radford, 1983).
(2) A temporary, pre-ictal amnesia for events in the hours and days preceding the attack. In a few cases, this may extend into a retrograde amnesia for several years, but such prolonged retrograde amnesia usually shrinks following the attack to a brief, residual pre-ictal amnesia.
(3) A perplexed state associated with repetitive questioning about one's plight. The individual tends, however, to be alert, to retain personal identity, and he is often able to carry out complex motor tasks.
(4) The patient is invariably left with memory loss for the episode itself and for any events which occurred during the episode.

In many cases, the aetiology of the transient global amnesia cannot be precisely indicated, nor the anatomical locus of any disturbance delineated, but some exceptions to this have been reported (*see* p. 54). It is, however, important to point out that evidence of focal vascular disturbance in patients with transient global amnesia may simply reflect coexistent cerebral dysfunction, and may not necessarily point to the neurological mechanisms underlying this type of transient memory disorder. Jensen and Olivarius (1980) found that from a series of 28 patients who had transient global amnesia, there were 10 cases with symptoms suggesting transient ischaemia in the vertebrobasilar system, these being episodic vertigo and transient visual disturbances. Angiography was carried out in four cases, and in three there was evidence of vascular pathology in one or both carotid arteries (*see* Robinson and Long, 1972). The patients were followed up over a period averaging 77 months. Three patients developed infarction in the distribution of the basilar artery, one patient had a right hemisphere stroke, and two had a small infarct in the brainstem. Only three of the subgroup of 10 patients had no permanent memory deficits.

Mathew and Meyer (1974) reported a series of 14 patients who suffered one or more attacks of transient global amnesia. Four-vessel angiography was carried out in 12 of the patients, and in most cases arteriosclerotic lesions were found in the vertebrobasilar or posterior cerebral arteries. Stenotic and occlusive lesions in the posterior cerebral arteries are often present, and were bilaterally distributed. Regional cerebral blood flow studies were also carried out, and in addition to a generalized reduction in cerebral blood flow, focal reductions were noted in the mid- and posterior-temporal regions. Recurrent attacks of transient global amnesia were noted in eight patients during a follow-up period of 30 months. All patients with recurrent episodes showed poor memory performance on anterograde memory tests. Two patients developed 'amnesic stroke', with clinical signs of acute infarction in the distribution of the posterior cerebral artery. Cochran *et al.* (1982) described seven patients who experienced transient global amnesia while undergoing cerebral angiography. They concluded that in most of the cases impaired circulation in the posterior cerebral arteries could be directly or indirectly implicated in the aetiology of the amnesic episode.

Transient ischaemic attacks associated with carotid artery disease

Patients with a history of transient ischaemic attacks may show memory impairment, and this is often accompanied by evidence of bilateral carotid artery disease. In general, reports of memory functioning in patients with carotid artery disease are difficult to interpret. This is in part due to the heterogeneous nature of such patients – in a number of studies (e.g. Parker *et al.*, 1983; Van Den Burg *et al.*, 1985) a proportion of patients have incurred cerebral infarction, and the severity and pattern of memory impairment will obviously depend on the number of such patients within a particular sample, and also on the location, size and recency of the cerebral infarct in individual cases. Where patients with minor stroke are considered as a separate group, they tend to show poorer memory performance than patients with a history of transient ischaemic attacks but without focal infarction (Sinatra *et al.*, 1984). However, in cases with established cerebral infarcts memory functioning may be normal if collateral circulation is well-developed, as in some cases of Moya-Moya disease, where there is bilateral impairment in carotid artery blood flow due to developmental anomalies (Bornstein, 1985). The generalized versus focal nature of any memory impairment will also depend on the laterality and extent of stenosis in the carotid arteries (*see* Delaney, Wallace and Egelko, 1980). In addition, the type of control data used by investigators has tended to be somewhat variable, with some (e.g. Kelly, Garron and Javid, 1980; Van Den Burg *et al.*, 1985) using data from patients with peripheral vascular disease, and others (e.g. Williams and McGee, 1964; Hemmingsen *et al.*, 1982; Baird *et al.*, 1984) using published normative data. Allowing for these various qualifications, the majority of these studies have tended to report the absence of marked memory impairment in most patients with carotid artery disease.

Migraine

While the precise pathophysiological basis of migraine remains a matter of speculation (Pearce, 1984), a disturbance of cerebral blood flow may often occur, if only as a secondary reaction to some other form of neuronal dysfunction. Migraine sufferers have been reported to complain of severe headaches or neurological symptoms (e.g. visual disturbance) in association with transient episodes of memory loss (Caplan *et al.*, 1981), and Jensen and Olivarius (1981) indicated that in six out of seven cases of migraine sufferers who experienced an episode of transient global amnesia, there was evidence of vertebrobasilar deficiency. Some researchers (Crowell *et al.*, 1984) have further argued that in such cases transient global amnesia 'may be a manifestation of an abnormal redistribution of blood during the vasodilatory phase of migraine'. Several studies have found evidence for more persistent memory impairment in patients with a history of migraine. Zeitlin and Oddy (1984) reported impaired verbal recognition memory performance in a group of migraine sufferers, although the authors regarded their observations as somewhat tentative. Hooker and Raskin (1986) found impaired memory performance on a delayed verbal recall task in patients with either classic or common migraine, the former patients being characterized by the presence of focal neurological disturbance in association with the migraine attack.

Management of memory deficits

Psychological techniques

Although there is now a considerable body of literature on psychological methods to improve memory function in brain-damaged patients (e.g. Wilson and Moffatt, 1984), relatively few studies have focused on attempts to improve memory function in patients with cerebrovascular disease. A number of these have tended to concentrate on changing patients' coding strategies (e.g. Kapur, 1979). In a detailed single-case study, Wilson (1982) reported a systematic attempt to improve memory in a patient who had bilateral cerebral infarction, probably involving both posterior cerebral arteries. Wilson attempted memory retraining in four problem areas; the patient's daily time-table, remembering people's names, remembering a shopping list, and remembering short routes. The first three of these did show evidence of improvement, but the last memory difficulty remained impervious to significant change. One of the techniques used by Wilson was visual imagery, and this was particularly helpful in improving the ability of this patient, and of several other patients with cerebrovascular disease described later (Wilson, 1987), to learn people's names.

Gasparrini and Satz (1979) also described the successful use of imagery techniques, on this occasion to improve verbal memory in patients with left hemisphere cerebrovascular disease. They found that in certain test conditions visual imagery was more successful at improving memory than other procedures. Such conditions included situations where the therapist went through the imagery procedures stage by stage and when items to be remembered were restricted to concrete nouns. A further visual mnemonic strategy for improving memory function in patients with left hemisphere vascular pathology was briefly described by Leftoff (1981). Drawing on the finding that these patients performed better on serial retrieval of visually presented word list material compared to other modalities, they encouraged patients to 'chunk' verbal information onto spaces on a visual array, and to use this strategy at time of retrieval. They reported improvement in list learning performance, and some evidence for generalization across memory tasks, although this aspect of their study was limited to two subjects.

In contrast to visual/visuospatial strategies such as these, Gianutsos and Gianutsos (1979) used practice in verbal mnemonics (making up a short meaningful story around three target words) to improve short-term verbal memory in three patients with right hemisphere cerebrovascular accidents. Memory training and assessment paradigms were similar, in that both employed a Brown–Peterson distractor paradigm. Although there was some evidence for transfer of training, in that the Wechsler memory quotients of the three patients improved, no control patients were repeat-tested, and improvements were largely restricted to the digit span and visual reproduction subtests of the Wechsler Memory Scale.

Using relatively novel retraining procedures derived in part from experimental memory research, Schacter, Rich and Stampp (1985) found some improvement in memory functioning in a group of four patients, two of whom had memory deficits subsequent to rupture of anterior communicating artery aneurysms. The particular technique which Schacter, Rich and Stampp described was a 'spaced retrieval' technique whereby patients were taught to retrieve information at increasingly long intervals after its initial presentation. As in the earlier studies, the observed improvement appeared to be maximal only in certain situations, namely, where the amount of information to be retained was relatively small, and where testing was carried out after fairly short retention intervals. Wilson (1987) has described an attempt to improve the memory of a patient with an anterior communicating artery aneurysm for details about his own clinical condition by using techniques which essentially involved his reading the information in a structured question-and-answer format, and incorporating repeated testing of retention for the material; she found some limited improvement in the patient's memory for this information.

Medical treatments

Relatively few studies have examined the possible beneficial effects of drugs on memory deficits in patients with cerebrovascular disease, and those carried out have mainly been restricted to patients with generalized disease. In addition, compared to the studies discussed in the sections above and below, memory testing has generally been less extensive. Most of the investigations described here have focused on drugs which are intended to improve cerebral blood flow. Several studies have considered the effects of cyclandelate in patients with deterioration in cognitive function related to generalized cerebrovascular disease (Ball and Taylor,

1967; Fine *et al.*, 1970; Young, Hall and Blakemore, 1974). Beneficial effects were usually found in the 'drug' as opposed to 'placebo' condition, but the effect was generally slight and restricted to certain memory tasks, and one study (Westreich, Alter and Lundgren, 1975) did not find any differences in degree of improvement in memory performance between placebo and drug conditions. Similar, somewhat disappointing, results were obtained by Smith, Philippus and Lowrey (1968) who observed only minor improvement in memory functioning of patients with moderate cerebral atherosclerosis who received papaverine hydrochloride to improve cerebral blood flow. Bouvier, Passeron and Chupin (1974) found some improvement on subtests of the Wechsler Memory Scale in patients receiving Praxilene (naftidrofuryloxalate), but the patient group was poorly documented, with only a general statement that their dementia was 'due mainly to reduction in cerebral blood flow'. Rivera *et al.* (1976) reported improved memory test performance in patients with vertebrobasilar insufficiency who were administered betahistine hydrochloride, a cerebral vasodilator. However, some improvement was also evident in the placebo condition, and the increase in memory test scores was only statistically significant in one of the two cross-over conditions.

The effects of hyperbaric oxygen on memory functioning in elderly patients with generalized cerebrovascular disease have also been somewhat disappointing. Thompson *et al.* (1976) did not find any improvement, following such therapy, in scores on the Wechsler Memory Scale or the Benton Visual Retention Test.

Surgical procedures

The most frequently used surgical procedure to improve memory functioning in patients with cerebrovascular disease has been carotid endarterectomy. This procedure consists of exposing the carotid bifurcation in the neck, opening the carotid artery and removing the offending atheromatous plaque. There is considerable evidence for the efficacy of this type of surgery for improving memory function (e.g. Horne and Royle, 1974; Kelly, Garron and Javid, 1980; Owens *et al.*, 1980; Hemmingsen *et al.*, 1982; Jacobs *et al.*, 1983) and against any significant beneficial effects (e.g. Williams and McGee, 1964; Parker *et al.*, 1983; Brinkman *et al.*, 1984; Van den Burg *et al.*, 1985). Asken and Hobson (1977) reviewed a number of studies which examined the effects of carotid endarterectomy on cognitive functioning, and concluded that the evidence for and against improvement after surgery was equivocal, partly due to inconsistent findings and methodological shortcomings in studies. These shortcomings have included lack of appropriate control patients and inadequate follow-up information.

The study by Parker *et al.* (1983), which failed to find improvement in memory, was particularly rigorous in that their control group did have carotid artery disease, but did not undergo endarterectomy. The two carotid artery disease groups were also similar in terms of history of previous stroke, and in the interval from the last arteriogram. In addition, neuropsychological testing was carried out 'blind' and the examiner did not know the group of the patient that he was assessing.

In those studies which have found improvement in memory functioning after carotid endarterectomy, the mechanisms of such improvement remain unclear. For example, in a well-controlled study which did observe improved memory functioning, Boysen *et al.* (1985) only found limited changes in cerebral blood flow after surgery. They hypothesized that a cessation of microembolization or an increase in cerebral perfusion pressure may underlie the improvements in cognitive functioning which they observed.

A second surgical procedure which has been evaluated with respect to its possible beneficial effects on memory, is extracranial to intracranial (EC/IC) bypass surgery. In this procedure, the superficial temporal artery is joined to a branch of the middle cerebral artery using microsurgical techniques. Nielsen *et al.* (1985) found evidence of a slight improvement in memory function after extracranial to intracranial bypass surgery which was carried out to reduce transient ischaemic attacks associated with internal carotid artery disease. Although control subjects were also tested, repeat testing was unfortunately not carried out to parallel that performed on neurological patients receiving surgery. In an earlier study by Binder *et al.* (1982), where control subjects were tested a second time, no significant difference was found in favour of the bypass group, although there was evidence suggestive of improvement in memory performance as a result of surgery.

Distinctive features of memory disorders in patients with cerebrovascular disease

Comparisons between patients with cerebrovascular lesions and those with other types of cerebral pathology need to take into account both the site and size of the vascular lesion and also the recency of any vascular episodes which have occurred. Few studies have compared focal areas of cortical or subcortical infarction/haemorrhage with equivalent focal lesions caused by other pathology, such as cerebral tumour or penetrating head injury. Some comparisons have, however, been made between patients with particular arterial disease and those having some other cerebral pathology. (The clinical differentiation of cerebrovascular and epileptic forms of transient memory loss is discussed on p. 192.)

Corkin *et al.* (1985) compared the memory performance of patients who suffered rupture of anterior communicating artery aneurysms with that of a range of neurological patients, including head-injured patients, a group of anoxic patients and a group of patients with herpes encephalitis. Three single-case studies were also incorporated in the study. Patients were selected for inclusion in the study if they were 'globally amnesic upon clinical observation', did not have focal memory deficits or dementia, and appeared to have normal language comprehension and perceptual processing abilities. The memory impairment of patients with anterior communicating artery aneurysm was found to be less marked than that of patients from the other aetiological groups. Further comparisons between the patients with aneurysms and those with blunt head injury failed to indicate any differences in pattern of memory performance between the two groups. However, the IQ levels of patients with anterior communicating artery aneurysms were higher than that of other groups of patients, and this may have accounted for part of the superiority in memory performance, and may possibly have masked any qualitative differences with other aetiologies. Butters *et al.* (1984) also noted superior performance in a single-case study of a patient with an aneurysm of the anterior communicating artery, when his short-term verbal memory or his verbal paired-associate learning performance was compared with that of patients with alcoholic Korsakoff's syndrome. On retrograde amnesia tests, this patient also performed better than an encephalitic patient, and his performance was little different from that of normal control subjects. However, his unusually high IQ of 141 may have contributed to part of this difference in memory performance, especially in the comparison with patients with alcoholic Korsakoff's syndrome, who typically have IQ scores in the average range. Parkin *et al.* (1987) have pointed to features of the memory performance of their patient with anterior communicating artery aneurysm which distinguished him from patients with alcoholic Korsakoff's syndrome; these included the absence of retrograde amnesia in their patient, a less rapid rate of forgetting (although a ceiling effect somewhat limits the significance of this finding), and greater facilitation of paired-associate learning by verbal/imagery mediation techniques.

Perez *et al.* (1975) compared the performance of three groups of patients on the Wechsler Memory Scale – patients with multiple infarctions, those with vertebrobasilar insufficiency, and a group of patients with primary degenerative dementia. In general, the latter patients had much poorer memory scores than the two former groups with cerebrovascular disease, and the difference between degenerative and vertebrobasilar pathology was particularly marked. The differences between the two cerebrovascular groups did not reach statistical significance, although there was a tendency for the multi-infarct patients to perform at a somewhat lower level than those with vertebrobasilar insufficiency. Johannesson *et al.* (1979) have provided evidence which suggests that isolated short-term memory deficits are more likely to occur in patients with cerebrovascular disease than patients with primary degenerative dementia, although it is possible that the latter patients in their study were simply at a more advanced stage of dementia than patients in their cerebrovascular disease group. Shindler, Caplan and Hier (1984) also found more impaired memory performance, in the form of a higher rate of prior intrusions, in elderly patients with primary degenerative dementia than in patients with stroke-related dementia. In addition, differences in pattern, as opposed to severity, of memory deficits have been noted between patients with vascular and degenerative dementia. Muramoto (1984) found that while elderly patients with primary degenerative dementia performed much worse on a visuospatial learning task compared to an auditory-verbal learning test, patients with multi-infarct dementia performed at a similar level on both tasks.

Summary

Memory deficits after cerebrovascular lesions in the territory supplied by the anterior cerebral artery or its branches have been well documented, although in most cases such deficits have been found to be relatively mild or transient. Some instances of amnesia have been reported, especially after ruptured aneurysms in the anterior communicating artery, and in some patients confabulation has also been observed in the early stages of recovery. Detailed studies of memory functioning in patients with lesions involving the middle cerebral artery have been less frequently reported, and have mainly focused on acute disturbances of memory function, as in acute confusional states. Memory deficits have been frequently reported in patients with vascular lesions in the territory of the posterior cerebral artery. In most cases, additional cognitive impairment such as visual or language disturbance, has accompanied the memory loss. Whether amnesia can follow a unilateral infarction of the posterior cerebral artery remains a matter of some debate, although most cases with post-mortem verification of the lesion pathology have reported that amnesia occurs only after bilateral infarction. In the case of lesions involving the vertebrobasilar artery, memory deficits have been milder than those associated with the posterior cerebral artery, and often take the form of episodes of transient memory loss.

Focal vascular lesions of the cortex result in memory deficits which are, in general, consistent with inter- and intra-hemispheric specialization of function. Thus, left- and right-sided vascular lesions have been shown to result in verbal or visuospatial memory deficits respectively, with lesions of the right parietal lobe, either temporal lobe, and hippocampus tending to be most frequently associated with persistent memory disturbance. However, a few studies have noted the absence of significant hemispheric-specificity of pattern of memory deficits, and this may be due in part to factors such as contralateral reduction in cerebral blood flow which can accompany unilateral cerebral infarction. In the case of subcortical structures, vascular lesions of the thalamic nuclei have been particularly well studied. In most instances, left thalamic, right thalamic and bilateral thalamic lesions have resulted in verbal, visuospatial and generalized memory impairment respectively, but a few cases have been reported of relatively generalized memory impairment after apparent unilateral thalamic infarction. It will be important to see if further studies, with post-mortem verification of lesion localization, confirm such findings.

Bithalamic infarction has usually been accompanied by a significant degree of retrograde and anterograde amnesia, and while this appears to be have been more frequent and more severe than that reported in cases of unilateral thalamic infarction, no systematic comparisons appear to have been reported in this regard. Patients with more generalized cerebrovascular pathology, as in the case of 'multi-infarct dementia' or bilateral carotid artery disease, have been found to display a variable degree of memory impairment. This may be due in part to the relatively heterogeneous nature of such groups of patients. In general, it appears that memory deficits in both of these conditions are relatively mild or moderate in severity, and this is particularly evident when patients are compared with those having primary degenerative cerebral pathology.

Transient episodes of memory loss are often associated with acute disturbance in the posterior or vertebrobasilar arteries, and a proportion of these patients may be left with persistent memory deficits. However, residual memory impairment in association with carotid artery disease tends to be somewhat more variable, and may often be determined by whether areas of cerebral infarction are also present. Both transient and persistent memory disorders have been noted in some migraine sufferers, but the precise cerebrovascular basis of any such difficulties remains uncertain.

Attempts to improve memory impairment in patients with cerebrovascular disease have encompassed a variety of psychological, medical and surgical procedures. Psychological studies have used a number of techniques, ranging from the use of visual imagery to the implementation of more sophsticated procedures such as the use of 'spaced-retrieval' practice. In general, any improvements in memory functioning have been relatively mild and/or task-specific, and little evidence is available as to whether psychological techniques can bring about long-term improvement in significant aspects of a patient's everyday memory functioning. Studies of drug treatment of memory disturbance in cerebrovascular disease have found only limited benefits of such therapy. Evidence with regard to the effects of surgical intervention is somewhat more controversial, with a number of studies reporting improvement after surgery while other studies have found no such improvement. Differences in patient populations, and variability in the use of control groups to allow for practice-effects in repeat testing, may partly explain such differences. In general, comparisons of cases of amnesia or dementia due to cerebrovascular disease with similar cases resulting from other aetiologies have indicated the milder severity of memory disorder in the former patients. However, only a limited amount of relevant data is available, and some of this suffers from poor matching of patient groups, so this observation must be regarded as tentative.

Chapter 3

Cerebral tumours

The effects of brain tumours on cerebral functioning are multifactorial: in addition to the destructive effects of intrinsic brain tumours, factors such as displacement of neighbouring cerebral structures, generalized cerebral oedema, disturbance of cerebral blood flow, and disturbance in the flow of cerebrospinal fluid, may be present and therefore any of these variables may contribute to impairment in the memory performance of a patient with a cerebral tumour. Studies of cerebral blood flow and brain metabolism in patients with cerebral tumours have yielded evidence of considerable abnormality of cerebral function, often greater than that evident on CT scanning, and sometimes spreading to the other hemisphere (e.g. Beaney et al., 1985). Further, variables, such as the pathology of the tumour, are also likely to play some part in determining the extent of the associated cognitive deficit (Hom and Reitan, 1984), but there is, as yet, a dearth of systematic evidence in respect of any such effects on memory functioning.

The three main types of brain tumour pathology consist of gliomas (intrinsic tumours arising from glial cells in the brain), metastases (intrinsic or extrinsic tumours which are secondary to a primary tumour elsewhere in the body) and meningiomas (extrinsic tumours which arise from the meninges). Most of the studies discussed in this chapter have assessed patients with one of these types of tumour. It may, however, be worth noting that non-metastatic cerebral complications of tumours elsewhere in the body have occasionally been associated with memory disorders. Corsellis, Goldberg and Norton (1968) described three patients with bronchial carcinoma who had marked memory disorder in association with an encephalitic-type of illness which resulted in destruction of the temporal lobe and adjacent limbic system structures. Memory disorder may also occur as a rare accompaniment of Hodgkin's disease (Carr, 1982). Duyckaerts et al. (1985) have described in some detail a patient with Hodgkin's disease who displayed anterograde amnesia, with no evidence of any confabulation nor any retrograde amnesia. Post-mortem investigations revealed selective, bilateral pathology in the hippocampus and amygdala. The authors were unable to indicate any possible aetiology for this pathology, and pointed to the lack of inflammatory changes in the brain of their patient.

Although a number of authors have alluded to memory disorders in patients with brain tumours (e.g. Hecaen and Ajuriaguerra, 1956; Mulder and Swenson, 1974), much of this evidence has been based on clinical observations or subjective reports by patients. In this chapter, I will mainly concentrate on studies which have reported detailed memory testing of patients.

Cortical tumours

While a good deal of evidence is available on the effects of focal cortical lesions on memory functioning (Luria, 1976; Walsh, 1978), there has been comparatively little work on the effects of such lesions when the aetiology is restricted to cerebral neoplasia. Transient loss of memory has occasionally been reported in patients with tumours of the left hemisphere (Lisak and Zimmerman, 1977; Ross, 1983) and right hemisphere (Meador, Adams and Flanigan, 1985), usually with direct or indirect medial temporal lobe involvement. In some of these patients, an initial episode of transient global amnesia was subsequently followed by focal and more persistent neurological signs. Persisting memory deficits have been more frequently studied than transient memory disorders.

In general, the hemispheric side of tumour has been related to the material-specific nature of the memory deficit in the same way as in other types of cerebral pathology, with verbal memory deficits following left hemisphere pathology, and non-verbal memory impairment resulting from right hemisphere pathology. However, a few atypical observations have been reported, and these may to some extent be specific to cerebral tumours.

In a study by Meyer and Falconer (1960), auditory verbal memory deficits were noted in patients with left temporal lobe tumours, but there was no evidence of corresponding non-verbal deficits in patients with right temporal lobe tumours. In this study, it is possible that the findings may have been partly due to the small number of cases and the fact that the non-verbal memory tests mainly consisted of immediate recall of visual patterns, which were amenable to some degree of verbal coding. In another study, where the patient sample ranged from children to adults, Cavazzuti *et al.* (1980) found impaired performance on both verbal and non-verbal memory tests in patients with right temporal lobe tumours. In most of the patients with left temporal lobe tumours, there was evidence of verbal memory impairment and mild non-verbal memory deficit. In a study of a series of patients with left hemisphere lesions, most of which were tumours, Coughlan (1979) found significant verbal memory deficits, using both recall and recognition tests. Similar memory deficits were found in patients whose lesions were restricted to the temporal lobe and in patients whose lesions were sited in other areas of the brain. Patients with dysphasia did not differ from other patients in their pattern of memory deficits. However, it appears that some of Coughlan's patients were tested preoperatively and some tested postoperatively, and so it is not possible to say with confidence whether any deficits were due to the effects of a whole or incomplete tumour mass, or to any effects of neurosurgical intervention.

In the case of frontal lobe tumours, there is a relative dearth of studies which have focused specifically on this group of patients. In my experience, patients with frontal lobe tumours less commonly present with subjective symptoms of memory difficulty compared with patients with tumours in the temporal lobe. In terms of test deficits, frontal lobe tumours may result in memory impairment, but this impairment tends to be highly variable and is dependent on a number of factors, including the size of the tumour – large, bilateral frontal tumours will tend to displace neighbouring structures and/or cause obstructive hydrocephalus (*Figure 3.1*), thus resulting in greater memory impairment than smaller frontal tumours; site of the tumour – some subfrontal tumours may lead to marked memory impairment through their proximity to limbic system structures; and the pathology of the tumour – frontal meningiomas will generally result in less memory

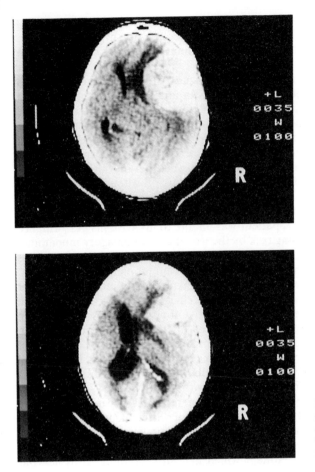

Figure 3.1 CT scan showing large right frontal meningioma, with some associated hydrocephalus, in a 67-year-old woman with marked memory impairment

impairment than gliomas of the frontal lobe, perhaps due to the greater cerebral oedema which is usually found with the latter tumours. In general, a pure amnesic syndrome rarely occurs after frontal lobe tumours – where the tumour is significant enough to lead to marked memory impairment, then there will usually also be evidence of generalized cognitive dysfunction.

Turning to studies of changes in memory function after removal of cortical tumours, apart from a few clinical reports of improvement in cognitive function after tumour removal (e.g. Chee et al., 1985), few systematic investigations have been carried out on memory function before and after surgery. An exception to this is the study by Cavazzuti et al. (1980) referred to earlier, where patients were assessed preoperatively and 10–12 months postoperatively. They found that 'contralateral memory functioning', e.g. non-verbal memory in patients with left temporal lobe tumours, improved after surgery, but 'ipsilateral memory functions', e.g. verbal memory performance in the same set of patients, showed a deficit after surgery. In the study by Meyer and Falconer (1960) also referred to earlier, some of the left hemisphere tumour patients did improve following surgery, but others did not show any change in memory function. The authors indicated that it was the patients in whom the surgical procedure did not involve removal of normal temporal lobe tissue who showed improvement subsequent to surgery. However, the absence of repeat testing of control subjects limits the significance of these findings.

Some patients may show persistent memory difficulty which may be evident both in the early postoperative period (Canavan, Janota and Schurr, 1985) and some time after the initiation of treatment for a cerebral tumour (Hochberg and Slotnick, 1980). Wilson (1981) has described a patient who had persistent memory difficulty several years after treatment for a left parietotemporal astrocytoma. He was taught to learn the names of familiar people by coding the name in the form of a visual image, and this learning was maintained over an 8-week period during which the patient was not receiving rehabilitation. A less successful attempt to use visual imagery was reported by Jones (1974) in the case of a patient with an astrocytoma which was primarily left temporal in location, but also appeared to extend across the hippocampal commissure. This patient was unable to improve his performance on a verbal paired-associate learning task by the use of a visual imagery mnemonic.

In some brain-tumour patients assessed after the initiation of treatment, it is difficult to distinguish between the effects of the brain tumour on memory function, and the effects (detrimental or beneficial) of radiation or chemotherapy. A number of studies of neuropsychological functioning in children have focused on the possible side-effects of cancer treatment on cognitive functions. While impairment in intelligence test performance has been reported in children receiving radiation and other forms of therapy for treatment of cerebral tumours (Duffner, Cohen and Thomas, 1983) or acute lymphocytic leukaemia (Eiser, 1978; Moss, Nannis and Poplack, 1981), only a few reports have specifically commented on disturbances in memory functioning (Goff, Anderson and Cooper, 1981; Meadows et al., 1981; Kun, Mulhern and Crisco, 1983). The extent of memory testing in these studies was, however, relatively limited. Considerable research remains to be carried out on the effects of surgical and non-surgical treatments, both early and late in the disease process, on memory functioning in patients with brain tumours, or in patients receiving prophylactic treatment which may involve the central nervous system.

Subcortical tumours

Marked memory impairment has been reported in most studies of patients with subcortical tumours, especially where these are located in or around the third ventricle (Delay, Brion and Derouesne, 1964; Angelergues 1969; Assal et al., 1976). In many patients with third ventricle tumours, more general changes in the level of arousal and metabolic functions may also be present, and changes in these may sometimes parallel fluctuations in the severity of the memory disturbance (Luria, 1976). Both transient and persistent memory difficulties have been reported in patients with third ventricle tumours. In the case of transient memory disturbances, which have usually resembled transient global amnesia (see p. 62), the underlying pathology has generally consisted of a glioma in the limbic system or neighbouring structures (Aimard et al., 1971; Boudin et al., 1975), although other types of pathology, such as a pituitary adenoma, have also been reported (Hartley, Heilman and Garcia-Bengochea, 1974). Most tumours have been bilateral, but some researchers have argued that a unilateral tumour, with or without additional vascular pathology, can result in transient global amnesia. For example, Findler *et al.* (1983) reported a case of transient global amnesia associated with a metastasis in the right posterior thalamic region. They concluded that in patients with a unilateral brain tumour, the aetiology for the transient global amnesia was probably vascular, with compromise of blood flow in the hemisphere not affected by the tumour. Findler *et al.* did not, however, present any convincing evidence for transient vascular disturbance in the left hemisphere of their patient. In an earlier study by Shuping, Toole and Alexander (1980), transient global amnesia was associated with a glioma in the left hippocampus, without any history of cerebrovascular disease in this patient. Shuping *et al.* implicated pressure on the left posterior choroidal artery as critical in the aetiology of the patient's amnesia. They speculated that if there were bilateral posterior choroidal artery ischaemia, there would probably also have been posterior cerebral artery involvement, with subsequent 'cortical blindness', and this was absent in their patient.

Turning to studies of persistent memory difficulty in patients with subcortical tumours, Williams and Pennybacker (1954) found that in cases where the tumour involved the area around the floor and walls of the third ventricle, there was usually significant memory impairment, but where the tumour was located further forward, memory impairment was absent. In four of the 180 patients studied, the memory disturbance and site of lesion were well defined, and in three of these cases there was a moderate degree of hydrocephalus in addition to the third ventricle tumour. For these four patients, significant impairment was also reported in remote memory and ability to 'learn new sensory-motor habits'. Williams and Pennybacker did not find a great deal of evidence to support the role of raised intracranial pressure in contributing to the memory impairment, since reduction of intracranial pressure (e.g. by ventricular tapping) did not bring about any change in memory performance. In addition, in a comparison of memory deficits in patients with third ventricle tumours, and those who had posterior fossa tumours, the incidence of memory disturbance was much smaller in the latter group of patients. One of the limitations of the study by Williams and Pennybacker was the relatively small number of patients in whom formal memory testing was reported, and the fact that the basis for determining the presence and degree of memory impairment was not always described in detail.

Support for some of the neuroanatomical observations made by Williams and Pennybacker has come from a study restricted to patients with craniopharyngiomas (Banna, 1973). Impaired memory was noted as a significant symptom in six out of 84 patients with craniopharyngiomas, and in these patients tumour growth was mostly in the posterior direction towards the brainstem and hippocampus, with the aqueduct being displaced posteriorly. Three of these six patients showed some degree of hydrocephalus. Banna reported that short-term memory was usually impaired, with remote memory being less significantly disturbed, but no detailed testing was described. Kapur (1985) found a marked tendency for perseverative responses on a short-term verbal memory task in a patient with a craniopharyngioma (*Figure 3.2*) and contrasted this with the relative absence of such responses in a patient with an anterior corpus callosum tumour, who nonetheless perseverated on a card sorting task. Kahn and Crosby (1972) reported marked memory impairment in a small group of patients with craniopharyngiomas which appeared to compress the mamillary bodies. One patient died within 2 weeks of surgery, and of the remaining four patients, three showed clinical evidence of

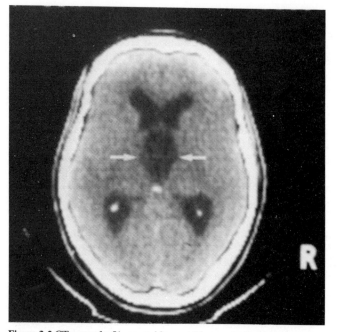

Figure 3.2 CT scan of a 51-year-old man with memory impairment associated with a craniopharyngioma (from Kapur, 1985. Reproduced by permission of Masson Italia Periodici Srl)

significant improvement in memory functioning after removal of the tumour. Similarly, Cavazzuti *et al.* (1983) reported short-term and long-term memory deficits in children with craniopharyngiomas, especially where there was hydrocephalus and/or distortion of the third ventricle. Detailed data comparing pre-and postoperative testing were not provided, although the authors did report that memory deficits tended to disappear after percutaneous drainage and/or radiotherapy or surgical excision of the tumour. However, on a few tests, such as immediate recall of prose material, deficits tended to persist, regardless of the type of treatment received, and the authors reported an instance of deterioration in memory functioning which appeared to follow a period of radiotherapy. The authors also noted that more radical surgery with an approach via the frontal lobes resulted in significant behavioural side-effects, and thus they favoured more conservative methods of treatment.

In a single-case study, notable for the detailed memory testing carried out, and for the neuropsychological insights which this offered, Ignelzi and Squire (1976) reported a patient who suffered both anterograde and retrograde amnesia as the result of a cystic craniopharyngioma. Included in their test battery was a recognition memory test covering both verbal and non-verbal material, delayed recall (24 hours) of the Rey-Osterreith figure, and a remote memory test based on a questionnaire. They showed that while there was memory impairment prior to drainge of the cyst, after drainage the patient was within the normal range for the recognition memory test, in the lower third of the normal range for the Rey-Osterreith delayed recall, and within the normal range for the test of remote memory. Ignelzi and Squire hypothesized that it was pressure exerted by the cyst on structures such as the thalamus which produced the memory deficit. The fact that remote memory and new learning improved in parallel suggested to Ignelzi and Squire that similar mechanisms may have played a role in both processes.

Tumours of the thalamus (*Figure 3.3*) have represented one of the common sources of material for the study of amnesia of neoplastic origin, although there are also descriptions of memory impairment related to tumours affecting other limbic system structures, such as the hypothalamus (Reeves and Plum, 1969; Beal *et al.*, 1981), hippocampus (Smith and Smith, 1966), fornix (Heilman and Sypert, 1977) and structures adjacent to the corpus callosum, such as the septum pellucidum (Bedou, Caruel and Pertuiset, 1972). In these studies, it is difficult to be certain of the circumscribed nature of the lesion (CT scan evidence was not usually available for most patients), and it is possible that pressure on thalamic nuclei, or on connections to such nuclei, may have played a role in the observed memory deficits. In this respect, negative cases (tumours which destroy limbic structures without producing amnesia, e.g. Woolsey and Nelson, 1975) carry more weight than the former studies. A further limitation, which applies to both the positive and negative studies reported above, is the lack of detailed memory testing carried out.

Since obstructive hydrocephalus is often a complicating feature of subcortical tumours which result in amnesia (e.g. Sprofkin and Sciarra, 1952), it is useful to document those cases, such as that of Ziegler, Kaufman and Marshall (1977), where hydrocephalus was absent. In their patient, where there appeared to be abrupt onset of memory impairment, the tumour was found at post-mortem to involve the thalamus bilaterally, and extend into the medial aspects of both temporal lobes posteriorly. The patient did not display any evidence of

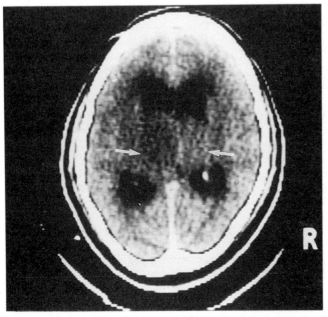

Figure 3.3 CT scan showing a bithalamic tumour in a 36-year-old man with marked memory disorder

confabulation, and did in fact have considerable insight into his disability. There was clinical evidence of retrograde amnesia over the 10 years or so prior to the onset of his illness.

Significant anterograde and retrograde amnesia was also noted in the case reported by McEntee, Biber and Perl (1976) where there was post-mortem evidence of a bilateral metastatic tumour which had invaded the medial and posterior thalamus, but with no apparent involvement of the mamillary bodies or anterior thalamus. Butters (1984a) has reported a patient with a thalamic tumour which appeared to be limited to the right medial thalamus, and in which there did not appear to be any associated hydrocephalus. He found evidence of retrograde amnesia, which was equally severe for the various decades studied. On short-term verbal memory tests, the patient showed release from proactive interference. In general, other deep-seated neoplasia, such as pituitary tumours, only give rise to memory symptoms when they expand to such an extent that they exert pressure on other subcortical regions (Luria, 1976). This also, to some extent, applies to tumours such as those in the region of the pineal gland (*Figure 3.4*) and tumours of the corpus callosum (*Figure 3.5*).

Subcortical space-occupying lesions other than primary tumours have been noted to result in marked memory difficulty. Colloid cysts, which grow around the area of the third ventricle, are an example of such lesions (*Figure 3.6*). Lobosky, Vangilder and Damasio (1984) reported three cases of third ventricle colloid cysts. In two of these, memory impairment was a presenting feature of the condition, and one patient, whose CT scan showed significant hydrocephalus, had generalized

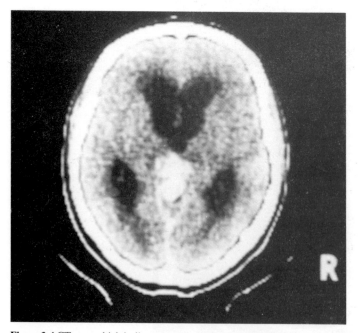

Figure 3.4 CT scan which indicates a mass in the pineal region, diagnosed clinically and radiologically as a pinealoma. This 37-year-old man displayed significant memory impairment which showed some improvement after a shunt was inserted to relieve hydrocephalus

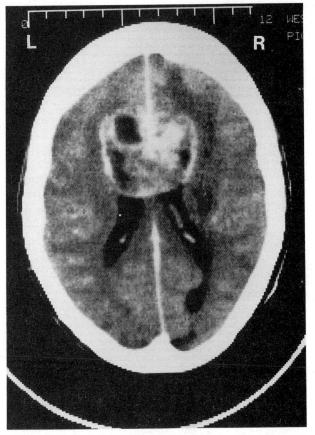

Figure 3.5 CT scan showing a tumour of the corpus callosum in a 67-year-old woman. The tumour invaded both sides of the middle portion of the corpus callosum, and was associated with a moderate degree of memory impairment

cognitive dysfunction together with amnesia and confabulation. This did not improve with ventricular shunting, but after removal of the cyst the patient did show a slight improvement in memory. The other patient with impaired memory did not show any change in level of memory functioning after surgery. The authors emphasized the importance of radical surgery in patients with colloid cysts, even in the absence of any associated hydrocephalus. Arachnoid cysts, especially where they are located in the anterior cranial fossa, have also been noted to produce impairment in memory functioning (Lang *et al.*, 1985).

Distinctive features of memory disorders in patients with cerebral tumours

Few published data are available on direct comparisons between memory disorders in patients with cerebral tumours and those shown by patients with other forms of

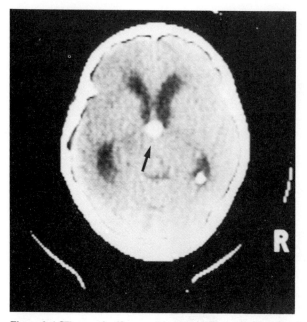

Figure 3.6 CT scan of a 62-year-old woman with a colloid cyst and evidence of moderate memory impairment

cerebral pathology. However, it is possible to make some tentative observations on the basis of existing evidence, and in a few instances I have supplemented these with some unpublished data.

Patients with frontal lobe tumours often represent a diagnostic puzzle in terms of their differentiation from other conditions, and it may be useful to consider briefly any distinctive features of their memory functioning. Such patients show significant individual variation in the presence, extent and awareness of memory disorders. Small, unilateral, extrinsic tumours, especially if they are located in the dorsolateral frontal region may be accompanied by minimal memory impairment. On the other hand, significant memory deficits may often be found in patients with larger frontal tumours, tumours which are intrinsic, those which are bilateral and those located in more medial or orbital structures of the frontal lobes. If marked memory impairment is present, this may often be present without the patient showing appropriate awareness or concern. Patients with frontal lobe pathology, especially where this is bilateral, may resemble patients with primary degenerative dementia in showing some degree of memory impairment, evidence of affective changes such as depression, and a slowing down in behaviour.

A comparison of the short-term memory performance of patients with bifrontal neoplasia and patients with primary degenerative dementia is shown in *Figure 3.7*. In this study (Kapur, unpublished data), a group of 10 patients with bifrontal pathology, 12 patients with primary degenerative dementia and eight control subjects were given a Brown–Peterson short-term verbal memory task, based on one used in a separate study of memory disorders in frontal lobe and subcortical tumours (Kapur, 1985). As can be seen, only 40% of bifrontal patients were

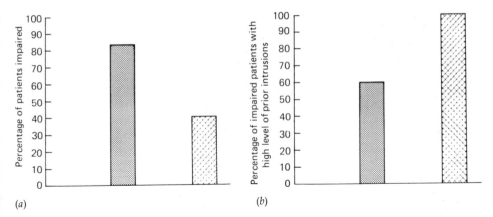

Figure 3.7 Short-term verbal memory performance of patients with bifrontal tumours and patients with primary degenerative dementia. (*a*) The percentage of patients impaired on the task; (*b*) the proportion of those impaired patients who displayed a high level of prior intrusion errors. ▨ Primary degenerative dementia; ▧ bifrontal tumours

impaired on the task (with scores of more than two standard deviations below that of control subjects), whereas 83% of patients with primary degenerative dementia showed such impairment. All four of the bifrontal patients who were impaired had high levels of prior intrusion errors, whereas this was evident in just one-half of the patients with dementia. It seemed therefore that short-term memory deficits were more common in patients with primary degenerative dementia, but that susceptibility to interference was more closely associated with such impairment in patients with bifrontal tumours.

Tumours around the area of the third ventricle may also result in memory deficits similar to those in other neurological conditions. The patient with a right thalamic tumour reported by Butters (1984a) differed from patients with alcoholic Korsakoff's syndrome in that he showed release from proactive interference (improvement in short-term verbal memory when there was a change in the category of material to be learned) which is typically absent in patients with Korsakoff's syndrome. In addition, his retrograde amnesia differed from that of the alcoholic patients in that it did not show a temporal gradient, i.e. the retrograde memory loss was equally marked across decades.

Summary

Cortical tumours have been shown to result in hemispheric-specific memory deficits related to the verbal/visuospatial nature of the material, but in some cases both types of memory deficit have been observed after unilateral tumours. Although this may be partly related to the nature of the test material used, and possibly also to the precise intra-hemispheric location of the tumour, there is some evidence to suggest that a focus of abnormal activity in the contralateral hemisphere may contribute to such patterns of memory deficits. While a number of studies have reported on the deleterious effects of temporal lobe tumours on memory functioning, there is a dearth of evidence relating to the corresponding effects of frontal lobe tumours.

Improvement in memory functioning has been reported after removal of temporal lobe tumours. In some cases, persistent memory deficits after brain tumour surgery may remain, and the latter may be related to variables such as extent of normal tissue removed at time of surgery, presence of postoperative vasospasm and postoperative irradiation treatment. However, detailed documentation of the precise role of such factors remains to be carried out.

Subcortical tumours may result in memory impairment either by direct effects on structures in the limbic system or as a result of factors such as ventricular dilatation, raised intracranial pressure, etc. Amnesia, as an episodic disturbance or, more commonly, as a persistent deficit, often occurs in tumours around the area of the third ventricle. Craniopharyngiomas accompanied by distortion/dilatation of the ventricular system, and craniopharyngiomas in a more posterior location, have been accompanied by memory deficits, which in many cases show improvement after surgical intervention. Thalamic tumours have also been commonly associated with memory impairment, and this impairment has tended to cover both anterograde and retrograde memory functioning.

Chapter 4

Penetrating head injury

Patients with penetrating head injury, where the skull and dura mater are perforated by a missile or missile fragments, form a relatively distinct population of head-injured subjects, with the pathology of the resultant brain lesion being quite different from that found in the more common 'blunt' head injury. In addition to obvious differences related to the more generalized damage characteristic of blunt head injury, and the more focal damage of penetrating injury, there are other differences, such as the absence of favoured loci for lesions in penetrating head injury compared to the high frequency of temporal and frontal contusions in blunt head injury. In addition, it is important to note that within the category of penetrating head injury there are considerable differences between types of missile wound. For example, the low velocity shrapnel wounds of the Second World War (Russell, 1971) probably caused more limited cerebral lesions than those which have resulted from high velocity bullet wounds characteristic of modern warfare, since the latter may often produce generalized cerebral oedema and lesions some distance from the main trajectory of the missile (Allen, Scott and Tanner, 1982).

Pre-traumatic and post-traumatic amnesia

Penetrating head injury, even when it is accompanied by significant brain damage and blood loss, may in some cases present in a dramatic fashion, with the patient fully conscious and able to narrate in detail the circumstances of the injury. This is in sharp contrast to even minor forms of closed head injury where there may be complete amnesia for events surrounding the injury. A number of studies have documented both the minimal duration of pre-traumatic amnesia and post-traumatic amnesia in cerebral missile wounds and also the relationship between the occurrence of each type of memory loss (e.g. Teuber, 1969, 1975; Russell, 1971). In a study of 100 patients with cerebral missile wounds, Teuber (1968, 1969) reported the incidence and pattern of traumatic amnesia. In 93 patients, amnesia could be accurately classified. Around two fifths of the patient sample had no amnesia for the injury (*Table 4.1*). While isolated post-traumatic amnesia did occur in some patients, no instance was found of a patient with isolated pre-traumatic amnesia. Teuber also observed that persistent anterograde amnesia was always associated with some degree of pre- and post-traumatic amnesia. Islands of memory in the period of post-traumatic amnesia were found in 22 patients and in the period of pre-traumatic amnesia were found in two patients. Of the nineteen patients with

Table 4.1 Incidence (%) of traumatic amnesia in patients with penetrating head injury (Teuber, 1969)

No pre- nor post-traumatic amnesia	Isolated post-traumatic amnesia	Isolated pre-traumatic amnesia	Both pre- and post-traumatic amnesia
41	16	0	43

persistent everyday memory difficulties, 10 had lesions in the diencephalic/mesencephalic region and nine showed evidence of bilateral posterior lesions accompanied by bilateral constriction of the visual fields. Teuber (1975) confirmed this pattern of findings in a further series of patients, and noted five patients who had post-traumatic amnesia of greater than one week, but did not show any evidence of pre-traumatic amnesia.

In his study of gunshot wound cases, Russell (1948) also found a significant proportion (22%) of patients without amnesia for the incident, and further observed that there seemed to be a dearth of cases with left posterior parietotemporal injury where there was no amnesia. Russell looked more closely at injuries which damaged one optic radiation without injury to the sensory motor system (excluding injuries within 5 cm of the midline). There were 45 such cases with 19 in the right and 26 in the left side of the brain, and a greater duration of post-traumatic amnesia was noted in patients with left hemisphere injury. Russell further examined a total of 22 cases where the missile penetrated directly into the brain over the anterior part of the optic radiation, and again he found longer post-traumatic amnesia in the left hemisphere group; it seemed that these patients accounted for most of the variance in the simple left versus right hemisphere comparison. Russell pointed out that a long duration of post-traumatic amnesia was associated with early dysphasia in patients with left temporal lesions, but that there was no such association after injury to other parts of the left hemisphere. He hypothesized that wounds of the left temporal lobe might inactivate the underlying hippocampal region, and thus cause some degree of traumatic amnesia.

In a detailed study of a small number of selected amnesic patients, who had sustained a penetrating head injury during wartime approximately 30 years earlier, Jarho (1973) confirmed Teuber's (1968) observation of diencephalic involvement and significant pre- and post-traumatic amnesia in those patients who had marked anterograde memory impairment following cerebral missile wounds. Jarho's selection criteria for including patients in his 'amnesic syndrome' group were that patients should have a severe recent memory loss, there should be no impairment of remote memory, there should be minimal additional cognitive impairment and the patients should be disorientated for time. In his control group, patients had incurred a penetrating missile wound in the diencephalon, but the resulting lesion was unilateral. Some of Jarho's observations were based on case note data rather than direct clinical examination, and he did not report the use of formal tests of retrograde amnesia to evaluate the long periods of pre-traumatic amnesia which he noted in a few patients.

Jarho estimated 'total duration of unconsciousness and confusion' on the basis of the hospital records and this duration was over 21 days in four out of the six amnesic patients, and over 21 days in only one of the control patients. He reported two types of data relating to pre-traumatic amnesia in the bilateral missile injury patients, one set of which was collected in the primary stage of the injury (early

1940s), and the other set which was gathered at the time of examination (1971). In five of the six amnesic patients where data were available, pre-traumatic amnesia in the primary stage varied between 3.5 months and 4 years, while in 1971 it ranged from no pre-traumatic amnesia to 4 years. Since no distinction was made between immediate pre-traumatic and longer-term retrograde amnesia, these two aspects of pre-traumatic amnesia presumably merged in the case of his missile wound patients. In two of the amnesic patients, the length of pre-traumatic amnesia did not change from an initial duration of 4 years. Jarho noted that the two patients in whom pre-traumatic amnesia shrank over the years also showed improvement in their anterograde amnesia; one patient, in whom the pre-traumatic amnesia shrank completely, seemed to recover clinically from his anterograde amnesia. Jarho hypothesized that similar cerebral structures and mechanisms might underlie pre-traumatic amnesia and anterograde amnesia, and that persistent, extensive pre-traumatic amnesia correlated with a subsequent amnesic disorder. In the control patients with unilateral diencephalic lesions, no detailed information was presented, but Jarho pointed out that pre-traumatic amnesia 'extended 30 to 60 minutes in only one control patient', implying that this was the maximum duration of pre-traumatic amnesia in the control patients.

In a recent study of 342 Vietnam veterans who incurred a penetrating head injury, Salazar et al. (1986b) confirmed the major observations of earlier research relating to the frequent absence of impaired consciousness or amnesia at the time of such an injury, the occurrence of isolated post-traumatic amnesia, and the singular absence of any case of isolated pre-traumatic amnesia. Prolonged unconsciousness was more closely associated with injury to the left hemisphere, especially to structures such as the left forebrain, and estimated volume of brain loss was higher in patients with prolonged unconsciousness. There was a slightly greater tendency for patients classified as 'alert' shortly after injury, but who subsequently displayed prolonged post-traumatic amnesia, to have some evidence of temporal lobe injury, but there was no tendency for left or right temporal injury to differ in this respect.

A few case studies of patients with marked memory deficits have tended to confirm the observations noted in the larger-scale studies reviewed above. A particularly unusual form of missile wound, caused by a fencing foil injury, was first reported by Teuber, Milner and Vaughan (1968), and has subsequently been the subject of a number of neuropsychological investigations. This patient (N.A.) incurred a focal subcortical injury in December 1960 from a foil which entered the right nostril and subsequently lodged in the left side of the brain. Although it appears that the main lesion caused by the injury was in the left thalamic region (Squire and Moore, 1979), evidence from positron emission tomography has indicated depressed cerebral metabolic activity in other left hemisphere structures, especially the left caudate area (Metter et al., 1983). In addition, there remains some controversy as to the precise location and extent of damage which might be caused by the type of penetrating missile injury which N.A. sustained (Weiskrantz, 1985; Zola-Morgan and Squire, 1985).

The original description by Teuber, Milner and Vaughan (1968) indicated that the patient had an initial pre-traumatic amnesia of 2 years which decreased to a couple of weeks over a 30-month period. In the months immediately after the injury, there also appeared to be a long period of very poor memory, although a specific estimate of post-traumatic amnesia appears not to have been documented at this stage. It would seem that his amnesia for events around the time of the injury did improve further, since in a subsequent report (Kaushall, Zetin and Squire,

1981) he was able to describe the circumstances immediately before and after the incident. Grafman *et al*. (1985) reported a case of injury to the fornix region after a missile injury, and their patient had a post-traumatic amnesia of around 2 months. He was asleep at the time of the injury, and the only indication of his pre-traumatic memory functioning was of his report of waking to the sound of exploding mortar rounds.

Anterograde memory deficits

Patients with cerebral missile wounds, especially where the missile is of low velocity, represent an ideal sample for the detection and elucidation of focal memory deficits. Hemispheric asymmetry of memory function is clearly illustrated by such findings and it is unfortunate that more studies of such patients have not been conducted, and that such evidence is not cited more frequently in discussions of hemispheric specificity of memory function. Although occasional reference had been made to clinically obvious memory deficits after penetrating cerebral wounds which affected temporal lobe and hippocampal regions (e.g. Russell and Espir, 1961), or structures adjacent to the third ventricle (Bender *et al.*, 1949), the large-scale study by Newcombe (1969) of 153 patients with missile wounds was one of the first to report a detailed analysis of focal memory deficits after penetrating head injury. She administered a large number of verbal memory tasks and a smaller number of non-verbal memory tests and found that patients with left hemisphere missile injury showed deficits on verbal memory tasks and patients with right hemisphere injury performed poorly on non-verbal memory tasks. She also observed some differences in pattern of memory symptoms in the two groups – three patients in her group with right hemisphere injury reported mild difficulties in topographical orientation and one of the patients reported that he found it particularly difficult to learn his way around in an unfamiliar place while on holiday, although once he had learned the route he was able to retain it. On the other hand, memory symptoms reported by left hemisphere-damaged patients tended to be related to more verbal situations such as recalling people's names.

Verbal memory deficits

Some of the most interesting findings from the study by Newcombe (1969) relate to the effects of lesions within a cerebral hemisphere, and how some of her observations differed from those obtained from studies of patients with other aetiologies. Newcombe found that patients with lesions involving the left parietal and occipital regions were particularly impaired on verbal paired-associate learning and nonsense syllable learning tests, whereas patients with left temporoparietal injury performed poorly on tests of memory span for verbal material and a test of letter recall after a short delay.

In the case of story recall, patients with 'mixed' lesions (frontotemporal, frontoparietal or frontotemporoparietal) showed impairment on both immediate and delayed (one hour) recall, while patients with temporal or temporoparietal lesions performed within normal limits. It is notable that on most of these verbal memory tasks, including a paired-associate learning test, patients with frontal injury did not show significant impairment (*see* Ghent, Mishkin and Teuber, 1962). One task where, in common with other left hemisphere lesion groups, they did perform poorly, was a nonsense syllable learning task, in which patients had to recall a list of nonsense syllables both immediately after and then 5 minutes after a 3 minute learning period. A number of the patients with left hemisphere injury were also dysphasic, and Newcombe noted that dysphasic patients were worse than non-dysphasic patients on letter span and 'selective noun span', where the patient had to listen to two overlapping lists of words and indicate for the second list which word was omitted from the first. She also noted that dysphasic patients performed worse on story recall, both immediate and delayed, but that on other memory tests such as paired-associated word learning, nonsense syllable learning, and digit span there was no difference between these two subgroups.

Lesion pathology in Newcombe's patients was largely limited to the cortex and adjacent white matter, but some missile wounds did transgress the lateral ventricles. An analysis of the relationship between verbal memory performance and depth of penetration of the missile (less than 3 cm, equal to or more than 3 cm, or involving the lateral ventricle) failed to yield any significant association except in the case of delayed letter recall, where deeper lesions resulted in greater impairment. Estimated amount of brain tissue loss, a further measure of severity of injury, was also found by Newcombe to be unrelated to verbal memory test performance, and a later study by Teuber (1975) did not find any difference on a paired-associate learning task between missile wound patients with short, intermediate or long periods of post-traumatic amnesia. Using a somewhat different measure of severity of penetrating head injury, namely level of consciousness ('alert' or 'impaired') at time of hospital admission, Kapur (1975, unpublished data) was able to show marked effects of severity of injury on delayed word-list recall (*Figure 4.1*). In addition to the differences in measures of severity of

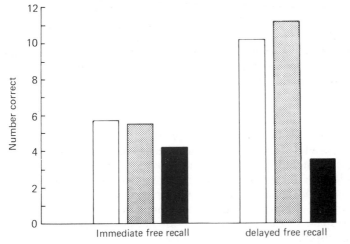

Figure 4.1 Verbal memory functioning, in relation to level of consciousness at time of hospital admission, of a group of patients with penetrating head injury. The 'alert' and 'impaired' groups $n = 14$ and $n = 16$ respectively) were matched for age (28.8 and 32.6 years respectively) and for months post-injury at which the assessment took place (27.7 and 27.8 respectively). The verbal memory task consisted of immediate and delayed recall of word-list material. Each patient heard five consecutive lists of 12 one-syllable high frequency nouns, which were presented at the rate of one word every 2.5 seconds. After the presentation of each list of 12 words, patients were given 60 seconds for free recall of the words. This procedure was followed for each list, and one hour after recall of the fifth list an unexpected delayed recall for all five lists was requested. □ Control; ▨ alert on admission; ■ impaired consciousness on admission

injury and method of memory assessment, this study also differed from earlier research in its population of penetrating head injury patients. Kapur's study, carried out in Belfast, included a significant proportion of patients with high velocity gunshot wounds, and it is possible that remote effects of this type of injury (*see* Allen, Scott and Tanner, 1982) resulted in a subgroup of patients who were particularly disabled from the neuropsychological point of view.

Newcombe's conclusion that deep missile wounds did not necessarily result in more significant memory deficit has drawn some support from the observations of Bakare and Adeloye (1972) in their study of Nigerian patients with missile wounds. Patients with tangential missile wounds in fact performed worse than patients with penetrating lesions on a test of delayed picture recall, and the authors hypothesized that this may have been due to a shower of bone fragments from the tangential injury affecting larger areas of the brain. Some patients with unilateral missile injury affecting deeper regions of the brain may nonetheless display focal memory deficits. In a recent study, where the penetration of the missile could be pinpointed using CT scan technology, Salazar *et al.* (1986a) found that patients with left or right basal forebrain lesions, where there was usually some additional pathology to the hippocampus and amygdala, tended to perform less well on verbal and non-verbal memory tests compared to other cognitive tasks; however, impaired performance relative to control subjects was usually mild and patchy, and the only significant deficit was shown after right basal forebrain injury on a verbal free recall task.

Non-verbal memory deficits

Turning to the effects of cerebral missile wounds on non-verbal memory deficits, these have generally followed right hemisphere injury, although occasional cases have been reported where the lesion was predominantly in the left posterior region (Spalding and Zangwill, 1950). The principal non-verbal memory test which Newcombe (1969) administered was a maze-learning test, where the patient had to learn a path consisting of 10 choice points (a practice path of six choice points was given initially). The path was quickly demonstrated in one move without pausing at the choice points. Patients were given a maximum of 25 trials to learn the maze, the learning criterion being three successive error-free trials. Delayed recall was tested one hour later. The right hemisphere damaged group was significantly impaired on this test, with the right parietal and right posterior subgroups showing more marked impairments. However, it should be borne in mind that more anterior penetrating head injury may sometimes result in impairment on this type of memory task. *Figure 4.2.* shows a case of bifrontal penetrating injury, seen by the present author. This patient, who recieved a gunshot wound, performed very poorly on a task similar to Newcombe's maze-learning test, but performed well on a verbal memory task and in most other aspects of cognitive functioning.

Some right and left hemisphere-damaged patients in Newcombe's study who had reached criterion on the initial maze-learning test were again assessed after one hour, but there was no difference in performance between right and left hemisphere damaged-groups (no control data appear to have been collected for this delayed version of the test). Newcombe found that patients with right hemisphere lesions who had a visual field defect performed less well on the maze-learning test than those without a visual field defect. She also reported a dissociation in the right hemisphere group between performance on a 'visual closures' test (where patients

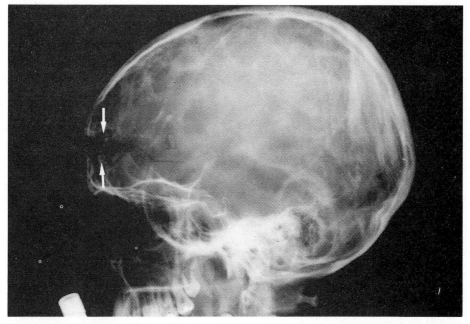

Figure 4.2 Skull X-ray of a 15-year-old patient who incurred a gunshot wound (probably low velocity) in 1973. The path of the lesion (arrowed) was from the left to the right dorsolateral frontal region, with the bullet traversing the skull. A maze-learning test, identical to that described in Chapter 1 (*Figure 1.2*) was administered 29 months after injury. He could not learn the maze after 25 trials. His immediate and delayed (30 minute) performance on a word list recall task was within normal limits, and his only other deficit was impaired performance on a verbal fluency task (Reproduced by permission of Mr D. S. Gordon)

had to categorize pictures of silhouetted faces) and the maze-learning test, with temporal lobe lesions being associated with poor performance on the closures test and parietal and posterior lesions being associated with poor performance on the maze-learning test. In contrast, there was no difference between dysphasic and non-dysphasic left hemisphere-injured patients in performance on the maze-learning task. As in the case of verbal memory tests, neither depth of lesion nor amount of tissue loss showed any relationship to level of impairment on the maze-learning task. On a similar maze-learning test, Kapur (1975, unpublished data) found that, as in the case of delayed verbal memory (*see* p. 87), there was a relationship between memory performance and a measure of severity of injury, as indicated by level of consciousness at time of hospital admission (*Figure 4.3*).

A follow-up study by Ratcliff and Newcombe (1973) replicated the maze-learning deficit found by Newcombe (1969) in the right posterior group and also reported a similar, although less severe, impairment in patients with bilateral posterior injury. This impairment contrasted with a marked difficulty shown by the latter subjects in performing a locomotor spatial orientation task where subjects had to follow a path in a large room on the basis of a visual map. On this task, patients with bilateral lesions were significantly worse than those with unilateral lesions of either hemisphere. Newcombe did not find any deficits on two other non-verbal memory tests which she administered to her missile wound patients – a memory-for-designs test (Newcombe, 1965) and a recurring figures recognition memory task. However, Teuber and Weinstein (1954) did find impaired recall of

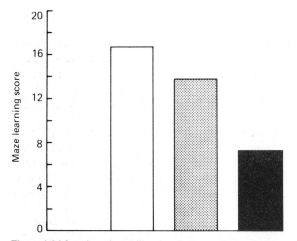

Figure 4.3 Maze-learning ability, in relation to the level of consciousness at the time of hospital admission, of a group of patients with penetrating head injury. These patients were the same as those described earlier (*see Figure 4.1*). The maze-learning test (*see Figure 1.2*) was similar to that used by Newcombe (1969). The patient was required to learn a path to a criterion of three successive error-free runs (a much shorter practice path was also given initially). The path which the patient had to follow was outlined once by the examiner. The patient was then given the stylus and asked to trace out the path. A click and a red light accompanied each erroneous turn, and when the end of the maze was reached a green light was illuminated. Performance was scored as 26 less the number of trials which the patient took to achieve criterion performance. If criterion performance was not reached by 25 trials, the test was discontinued and the patient was given a score of zero. □ Control; ▨ alert on admission; ■ impaired consciousness on admission

designs presented to missile wound patients in the tactile modality, with posterior cerebral injury resulting in the greatest deficit, and in the more recent study by Salazar *et al.* (1986a) referred to earlier, right forebrain injury did result in poor performance on a memory task involving recognition of recurring figures.

Other types of non-verbal memory functions have been implicated in the sequelae of right hemisphere missile injury. Yin (1970) and Grafman *et al.* (1986) reported impaired faces recognition memory after right hemisphere injury. Yin assessed recognition memory for faces and pictures of houses where the stimuli were presented in normal or inverted positions. He demonstrated a recognition memory deficit in patients with right posterior injury for faces presented in normal position and tested in this position, but minimal impairment for pictures of houses. When faces were presented in the inverted position, patients with unilateral injury in regions other than the right posterior area performed significantly worse than controls, whereas the performance of patients with right posterior injury was comparable with that of controls. In the study by Grafman *et al.* (1986), patients were shown 12 faces and then presented with 24 faces from which they had to select the original 12. Patients with right hemisphere or bilateral lesions performed worse than control patients, with poorest scores coming from patients with right temporal lobe injury. Midline lesions were also closely associated with impaired delayed recognition of unfamiliar faces and the structures which were most closely implicated in this deficit included the left and right internal capsules and the right caudate body. As in the case of Newcombe's observations with respect to maze learning, there was no relationship between size of lesion and severity of memory deficit.

Combined verbal and non-verbal memory deficits

Patients with penetrating head injury who display both verbal and non-verbal memory deficits have usually incurred bilateral or multifocal lesions. In some cases, the relevant lesions will have involved the diencephalic region, and in those patients who survive such injury there may often be deficits related to both subcortical and cortical damage, each of which may in turn vary according to the precise trajectory of the missile. Other complications such as abscess formation or subsequent epilepsy may provide additional sources of cognitive dysfunction. As a result, those patients with severe, global memory deficits resulting from penetrating missile wounds may also show signs of additional cognitive impairment or even a marked dementia. The former pattern of neuropsychological functioning characterizes the series of missile injury patients described by Hillbom and Jarho (1969), and later in more detail by Jarho (1973). Two factors which cloud the significance of the amnesic syndrome of these patients are the presence of additional cognitive deficits (e.g. impaired copying and naming abilities), and the fact that his selection criteria were based on case-note information rather than formal neuropsychological testing.

The cognitive testing of patients was carried out and reported by Lehtonen (1973) who administered a number of memory tests. These included a sequence learning task, where a patient had to press a series of up to five buttons on a display according to a certain sequence, with the sequence consisting of between two and five steps (recall and relearning after 60 minutes was also incorporated in the testing procedure); the paired-associate subtest of the Wechsler Memory Scale; the Benton Visual Retention Test; recall of the Rey-Osterreith figure one hour after initial copying; presentation of a story followed by recall and then questions about the story (after one hour this recall and prompted recall was repeated and this was again repeated the following day). Lehtonen found marked impairment on all of these tests, with patients with bilateral diencephalic injury performing significantly worse than control patients who had unilateral lesions, particularly on tests requiring delayed recall.

An example of a penetrating head injury patient, who displayed marked asymmetric memory difficulty in the context of some generalized cognitive dysfunction, is shown in *Figure 4.4*. This patient incurred a penetrating missile wound in which the bullet entered the left side of the skull and then broke up into fragments, the largest of which lodged in the right temporal region. Consequently he showed marked memory impairment on a non-verbal maze-learning test, with milder deficits on a test of verbal memory.

In the case of the patient N.A. (with the fencing foil injury) referred to earlier, the initial series of neuropsychological investigations carried out by Teuber, Milner and Vaughan (1968) between 4 and 7 years after the injury showed that the patient had severe verbal memory deficits and mild to moderate non-verbal memory impairment. The verbal memory impairment was similar to that of amnesic patients, but the non-verbal impairment was at a level similar to that of right temporal lobectomy patients rather than patients with amnesia. Other aspects of the patient's condition noted by Teuber, Milner and Vaughan included the patient's apparent unresponsiveness to painful stimuli, impotence, and an impairment of upward gaze. Most of these seem to have cleared up by 1976 (Squire and Slater, 1978), although a mild paralysis of upward gaze appears to have remained (Zola-Morgan and Squire, 1985). Subsequent studies by Squire and his

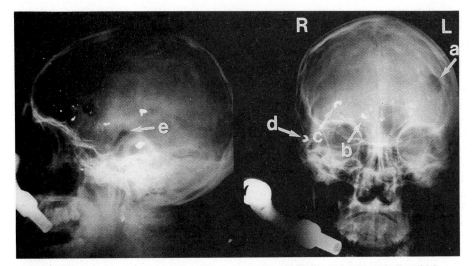

Figure 4.4 Multi-focal lesions in a patient with a penetrating head injury caused by a bullet which entered on the left side (*a*) and then broke up into fragments which can be seen in the right temporal region (*b,c,d*), and also in the midline and in some medial parts of the left hemisphere. Some air can also be seen in the right temporal horn (*e*)

colleagues have confirmed the marked verbal memory impairment, with much milder non-verbal memory deficits. On one task, remembering the location of a circle on a line, N.A. performed normally (Squire and Slater, 1978). On verbal recognition memory tasks, N.A. was significantly impaired, but showed normal effects of encoding instructions with superior retention under 'semantic' encoding instructions (Wetzel and Squire, 1980). In a further series of studies, Squire (1982) reported that on short-term verbal memory tasks the patient performed like control subjects and displayed release from proactive interference. Squire (1982) also reported that N.A. was not impaired in making temporal order memory judgements. He has also shown a normal rate of forgetting for sentence material (Squire, 1981), and intact ability to learn skills such as reading mirror-reversed words (Cohen and Squire, 1980).

Grafman *et al.* (1985) reported isolated, generalized memory impairment in their patient with bilateral fornix lesions referred to earlier, although the overall level of memory impairment was probably in the mild to moderate rather than severely impaired range. The patient showed moderate impairment on verbal and pictorial paired-associate learning tests and a similar level of impairment on recognition memory for geometric or nonsense figures. On some verbal recognition memory tests, however, his performance was either normal or only mildly impaired. Although the focal damage to the fornix region was exceptionally well documented by Grafman *et al.*, it is possible that left frontotemporal and right parietal injury caused by the trajectory of the missile may also have played a part in the patient's memory deficits.

Retrograde memory deficits

Few studies have formally tested for the presence of retrograde memory deficits in patients with unilateral penetrating head injury. Grafman *et al.* (1986), in the study referred to above, presented 30 photographs of faces that were famous in the 1960s or 1970s, and the patient had to name each face with or without acoustic or semantic cues. Somewhat surprisingly, patients with right hemisphere lesions performed better than patients with left hemisphere lesions. Patients with bilateral lesions and patients with left temporal lobe lesions scored lower than control subjects, with the left temporal group obtaining the lowest scores. Grafman *et al.* also noted that left temporal and left temporal-occipital white matter involvement showed the closest correlation with impaired performance on the retrograde amnesia test. In a single-case study of a patient with bilateral fornix injury, Grafman *et al.* (1985) could not find any impairment on a faces retrograde amnesia test, and the patient's verbal retrograde memory functioning appeared to be only marginally impaired.

The patient N.A. has been found to show normal performance on most recall and recognition tests for information relating to public events in the decade prior to his head injury in 1960 (Squire and Slater, 1978), whereas events in the early 1970s were poorly retained on recall and recognition testing (Squire and Slater, 1977). In addition, knowledge of some autobiographical events which occurred prior to his injury also appeared to be relatively intact (Kaushall, Zetin and Squire, 1981). However, on tests requiring detailed recall of public events he has shown some impairment for pre-injury information (Cohen and Squire, 1981). When asked to recall specific autobiographical events in response to single words (e.g. 'flag'), the memory performance of both N.A. and control subjects was helped by probing from the experimenter, but N.A. still displayed significant impairment on most conditions; this impairment was particularly evident when the specific content of subjects' responses was scored (Zola-Morgan, Cohen and Squire, 1983).

Distinctive features of memory disorders in penetrating head injury

Penetrating head injury compared with blunt head injury

Few formal comparisons have been made between memory functioning in patients with penetrating head injury and those associated with other disease states. This may be due in part to the relative infrequency of such patients in routine clinical practice, although it may also reflect a lower incidence of significant memory impairment in this population of patients. In the case of traumatic amnesia, i.e. memory loss for events around the time of the injury, this may be absent in many patients with penetrating head injury, even where a significant degree of brain damage has occurred. This is in contrast to the usual finding in blunt head injury, where traumatic amnesia may accompany cases of relatively mild head injury. Although no studies have specifically reported on comparisons between traumatic amnesia in penetrating and blunt head injury, some relevant observations can be made on the basis of existing evidence. Thus, as was indicated earlier (p. 84), the findings of Teuber (1969) yielded an incidence of 41% of patients with penetrating head injury with no traumatic amnesia, whereas the series of Russell and Nathan (1946) of over 1000 patients with 'accidental' head injury (which excluded gunshot wound cases, and largely comprised patients with blunt head injury), the corresponding incidence was 9.6%. Detailed assessment of pre-traumatic amnesia in a subgroup of 200 of these patients yielded a 5.5% incidence of isolated pre-traumatic amnesia, whereas almost three times this frequency (16%) of isolated pre-traumatic amnesia was evident in Teuber's series of patients with penetrating head injury.

The relationship between traumatic amnesia and subsequent recovery of anterograde memory functioning may differ between blunt and penetrating head injury, although this has not been formally evaluated. It is quite conceivable that some patients with penetrating head injury without any traumatic amnesia may show persistent memory impairment, although this is likely to be focal and mild or moderate in severity. Where there are marked, generalized memory deficits, then, as Teuber (1969) has pointed out, these are likely to be accompanied by both pre- and post-traumatic amnesia. By contrast, in the case of blunt head injury, one would seldom encounter persistent memory difficulties without significant traumatic, especially post-traumatic, amnesia.

Turning to anterograde memory functioning, in my experience complaints of everyday memory difficulty are more frequent after blunt than penetrating head injury (*Figure 4.5*). This may be due in part to the lack of everyday memory

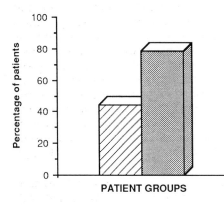

Figure 4.5 Incidence of complaints of everyday memory difficulty in two groups of patients: one group of 23 patients with blunt head injury, ▨ (mean age = 33.8 years, mean months post injury = 24.7), and a second group of 25 patients with penetrating head injury (mean age = 30 years, mean months post injury = 27.3), ▨

symptoms associated with some forms of focal right hemisphere injury, and the restricted locus of lesions in most patients with penetrating head injury, whereas those with blunt injury will invariably have some degree of bilateral cerebral pathology. However, it may also reflect real differences in severity and type of memory deficits between the two populations.

Black (1973) reported significantly lower memory scores, as evident on the Wechsler Memory Scale, in a group of patients with blunt injury compared to a group of subjects with penetrating injury, with the memory quotients of the latter group being within normal limits. No attempt was made however to match the two groups of patients for severity of injury. Focal memory deficits are probably more common in patients with penetrating head injury, and generalized memory impairment more prevalent in blunt head injury, although only a limited amount of comparative data has been reported for these two populations. Yin (1970) has reported data which indicate that for some types of specific memory deficit, namely memory for faces, patients with penetrating head injury in the posterior regions of the brain tend to perform less well than patients with blunt head injury. In particular, memory for upright and for inverted faces was lower in patients with right and left posterior injury respectively, compared to patients with blunt head injury. Unfortunately, no detailed analysis of the data was reported, and although both groups of patients incurred their head injury in combat, it is not possible to ascertain whether the two sets of injury were of similar severity.

Penetrating head injury compared with other neurological conditions

Traumatic amnesia in penetrating head injury has seldom been compared with non-traumatic, 'ictal' amnesia seen in other neurological conditions such as subarachnoid haemorrhage, epilepsy, etc. In the case of anterograde memory functioning, some indirect comparisons have been made, and these will be briefly reviewed. In a study of cerebral missile wounds, Newcombe (1969) attempted to reconcile the relative lack of marked verbal memory deficits after left temporal lobe injury with the significant deficits noted by Milner in a series of temporal lobe epilepsy and temporal lobectomy patients (Milner, 1962), and suggested that this may have been due to the relatively small number of purely temporal lesions in her own (Newcombe's) study and the fact that the missile injuries in her sample were mostly lateral-temporal, whereas Milner's temporal lobe epilepsy patients had mesial-temporal lesions. Newcombe's observation of a right parietal/right posterior predominance for maze-learning impairment also conflicted with data gathered by Milner. In another study, of cortical ablation for the relief of epilepsy, Milner (1965) had found that it was patients with right temporal lobe excision, and also patients with large right frontal or right posterior ablation, who performed poorly on the maze-learning task. However, Newcombe attributed the discrepancy with her own observations to the fact that there were no large right frontal lesions in her group and that Milner's right parietal group was somewhat small and the respective lesions appeared to be limited in extent. In addition, the particular maze used by Milner was somewhat longer than that of Newcombe and perhaps more taxing to perform for patients with frontal lesions. Nevertheless, in spite of these differences, both studies demonstrated deficits in maze learning in patients with right hemisphere pathology.

The patient N.A., described in detail earlier (p. 85), has been compared to other clinical populations, in particular patients with cortical ablation and patients with alcoholic Korsakoff's syndrome. The relative selectivity of his memory impairment, with greater impairment on verbal than non-verbal memory tests, was evident in the initial study by Teuber, Milner and Vaughan (1968), where his verbal memory scores were much poorer than patients with left temporal lobectomy, and similar to those of a well-documented amnesic patient; by contrast, his non-verbal memory test scores were similar to those of patients with right temporal lobectomy, and outside the range associated with an amnesic syndrome. Squire (1982) showed that N.A. displayed 'release from proactive interference' (improved memory performance when there was a change in the category of material to be learned), whereas this feature was absent in a group of patients with alcoholic Korsakoff's syndrome. He also observed that N.A. was much better at making temporal order judgements (indicating which of two previous lists of sentences, separated by a 3-minute interval, contained a target sentence) than patients with Korsakoff's syndrome, even though recognition memory for the sentences was at a similar level in both aetiologies. On a test of memory sensitive to frontal lobe ablation (Petrides and Milner, 1982), where subjects have to point to a different item on each successive page of items, N.A. performed much better than patients with alcoholic Korsakoff's syndrome, although no control data were presented by Squire to indicate if his performance was impaired relative to control subjects. In the case of his memory for events prior to his injury, his relatively limited retrograde amnesia contrasts quite sharply with the extensive retrograde amnesia seen in other conditions such as alcoholic Korsakoff's syndrome and herpes encephalitis.

Summary

It is apparent from the studies reviewed above that penetrating head injury can be highly selective in its effects; traumatic amnesia may be absent, and post-traumatic amnesia may occur in isolation; quite specific memory deficits may be apparent, and these may be dissociable from performance on other related cognitive tasks; and in a few patients the severity of memory deficit may be on a par with that found in the alcoholic Korsakoff amnesic syndrome. However, none of the studies reviewed in this chapter has been able to demonstrate an isolated, global amnesic syndrome. Where memory deficits are isolated, they tend not be global or severe enough to warrant the label 'amnesia' as it is used in the prototypical amnesic syndrome. Where the amnesia is global and severe, there is invariably evidence of additional cognitive impairment such that the patient may resemble a case of dementia rather than pure amnesia.

Some of the findings discussed in this chapter have raised intriguing questions about the nature of memory loss, e.g. do generalizations such as 'no pre- without post-traumatic amnesia' or 'no significant anterograde amnesia without pre- and post-traumatic amnesia' indicate that similar mechanisms underlie the types of memory loss in question? No firm evidence has yet been gathered to link pathophysiological aspects of penetrating head injury with subsequent memory disorders. As indicated at the beginning of the chapter, penetrating head injury will often vary in the type of severity of brain damage it causes. More information needs to be gathered to relate such differences to recovery of memory function, as has been done in the case of studies of blunt head injury. In addition, few systematic comparisons have been made of memory functioning after penetrating and blunt head injury. The few existing studies (Yin, 1970; Black, 1973) have not attempted to match the two groups for severity of injury nor sought to identify patients with blunt head injury in whom there is evidence of more focal cerebral damage.

Finally, patients with memory deficits resulting from penetrating head injury would seem to be an ideal sample to consider the effects of therapeutic measures for improving memory, since other cognitive functions and aspects of memory may often be intact.

Chapter 5

Blunt head injury

While patients with penetrating head injury fall within a relatively homogeneous group, other head-injury patients represent a more heterogeneous population. The term 'blunt head injury' will be used to describe this broad category of patients, and I will be including within this category studies of patients with 'closed' head injury. While the cerebral pathology resulting from blunt head injury entails a significant degree of generalized brain damage, focal cerebral lesions may also be evident after this type of injury. This may result from localized skull fracture or from the development of a focal intracerebral or extracerebral haematoma. In addition, however, areas of focal cerebral contusion are frequently found in temporal lobe and basal-frontal regions after blunt head injury (*Figure 5.1*).

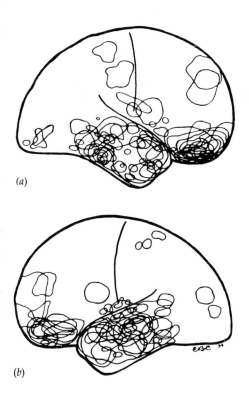

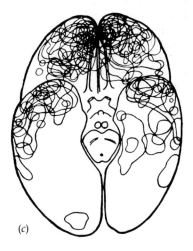

Figure 5.1 Temporal and basal-frontal regions which are the most common sites of cerebral contusion in patients with blunt head injury (from Courville, 1945. Reprinted by permission of Pacific Press Publishers Association)

Pre-traumatic and post-traumatic amnesia

Memory loss for events around the time of the injury accompanies cases of blunt head injury where significant cerebral concussion has taken place. In most instances, loss of consciousness accompanies the injury, but in a few cases the patient may not lose consciousness yet will subsequently display both pre- and post-traumatic amnesia (Fisher, 1966; Haas and Ross, 1986). The mechanisms of this amnesia are unclear, but it is possible that there is some overlap with the phenomenon of 'transient global amnesia' and that the head injury acts as a trigger to initiate a separate pathological process.

The following sections will consider memory loss for events immediately preceding and subsequent to the head injury, and also memory functioning during the early post-traumatic period.

Pre-traumatic amnesia

Pre-traumatic amnesia has traditionally been defined as memory loss for events which immediately preceded the head injury. The estimate of pre-traumatic amnesia is usually obtained months or years after the injury and is often difficult to obtain with precision, especially when the patient's daily schedule prior to the injury was fairly routine. It is also unclear whether the memory loss should be absolute or whether partial memory for events may also be subsumed under the period of pre-traumatic amnesia. Nor is it generally agreed whether such amnesia should include more general memory loss which may be present for events, months and years prior to the injury, but which may be discontinuous with a period of pre-traumatic amnesia. Pre-traumatic amnesia is frequently short in duration, and can usually be counted in minutes or hours rather than days or weeks (Eden and Turner, 1941). In many cases of mild blunt head injury, pre-traumatic amnesia may be absent, leaving an isolated period of post-traumatic amnesia (Crovitz, Horn and Daniel, 1983). Russell (1935) suggested that residual pre-traumatic amnesia seldom lasted more than a week, and that instances where the duration was in years probably had a hysterical basis. He also noted that in a few cases pre-traumatic events might be remembered in the early post-traumatic period but be lost from memory after the period of post-traumatic amnesia. Symonds (1962) described two patients with blunt head injury, one of whom had a pre-traumatic amnesia of 3 months and the other of one year, but he did not believe there was a hysterical basis to the amnesia in either of these patients.

Wasterlain (1971) suggested that patients with long periods of pre-traumatic amnesia (which he defined as more than 10 minutes) tended to have more severe head injuries with evidence of considerable cerebral contusion. Russell and Nathan (1946) assessed pre-traumatic and post-traumatic amnesia in a large series of patients, including cases of gunshot wounds and cases of 'accidental head injury' (mostly blunt head injury). In the latter group of patients, pre-traumatic amnesia lasted less than 30 minutes in over 80% of the series, and was also found to be less than 30 minutes in about 50% of the patients who had post-traumatic amnesia exceeding 7 days. A small number of patients (11/200) had no pre-traumatic amnesia despite a post-traumatic amnesia of up to 7 days. There did not therefore appear to be much of a correlation between the duration of the pre-traumatic amnesia and that of post-traumatic amnesia. However, Blomert and Sisler (1974) examined patients shortly after a mild head injury and found a stronger correlation between duration of pre-traumatic and post-tramatic amnesia. When post-traumatic amnesia was less than one hour, pre-traumatic amnesia was always under one minute.

On the basis of their observations of head-injured patients Williams and Zangwill (1952) hypothesized that two types of pre-traumatic amnesia may exist: '(1) A short and usually complete retrograde amnesia; (2) More diffuse and widely distributed disturbances of memory for pre-traumatic events'. The suggestion that a short pre-traumatic amnesia and a more general retrograde amnesia may be dissociable and rely on different neural mechanisms has not been systematically followed up by subsequent research workers, even though it has been alluded to in other studies of patients with blunt head injury (Benson and Geschwind, 1967).

Some recent evidence has, however, been gathered to support the presence of a more general retrograde memory loss in head injury patients. Using a questionnaire relating to television programmes which had been broadcast in the years prior to the injury, Levin et al. (Levin, Grossman and Kelly, 1977; Levin, Papanicolaou and Eisenberg, 1984) found impaired memory during the post-traumatic period for programmes which had taken place over a period of around 12 years prior to the injury, and did not find any evidence of a temporal gradient in the memory loss. In a subsequent report (Levin et al., 1985), a similar impairment was also observed in patients who were assessed after the period of post-traumatic amnesia. The remote memory loss shown by patients during post-traumatic amnesia, was also evident for autobiographical events (e.g. name of primary/secondary school attended). However, when autobiographical memory was sampled, they did find better recall of earlier compared to more recent events by patients tested during the post-traumatic period. It is worth pointing out that the questionnaire method employed in the earlier studies (Levin, Grossman and Kelly, 1977; Levin, Papanicolaou and Eisenberg, 1984) used a recognition format and it is possible that recall procedures would have produced a temporal gradient in the retrograde amnesia. Further, head-injury patients tend to be relatively young subjects, and so time periods which can be validly sampled may not stretch back far enough for any gradient effect to be manifest. Crovitz (1986) has also outlined, in the form of a detailed single-case interview, the use of cue words to stimulate recall of autobiographical information by a patient who suffered a severe blunt head injury. A further manifestation of retrograde memory deficits after blunt head injury may be in the form of an inability to recognize faces which were familiar to the patient prior to his head injury. Levin and Peters (1976) have reported one such case, although this patient showed significant cognitive impairment in addition to his deficit in faces recognition.

Russell (1935) first reported the condition of 'shrinking' pre-traumatic amnesia and described a patient with a closed head injury who had an initial pre-traumatic amnesia of at least 5 years which, over a period of 10 weeks, eventually shrank to a matter of a few minutes. Russell and Nathan (1946) confirmed this pattern and found that the recovery of pre-traumatic amnesia was in chronological order, with items in the distant past recovering first. Williams and Zangwill (1952) pointed to some degree of variability in the chronological sequence of remembered events, and indicated that cueing might often help patients to recover lost memories. Although shrinkage of pre-traumatic amnesia usually parallels the resolution of post-traumatic amnesia, the latter may terminate well before pre-traumatic amnesia shrinks to its final duration (Russell, 1971), and significant pre-traumatic amnesia may remain in a few isolated cases (Goldberg et al., 1981).

The converse to shrinking pre-traumatic amnesia has been noted in football players with minor concussion who can recall pre-traumatic information immediately after the injury but have amnesia for the same information if questioned minutes later (Lynch and Yarnell, 1973). The phenomenon of shrinkage of pre-traumatic amnesia has led some investigators (e.g. Benson and Geschwind, 1967) to suggest a retrieval deficit as the major mechanism underlying this form of temporary memory loss, although other explanations such as interference with normal rehearsal processes (Williams, 1969) may also be feasible.

Post-traumatic amnesia

Post-traumatic amnesia refers to the period subsequent to the head injury for which the patient has loss of memory. Russell (1932) alluded to some of the difficulties in equating loss of consciousness with loss of memory, but it was not until several years later that Symonds and Russell (1943) specifically defined the duration of post-traumatic amnesia as ending 'at the time from which the patient can give a clear and consecutive account of what was happening around him'. They emphasized the dangers of underestimating the duration of post-traumatic amnesia by using 'islands of memory' to indicate the end of the amnesia, or by assuming that if the patient is aware of things going on around him, he may necessarily be able to recall these at a later date. A number of authors (e.g. Whitty and Zangwill, 1977) have noted that a 'lucid interval' may be present early in the period of post-traumatic amnesia where there has been minimal initial concussion. This may be due to a highly emotional event which has remained imprinted in the patient's memory, or to a period preceding the delayed development of vascular lesions such as an extradural haematoma, which may subsequently result in a period of amnesia due to cerebral compression.

The duration of post-traumatic amnesia will vary with severity of the head injury, and therefore 'typical' durations are somewhat misleading. Russell and Nathan (1946) noted that in a series of over a thousand 'accidental' head injuries, 70% of cases had post-traumatic amnesia lasting between one hour and 7 days. Even in patients with a post-traumatic amnesia lasting more than one week, as in the series reported by Roberts (1979), a relatively wide distribution of duration of post-traumatic amnesia was evident, with one-third of patients having a post-traumatic amnesia duration of 28 days or more. Russell and Smith (1961) observed that the distribution of length of post-traumatic amnesia in older patients was skewed towards prolonged periods in this age group. As Levin, Benton and Grossman (1982) have pointed out, the total duration of post-traumatic amnesia will include some period of coma and a further period of impaired memory. The relative lengths of these may be variable, and in some patients such as the elderly head injured, a short period of coma may be followed by a relatively protracted period of poor memory, resulting in a long overall duration of post-traumatic amnesia (Von Wowern, 1966).

Dissatisfaction with retrospective estimates of post-traumatic amnesia has led investigators to seek more accurate observations of memory functioning during this period and to obtain concurrent measures of post-traumatic amnesia. In a longitudinal study of patients with mild head injury, Gronwall and Wrightson (1980) noted a dissociation between recovery of orientation (mainly orientation for time and place) and recovery from post-traumatic amnesia, and therefore disputed the functional equivalence of disorientation and post-traumatic amnesia. Similar findings were reported by Sisler and Penner (1975) in patients with more severe head injury. Somewhat different conclusions were reached by Fortuny *et al.* (1980) in their study of post-traumatic amnesia in head-injured patients. They supplemented questions regarding orientation for time and place with a picture recall task, and also tested patients' memory for the examiner's name. They defined the termination of post-traumatic amnesia as the point when the patient had three successive days of correct recall on such items, and found that this brief test yielded estimates of post-traumatic amnesia that correlated with retrospective estimates made by neurosurgeons.

Levin, O'Donnell and Grossman (1979) designed a test of orientation specifically for the study of head-injured patients – the Galveston Orientation and Amnesia Test (GOAT). It included orientation for time and place, and the patient's memory for events around the time of the injury, mode of transport to hospital, etc. Using this instrument to monitor post-traumatic amnesia and its termination, they found that in a series of 52 patients with significant closed head injury there was a median post-traumatic amnesia of 14 days. They found a correlation between duration of post-traumatic amnesia and ratings on components of the Glasgow Coma Scale. Post-traumatic amnesia which persisted beyond 2 weeks was associated with CT scan findings indicative of diffuse injury or bilateral lesions, whereas GOAT scores which improved more rapidly tended to be found in patients with focal mass lesions. In terms of correlation with the Glasgow Outcome Scale (Jennett and Bond, 1975), patients with post-traumatic amnesia of less than 2 weeks achieved good recovery, while longer intervals were associated with prolonged disability. They found that their instrument was particularly useful in patients with very brief periods of coma (one or 2 hours) which were then followed by prolonged confusional states that may have included periods of fluctuating memory functioning. Levin, Papanicolaou and Eisenberg (1984) reported some further data relating duration of coma to duration of post-traumatic amnesia defined by GOAT scores, and they found that there was a relatively weak relationship between the two, with some instances of prolonged post-traumatic amnesia following relatively brief periods of coma. They suggested that the factors which determine the duration of post-traumatic amnesia may be quite different from those variables which influence the duration of coma. Apart from considering memory functioning after blunt head injury as a means of defining the period of post-traumatic amnesia, other investigators have examined memory performance in its own right. Cronholm and Jonsson (1957) reported impaired memory scores on the Benton Visual Retention Test in patients examined within the first 24 days of a closed head injury, the severity of which was not indicated by the authors but stated to have 'varied considerably' between patients. Dunn and Brooks (1974) observed that patients' verbal recall scores during the period of post-traumatic amnesia could be improved with semantic cues, and suggested that difficulties in retrieval may characterize memory problems in the post-concussion phase.

In addition to general impairment in memory functioning in the post-traumatic period, confabulation and other forms of paramnesia may be present. As was pointed out earlier (*see* p. 20), there are difficulties in interpreting reports of confabulation due to the lack of standardized procedures for assessing confabulatory responses and the practical difficulties in ascertaining the extent to which patients' responses are based on real or imaginary past experiences. Whitty and Zangwill (1977) indicated that a mild form of paramnesia or confabulation may exist in most instances of post-traumatic amnesia, but that occasionally an instance of marked confabulation may occur in the presence of relatively normal behaviour in other spheres of activity, as opposed to confabulation which may be present as part of 'general traumatic confusion'. In the former cases, there is usually subsequent evidence of prolonged post-traumatic and pre-traumatic amnesia and other neurological signs of severe brain injury. A focal confabulatory syndrome was noted to have been present in only 38 out of 1931 cases of blunt head injury observed during the Second World War (Whitty and Zangwill, 1977). Six of these showed confabulation persisting for more than 2 or 3 days, with the content of the confabulation mainly comprising misrecall of real experiences; e.g. events placed in the wrong temporal/spatial context. There was a rather facile euphoria in most of these patients which tended to disappear as recovery continued.

In a study which included both patients with blunt head injury and those with penetrating head injury (gun-shot wounds), Weinstein and Lyerly (1968), found confabulation in 60% of patients. This was defined as invention of a story about a past event or gross distortion of an actual occurrence, and was elicited by direct questions about the patients' disability and the circumstances surrounding their admission to hospital. While florid, spontaneous confabulation is invariably restricted to the early stages of the post-traumatic period, in a few instances a patient examined several months after injury may confabulate in response to specific questions probing his memory for past events; these patients, such as the one described by Baddeley and Wilson (1986), usually have evidence of significant frontal lobe pathology as a result of their head injury.

The condition known as 'reduplicative paramnesia', which was earlier discussed in Chapter 1, has also been observed in head-injured patients. Paterson and Zangwill (1944) reported spatial disorientation, which included features of 'reduplicative paramnesia' in two patients who incurred severe head injury. The patients' disorientation for place, which lasted 1–2 weeks, included confusing their present location with a place in which they had previously been. Benson, Gardner and Meadows (1976) reported an even longer duration (several months) of reduplicative paramnesia in their three patients with severe closed head injury. These patients consistently mislocated the hospital to another site which had been significant to them at an earlier stage in their lives, even after memory for everyday events seemed to have returned to normal. Benson, Gardner and Meadows implicated right hemisphere and frontal pathology in mediating the form of spatial disorientation present in their patients. Staton, Brumback and Wilson (1982) reported a case who showed reduplicative amnesia which included features of the 'Capgras syndrome', following a severe head injury which resulted in a number of cerebral lesions, including right hippocampal and temporal lobe damage. As part of this syndrome, their patient failed to recognize familiar people, even family members, and also believed that the real person had been replaced by a double. He also had a number of *déjà vu* experiences.

Anterograde memory deficits

Memory symptoms and impaired memory test performance are among the most common sequelae of blunt head injury, even in those patients who otherwise appear to have made a good recovery from their injury (Stuss *et al.*, 1985). In view of the most frequent sites of cerebral contusion in blunt head injury (*see Figure 5.1*), namely the temporal and basal-frontal regions, it is not surprising that memory impairment is the most marked and persistent impairment after blunt head injuries. Everyday memory symptoms which are present several years after a severe head injury may often be more reliably reported by an observer than by the patient himself (Sunderland, Harris and Gleave, 1984), perhaps due in part to the head-injured patient sometimes forgetting instances of his own memory lapses! Memory symptoms described by patients or their close family members are in general similar to 'normal' memory symptoms, ranging from difficulties in remembering people's names to forgetting where articles have been put. In general, there is only a slight correlation between memory symptoms and memory test performance (Kapur and Peason, 1983), and where a correlation has been found it has been limited to certain memory tasks such as story recall, and to patients who are assessed several years after the head injury (Sunderland, Harris and Baddeley, 1983). Russell (1932) and Russell and Smith (1961) pointed to clinical evidence for the presence of memory deficits after the initial period of traumatic amnesia, but did not report any detailed memory testing. Recently there has been a mushrooming of investigations of memory function after blunt head injury, with a large number of these emanating from Brooks and his colleagues in Glasgow. In a study of patients who were mostly seen within 2 years of injury, Brooks (1976) found normal or near normal performance on digit span but impaired recall on reverse span, impairment in immediate and delayed recall of a short story, and in paired-associate learning. Thomsen (1977) assessed verbal learning within 3 years of injury in patients with severe closed head injury, 19 of whom were still dysphasic. Both dysphasic and non-dysphasic patients were worse than controls on learning a complete sentence, learning 10 unrelated words, or recalling a short story; on most measures, patients with dysphasia were worse than patients without. Brooks (1975) showed that in word-list recall it was the long-term memory component of the task which was most impaired in head-injured patients. Lower levels of clustering and subjective organization were noted to be present in the verbal free recall of patients with blunt head injury who were examined during a course of rehabilitation after severe head injury (Levin and Goldstein, 1986). Fodor (1972) reported that in her patients, who were studied shortly after their head injury, delayed recall of related material was one of the more sensitive measures of their memory deficit. However, this study has been criticized for confounding measures of premorbid and current intellectual level (Schacter and Crovitz, 1977), and it also suffered from floor effects for delayed recall of unrelated material.

Brooks (1974b) examined continuous recognition memory performance with non-verbal stimuli in patients seen one to 32 months after injury. Interpreting his data in terms of signal detection theory, he suggested that head-injured patients were significantly more unwilling to guess than control subjects on the test. However, Richardson (1979a) disputed Brooks' use of signal detection theory and reinterpreted his data as indicating no change in response bias after head injury. Hannay, Levin and Grossman (1979) found that the number of false positive responses by head-injured patients on a similar continuous recognition memory task was greater than that by control subjects, but that a combined measure of hits and false positives, i.e. the total number of correct responses, was the factor which best discriminated head-injured from control subjects. Using the selective reminding technique (Buschke and Fuld, 1974), Levin et al. (1979) assessed word-list recall of severely head injured patients seen at least 6 months after injury. They found that memory test scores showed a fairly close relationship with severity of disability, as measured by the Glasgow Outcome Scale. Brooks (1984) pointed out that this sample of patients was not random, since it was restricted to the ages of 16–50 years and excluded patients with a history of alcoholism, drug abuse or neuropsychiatric disorders.

Patients with relatively mild head injury (usually with post-traumatic amnesia between a few minutes and a few days) have also been found to show impaired memory functioning (Gronwall and Wrightson, 1981; Barth et al., 1983), although this evidence is subject to some qualifications. In general, such deficits appear to have been limited to the first few months after injury, and one study (McLean et al., 1983) only found significant memory impairment if this was tested a few days after injury. Another investigation (Gentilini et al., 1985) did not find any evidence of memory impairment in patients with mild head injury who were assessed one month after injury. Richardson (1979b) found a deficit in recall of concrete but not of abstract words after mild head injury, and subsequently obtained similar findings in a group of 30 patients, 22 of whom had incurred a mild blunt head injury and eight of whom had a moderately severe blunt head injury (Richardson and Snape, 1984). A similar pattern of memory deficits was observed by Richardson and Barry (1985) in a group of patients with mild blunt head injury who, nonetheless, performed normally on tests of memory for faces and memory for pictures. These researchers also observed that if blunt head injury and control patients were instructed to use visual imagery to remember the words, the former no longer showed a deficit relative to control patients. Richardson (1984) also observed that in patients with blunt head injury the pattern of intrusion errors during recall of a word-list was unrelated to the concreteness of the material in the word-list, whereas such a relationship was readily apparent in the performance of control subjects. It is important to point out that in all of these studies by Richardson, patients were examined within the first few days after their head injury, and so such deficits should not necessarily be regarded as reflecting permanent sequelae of a minor blunt head injury.

Boxers represent a unique subset of the population of patients with mild blunt head injury, since one is usually concerned with the cumulative effects of a large number of minor head injuries rather than a single episode of concussion (Roberts, 1969). In considering this group of patients, it is important to make allowance for any history of alcohol abuse and also any limitations in the subject's premorbid intellectual level. Thomassen et al. (1979) found evidence for a deficit in a word-list learning task in a group of former boxers, but this deficit was no longer evident when allowance was made for educational and vocabulary level of the boxers. More recently, McLatchie et al. (1987), in a more detailed investigation of memory functioning, found that a subgroup of active boxers (7 out of 16 for whom data were available) showed impaired memory functioning.

In summary, there appears to be no doubt that significant impairment on a range of memory tasks, but especially those with a long-term component, can occur as a sequel of blunt head injury. What is of greater interest, however, is the extent to which residual memory deficits can be predicted on the basis of particular features of the head injury or the head-injured patient. This will be examined in the following sections.

Features of the comatose period

Interpretation of studies reporting correlations between the comatose state of patients after head injury and subsequent memory performance, need to take account of the difficulties in obtaining valid and reliable measures of head-injured patients' cerebral function while they are in a comatose state, especially where such measures have been made on a retrospective basis. Such difficulties have to some extent been alleviated with the introduction of scales such as the Glasgow Coma Scale (Teasdale and Jennett, 1974). Levin, Grossman and Kelly (1976) and Hannay, Levin and Grossman (1979) found a relationship between coma duration and short-term recognition memory for visual patterns, but this relationship was somewhat variable – patients with severe head injury performed worse than those with mild or moderate head injury in the study by Levin *et al.*, whereas in the investigations by Hannay *et al.*, patients with moderate and severe head injury did not differ in memory performance, although both groups were more impaired than a group with mild head injury. Lezak (1979) did find some relationship between coma duration on auditory verbal learning; patients with coma of longer than 2 weeks were much more likely than those with coma of shorter duration to show impaired memory 3 years after injury. Brooks *et al.* (1980), using the Glasgow Coma Scale, did not find any significant relationship between coma duration and performance on a range of memory tasks. Levin *et al.* (1979) reported a close relationship between features of the comatose state, namely, presence of oculomotor deficit and impaired motor functioning in the early stages of recovery, and impaired performance on both storage and retrieval measures of word list learning. Dye, Milby and Saxon (1979) also found poor tactile memory performance in patients with coma and additional motor and ocular signs, compared to those with less severe neurological deficit after injury. In general, therefore, the relationship between coma duration and residual memory functioning has been shown to be relatively inconsistent, although it appears that some features of the comatose patient, e.g. particular neurological signs, may be predictive of future memory performance.

Features of the post-traumatic period

In his study of continuous recognition memory, Brooks (1974b) found that the duration of post-traumatic amnesia showed a significant negative correlation with efficiency of recognition memory, but in a later study (Brooks, 1975), he found that the post-traumatic amnesia showed a weak relationship with short-term and long-term memory for word list material. In a subsequent larger-scale study of 82 patients, Brooks (1976) found that performance on the story recall and paired-associate learning subtests of the Wechsler Memory Scale was significantly related to the duration of post-traumatic amnesia, and that patients with more than 7 days of amnesia performed significantly worse than controls. In another investigation by Brooks *et al.* (1980) using paired-associate learning, story recall and visual design recall (recall of the Rey-Osterreith figure), a further effect with regard to post-traumatic amnesia and memory/learning tasks was found, and this relationship was particularly marked in the case of delayed relearning of paired-associate items.

Smith (1974) did not find any significant relationship between post-traumatic amnesia and memory performance 10–20 years after injury, although her data suggest that patients with shorter post-traumatic amnesia, 21 days or less, performed somewhat better than those with longer amnesia on story recall. Van Zomeren and Van Den Berg (1985) noted that a cut-off point of post-traumatic amnesia of 13 days was most reliable in distinguishing those patients with blunt head injury with symptoms of everyday memory difficulty. Parker and Serrats (1976) used a classification of post-traumatic amnesia based on assessment of memory functioning during the post-injury period. This assessment comprised 'a simple question and answer test given daily', but no further details of the test were provided. They estimated that 92% of patients with post-traumatic amnesia of 24 hours or less reached normal memory by 2 years, whereas only 50% of those with post-traumatic amnesia longer than one month recovered normal memory functioning. Over shorter periods of post-traumatic amnesia (from a few seconds to a few days), Gronwall and Wrightson (1981) found that durations of the amnesia which were less than one hour were similar to those for one to 24 hours in terms of their effects on Wechsler Memory Scale performance, but patients with post-traumatic amnesia of more than one day were impaired compared to those with a shorter duration. A further relationship between duration of post-traumatic amnesia and memory for word list material, more especially with regard to storage than retrieval measures of performance, was observed in a further group of patients whose duration of amnesia varied between several hours and several days.

Features of the cerebral injury

A number of studies have failed to find any significant effect of the presence of skull fracture on residual memory deficit (e.g. Klove and Cleeland, 1972; Brooks, 1976; Brooks et al. 1980). Brooks (1975) did find an effect on one measure of memory performance – 20 seconds delayed recall of word list material – with greater impairment in patients with skull fracture. Smith (1974) found that the site of skull impact affected the degree of recovery of memory function. She found that patients with right-sided impact performed worse than those with left-sided impact on tests of story recall and recall of visual designs, but that on the latter test patients with left-frontal impact performed particularly poorly. She interpreted some of her findings as reflecting contre-coup effects, but it is unclear why these should have appeared to occur for some impact sites and not for others. Brooks (1984) also disputed some interpretations of Smith's data, and in his own study (Brooks et al., 1980) did not find any significant findings either with regard to the presence of skull fracture or whether it was on the left or right side, although patients with operated haematomas performed better than non-operated patients, possibly reflecting more limited, focal damage in the operated patients. Left and right sided haematoma cases did not show any differences in pattern of memory performance.

   In general, patients with focal intracranial haematomas tend to perform more poorly than patients with blunt head injury with normal CT scans or small ventricles (Timming, Orrison and Mikula, 1982). Patients with subdural haematomas, when compared to those without haematomas, have been found to perform worse on memory tests, and this may be related in part to the greater degree of cortical atrophy which accompanies such haematomas and to the frontal distribution of such lesions (Cullum and Bigler, 1985). Milner (1969) found that patients with left temporal epileptic foci after blunt head injury were particularly impaired on delayed recall of story and paired-associate material. Warrington and Shallice (1969) reported an isolated verbal memory deficit in a patient who had a left parietal subdural haematoma following a blunt head injury. Their patient showed significant short-term, mainly repetition, verbal memory deficits in the context of normal performance on long-term verbal memory tasks. Lezak (1979), using verbal memory tasks, noted that in the early recovery period, patients with greater left-hemisphere involvement tended to have lower test scores than other patients.

Brooks (1976) found that patients with persistent neurological signs did not score worse on the Wechsler Memory Scale. In the study by Levin *et al.* (1979) referred to earlier, patients showing signs of brainstem damage performed poorly on memory tasks, possibly reflecting greater severity of diffuse rather than focal brain damage. Klove and Cleeland (1972) found that the presence of persisting neurological signs was significantly associated with poor performance on a tactile memory task. Smith (1974) reported that patients with abnormal motor responses soon after injury (for example, decerebrate response), were more likely to show severe verbal learning deficits at follow-up, although this was only found in right-sided impact cases, but Brooks (1984) questioned whether the raw data in fact warranted such conclusions. Levin *et al.* (1979) reported that early hemiparesis, bilateral non-reactive pupils, and more particularly, oculovestibular deficit were associated with poor memory storage and retrieval months or years after injury. Levin and Eisenberg (1979c) carried out a study (reported in Levin, Benton and Grossman, 1982) in which they classified head-injured patients into mild, diffuse, complicated by a lateralized mass lesion, or associated with a bilateral mass lesion. Patients were assessed after they had come out of post-traumatic amnesia or at least had reached a stable plateau of recovery. Thus, mildly injured patients were seen a shorter period (median 16 days) after injury than patients with more severe injury (median 42 days). They administered a word-list recall test and found significantly better performance in patients with mild blunt head injury and those with right hemisphere mass lesions, compared to patients with more diffuse injury. Patients with left hemisphere lesions, especially those involving the left temporal lobe, performed less well than other patients. Within the right hemisphere group, there was no evidence of more marked memory impairment with temporal lobe involvement, and Levin, Benton and Grossman (1982) also indicated that they did not think a measurable language deficit was a necessary or sufficient condition for impaired performance on the word-list recall task. Jetter *et al.* (1986) presented evidence implicating frontal lobe damage after blunt head injury in impaired delayed (24 hours) recall of verbal material, but interpretation of their study is complicated by the presence of some non-traumatic aetiologies in their sample, and by the presence of bilateral pathology in some patients with frontal lesions, but not in any of the patients with lesions outside the frontal area.

Evidence of more diffuse cerebral pathology in blunt head injury is more difficult to quantify, but some attempts have been made to relate severity of memory impairment with measures of ventricular dilatation, which may often follow cases of blunt head injury. Levin *et al.* (1981) found a relationship between degree of ventricular dilatation and performance on tests of verbal recall and picture recognition memory. Bigler *et al.* (1984) also reported a significant correlation between memory performance and degree of ventricular dilatation in patients with blunt head injury, and later studies (Cullum and Bigler, 1986; Massman *et al.*, 1986) showed a relationship between severity of memory impairment, and measures of both cortical atrophy and ventricular dilatation. Verbal paired-associate learning showed the strongest correlation with these indices of cerebral injury and, in the case of cortical atrophy, it appeared that left frontal cortical atrophy accounted for much of the relationship with severity of memory impairment.

A single-case study of a patient with residual left frontal and right temporal pathology after a severe blunt head injury (Zatorre and McEntee, 1983) yielded evidence of a marked, relatively pure, amnesic syndrome. Some of the features of this syndrome resembled those found in studies of patients with alcoholic Korsakoff's syndrome (e.g. evidence of impaired semantic encoding of verbal information during verbal memory performance). Bauer (1982) has also reported a case of bilateral, cerebral lesions following a severe blunt head injury, although in this patient the intracerebral haematomas, which were sited in both posterior temporal regions, developed after a minor surgical procedure carried out 6 days after injury, and so it is not possible to relate the pathology specifically to the effects of the head injury. The patient showed marked memory impairment, which included inability to recognize familiar faces, together with topographical memory loss and impaired memory test performance, more especially for visual, non-verbal material. These memory deficits were still apparent about 18 months after the injury.

Effects of age

The effects of age on memory function after head injury are complicated by a number of factors. Measures of severity of injury such as the length of post-traumatic amnesia appear to be longer in elderly subjects (Russell, 1971), and so correlations between age and residual memory function need to take this into account. In addition, the type of head injury incurred by children (e.g. pedestrian accidents, falls) tend to be different from those sustained by adults (e.g. deceleration injury as driver/passenger in car, motor-bike accidents), and it is possible that the type and severity of injury may not be the same in the two populations. A final point to note is that the effects of age need to be distinguished from those of cumulative occurrences of head injury over a period of time. In the case of boxers, for example, Roberts (1969) found that performance on memory tests correlated with age, but not with length of career, whereas incidence of subjective or observed memory symptoms did show a relationship with length of career. Kear-Colwell and Heller (1980) reported that younger head-injured patients (less than 35 years old) were more severely impaired than older patients on some of the verbal subtests of the Wechsler Memory Scale, but unfortunately they did not allow for possible differences in severity of injury between the two groups. Brooks et al. (1980) found little evidence, apart from performance on one delayed recall task, for a relationship between age and residual memory function, although this study did not include many older patients. Brooks (1972, 1974a) observed that the relationship between post-traumatic amnesia and memory performance was more marked in elderly patients, but this finding was not confirmed in a follow-up investigation (Brooks, 1976). Lezak (1979) did not find any effects of age on recovery of memory function, although her sample did not include any patient over 41 years of age.

Several studies have focused on the effects of head injuries in children. Richardson (1963) reported poor memory performance in children who incurred severe head injury up to 13.5 years earlier. This impairment was evident on tasks such as the Benton Visual Retention Test and tests of rote memory. Richardson commented that memory deficits often interfered with the children's subsequent academic and social adjustment. Subsequent studies have found impairments on other tasks such as word-list recall (Levin and Eisenberg, 1979a) and, less frequently, on continuous recognition memory tasks (Levin and Eisenberg, 1979b). Using patients with mild head injury as controls, Levin et al. (1982) found that memory deficits accompanied severe head injury in children and adolescents, and that at follow-up (usually several years later) this was more likely to persist in the head-injured children. Severity of injury (as estimated by duration of impaired consciousness) rather than presence of laterality of focal lesion, was related to the degree of memory deficit, and was also the critical measure from the point of view of memory recovery. Impairment on a task involving continuous recognition memory for pictures was mainly evident in the severely head-injured children, whereas both sets of patients showed deficits on word-list recall tasks.

In contrast to these studies, several investigators have reported relatively good recovery of memory function in children with blunt head injury. Vignolo (1980) assessed school children around 10 years after a moderately severe head injury, and found normal memory performance in most children, although in those who did he Benton Visual task. Chadwick *et al.* (1981a) found normahave a residual cognitive deficit this commonly occurred on a word-list recall 1 paired-associate learning performance in head-injured children with periods of post-traumatic amnesia greater than one week when they were examined one year after injury. It is not possible to ascertain whether differences in patient selection criteria underlie their findings, since their clinical classification of patients according to duration of post-traumatic amnesia has not usually been employed in other studies of head-injured children. It is also possible that if they had included more than one memory task, evidence of learning impairment might have been more forthcoming.

In a further study, this time with children who incurred focal blunt head injury, Chadwick *et al.* (1981b) found some relationship between clinical variables and memory performance where both verbal and non-verbal memory tests were used. Some patients with focal left and right injury did differ on verbal and non-verbal memory tests, but this was only evident in children who did not have evidence of generalized cerebral dysfunction (presumed to be present if there were signs such as prolonged unconsciousness or cerebral oedema). Patients with such signs performed worse than other patients on a range of tests, including a verbal learning task, although the absence of control subjects in this study limits the value of the findings.

Presence of compensation claim

The issue of whether the presence of an ongoing claim for compensation influences disability has been the subject of much controversy in the area of head injury (Miller, 1961; Miller, 1979; Kelly, 1981; Trimble, 1981). Although some studies (e.g. Stuss *et al.*, 1985) have alluded to the limited importance of litigation in influencing neuropsychological test profiles after blunt head injury, few systematic studies have however been carried out on this topic with reference to memory functioning. An exception to this is the investigation by McKinlay, Brooks and Bond (1983) who did not find any significant differences in memory performance or memory symptoms between those head-injured patients seeking compensation and a matched group of patients who did not have any legal claim pending.

Rate of recovery of memory deficits

While a few studies have examined recovery of memory functioning in the early period after mild head injury (e.g. Lindvall, Linderoth and Norlin, 1974), the majority of researchers have addressed the issue of recovery of memory function in cases of more severe head injury. Conkey (1938) found that the greatest improvement in memory occurred between the first and second assessments (between 30–40 days after injury). He further showed that the head-injured patients as a group had reached the level of controls by the fourth testing (8 months after injury). A limiting factor in this study was the small number of patients who remained throughout the investigation – four patients from an initial cohort of 25. Parker and Serrats (1976) found that 50% of patients with mild head injury showed normal verbal memory performance by one month after injury, and that this proportion rose to 84% and 92% one and 2 years post-injury respectively. In the case of the most severely injured patients (those with a post-traumatic amnesia for more than one month), none performed normally one month after injury, but 42% and 50% showed normal scores one and 2 years after injury respectively. Thus, regardless of the severity of the head injury, there was evidence to suggest that the major proportion of recovery of memory functioning took place in the first year after injury. A limitation of this study was that control subjects appear not to have been tested at the regular intervals at which repeat assessments were carried out on head-injured patients.

Groher (1977) tested patients on five occasions at intervals of 120 days from initial testing (one week after injury). Significant improvements were found from test to re-test, with the greatest change occurring between the first and second examinations, possibly coinciding with the termination of the period of post-traumatic amnesia. Lezak (1979) tested patients on four occasions during the first 3 years after injury; 0–6 months, 7–12 months, 13–24 months and 25–36 months. She found consistent improvements on digit span performance, with 83% of patients being normal on the fourth testing. On more difficult verbal learning tasks, there was generally some improvement in the first 12 months, but less consistent improvement after this period, and on some measures of verbal memory a large proportion of patients were still impaired on final testing after 3 years. At all time periods, Lezak found that patients with shorter duration of coma (less than 2 weeks) were more likely to show normal performance than patients with longer periods of coma.

Brooks and Aughton (1979) examined two groups of head-injured patients 3, 6 and 12 months after injury, and one of the groups was also examined one month after injury. At the 12-month testing, both groups of patients were significantly worse than controls who were tested and re-tested after a 6-week period (with comparisons being with the second assessment). This impaired performance was particularly evident on verbal paired-associate learning and complex figure recall, while on non-memory cognitive tests, head-injured subjects achieved normal scores at the 12-month testing. In general, the change in performance from test to re-test was relatively small, although in some head-injury patients, recall of a complex figure improved over the test sessions, while performance on verbal paired-associated learning showed, somewhat surprisingly, a drop from the 6-month to the 12-month assessment. Levin and Eisenberg (1979c) also followed up their patients and re-assessed them around 10 months after the initial assessment (which was usually 1–2 months after injury). Sixteen out of 22 patients with an initial retrieval deficit had improved by the time of follow-up.

Management of memory deficits

As in other aetiologies of cerebral dysfunction, no established therapies exist for bringing about significant and permanent improvement in the everyday memory functioning of head-injured patients, although some researchers have expressed scope for optimism (Newcombe, 1982). Prigatano et al. (1984) found higher

Wechsler memory quotients in a group of head-injured patients after a period of intensive rehabilitation, and this improvement was greater than that found in a control group who did not receive this therapeutic regimen. However, little detail was reported on which memory retraining techniques, if any, were used, nor whether the improvement generalized to everyday memory symptoms and was maintained at longer term follow-up. Individual case studies have indicated that some benefit may accrue from the use of specific mnemonic strategies such as visual imagery techniques (Glasgow *et al.*, 1977; Crovitz, 1979; Crovitz, Harvey and Horn, 1979) or introducing questions during learning (Crosson and Buenning, 1984). Wilson (1987) has also reported beneficial effects of these and similar techniques in the case of a range of neurological patients, many of whom had sustained a severe blunt head injury. However, any improvement shown by patients with blunt head injury has often been task-specific, and on long term follow-up there may be a decline in the initial improvement due to patients forgetting, or lacking the motivation, to use strategies in everyday settings (e.g. Crosson and Buenning, 1984).

Severely head-injured patients may show evidence of learning and transfer of training on simple perceptual-motor learning tasks (Miller, 1980), and may also be able to learn the simple procedures involved in performing basic operations on a microcomputer (Glisky, Schacter and Tulving, 1986a). In a further study, Glisky, Schacter and Tulving (1986b) showed that three patients with blunt head injury were able to acquire a limited computer vocabulary by gradually reducing, over successive trials, the number of letters required to identify the words in the vocabulary. However, in most of these studies head-injured patients have still performed at a lower level than control subjects, and it remains to be seen if such training can lead to meaningful rehabilitation in everyday work settings. Goldberg *et al.* (1982a,b) reported a case study where pharmacological means were used to try to improve memory functioning in a double-blind study of a head-injured patient. They found that a combination of physostigmine and lecithin resulted in a higher Wechsler memory quotient and improved word list recall, although performance on the Benton Visual Retention Test remained unchanged. A related study, although not directly concerned with attempts to improve memory functioning, was carried out by Dikmen *et al.* (1984). They looked for any differences in memory functioning between patients with blunt head injury receiving or not receiving anticonvulsant medication (phenytoin), but both groups performed at a similar level on a range of memory tasks.

Distinctive features of memory disorders in blunt head injury

While a large amount of data has been collected on memory functioning in patients with blunt head injury, few direct comparisons have been made with memory disorders in other neurological conditions. Although many other conditions tend to affect an older age group than head-injured patients, some illnesses, such as subarachnoid haemorrhage, overlap with blunt head injury in the population which is affected. This section will, therefore, include more general observations on indirect comparisons which can be made on the basis of existing evidence in the literature.

In the case of traumatic amnesia, i.e. loss of memory for events around the time of the injury, some comparisons can be made between such memory loss in blunt head injury and analogous observations which have been made in the case of penetrating head injury. These have been summarized in the chapter dealing with penetrating head injury (*see* p. 93), and will not be repeated here. Schacter and Crovitz (1977) pointed to the desirability of comparing the memory loss in traumatic amnesia with that seen in conditions such as transient global amnesia, which usually have a cerebrovascular basis. While both conditions share features such as marked memory impairment with some degree of retrograde amnesia during the post-ictal period, there are a few distinguishing features of memory functioning. First, the most striking difference is the alert state of the patient with transient global amnesia – the patient is usually able to maintain attention and carry out skills which do not tax his memory. In contrast, the patient with blunt head injury is invariably rendered unconscious by the cerebral injury. Second, in traumatic amnesia, marked anterograde memory impairment may extend for a longer period (up to several months) than the maximum length of memory difficulty seen in transient global amnesia, which usually does not exceed a few hours. Third, long-term recovery of memory functioning is at a much higher level in transient global amnesia than blunt head injury. Fourth, paramnesic phenomena, such as florid confabulation, tend to be more common in the post-traumatic period after blunt head injury than in the post-ictal period during an episode of transient global amnesia. Fifth, as Fisher (1982a) has pointed out, the duration of permanent pre-ictal amnesia tends to be somewhat longer in transient global amnesia compared with blunt head injury.

Turning to residual memory deficits after blunt head injury, few studies have formally compared such deficits with those found in other aetiologies. Exceptions to this include the investigation by Corkin *et al.* (1985) in which they compared a small group ($n = 5$) of selected patients with blunt head injuries with those of other aetiologies. Their patients were selected such that they might display a relatively pure, global amnesic syndrome. On verbal and non-verbal recurrent recognition memory tasks, the patients with blunt head injury performed worse than those with subarachnoid haemorrage or with herpes simplex encephalitis. Other memory tests (e.g. delayed recall of verbal and non-verbal material, paired-associated learning) did not reveal any significant differences in performance relative to other patient groups. Massman *et al.* (1986) found that in patients with blunt head injury, severity of memory impairment showed a relationship with degree of structural brain damage (as indicated by measures of cortical atrophy and ventricular dilatation), but that such a relationship was absent in a group of patients with primary degenerative dementia.

Comparisons between residual memory functioning after blunt head injury and penetrating head injury are discussed elsewhere (*see* p. 93), and some differences between observations of patients with blunt head injury and those with tuberculous meningitis are reviewed in Chapter 7.

Summary

The findings reviewed in this chapter have indicated that blunt head injury frequently leads to significant memory loss, both for events around the time of injury and as a persistent impairment of anterograde memory functioning. Memory loss for events post-dating the injury is usually more extensive than corresponding pre-traumatic memory loss. The extent of either type of memory loss will depend not only on the severity of the injury, but also on the sensitivity of the procedures used to assess the memory loss. In the case of pre-traumatic amnesia, the issue of possible dissociation between immediately pre-traumatic and more general retrograde memory loss remains unresolved. With regard to post-traumatic memory loss, in the individual case, retrospective estimates of duration of post-traumatic amnesia are subject to uncertainty and inconsistency. More research needs to be undertaken into procedures for the concurrent assessment of post-traumatic amnesia, and their predictive value for subsequent recovery of function. Residual memory deficits are a frequent sequel of blunt head injury, and the extent of these is in part related to the initial severity of injury, and to the stage of recovery at which memory functioning is assessed. The relationship with variables such as age and focal injury remains more complex, and it is possible that both positive and negative correlations with memory deficits can occur depending on the sample of patients and memory tests which are used.

Comparisons between memory functioning after blunt and penetrating head injuries are practically non-existent. More research also needs to be carried out on the role of attentional and volitional factors in the mediation of memory deficits after blunt head injury, especially as applied to 'everyday' situations. This is particularly pertinent for this population of neurological patients, since it is often necessary to predict the implications of memory test performance for aspects of occupational and educational adjustment. In general, poor memory performance will be expected to correlate with overall degree of disability (Brooks *et al.*, 1986), but it would be useful if more specific relationships could be established. The management of memory impairment in patients with blunt head injury remains an open question; no therapeutic procedures exist which can be offered as a reliable means of improving memory function in such patients, although in a few individual cases specific types of memory deficit may be amenable to partial improvement by psychological techniques.

Chapter 6

Degenerative, demyelinating and hydrocephalic dementias

This chapter considers memory functioning in patients with primary degenerative dementia, degenerative dementia associated with other neurological conditions, patients with CNS demyelination and patients with evidence of progressive cognitive dysfunction due to hydrocephalus. The term 'dementia' can sometimes be misleading, since it is occasionally used to refer to an impaired level of cognitive functioning (and as such could be used with reference to any clinical aetiology), or it is used in the form of a predictive diagnosis, often implying a specific degenerative pathology. In addition, because of the lack of commonly agreed and valid instruments for the assessment of cognitive deterioration, even those studies of patients from within a specific aetiology may not be strictly comparable, since the progressive nature of the disease can result in differences in severity and pattern of memory deficits depending on the stage of illness at which patients are examined (e.g. Corkin, 1982; Ober et al., 1985).

Primary degenerative dementia

The most frequently diagnosed type of degenerative dementia is Alzheimer's disease, although verification of the pathology can, as yet, only be made post-mortem, and significant issues in its diagnosis and classification remain unresolved (McKhann et al., 1984). The more neutral term 'primary degenerative dementia' will, wherever possible, be adopted here to describe idiopathic deterioration of cognitive function which would generally come under the rubric of Alzheimer's disease or Alzheimer-type dementia. The primary lesions associated with primary degenerative dementia consist of senile plaques, neurofibrillary tangles and granulovacuolar degeneration; these lesions appear to be most frequently found in the temporal and frontal lobes and in medial temporal structures such as the hippocampus. The use of a single term such as 'primary degenerative dementia' should not be taken as precluding the possibility that distinct subtypes of primary degenerative dementia may well exist (see Neary et al., 1986), perhaps with their own distinctive pattern of cerebral pathology.

Pick's disease is another form of primary degenerative dementia which can only be diagnosed with certainty at post-mortem. At the clinical level, it can sometimes be distinguished from Alzheimer-type dementia by features such as its later onset (peak between 50 and 60 years), slower course, higher prevalance among women, and by the early development of 'frontal lobe' dysfunction, which may take the

form of personality changes such as lack of spontaneity and facile hilarity (Lishman, 1987). In addition, some patients with Pick's disease may show selective language deficits and left temporal pathology as an early feature of their condition (Wechsler *et al.*, 1982). At the pathological level, the plaques and tangles associated with Alzheimer-type dementia are seldom found; neuronal loss appears to be predominate in the outer layers of frontal and temporal lobe cortex, and so-called 'balloon cells' are considered to be a commonly found feature of the neuronal degeneration (Lishman, 1987). Because of the lack of any reliable measures for differentiating these two forms of primary degenerative dementia, it is possible that some studies of patients with 'Alzheimer-type dementia' may have unwittingly included certain patients with Pick's disease. No formal studies of memory functioning appear to have been carried out on patients who were eventually proven to have suffered from Pick's disease, although a few researchers have commented on the relative sparing of memory functioning in the early stages of this disease compared to Alzheimer-type dementia (Robertson, Le Roux and Brown, 1958; Cummings and Duchen, 1981).

Memory symptoms offered by patients and family members, and impaired memory test performance are the most common and often the earliest features of primary degenerative dementia. Little systematic evidence has, however, been gathered on the detailed pattern of memory symptoms which patients report, or are observed to display, and how these may differ from those found in other types of progressive neuropsychological dysfunction. Some researchers have commented on relatives' reports of impaired everyday memory functioning as an early indicator of the disease process (Sulkava and Amberla, 1982; Semple, Smith and Swash, 1982), and certain symptoms, such as forgetting where things were put, have been noted in conjunction with analogous memory test deficits (Crook, Ferris and McCarthy, 1979). In this section, I will review a number of aspects of memory functioning in patients with primary degenerative dementia, namely presentation and retention test parameters which have been highlighted by investigators, retrograde amnesia, the relationship between memory functioning and clinical/biological aspects of the disease process, and the management of memory disorders of patients with primary degenerative dementia. I will focus mainly on more recent experimental investigations since many of the earlier studies lacked adequate control data or satisfactory clinical classification of patients (*see* Inglis (1958) for a review of some of these studies).

Presentation parameters

Patients with primary degenerative dementia have been found to show impaired performance on a variety of memory tasks, ranging from prose recall (Whelihan *et al.*, 1984; Bandera *et al.*, 1985) to tests such as delayed matching to sample, or memory for spatial position, which parallel those used in animal learning studies (Albert and Moss, 1984; Flicker *et al.*, 1984). In a number of instances, the memory impairment shown by patients with primary degenerative dementia may be secondary to more general cognitive deficits which are present, e.g. in some patients, their impaired memory on perceptual-motor memory tasks may be related to evidence of 'constructional apraxia' (Martin *et al.*, 1985b), and their deficits on tests of word list recall may be related to impaired semantic memory, as in category-item generation tasks (Weingartner *et al.*, 1983). In general, patients with primary degenerative dementia are more likely to show impaired performance on tasks which exceed their immediate memory span, or those which have a significant delay component (e.g. Osborne, Brown and Randt, 1982; Haxby *et al.*, 1985; Moss *et al.*, 1986). Even patients in the early stages of primary degenerative dementia may show marked impairments on delayed recall testing (Duara *et al.*, 1986). Miller (1973) found impaired performance in patients with primary degenerative dementia (mostly patients under 65 years and in the early stages of the illness) when they were asked to learn lists of words greater than their immediate span. Kopelman (1985), using a Brown–Peterson paradigm in patients with primary degenerative dementia, found poor performance in short-term memory for verbal material, even at delay intervals of 5 seconds, although it is of note that his patients also had low forward digit span scores, and were also impaired in the immediate recall of semantically anomalous sentences (Kopelman, 1986a). Wilson *et al.* (1983b) also reported impaired memory for verbal material where a relatively small number of items intervened between presentation and recall, and Morris (1986) noted impaired verbal short-term memory where the distractor task between presentation and retention was simply repeating the word 'the'. Impaired paired-associate learning also appears to be a sensitive indicator in the early stages of primary degenerative dementia, at least in elderly patients (Rosen and Mohs, 1982; Rosen, 1983).

A number of studies have focused on stimulus features which may influence the pattern of memory test performance. Miller (1972) found that the effect of acoustic similarity of verbal stimuli on recall was more marked in control patients than in patients with primary degenerative dementia. Weingartner *et al.*. (1981a) examined the effects of semantic organization of word-list material and presented lists of unrelated words, or lists where the words were clustered according to semantic categories. Control patients recalled significantly more related than unrelated words, but this difference was not evident in patients with primary degenerative dementia. Wilson *et al.* (1983a) found that verbal recognition performance in elderly patients with primary degenerative dementia benefited less from semantic encoding instructions than that of control subjects. In other types of memory tasks, however, patients with primary degenerative dementia appear to demonstrate relatively normal processing of semantic features.

Martin *et al.* (1985a), using free recall, cued recall and a variety of initial encoding instructions, found that patients with primary degenerative dementia showed effects of encoding instructions on verbal memory tasks similar to those in control patients (although absolute level of performance was predictably impaired). They therefore argued that the memory of patients with primary degenerative dementia may be quantitatively rather than qualitatively different from that of normal subjects. Some support for this hypothesis comes from the study by Kopelman (1985) referred to above, in which he also found that patients with primary degenerative dementia, when given sufficient presentation trials to equate initial learning level with control subjects, showed similar rates of forgetting over 24-hour and 7-day retention periods. Corkin (1985) also argued that her group of patients with primary degenerative dementia showed normal rates of forgetting for picture material, although these patients displayed an unusual pattern of performance: they showed a drop in performance from 10 minutes to 24 hours (this drop appearing to be greater than that demonstrated by control subjects), followed by an improvement in performance from 24 to 72 hours, while control subjects showed a drop in performance over this period. Where multiple modalities are incorporated in the stimuli to be learned, for example where subjects are asked to recall actions they recently performed, memory performance of elderly patients with primary degenerative dementia has been found to be superior to that shown by the more usual unimodal memory tests (Winblad *et al.*, 1985).

Retention test parameters

In general, free recall paradigms have been shown to be more sensitive in detecting memory deficits in patients with primary degenerative dementia than recognition or cued recall tasks. A number of studies have examined the pattern of free recall in patients with primary degenerative dementia, including the types of errors which they make. In the case of free recall of word-list material, Miller (1971) found that patients with dementia, unlike control subjects, did not show a primacy effect (whereby more items are recalled from the beginning than from the middle of the list). Thus, patients were impaired at recalling initial items, although there was also a tendency for words to be less well recalled throughout the serial positions. This pattern of deficit was observed even when the rate of presentation of words was slowed down. In a more recent study, however, Martin *et al.* (1985a) failed to find the pattern of 'primacy effect' deficit which had been observed by Miller. Diesfieldt (1978) found a primacy effect in some, but not all, elderly patients with primary degenerative dementia, observing that patients who did not show a primacy effect tended to be those who also performed poorly on delayed recognition memory for pictures.

Weingartner *et al.* (1981a) found that patients with primary degenerative dementia did not consistently remember information they had previously recalled on word-list recall trials. Impaired performance on serial learning of word lists became more marked as learning trials progressed. Consistent retrieval of items over the various test trials was more evident in controls than in patients with primary degenerative dementia (89% and 20% respectively). Organization in recall, in terms of pairs of words recalled together on successive trials, was also more evident in control subjects. Similar patterns of recall performance were noted by Sitaram *et al.* (1983) using verbal stimuli, and by Fuld (1980) using real objects as stimuli to be learned over a series of trials. A number of researchers have also noted that patients with primary degenerative dementia tend to produce a greater-than-normal proportion of intrusion errors during free recall (e.g. Miller, 1978; Fuld, 1982). Shindler, Caplan and Hier (1984) examined patients with dementia from a variety of aetiologies, including vascular dementia and communicating hydrocephalus, and observed that elderly patients with primary degenerative dementia produced the largest number of intrusions, although within the group severity of dementia did not correlate with number of intrusions. Hart, Smith and Swash (1986) noted a higher proportion of intrusions errors in elderly patients with primary degenerative dementia who performed on a picture memory task, although they did not find any evidence for a specific tendency for such patients to show more prior list intrusion errors than other types of intrusion errors.

In cued recall paradigms, patients with primary degenerative dementia show less marked memory impairment than in free recall, and some studies have even reported normal cued recall performance. Miller (1975) asked patients with primary degenerative dementia to read aloud and remember lists of 10 common words, with each list being presented three times. Following a delay, three types of retention test were given: recall, recognition and cued recall. There were significant deficits in the demented group for recall and recognition but not for cued recall.

Morris, Wheatley and Britton (1983) found that elderly patients with primary degenerative dementia performed at the same level as controls when the first three letters of each word were used as cues for cued recall, but that patients were significantly impaired in forced-choice recognition performance. In contrast to these findings, Davis and Mumford (1984) found that in elderly patients with primary degenerative dementia there was impairment in free recall and also where recall was cued by category cues or letter cues. They observed that control patients performed better with letter cues or category cues than with free recall, and that letter and category cues had an equivalent enhancing effect. However, in the case of patients with primary degenerative dementia, recall with letter cues was better than free recall, but recall with category cues was not. An important aspect of their findings was that patients with primary degenerative dementia were not helped any more than controls by recall cues. It is possible that the older age of their patients, or differences in the types of cues used, may have contributed to the difference between their findings and those of other studies, although it is worth noting that Semple, Smith and Swash (1982) have also found impaired performance in cued recall using similar procedures, and testing similar types of patients with primary degenerative dementia, to those described by Miller (1975).

It is important to note that in both the studies by Miller (1975) and by Morris, Wheatley and Britton (1983), which found evidence for normal cued retention, no control data were gathered to allow for correct naming of the words on the basis of the letter cues alone, without reference to any memory task. A more critical point is that patients in these two studies appeared to have been given recall instructions which made explicit reference to the items presented initially (although in Miller's study, if a subject could not indicate a word in response to the letter cue 'he was then asked, but not forced, to guess' (1975). The fact that normal cued retention was found under such conditions is somewhat surprising, since in the case of amnesic patients it would appear that it is only when memory is 'implicitly' rather than 'explicitly' tested, i.e. when the retention test is presented as a form of a guessing task, that normal memory functioning is most likely to be found (Graf, Squire and Mandler, 1984). Relatively few formal studies of 'implicit memory' have been carried out in patients with primary degenerative dementia, and those which have been conducted have employed small numbers of subjects. Moscovitch (1982a) reported the performance of three patients with primary degenerative dementia (although the actual test data combined their performance with that of an anoxic patient) on a lexical decision task, where subjects were asked to judge whether a string of letters formed a word. If some words are repeated during test trials, a reduction in latency of response is generally found in normal subjects. Moscovitch found that patients with dementia showed such a facilitation effect across trials, in spite of their impaired recognition memory for the words. Martin (1987) has provided evidence of normal improvement in maze learning in one of three patients with primary degenerative dementia, in contrast to the patient's poor performance on a spatial position memory task.

On recognition testing, patients with primary degenerative dementia have generally been observed to show significant impairment, although to a lesser extent than in free recall tasks, and in a few instances normal recognition memory has been reported (Ferris, Crook and Clark, 1980). Wilson et al. (1982a) found both verbal and non-verbal (faces) recognition memory impairment in elderly patients with primary degenerative dementia, and argued that the former may have been related to linguistic and encoding deficits while the latter was independent of perceptual factors, response bias and linguistic ability. Vitaliano *et al.* (1984) administered the mini-mental state exam (Folstein, Folstein and McHugh, 1975) and the Mattis dementia rating scale (Mattis, 1976), and found that in elderly patients with primary degenerative dementia, items which assessed recall tended to distinguish mildly demented patients from controls, whereas recognition items were better at distinguishing the severity of dementia between mildly and moderately impaired patients. However, a study by Branconnier *et al.* (1982), which specifically examined verbal recall and recognition memory performance in elderly patients with primary degenerative dementia, found that recognition test performance, in particular the occurrence of false positive responses, discriminated dementia patients from control subjects more accurately than did recall measures.

Miller (1977) has reported verbal recognition memory data where the number of distractor items at retention testing was systematically varied. There was a significant effect related to number of response alternatives, such that patients with primary degenerative dementia performed worse when the number of choices was eight than when it was two (*see also* Miller, 1978). He also examined patients' performance where the distractor items were either acoustically or semantically similar to the target, and found no difference in pattern of errors between control subjects and patients in terms of the type of distractor items chosen. However, Martin *et al.* (1985a) did note that there was a greater tendency for patients with primary degenerative dementia to choose semantic distractor items on a recognition memory task. Wilson *et al.* (1983a) did not find a greater than normal tendency for false positive responses to high-frequency words, but observed that patients with dementia differed from controls in not displaying superior recognition memory for rare words. Whitehead (1975) found that patients with primary degenerative dementia performed better on forced-choice than free-choice recognition memory testing from pictures or words, but no control group was included, and so it is difficult to be certain of the precise significance of this finding.

Retrograde memory deficits

Relatively few studies have been carried out on remote memory functioning compared to anterograde memory performance in patients with primary degenerative dementia. Wilson, Kaszniak and Fox (1981) administered an events questionnaire and a famous faces memory test to elderly patients with primary degenerative dementia, and found marked impairment on both tasks. The remote memory loss was evident over all time periods sampled, but was somewhat poorer for more recent items, possibly reflecting the stage of onset of learning difficulties. Moscovitch (1982a), however, using a famous faces memory test, only found retrograde memory impairment in patients with primary degenerative dementia for items from the 1970s. Morris and Kopelman (1986) have pointed to clinical variables (mild severity of dementia) and procedural factors (subjects were given cues to assist their recall) in Moscovitch's study which may have contributed to the differences between his findings and those of other researchers. Corkin *et al.* (1984) and Sagar *et al.* (1985) also reported impaired remote memory in patients with primary degenerative dementia, this impairment being uniform across the previous 40 years which were sampled, and found that this was evident not only in tasks similar to those used by Wilson, Kaszniak and Fox, but also in the patients' ability to recall specific autobiographical episodes from the distant past.

Relationship between memory functioning and neurobiological variables

In recent years, there have been increasing numbers of multidisciplinary studies of patients with primary degenerative dementia, and these have provided important clues to the pathophysiological basis of cognitive deterioration due to primary degenerative disease. A number of early studies by Blessed and his colleagues (e.g. Blessed, Tomlinson and Roth, 1968) found a correlation between the number of senile plaques and performance on clinical tests of cognitive function, these tests usually comprising orientation, concentration and simple memory tasks. Clinical tests such as these cannot be classified as 'pure' memory tasks, and often lack any degree of neuropsychological sophistication. However, this early work did offer useful pointers for subsequent research on primary degenerative dementia. More recent studies have lent some support to earlier observations. Fuld *et al.* (1982) found that intrusions during psychological test performance, defined as items which were produced from an earlier test to a later test (excluding perseverations or guesses), correlated with levels of choline-acetyltransferase in the cortex of patients with primary degenerative dementia who came to autopsy and also correlated with number of senile plaques. They found that patients most frequently intruded items on a mental status test and verbal fluency test.

The introduction of computerized tomography (CT) has provided a stimulus to research workers to examine the relationship between measures of cerebral degeneration and psychological test performance. However, on the one hand, there have been technical difficulties in obtaining reliable estimates of cerebral atrophy from conventional CT scan images and, on the other hand, memory tests which have been used have sometimes been relatively crude, and have often been administered as part of a heterogeneous 'mental test battery' or 'dementia scale'. It has, therefore, not always been possible to come to firm conclusions about the relationship between CT scan measures and memory functioning. In my own experience, there is considerable variability in the relationship between CT scan appearances in primary degenerative dementia and memory functioning. Some of this variability is highlighted in *Figures 6.1* and *6.2*.

Kaszniak, Garron and Fox (1979) found that both younger and older patients with primary degenerative dementia having cerebral atrophy (a combination of ventricular dilatation and cortical atrophy) performed worse on subtests of the Wechsler Memory Scale than matched patients without evidence of atrophy. They pointed out that differences between the groups were no greater in young than in older patients. Jacoby and Levy (1980) found no significant relationship between performance on most clinical tests of memory and orientation and measures of cortical atrophy or ventricular dilatation in elderly patients with primary degenerative dementia, although one significant correlation did arise between a measure of dilatation of the frontal horns and a composite measure of disorientation for age, time and place. Likewise, Eslinger *et al.* (1984) did not find any significant relationship, in a group of elderly patients with primary degenerative dementia, between three measures of ventricular dilatation and performance on a range of memory tests. Bigler *et al.* (1985) also failed to discover any relationship between memory test scores and ventricular dilatation in patients with primary degenerative dementia. A similar absence of correlation on most tests was noted by these researchers in the case of cortical atrophy measures, although verbal paired-associate learning performance did significantly differentiate patients with high and low levels of cortical atrophy. De Leon *et al.* (1980) observed a

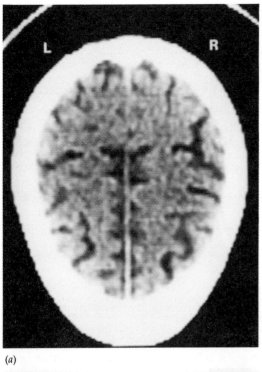

(a)

(b)

Figure 6.1 CT scan of a 64-year-old patient with primary degenerative dementia with marked memory impairment associated with considerable cerebral atrophy

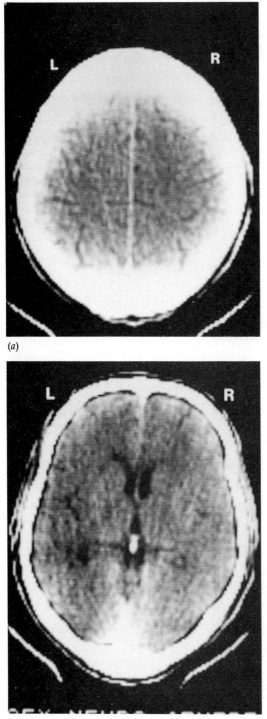

(a)

(b)

Figure 6.2 CT scan of a 61-year-old patient with primary degenerative dementia with marked memory impairment but with minimal evidence of cerebral atrophy

relationship between degree of ventricular dilatation, especially enlargement of the third ventricle, and performance on a wide range of verbal and non-verbal memory tests, but found an absence of any such relationship in the case of cortical atrophy. An even more specific relationship was reported by De Leon and George (1983), who found a significant relationship between estimated volume of subarachnoid CSF in temporal regions, and performance of patients with primary degenerative dementia on tests of memory functioning.

A few cautionary points need to be borne in mind when considering such brain–behaviour correlations. First, although some correlations may prove to be statistically significant, they may account for a relatively small amount of the total variance (e.g. George et al., 1983). Such correlations also tend to mask degrees of overlap between patient groups and, more importantly, may mask evidence for double dissociations (e.g. enlarged ventricles coexisting with normal memory functioning, and normal ventricles coexisting with impaired memory functioning). Finally, the presence of such correlations provides little information as to the mechanisms underlying memory dysfunction. Such mechanisms may even be independent of those underlying ventricular dilatation, but simply be affected by similar factors.

Studies using computerized tomography have been complemented by imaging procedures which enable measurements to be made of regional cerebral blood flow, or more recently, of cerebral metabolic activity. Hagberg and Ingvar (1976) examined regional cerebral blood flow in patients with primary degenerative dementia, in some of whom post-mortem findings were subsequently available. Patients with relatively isolated memory deficits – elicited by a range of verbal and non-verbal memory tests – showed a focal reduction in cerebral blood flow in the temporal lobes. In a later report on this subgroup of patients, Hagberg (1978) concentrated on left hemisphere regional blood flow patterns in relation to memory test performance, and noted specific sets of correlations. Paired-associate learning correlated with flow in temporal and parietal areas; memory for objects and memory for simple designs correlated with flow in the temporal and inferior frontal regions; and performance on a more difficult memory-for-designs test correlated with flow in temporal regions alone.

One of the most recent procedures used to study cerebral metabolism in patients with primary degenerative dementia is positron emission tomography (PET). Cutler et al. (1985) showed that patients with mild to moderate primary degenerative dementia, who displayed significant memory deficits as part of their neuropsychological impairment, had significant bilateral reductions of metabolic activity in mid-frontal, superior parietal and inferior temporal regions, as indicated by their PET scans. The authors pointed out that their inability to find reduced metabolic activity in regions such as the hippocampus or amygdala may have been due to technical factors, including limitations in their measurement procedures for relatively small areas such as those taken up by these structures. An absence of metabolic asymmetry in PET scans in amnesic patients with primary degenerative dementia was also noted by Foster et al. (1983), in contrast to the focal reductions in glucose metabolism in the left and right hemisphere of patients with primary degenerative dementia with disproportionate language deficits or constructional apraxia respectively. However, the significance of this study is limited by the lack of data on metabolic activity from control subjects. In an investigation which did include control subjects, Haxby et al. (1986) reported that patients in the early stages of primary degenerative dementia who had isolated memory deficits, nonetheless displayed abnormal measures of neocortical (mainly parietal) glucose metabolism. These authors also commented on the difficulty in measuring metabolic activity in discrete limbic system structures, and it is of note that one case has been reported of a patient with primary degenerative dementia whose identical twin appeared to show early signs of dementia in the form of impaired performance on delayed recall tasks, in the absence of any abnormality on a range of neurological imaging procedures, which included PET scanning (Luxenberg et al., 1987). It would appear, therefore, that the precise pathophysiological basis of isolated memory impairment in patients with primary degenerative dementia may remain a matter of speculation until more refined imaging data are available.

Management of memory deficits

A large variety of possible therapies has been considered for the treatment of primary degenerative dementia, ranging from drug treatments (Crook, 1985; Hollister, 1985) to psychological intervention (Powell-Procter and Miller, 1982; Whitehead, 1984). The reader is referred to these sources and to recent volumes (e.g. Corkin et al., 1982; Reisberg, 1983; Wurtman, Corkin and Growdon, 1984; Roth and Iversen, 1986) for more detailed documentation of attempts to improve memory functioning in primary degenerative dementia. Many reports have, however, failed to carry out detailed memory testing, or appropriate repeat testing of control subjects using neuropsychological tests with equivalent parallel forms. In addition, there has been only limited long-term follow-up of patients to ascertain if any treatment effects found in the laboratory can be translated into some form of rational treatment at the clinical level. Some studies will be reviewed here to give a broad overview of the types of results which have been found in therapeutic trials of memory functioning in primary degenerative dementia.

The majority of studies have focused on drugs which have an effect on the cholinergic system in the brain. In an early study with negative results, Ferris et al. (1979) administered choline chloride daily over a 4-week period to elderly patients with primary degenerative dementia with mild to moderate cognitive impairment, but found no improvement in memory test performance. Subsequent studies using physostigmine have, however, had more success. Smith and her colleagues (Smith and Swash, 1979; Smith, Semple and Swash, 1982) found evidence of a decrease in prior intrusions on tests of verbal recall in patients with primary degenerative dementia after administration of physostigmine. These findings were supported by similar observations in a study carried out by Thal et al. (1983), who administered gradually increasing daily doses of oral physostigmine and lecithin. They found improvement in memory performance in six out of eight patients with Alzheimer's disease and noted improvement in 'total recall' and 'retrieval from long-term memory' on the selective reminding test (Buschke and Fuld, 1974), together with a concomitant decrease in intrusion errors. A further experiment by Thal et al. (1983), with a double blind cross-over trial comparing physostigmine to placebo, produced similar results. Thal et al. observed that the decrease in intrusions correlated closely with increasing inhibition of cholinesterase activity in CSF, suggesting that the degree of improvement in memory was related to the amount of physostigmine in the brain. A follow-up study (Thal et al., 1984) confirmed most of these findings, but a longitudinal study of individual patients indicated diminishing effects of therapy as the dementia progressed.

Analogous memory improvement, this time with a decrease in false-positive responses on a recognition memory task, was observed by Davis *et al.* (1982) after administration of physostigmine to subjects with primary degenerative dementia. Peters and Levin (1982) and Levin and Peters (1984) have reported a significant improvement in memory over intervals ranging between 3 and 18 months following the initiation of physostigmine and lecithin treatment, this improvement being evident on a word-list learning task. Davis and Mohs (1982) found evidence of improvement in some aspects of memory performance after administration of physostigmine to patients with primary degenerative dementia. They tested patients on a range of memory tasks, including a famous faces retrograde amnesia test, digit span test, and recognition memory tests for words and for pictures. Although there was no facilitating effect on digit span or a famous faces retrograde memory test, significant improvement compared to the placebo condition was evident on tests involving long-term retention. It is worth noting, however, that compared to control subjects, patients in this study were still impaired on memory testing even while receiving physostigmine, and this important observation has also been made by other researchers (e.g. Christie, 1982). In a later study (Mohs *et al.*, 1985), it was pointed out that while some improvement in memory test scores was evident after administration of physostigmine, in only two out of 16 patients was the improvement large enough to be clinically evident to medical staff or relatives. Conversely, Caltagirone, Gainotti and Masullo (1982b) found that after administration of physostigmine for one month a few dementia patients showed slight improvement at the behavioural level without any overall change in memory test scores after treatment. A further qualification is that any beneficial effects of physostigmine may be dose dependent (Beller, Overall and Swann, 1985), though even where individual optimal doses have been administered little benefit from the drug has been observed (Caltagirone *et al.*, 1983). Improvement in only one out of six patients with primary degenerative dementia was noted in a study of a new cholinergic drug, RS86 (a direct muscarinic agonist) reported by Wettstein and Spiegel (1985).

Some research workers have examined memory functioning after lecithin (Signoret, Whiteley and Lhermitte, 1978) or a combination of lecithin and other compounds (Kaye, Sitaram and Weingartner, 1982; Sitaram *et al.*, 1983) and found improvement to be restricted to patients in the early stages of primary degenerative dementia with less severe accompanying memory deficits. Other investigators have failed to find significant long-term improvement in memory after lecithin administration (Brinkman *et al.*, 1982; Dysken *et al.*, 1982; Heyman *et al.*, 1982; Sullivan *et al.*, 1982; Little *et al.*, 1985). Other drugs, such as vasopressin or its analogues (Chase *et al.*, 1982; Kaye *et al.*, 1982; Tinklenberg *et al.*, 1982), L-dopa (Adolfsson *et al.*, 1982), piracetam (Ferris *et al.*, 1982; Growdon, Corkin and Huff, 1985), and naltrexone (Hyman, Eslinger and Damasio, 1985) have had minimal or variable effects on memory functioning in primary degenerative dementia. Hydergine has been widely used in clinical trials for the treatment of both degenerative and vascular dementia (Loew and Weil, 1982). Few studies have incorporated systematic memory testing as part of the assessment procedures, and one study (Yesavage, Wesphal and Rush, 1981) which employed a word-list learning test found hydergine to be of significant benefit only when accompanied by cognitive retraining.

Other forms of intervention to improve memory functioning in primary degenerative dementia have been less well documented. For example, patients in trials of 'reality orientation' therapy (e.g. Hanley, McGuire and Boyd, 1981) have often been of mixed aetiology, with minimal neurological information being provided, and thus it is often not possible to determine whether any change is specific to a particular cerebral disease. In general, as indicated by reviews such as that of Powell-Procter and Miller (1982), there is little evidence that psychological techniques have a significant permanent beneficial effect on memory functioning in primary degenerative dementia. Thompson *et al.* (1976) evaluated the effects of repeated exposure to hyperbaric oxygen on memory functioning in patients with primary degenerative dementia, and did not find any significant changes in memory test scores before and after a 15-day period of therapy. Goldfarb *et al.* (1972) found a similar, disappointing outcome after hyperbaric oxygen therapy in their group of elderly patients, some of whom were presumed to have degenerative dementia.

Huntington's disease

Although some authors (e.g. Lishman, 1987) have pointed to the relative infrequency of memory deficits in patients with Huntington's disease, more recently a large body of evidence has accumulated to support the presence of significant memory impairment over a range of anterograde and retrograde memory tasks, and one study (Lyle and Gottesman, 1977) has even reported differences in a design-recall task, between subjects who did or did not develop Huntington's disease a number of years after initial testing. As in the case of other progressive dementias, the stage of illness at which patients are examined may be critical to the type and severity of memory deficits (Butters *et al.*, 1978; Fisher *et al.*, 1983). In the case of Huntington's disease, this is often easier to document due to the frequent, but not invariable, concomitance of movement disorder as part of the patient's progressive clinical condition.

Anterograde memory deficits

Studies of anterograde memory functioning in Huntington's disease have found that patients may be impaired on a range of memory tasks, comprising a variety of test paradigms. Thus, Moses *et al.* (1981) reported impaired memory in patients with Huntington's disease, both those in the early and late stages of the disease, on verbal memory tasks such as word list and sentence recall, and on other types of memory tasks such as memory for pictures, memory for acoustic rhythms, memory for hand positions and word-picture paired-associate learning tasks. Fedio *et al.* (1979) found that both recall of a complex figure and maze-learning ability were impaired in patients with Huntington's disease. They also reported some impairment in maze-learning performance by subjects at risk of developing the disease, although Wexler (1979) did not find any convincing memory deficits in his group of 'at risk' subjects. Researchers have explored the effects of variation in task-demands on the memory performance of patients with Huntington's disease. Both Caine *et al.* (1978) and Weingartner, Caine and Ebert (1979b) noted that, in contrast to control subjects, patients with Huntington's disease did not show superior memory performance for high versus low imagery words. However, Beatty and Butters (1986) found similar effects of imagery on word-list recall of patients with Huntington's disease and control subjects, and they also reported similar patterns of verbal short-term memory performance in the two groups. Weingartner, Caine and Ebert (1979a) found that verbal memory performance of patients with Huntington's disease was not helped, unlike control subjects, by slowing down the rate of presentation of stimuli, such that subjects had more opportunity to rehearse items. Similarly, Butters and Grady (1977) showed no beneficial effects of pre-distractor rehearsal on the short-term memory for verbal stimuli in patients with Huntington's disease. Butters, Tarlow and Cermak (1976) reported that patients with Huntington's disease were relatively impervious to the effects of massed versus spaced presentation trials.

In the case of non-verbal stimuli such as faces, Butters et al. (1984) found that unlike control subjects and neurological patients of other aetiologies, patients with Huntington's disease did not show improved memory in response to specific encoding instructions such as judging the likability of a face. In contrast to these negative findings, Butters et al. (1983) did find that providing verbal mediation, in the form of story material to aid recall of a pictorial scene, did help the memory performance of patients and, in a subsequent study, Martone, Butters and Trauner (1986) found normal picture memory performance in patients with Huntington's disease after increased exposure to stimuli on presentation trials. Wilson et al. (1987) have also argued, on the basis of the verbal memory performance of their group of patients with Huntington's disease, that these patients showed evidence of retention of normal semantic coding of information.

Studies of memory functioning in patients with Huntington's disease have also highlighted unique features of their responses during retention testing. Meudell, Butters and Montgomery (1978) observed that, in contrast to patients with Korsakoff's syndrome, errors by subjects with Huntington's disease in verbal short-term memory tasks were predominantly omissions rather than prior intrusions. Fedio et al. (1979) observed that patients with Huntington's disease were more likely than control subjects to forget or ignore instructions not to make diagnonal moves during learning of a path on a maze. Caine, Ebert and Weingartner (1977) noted that category cues had little beneficial effect on the verbal free recall scores of patients with Huntington's disease, in contrast to their enhancing effect on the scores of control patients and patients with Parkinson's disease. A number of research workers (e.g. Caine et al., 1978; Weingartner, Caine and Ebert, 1979b) have reported that in word-list recall, patients with Huntington's disease offered less consistent retrieval of correct responses over learning trials than did control subjects. In some recognition testing situations, such as recognition memory for words seen over a period of several days, these patients may show normal performance, while at the same time displaying impairment on perceptual learning tasks with a recall component (Martone et al., 1984). However, this normal performance may be task-specific, since in other recognition memory paradigms, such as those which follow multiple free recall trials (Caine, Ebert and Weingartner, 1977; Butters et al., 1985; Caine et al., 1986), or those using less verbal materials (Moss et al., 1986), patients with Huntington's disease have been found to be impaired. They have also been found to show more false positive responses than control subjects on a picture memory task (Martone, Butters and Trauner, 1986).

Many patients with Huntington's disease show some degree of cerebral atrophy, and while this is frequently non-specific it may occasionally be more marked in the region of the caudate nuclei. Sax et al. (1983) found that a measure of this caudate atrophy, as indicated by CT scan indices, correlated with performance on the

Wechsler Memory Scale. In comparison, a measure of dilatation of the frontal horns of the lateral ventricles showed minimal relationship with performance on subtests of the Wechsler Memory Scale.

Retrograde memory deficits

Much less research has been carried out on retrograde compared to anterograde memory functioning in patients with Huntington's disease. A few relevant observations have emanated from a single group of research workers who have found definitive evidence for retrograde memory loss. Albert, Butters and Brandt (1981a) administered remote memory tasks assessing memory for famous faces or public events and sampled decades from the 1930s to the 1970s. They found that patients with Huntington's disease were markedly impaired on both sets of tasks, and also indicated that unlike patients with alcoholic Korsakoff's syndrome, those with Huntington's disease were equally impaired for all decades, and their performance did not show a temporal gradient whereby items from earlier decades were relatively spared. In a further study, Albert, Butters and Brandt (1981b) showed that a similar, but less marked pattern of deficits was evident in recently-diagnosed patients.

Parkinson's disease

While the clinical features of Parkinson's disease may be found following a variety of aetiologies, by far the most commonly studied is that which occurs as a result of idiopathic degeneration in the basal ganglia and in the substantia nigra. It is this variety of Parkinson's disease which will be considered in this section. Contrary to Parkinson's original dictum, it is now recognized that a proportion of patients suffering from Parkinson's disease may show evidence of dementia (Boller, 1980), and a number of studies have provided detailed evidence of memory dysfunction in such patients. Tweedy, Langer and McDowell (1982) noted impaired performance on a range of verbal memory tasks, ranging from free recall, cued recall, recognition memory and short-term memory using a Brown–Peterson paradigm. Patients with Parkinson's disease benefited from semantic cues, and from changes in category of material, less than control subjects on the short-term memory task. Similarly, Horn (1974) found impaired performance in patients with Parkinson's disease on a recall task where category cues were provided at recall. Most of Horn's patients suffered from a variable degree of depression, and it is notable that the impairment which she found in patients relative to normal control subjects disappeared when the patients with Parkinson's disease were compared to age-matched paraplegic control patients. Using both verbal and visuospatial memory tests, Chouza et al. (1984) noted that moderate and severe memory impairment was found in 54% of patients with hemi-parkinsonism, and in 68% of patients with bilateral parkinsonism. In patients with left hemi-parkinsonism, they found evidence of greater visuospatial memory deficit, suggesting the presence of greater right hemisphere abnormality. In two of their patients with severe memory impairment, there was evidence of moderate hippocampal atrophy.

Several studies encompassing a variety of paradigms and test materials, have reported normal recognition memory performance in patients with Parkinson's disease and thus raised the possibility that any anterograde memory deficits in these patients may be specific to certain retention testing situations (e.g. Asso *et al.*, 1969; Caine, Ebert and Weingartner, 1977; Lees and Smith, 1983; Flowers, Pearce and Pearce, 1984). It is possible, therefore, that tests which require a greater degree of 'cognitive effort' and active attention (variables which, it is worth noting, may be particularly affected by any depression present in a sample of patients with Parkinson's disease) are more likely to yield evidence of memory impairment in Parkinson's disease. In the series of memory tests given by Pirozzolo *et al.* (1982), all of which required some form of recall, Parkinson's disease patients performed much worse than control subjects. Huber, Shuttleworth and Paulson (1986) reported normal digit span scores but impaired verbal paired-associate learning in a group of patients with primary degenerative dementia. Taylor, Saint-Cyr and Lang (1986) found impaired word-list recall in patients with Parkinson's disease, with this deficit being mainly apparent for words from the middle of the list. In this study, and in a further investigation (Taylor *et al.*, 1986), minimal differences between patients with Parkinson's disease and control subjects were found in their performance on subtests of the Wechsler Memory Scale. They did, however, note that depressed patients with Parkinson's disease had lower digit span and visual reproduction scores than non-depressed patients, although both subgroups performed within the normal range on these and other memory tests. Learning of perceptual-motor skills, such as tracking a target with a joystick, has been found to be impaired in patients with Parkinson's disease (Frith, Bloxham and Carpenter, 1986). These authors observed that the main learning deficit appeared to occur in the initial practice session, whereas their findings from delayed testing indicated that any learning which had taken place was relatively well retained by patients with Parkinson's disease.

Impaired memory has also been noted on tests of remote memory. Warburton (1967) found deficits mainly in older patients with Parkinson's disease using a simple questionnaire for personal autobiographical events, and Freedman *et al.* (1984b), using more sophisticated tests of remote memory for public events and famous faces, observed a retrograde amnesia which was constant in severity over the decades which were sampled. Sagar *et al.* (1985) have pointed to a specific deficit in the temporal dating of past events which patients with Parkinson's disease appear to have. Huber, Shuttleworth and Paulson (1986) observed that remote memory deficits were only present in patients with Parkinson's disease who showed evidence of intellectual impairment, as indicated by performance on a 'mini mental-state' test (Folstein, Folstein and McHugh, 1975).

Patients with Parkinson's disease may show marked fluctuation in their movement disorder, the absence/presence of which has been referred to as an 'on/off state'. Girotti *et al.* (1986) did not find any corresponding variation in performance on a story memory task, and Taylor, Saint-Cyr and Lang (1987) did not find any evidence of memory deficits across any of their subgroups of patients with Parkinson's disease who were categorized according to the presence of and response to treatment. However, Delis *et al.* (1982) did find a relationship between the on/off phase and memory performance if retention testing had a delayed component. Some aspects of short-term memory performance in patients with Parkinson's disease have also been reported to be faster in those patients who were receiving drugs which alleviated motor symptoms when testing was carried out (Rafal *et al.*, 1984). Several researchers have noted a relationship between memory impairment and the duration of the disease (Hietanen and Teravainen, 1984), functional severity of the disease (Scholz and Sastry, 1985) and age of patients

(Wilson *et al.*, 1980). Mortimor *et al.* (1982) were unable to find a relationship between verbal memory performance and aspects of motor dysfunction in Parkinson's disease, but did discover a positive relationship between degree of bradykinesia and performance on a spatial orientation memory task. Villardita *et al.* (1982) reported a lack of association between the presence of memory deficits in patients with Parkinson's disease and their performance on copying or visuoperceptual tasks.

The pathophysiological basis of cognitive dysfunction in patients with Parkinson's disease remains a matter of controversy; for example, while Globus, Mildworf and Melamed (1985) reported both reduced cerebral blood flow and impaired performance on a range of memory tasks, they could not find any correlation between the two sets of deficits. Portin, Raininko and Rinne (1984) found a significant correlation between memory test performance and CT measures of 'central atrophy' (assessed by degree of ventricular dilatation) and atrophy of the insular cortex, but not with other aspects of cortical atrophy. At the level of particular subcortical nuclei, Chui *et al.* (1986) have reported a patient with Parkinson's disease with significant memory impairment and in whom post-mortem analysis of brain tissue indicated lesions in the anterior temporal cortex, amygdala and hippocampus, with relative sparing of the nucleus basalis.

In the early 1960s, Talland (1962) observed that auditory verbal memory impairment in patients with Parkinson's disease was mainly present in those patients receiving medication (usually a variety of drugs) to relieve their symptoms. In recent years, a large number of studies have focused on the effects of L-dopa on memory functioning, and conflicting findings have often emerged. The interaction of severity of disease state with dose-levels and duration of L-dopa administration, and possibly also individual differences in response to L-dopa may, in part, underlie the divergent findings. Some investigators (e.g. Donnelly and Chase, 1973) have reported improvement in memory functioning in Parkinson's disease after the initiation of L-dopa therapy, although other investigators have noted such improvement to be specific to certain patients (O'Brien *et al.*, 1971) or to certain memory tests (Marsh, Markham and Ansel, 1971). There is also evidence that L-dopa may impair verbal memory in patients with Parkinson's disease (Halgin, Riklan and Misiak, 1977). Some researchers (Bowen, Brady and Yahr, 1973) have found the duration of L-dopa therapy to be unrelated to memory test performance, although other studies (Riklan, Whelihan and Cullinan 1976) have reported that patients on long-term L-dopa therapy perform worse on short-term memory tasks than patients on therapy of more limited duration. The mechanisms of any deterioration are unclear, and it is possible that simple changes in the therapy regimen may themselves bring about some deterioration in memory (Agnoli *et al.*, 1984). The effects of drugs other than L-dopa have seldom been examined, although one study (Garcia *et al.*, 1982) found evidence to suggest improved memory function in patients with Parkinson's disease after administration of lecithin.

Demyelinating disease

Impaired memory functioning in demyelinating disease, in particular multiple sclerosis (MS) has, in recent years, become a well-recognized, although relatively infrequent, feature which may be manifest even in the early stages of the illness

(Young, Saunders and Ponsford, 1976). Areas of demyelination may be evident as plaques on CT scanning, with such plaques often being most prominent in periventricular regions. The presence of plaques in patients with MS may often be more readily discernable by imaging procedures based on magnetic resonance (*Figure 6.3*). The relationship between areas of demyelination in the brain and memory functioning remains to clarified, e.g. all three patients with MS reported by Jennekens-Schinkel and Sanders (1986) had areas of demyelination on CT scanning and showed memory impairment, but there did not appear to be any straight-forward relationship between sites of demyelination and severity or pattern of memory impairment. Fewer studies have been reported on memory disorders in MS compared with cerebral degenerative diseases, but several systematic investigations have been carried out, and these will be summarized.

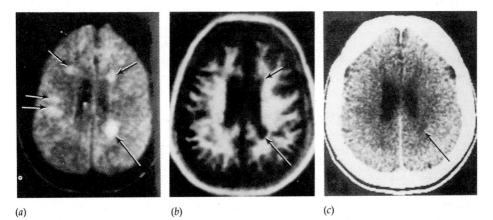

(a)   (b)   (c)

Figure 6.3 (*a*) CT scan and (*b* and *c*) NMR scans of a patients with multiple sclerosis. Note the periventricular lesions, which are evident in greater numbers on the NMR scans (from Young *et al.*, 1983. Reproduced by permission of Raven Press)

Jambor (1969) administered a number of memory tests as part of an overall battery of measures to examine cognitive functioning in MS, and found that learning and memory tasks, with the exception of digit span, were among the most sensitive measures in detecting neuropsychological impairment in his patients with MS. These tasks included tests of sentence learning, learning of word definitions and delayed recall of pictures. A subgroup of patients with MS, who had additional symptoms of depression and anxiety, was also found to be impaired compared to a control group of psychiatric patients without MS, but actually performed better than the non-depressed group with MS. Thus, memory impairment was unlikely to be due to concomitant mood disturbances. Staples and Lincoln (1979) also noted that on tests of immediate memory, such as digit span and immediate recall of designs, patients with MS did not differ from control subjects, whereas significant impairments were evident on tests of delayed memory such as a delayed prose recall or delayed recall of pictures. Staples and Lincoln estimated that around 60% of patients with MS in their sample showed evidence of memory impairment, and a similar, although slightly lower (46%) proportion of patients in a study by Brooks *et al.* (1984) had impaired performance on a faces-recognition memory test. On the basis of relatively limited memory testing, Bertrando, Maffei and Ghezzi, (1983) reported that 22% of their patients with MS had evidence of memory impairment.

A further indication that some, but not all, patients with MS may suffer from memory impairment arises from a recent study by Rao *et al.* (1984) who observed that it was possible to distinguish three groups of patients: one group who showed generalized cognitive impairment including memory deficits; a second group who showed mild memory deficit (this being associated with a higher incidence in the use of psychotropic medication and incidence of reactive depression); and a third group of patients who performed normally on memory tasks. Rao *et al.* used tests of word list and spatial position learning to assess for the presence of memory impairment, and were able to demonstrate in their patients increased sensitivity to retroactive interference and more marked impairment in visuospatial memory function. Both Beatty and Gange (1977) and Grant *et al.* (1984) found patients with MS to be impaired on several short-term and long-term memory tasks, and Grant *et al.* also noted a relationship between short-term memory performances and clinical features of the illness, such as duration of active disease, and whether the illness was active or quiescent at the time of the assessment. The importance of disease characteristics was also highlighted in a study by Heaton *et al.* (1985), who found significant impairment on verbal memory tasks in patients with 'chronic-progressive' as opposed to 'relapsing-remitting' MS. Few researchers have as yet hypothesized on the nature of the memory deficits found in MS, although Carroll, Gates and Rolden (1984) have argued for some form of semantic encoding deficit on the basis of their findings relating to impaired picture and verbal-recognition memory performance. Fewer MS than control patients used a mnemonic strategy to remember material in the verbal memory task, and those who did use a strategy made more false positive responses to related category items on recognition testing. Caine *et al.* (1986), however, reported normal serial position and visual-imagery effects in the verbal recall performance of patients with MS, even though the level of recall scores was significantly below that of control subjects.

Demyelinating disease may often show periods of remission and decline of clinical symptoms, and in some such cases memory testing may help to monitor, and sometimes predate, changes in cerebral function more accurately than CT or EEG evidence. A set of observations along these lines was reported by Bieliauskas, Topel and Huckman (1980) who found changes in memory performance, especially on some subtests of the Wechsler Memory Scale, over a 2-month period in a patient with presumed demyelinating disease. Unfortunately, repeat testing of control subjects was not reported, so it was not possible to delineate the interaction of any practice-effects with significant changes at the neurological level.

Other primary dementias

A few remaining primary dementias have been the subject of neuropsychological investigation of memory functioning. In the Steele–Richardson–Olszewski syndrome (otherwise known as progressive supranuclear palsy – PSP), neurological features include paralysis of external ocular movements, dysarthria, pseudobulbar palsy and dystonic rigidity of the neck and trunk. The principal sites of pathology appear to be in the basal ganglia, brainstem and cerebellum. Some cases may be accompanied by evidence of dementia. Albert, Feldman and Willis (1974), in a review of earlier studies and a discussion of five cases reported in the paper, pointed out that while some patients may show evidence of memory difficulties, when they were given additional time to respond their memory appeared to be much better. However, they did not report detailed memory test scores as such to substantiate this clinical impression, and this hypothesis remains attractive but lacking in experimental support. Kimura, Barnett and Burkhart (1981) reported a mean Wechlser memory quotient for her seven patients which was within normal limits, and found no difference between their scores and those of patients with frontal or occipital lesions. Maher, Smith and Lees (1985) reported verbal recognition memory impairment in four out of 19 patients with progressive supranuclear palsy, and evidence of somewhat more marked impairment on a faces-recognition memory task.

In the case of myotonic dystrophy, a familial condition in which there is progressive wasting and weakness of muscle groups, there have been occasional clinical reports of cognitive impairment in such patients (Lishman, 1987), but few systematic investigations of memory functioning have been carried out. Two exceptions to this are studies by Walker et al. (1984) and Stuss et al. (1987) which did not find any impairment in myotonic dystrophy patients compared to control subjects on the Wechsler Memory Scale. The relative insensitivity of this instrument does not preclude the possibility that future studies using more exacting procedures may indicate the presence of memory impairment in some patients with myotonic dystrophy.

There have been occasional clinical descriptions (e.g. Mitsuyama, 1984) of everyday memory difficulties as part of a progressive dementia in patients with motor neuron disease (amyotrophic lateral sclerosis). This condition is usually characterized by degenerative changes in the anterior horn cells of the spinal cord, motor nuclei of the brainstem, and the corticospinal tracts, and at the clinical level by progressive wasting of muscles. Pathology in cortical regions, apart from the motor cortex, is considered to be very rare, and there have been relatively few detailed assessments of memory functioning in such patients, apart from one study which found that only two out of 21 patients with amyotrophic lateral sclerosis showed evidence of memory impairment (Poloni et al., 1986).

Hydrocephalic dementia

Hydrocephalus may accompany a variety of neurological conditions, and result in periventricular lesions which affect structures, such as the hippocampus, that are critical to memory functioning (Granholm, 1976). Where hydrocephalus is secondary to disease states such as deep-seated cerebral tumours or cerebrovascular disease, it is clearly difficult to evaluate the role of ventricular dilatation per se in contributing to any memory dysfunction which may be present. Some degree of hydrocephalus may also accompany less acute conditions such as chronic alcohol abuse or cerebral degenerative disease, and here also it may be impossible to elucidate what effects, if any, may be related solely to ventricular enlargement. In this section, I will concentrate mainly on the condition known as 'normal pressure hydrocephalus', where ventricular dilatation is accompanied by CSF pressure which may be only intermittently raised (Pickard, 1982). In this condition, cognitive deterioration is usually accompanied by gait disturbance and urinary incontinence. The condition may sometimes resemble a dementing process in its presentation, and since it may coexist with other pathologies, it is important to

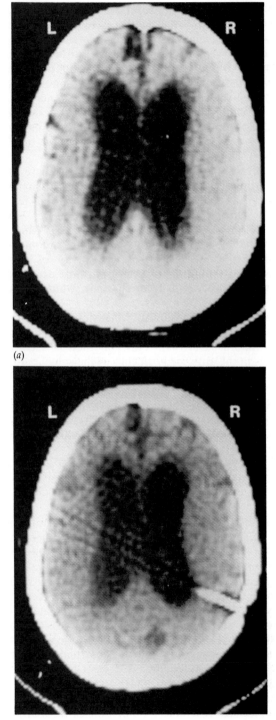

(a)

(b)

Figure 6.4 CT scan of a 65-year-old patient with a diagnosis of normal pressure hydrocephalus. (*a*) The ventricular dilatation which was evident prior to shunting showed only minimal reduction after shunting (*b*) in spite of improvement in memory functioning

consider additional sources of cerebral dysfunction which may be present, and also (as in the case of all progressive neurological conditions) the stage to which the illness has progressed in a given individual.

While a number of studies have reported the presence of memory difficulties in hydrocephalic dementia (e.g. Jeffreys and Wood, 1978), some researchers have found memory deficits to be absent or only mild in degree (Caltagirone *et al.*, 1982; Wikkelso *et al.*, 1982). It is possible that differences in patient populations accounted for some of the disparity between these findings. In addition, detailed memory testing of patients with hydrocephalic dementia has been reported only in a few studies. In some cases, preoperative assessment has lacked suitable control data for comparison presumably because researchers were mainly interested in focusing on postoperative changes in test performance. At the clinical level, confabulation has been postulated as part of a constellation of symptoms forming a unique feature of hydrocephalic dementia compared to other conditions such as alcoholic Korsakoff's syndrome or Alzheimer-type dementia (Gustafson and Hagberg, 1978; Berglund, Gustafson and Hagberg, 1979). These authors also reported preoperative memory deficits on tasks such as verbal paired-associate learning or the Benton Visual Retention Test (Benton, 1974).

Improvement in memory performance after shunting has been noted by a number of researchers (Jeffreys and Wood, 1978; Gustafson and Hagberg, 1978), although Thomsen *et al.* (1986) found no overall change in memory test scores, and in those patients who showed improvement at the neuropsychological level after shunting, changes in reaction time and visuospatial function were more noticeable than changes in memory functioning. In a detailed presentation of three single-case studies of patients with hydrocephalus but without the triad of symptoms (dementia, gait disturbance and incontinence) associated with normal pressure hydrocephalus, Ogden (1986) reported that the only patient to show major improvement in memory after shunting was the one with a short clinical history (2 weeks' duration). Some tests may be more sensitive than others in reflecting improvement in memory functioning; Gustafson and Hagberg (1978) showed that paired-associate learning showed the most marked improvement after shunting. Few investigators have compared changes in memory functioning after shunting with changes in degree of ventricular dilatation. In my experience, double dissociations may occur between the two, such that there may be absence of change in memory functioning in a patient whose CT scan shows marked reduction in ventricular dilatation, and conversely a patient may improve significantly on memory testing, yet the degree of hydrocephalus may appear unaltered (*Figure 6.4*).

Distinctive features of memory disorders in patients with dementia

A number of studies have compared memory functioning between various groups of patients with dementia, and between patients with dementia and those with less progressive forms of memory disorder. The first type of comparison needs to be considered in the light of the stage of progression of the dementing condition, since any differences between patient groups in this respect may confound differences in performance due to the aetiology in question. In addition, comparison with less progressive conditions, such as cerebral infarction, need to consider length of time since the most recent infarct, because this may also have an effect on memory functioning.

Primary degenerative dementia compared to depression

One of the most common referrals in clinical practice is for a differential diagnosis to be made between an idiopathic dementia and a depressive illness, since both groups of patients may offer symptoms of everyday memory difficulty and problems in work adjustment, but may display no focal neurological signs. In general, memory deficits in patients with primary degenerative dementia tend to be more marked than those found in patients suffering from depression (La Rue, 1982), although in the very early stages of primary degenerative dementia the level of memory impairment may be mild enough to raise doubts as to the presence of an underlying disease process. The significance of earlier studies which found greater severity of impaired performance of demented compared to depressed patients on tests of synonym learning (Kendrick, Parboosingh and Post, 1965) or recall of visual designs (Crookes and McDonald, 1972), is limited by the heterogeneous or undefined aetiology of the group of patients with dementia.

Larner (1977) compared elderly primary degenerative dementia with elderly depressed and elderly psychiatrically ill patients, and found that on a continuous recognition memory task, the latter two groups tended to adopt much more conservative criteria for accepting stimuli as target items, and that performance on this type of task was of more help in distinguishing patients with dementia than a paired-associate synonym learning test. A similar pattern of results was reported by Miller and Lewis (1977) using a non-verbal continuous recognition memory task. In terms of free recall performance, Gibson (1981) noted that in elderly patients with primary degenerative dementia, there was an absence of a primacy effect (i.e. better recall of earlier items in a list), either for free recall of pictures or words, but he found such an effect in depressed and normal control patients. Kopelman (1986a) found that patients with primary degenerative dementia were significantly worse than depressed patients in their recall of semantically anomalous sentences, with the depressed patients scoring in the normal range. A picture learning test, which involved repeated presentation and recall of overlapping sets of line drawings, has been reported to distinguish patients with dementia from those with depression (Kendrick, Gibson and Moyes, 1979). However, in the validation studies, no distinction appears to have been made by Kendrick, Gibson and Moyes between degenerative and vascular dementia, and the severity of dementia in the samples tested is not made clear. In addition, possible limitations of the test itself have been the subject of some debate (Skelton-Robinson and Telford, 1982; Kendrick, 1982). Weingartner et al. (1982a,b) argued that patients with depression and patients with dementia may differ in the types of deficits they show on memory tests. In contrast to depressed patients, patients with primary degenerative dementia showed impaired learning of related word-list material and seemed to be unable to use relational features to assist their recall. They further suggested that memory impairment in depressed patients may be more evident on tasks requiring considerable 'cognitive effort', possibly related to some impairment in 'arousal-activation' (Weingartner et al., 1981b), while patients with primary degenerative dementia may show impaired memory even when processing demands are minimal.

Primary degenerative dementia compared to other progressive neurological conditions

The differentiation of primary degenerative dementia and Huntington's disease will seldom pose any clinical problem in view of the genetic component and movement disorder associated with the latter condition. However, both sets of conditions can be accompanied by significant memory disturbance, and it may be useful to consider several studies which have compared the two forms of dementia.

Little evidence is available on the relative incidence of memory symptoms in primary degenerative dementia and Huntington's disease, although in my experience, everyday memory difficulties will be a more frequent presenting symptom among patients with primary degenerative dementia than Huntington's disease. While a large amount of data has accumulated on the separate memory performance in primary degenerative dementia and Huntington's disease, few studies have formally compared memory functioning in the two conditions. Butters *et al.* (1983) examined memory for pictorial material in patients with primary degenerative dementia or Huntington's disease and found that the latter patients' memory performance benefited by verbal mediation in the form of a story which linked items in the picture, whereas the memory performance of patients with primary degenerative dementia was relatively unaffected by such mediation. Butters *et al.* further observed that patients with primary degenerative dementia made significantly more perseverative responses than control patients on the memory task, but the differences between patients with Huntington's disease and control subjects did not reach significance. Butters (1985) also found a high level of prior intrusion errors in a task requiring successive recall of short stories by patients with primary degenerative dementia compared to those with Huntington's disease (*Figure 6.5*).

In a more recent study, Butters *et al.* (1986) found that patients with Huntington's disease showed higher recognition memory performance than patients with primary degenerative dementia on a short-term verbal memory task. They also observed that primary degenerative dementia patients displayed a greater memory loss than those with Huntington's disease for verbal material between two retention test trials administered 15 and 120 seconds after

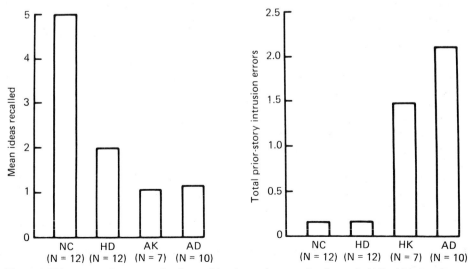

Figure 6.5 Memory performance of patients with primary degenerative dementia (AD: Alzheimer's disease), alcoholic Korsakoff's syndrome (AK) and Huntington's disease (HD) on a task requiring successive recall of short stories (from Butters, 1985. Reproduced by permission of Swets and Zeitlinger). NC = normal controls

presentation respectively. The patients with primary degenerative dementia were also less likely to show reminiscence (recall of words on trial 2 which were not recalled on trial 1). In a study which examined both word-list recall and how well patients could judge the frequency with which words were repeated in a long list, Strauss, Weingartner and Thompson (1985) found that both groups of patients were impaired in these two memory processes; however, in patients with Huntington's disease the memory for repeated words was better than that for non-repeated words, whereas in those with primary degenerative dementia memory performance showed no difference for the two sets of items.

In the case of retrograde amnesia, few data are available on direct comparisons between patients with primary degenerative dementia and Huntington's disease. There is evidence for significant remote memory deficits in both populations (Albert, Butters and Brandt, 1981b; Wilson, Kaszniak and Fox, 1981). These researchers have observed equivalent memory loss over all decades sampled, although one study (Moscovitch, 1982a) only found a deficit in patients with primary degenerative dementia for identification of famous faces from the 1970s.

Considering other degenerative dementias, only a few studies have compared patients with primary degenerative dementia with those suffering from Parkinson's disease. As was indicated earlier, anterograde memory impairment has been found in a number of studies of patients with Parkinson's disease, although in general this appears to be less marked, less frequent and more task-specific than that observed in corresponding studies of primary degenerative dementia patients. Pillon *et al.* (1986) compared the memory performance of patients with primary degenerative dementia, Parkinson's disease and progressive supranuclear palsy. While impaired memory performance was noted in all three groups, the former group was significantly worse than the other groups of patients on verbal memory tasks. Similarly, Huber *et al.* (1986) found impaired verbal paired-associate learning in both patients with Parkinson's disease and primary degenerative dementia but this was more marked in the latter patients. Freedman and Oscar-Berman (1986) made a specific comparison of memory functioning in patients with primary degenerative dementia and Parkinson's disease matched for degree of dementia. They used delayed response and delayed alternation procedures, analogous to those employed in animal studies. The delayed response task required the patient to remember the location of a penny in one of two plaques after zero delay, or delays ranging from 10 to 60 seconds. In the delayed alternation task, which more closely resembled a problem solving task, the penny was alternately located under the left and right plaques, and the subject had to reach a predefined criterion of successive correct responses. While patients with primary degenerative dementia were impaired on both the delayed alternation and delayed response tasks, those with Parkinson's disease were only impaired in the delayed response task. However, there was a significant degree of individual variation within the two groups of patients, with a number from both groups of patients scoring within the normal range. In the case of remote memory loss, the pattern of deficit reported for patients with Parkinson's disease (Freedman *et al.* 1984b) is similar to that shown by primary degenerative dementia patients, with the exception of the Moscovitch study described above.

Comparisons between the memory disorder associated with primary degenerative dementia and that found in dementia related to cerebrovascular disease are discussed elsewhere (*see* p. 68). Few comparisons have been reported between memory functioning in demyelinating conditions and that found in patients with primary degenerative dementia. In general, memory impairment would seem to be less extensive, both in its presence and severity, in demyelinating than primary degenerative conditions, but little 'hard' data are presently available to permit more specific statements to be made.

Patients with dementia related to hydrocephalus may sometimes show clinical similarities with patients with primary degenerative dementia. Gustafson and Hagberg (1978) noted that confabulation occurred more frequently in patients with hydrocephalic dementia compared with patients having primary degenerative dementia, and that memory loss for remote events was more frequent in the dementia patients than in patients with hydrocephalic dementia (the precise method of testing for either of these features was not reported). On formal memory testing, patients with hydrocephalic dementia showed less marked impairment, relative to control subjects, than patients with primary degenerative dementia.

Primary degenerative dementia compared to non-progressive neurological conditions

The memory functioning of patients with primary degenerative dementia has also been compared with that of patients with alcoholic Korsakoff's syndrome. Williams and Owen (1977) found that both groups of patients failed to remember any of four picture-word pairs; however, they did differ in their pattern of memory performance, in that the alcoholic patients appeared to remember words better than pictures, but no such difference was apparent in the performance of primary degenerative dementia patients who were equally poor at retaining either class of item. Weingartner et al. (1983) noted that the impaired memory performance of patients with primary degenerative dementia correlated with their deficits on semantic memory tasks (e.g. generating words of a certain category, or finding words which would complete a sentence). Such a relationship was not evident in the performance of patients with alcoholic Korsakoff's syndrome whose scores were similar to control subjects on the semantic memory tasks. Butters et al. (1983) noted the presence of perseverative responses during memory test performance in both patients with alcoholic Korsakoff's syndrome and primary degnerative dementia. Moss et al. (1986) found that patients with primary degenerative dementia performed significantly worse than those with alcoholic Korsakoff's syndrome on a 2 minute delayed verbal recall task, even though at 15 seconds delay both groups performed at a similar, but impaired level. Kopelman (1985) also noted a significantly lower performance in those with dementia on a verbal short-term memory task, although in his study this difference was evident at delay intervals as short as 2 seconds; patients with primary degenerative dementia also had impaired digit span scores, compared to the normal scores of patients with alcoholic Korsakoff's syndrome. In further studies of the same population of patients, dementia patients were poorer than alcoholic patients at repeating semantically anomalous sentences (Kopelman, 1986a), and on other verbal short-term memory tasks (Kopelman, 1986b). In the latter study, patients with alcoholic Korsakoff's syndrome were worse than patients with primary degenerative dementia on tests of orientation and memory for recent personal information. A further observation on poorer memory functioning in dementia compared to Korsakoff's syndrome was made by Strauss, Weingartner and Thompson (1985) who found that the latter, but not the former patients, showed better recall of words repeated several times in a long word-list, compared to those which occurred only once.

In the case of retrograde amnesia, a number of studies have found marked retrograde amnesia in patients with alcoholic Korsakoff's syndrome. As summarized earlier (*see* p. 119), there seems to be an equivalent memory loss in studies of retrograde memory functioning in primary degenerative dementia patients, although it would appear that the dementia patients are less likely than patients with alcoholic Korsakoff's syndrome to show a temporal gradient (better recall of items in the more distant past) in their pattern of memory performance.

Huntington's disease compared to other neurological conditions

Comparisons between memory functioning in Huntington's disease and that in primary degenerative dementia are discussed above. No studies appear to have been reported on the relative memory disorders of patients with Huntington's disease and Parkinson's disease. Significant anterograde memory impairment, more marked on recall than recognition memory testing, has been reported for both conditions. In addition, as indicated earlier in the chapter, both sets of patients have been reported to display extensive retrograde amnesia which affects previous decades regardless of proximity to the onset of the disease. One investigation (Caine *et al.*, 1986) compared memory functioning in Huntington's disease with that of patients suffering from MS. More marked memory impairment was evident over a range of tasks in patients with Huntington's disease, with this difference particularly evident on immediate and delayed recall of visual figures.

Turning to non-progressive neurological conditions, a large number of studies have compared memory functioning in Huntington's disease with the memory disorder associated with alcoholic Korsakoff's syndrome. Most of these studies have shown the memory performance of patients with Huntington's disease to be less affected by task variables such as spacing of learning trials, encoding instructions, rehearsal activity, etc. than the memory performance of patients with alcoholic Korsakoff's syndrome (Butters and Grady, 1977; Butters *et al.* 1978; Biber *et al.*, 1981). However, in one study (Butters *et al.*, 1983), the picture memory performance of patients with Huntington's disease was helped more by verbal mediation than that of patients with alcoholic Korsakoff's syndrome. In this study, it was also noted that the latter patients made more perseverative responses than patients with Huntington's disease. In a more recent investigation (Martone, Butters and Trauner, 1986), both groups of patients' picture memory performance was found to be helped to an equivalent degree by increased exposure on presentation trials, although patients with alcoholic Korsakoff's syndrome required longer exposure periods than those with Huntington's disease to reach the same level of performance as control subjects. Further evidence of dissociations between the memory performance of these groups of patients was provided by Martone *et al.* (1984). They found that patients with alcoholic Korsakoff's syndrome could show learning of mirror-reading skills, but poor recognition memory for the words used in the reading task. In contrast, patients with Huntington's disease were somewhat impaired in learning such skills, but showed good recognition memory for such words. In the case of the mirror-reading task, this dissociation mainly related to the reading of 'unique' words, i.e. those which were not repeated over successive trials. For repeated words, patients with Huntington's disease and control subjects showed similar savings between learning sessions, while patients with alcoholic Korsakoff's syndrome showed a lower score on this measure.

Distinctive features of memory functioning in other dementias

In the case of Parkinson's disease, few additional comparisons in respect of memory performance appear to have been reported, other than those already discussed above. Kimura, Barnett and Burkhart (1981), in their study of progressive supranuclear palsy, included a small group of patients with Parkinson's disease, and found similar (close to normal) Wechsler memory quotients in the two sets of patients. Similarly, in the study reported earlier, Pillon *et al.* (1986) found similar memory test scores in their patients with Parkinson's disease and their patients suffering from progressive supranuclear palsy. Little further comparative evidence on memory functioning in demyelinating disease is available. In the case of hydrocephalic dementia, comparisons with primary degenerative dementia which were made by Gustafson and Hagberg (1978) have been described above. Berglund, Gustafson and Hagberg (1979) included a group of patients with alcoholic Korsakoff's syndrome in their study of patients with hydrocephalic dementia. They found that marked, 'fantastic' confabulation and remote memory loss were more common in the hydrocephalic patients, although the methods for measuring these features were not described. On a memory-for-designs task, patients with alcoholic Korsakoff's syndrome, somewhat surprisingly, performed normally, whereas hydrocephalic patients were impaired. Both groups showed impairment on a verbal paired-associate learning task.

Summary

Primary degenerative dementia forms one of the most common sources of progressive deterioration of memory functioning in neurological disease. Memory impairment frequently represents the initial symptom which comes to the notice of patients and of their close relative or friends. Supraspan learning, delayed recall and paired-associate learning are among the tasks on which patients with primary degenerative dementia have shown particularly impaired memory performance. Whether the memory deficits of these patients represent a qualitative rather than simply a quantitative difference from that of age-matched control subjects remains a matter of some debate, since there is evidence in favour of both viewpoints. Their pattern of retrieval in verbal memory tasks differs from that of control subjects in several ways: an increase in the number of prior list intrusions, less organization in recall, and less consistent retrieval over repeated test trials. Some uncertainty remains as to whether patients with primary degenerative dementia show normal cued recall and whether their recall is helped by cues significantly more than the recall of control subjects. Impaired recognition memory performance has been reported in a number of studies of patients with primary degenerative dementia, and some of these studies have reported specific patterns of recognition memory performance, such as greater-than-normal number of false positive responses to particular types of items. In the case of retrograde amnesia, a few studies have found evidence of significant remote memory loss in these patients, this loss extending over a number of years pre-dating the onset of the illness.

Some investigations have noted specific correlations between memory functioning in patients with primary degenerative dementia and measures of cerebral structure or cerebral metabolic activity. In the case of cerebral structure, measures of ventricular dilatation/CSF volume have been found to be more closely related to memory functioning than measures of cortical atrophy. Measures of cerebral blood flow and cerebral metabolic activity in patients with primary degenerative dementia have tended to implicate temporal lobe structures in their impaired memory performance. A large number of studies have considered aspects of management of memory functioning in primary degenerative dementia, but a proportion of these are somewhat unsatisfactory from the methodological point of view. Most studies have focused on the effect of drugs on memory functioning in primary degenerative dementia, ranging from cholinergic drugs, such as physostigmine, to vasopressin and its analogues. While a few studies have reported significant improvement in memory functioning, in most cases any beneficial effects appear to have been relatively slight, with little evidence to indicate significant long-term benefits on the basis of a clinically acceptable form of drug administration.

Patients with Huntington's disease may show impaired memory functioning even in the early stages of the disease process. Experimental studies of memory performance of patients with Huntington's disease have indicated that such patients are relatively impervious to variation in memory task demands, compared to the pattern of performance shown by control patients or other neurological patients. Both anterograde memory deficits and retrograde memory impairment are more marked in patients with advanced disease compared to recently diagnosed cases. Recognition memory performance has sometimes been reported to be normal in a few studies of Huntington's disease.

In Parkinson's disease, normal recognition memory has also been reported by a number of investigators. It is possible that memory impairment in these patients may be more evident in tests requiring active effort and attention, as in most verbal recall tasks, and that the memory impairment shown by patients with Parkinson's disease may in part be related to the severity of any depression which is present. However, patients with Parkinson's disease are also impaired in retrograde memory tasks, and these tend to be less taxing and less influenced by the patients' affective state than tests of anterograde memory functioning. No clear picture has emerged with regard to the relationship between drug therapy, especially the administration of L-dopa and memory functioning in Parkinson's disease, with some studies reporting impaired memory performance and others reporting improved memory functioning in relation to drug administration.

The occurrence of memory impairment in demyelinating diseases has only recently been recognized as one of the possible cerebral complications of demyelination. Studies of patients suffering from multiple sclerosis have tended to show memory impairment to be restricted to subgroups of patients and some authors have attempted to define the nature of such subgroups. As in Parkinson's disease, memory impairment and MS may be related to the affective state of the patient, although such a relationship appears to be weaker in MS than in Parkinson's disease.

Dementia related to hydrocephalus, especially where this is 'idiopathic' and not secondary to a specific lesion which also disrupts brain function, represents a unique subgroup of patients with primary dementia. The presence and degree of memory impairment is, however, somewhat variable. Where this is present, some improvement may occur after shunting which has been carried out to relieve the hydrocephalus, although this improvement has sometimes been found to be restricted to certain patients.

Of the remaining primary dementias, only progressive supranuclear palsy appears to have been well documented with respect to the possibility of memory test deficits; however, such deficits have only been found in a small number of patients within one particular sample.

Chapter 7

Infectious, metabolic and related diseases

Infectious diseases

While infections of the central nervous system frequently lead to disorders of psychological function (Lishman, 1987), there have been relatively few detailed studies of memory deficits in such illnesses. Although memory symptoms have been reported in a wide range of infectious diseases, such as neurosyphilis (Dewhurst, 1969), cerebral abscess (Simpson and Swash, 1985) and acquired immune deficiency syndrome (AIDS) (Faulstich, 1986), well-documented case reports and group studies of memory disorder after CNS infections have mainly been limited to encephalitic illnesses, and in particular herpes simplex encephalitis. One of the first detailed case reports was that by Rose and Symonds (1960) who reported four cases of amnesia subsequent to encephalitis. In all four cases there were permanent residual sequelae which consisted of marked everyday memory impairment, significant retrograde amnesia, and minimal additional psychological deficits. The duration of retrograde amnesia varied between 2 and 20 years, although the authors felt that there was patchy retrograde amnesia for longer periods. They hypothesized that the most probable sites of involvement were the anterior portions of the temporal lobes. This investigation was, however, mainly a clinical study, and no specific psychological testing was reported. Drachman and Adams (1962) reported six cases of encephalitis, some of whom could be characterized as herpes simplex, and others as 'acute inclusion-body' encephalitis (although in one case there was the complication of coexisting frontal meningiomas). The two adult patients who survived had marked memory impairments. In one case, formal assessment was carried out, and this patient had a Wechsler memory quotient of 77, in contrast to an intellectual level in the 'bright–normal' range. In the three patients who came to post-mortem, asymmetrical temporal lobe lesions were noted together with some pathology in the frontal regions. An example of the type of pathology in encephalitic patients is shown in *Figure 7.1*, although it should be borne in mind that in a proportion of patients with encephalitis CT scanning may not demonstrate any abnormality. Other clinical studies of herpes and related forms of viral encephalitis (Hall, 1963, 1965; Talland, 1965b; Aimard *et al.*, 1979; Wechsler, Guisado and Bentson, 1974; Barbizet, Duizabo and Poirier, 1978; Foletti, Regli and Assal, 1980) have indicated the presence of anterograde amnesia, usually accompanied by some degree of retrograde amnesia, but most of these reports are of limited value due to the lack of detailed memory testing.

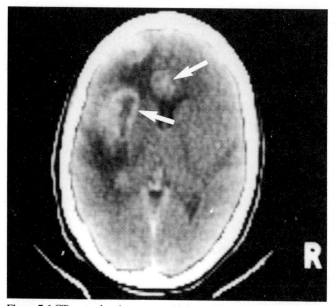

Figure 7.1 CT scans showing temporal lobe and frontal lobe lesions in a patient who developed marked memory difficulties after incurring a viral encephalitis. This was diagnosed to have most likely been due to a herpes virus

Turning to studies which have provided more extensive neuropsychological testing of encephalitic patients, Starr and Phillips (1970) reported marked impairment on most verbal and non-verbal memory tests which they administered to a patient with herpes simplex encephalitis. Features of their patient's pattern of memory performance included intact short-term memory on a Brown–Peterson paradigm, better recognition than recall performance on some verbal memory tasks, and the presence of prior intrusion errors. In contrast, motor learning tasks such as learning a simple maze or a piano tune appeared to be within their patient's repertoire. There was evidence of patchy retrograde amnesia, especially for events in the years immediately preceding the patient's illness, but no formal testing of this aspect of memory was reported. One of the limitations of the study was the lack of satisfactory control data for some of the experiments which were reported, e.g. in the maze-learning task, the control subject was approximately 20 years younger than the encephalitic patient!

Lhermitte and Signoret (1972) found impaired performance on a spatial learning task in encephalitic patients, but relatively intact performance on sequential learning tasks. The former test required patients to learn the spatial position of a set of nine pictures, with free and cued recall tested at delays of 3 minutes, one hour, 24 hours and 4 days. The latter tasks included a word-list learning task, learning a rule for placing simple two dimensional stimuli in a vertical and horizontal array and predicting the sequence of presentation of a set of coloured stimuli.

Cermak (1976) reported detailed memory testing of a patient who incurred herpes simplex encephalitis in 1971 at the age of 44 years. He retained a high premorbid IQ level but was markedly amnesic, with a 50 points difference between his Wechsler Adult Intelligence Scale IQ and Wechsler memory quotient. He performed normally on a Brown–Peterson verbal short-term memory task, and did not show any specific susceptibility to interference effects in his short-term memory performance. He displayed release from proactive interference, and his short-term motor memory was intact, but on a visual non-verbal short-term memory task he showed a deficit similar to that found in patients with alcoholic Korsakoff's syndrome. Over a period of one month, he retained learning of a short maze, although he would deny that he had ever done the maze-learning task before. Eight years after the initial assessment, Cermak and O'Connor (1983) reported a further series of investigations of the same patient (his age at testing in 1980/1981 was around 50 years). He continued to show marked anterograde amnesia in the context of normal short-term memory as had previously been demonstrated, and also a normal ability to analyse and encode semantic information. However, in tasks which exceeded his 'working memory' he tended to confuse strength of association of an item with recency of presentation. On the recognition part of a retrograde amnesia test which dealt with questions about past public events, he performed less well on items relating to the 1930s and 1940s than more recent items, whereas on the recall portion of the test, and on the faces memory portion there was a significant gradient in the opposite direction, i.e. more impaired performance on items in the 1960s and 1970s compared with 1930s and 1940s. In spite of his dense amnesia, S.S. has shown evidence of preserved learning on a number of tests of 'implicit memory', such as enhanced tachistoscopic recognition of previously presented words (Cermak et al., 1987).

In a study of an 18-year-old girl with herpes simplex encephalitis, Butters and Miliotis (1985) reported normal performance on a Brown–Peterson short-term memory task, impaired paired-associate learning, and retrograde amnesia for the previous 12 years, both for significant personal events and on tests covering public events or famous faces. Marked, generalized retrograde amnesia, which was not affected by the provision of cues, was also observed by Damasio et al. (1985a) in their patient with herpes encephalitis. This patient also displayed a dense anterograde amnesia, but showed some evidence of learning on a mirror tracing task, although no control data were presented for the latter task to indicate if such learning was within normal limits. Wood, Ebert and Kinsbourne (1982) also commented upon a dissociation in the memory functioning of their patient who incurred a probable herpes simplex encephalitis infection 5 years earlier. In spite of marked amnesia, their patient was able to demonstrate improvement in standard school achievement test scores over the years following her illness. There would appear, therefore, to be some evidence in favour of a certain degree of preserved learning in encephalitic patients who are left with an amnesic syndrome. Such preserved learning may, however, be somewhat selective; Kapur (1987b) reported normal pursuit rotor learning by a patient who incurred herpes encephalitis, but his performance on a perceptual learning task was lower than normal and he showed minimal 'priming' effects on two verbal retrieval tasks designed to reflect the effects of prior experience.

Patients with marked memory difficulties secondary to meningitis are rarely encountered, presumably due to the relatively benign nature of the illness. Zangwill (1977) has reported a case of amnesia in a patient with meningitis, in whom there was evidence, from air encephalography, of a lesion in the posterior horn of the left lateral ventricle. This patient showed marked memory impairment, but without any confabulation, and he performed normally on tests of vocabulary and non-verbal reasoning. His memory impairment was evident both on verbal and perceptual-motor learning tasks. He had a retrograde amnesia of at least several weeks, although Zangwill pointed out that its duration could not be precisely established.

A specific group of patients suffering from meningitis who have been frequently noted to show signs of significant memory impairment, are those who have been afflicted with tuberculous meningitis. The major study in this regard was carried out by Williams and Smith (1954). A number of interesting features were found in their patient population, including the observation that some patients with tuberculous meningitis may be left with a long period of retrograde amnesia, lasting months or years, but without any significant, residual anterograde amnesia. Duration of retrograde amnesia seemed to correlate with the period of 'confusion' subsequent to the onset of the illness, and memory deficits that were present in the early recovery period seemed to be disproportionate to any general intellectual deficit. Williams and Smith reported lucid episodes during some portions of the post-ictal period, with subsequent loss of memory for information acquired during the lucid period, and pointed out that a long period of post-ictal amnesia was nevertheless compatible with good subsequent recovery. Most of the patients described by Williams and Smith showed a good recovery from their illness in that they had few residual anterograde memory deficits. They all displayed amnesia for the period of the illness, and showed a gradual transition from the period of confusion and marked impairment back to normal memory.

Tuberculosis may also result in the development of granulomatous lesions in the central nervous system, which behave like space-occupying lesions and may lead to memory difficulties. In other conditions, such as cerebral sarcoidosis, such granulomatous lesions have been shown to be associated with memory test deficits (Thompson and Checkly, 1981), but no analogous studies have been reported in the case of tuberculoma.

A few studies have focused specifically on attempts to improve memory functioning in patients with infectious diseases of the brain. A psychological retraining study reported by Gianutsos (Gianutsos, 1981; Gianutsos and Grynbaum, 1983) dealt with a university professor who incurred herpes encephalitis. Intensive practice in short-term verbal memory tasks improved free recall performance, and advice on the use of mnemonic aids appeared to help his readjustment to academic duties. Wilson (1987) has reported some success in using psychological techniques to improve specific memory skills in a 59 year-old patient with a meningoencephalitic illness. She found that visual imagery techniques were helpful in improving retention of peoples' names, and that his delayed recall of short stories could be improved by encouraging critical reading of stories using a question-answer format combined with preview and retention testing. A pharmacological trial to improve memory functioning in an 18-year-old student with herpes encephalitis was carried out by Peters and Levin (1977), and a trial of hyperbaric oxygen was also reported in respect of the same patient (Levin and Peters, 1977). In these two studies, a short-term trial of physostigmine compared to placebo administration was found to facilitate verbal free recall with a concomitant decrease in number of intrusion errors; however, hyperbaric oxygen did not have a significant beneficial effect on the patient's memory functioning. Catsman-Berrovoets, Van Harskamp and Appelhof (1986) also found improved memory performance in their encephalitic patient who was administered physostigmine and lecithin; however, in spite of some improvement in verbal memory test scores, their patient remained clinically amnesic at the end of the treatment trial.

Metabolic diseases

Hypoxia

Cerebral hypoxia can occur in a variety of settings, ranging from general medical conditions such as cardiac disease to neurological conditions such as head injury. Since the degree of hypoxia itself may be difficult to measure accurately in most clinical situations, and is often presumed to occur from the clinical information available, relatively limited clinical evidence is available on the specific effects of hypoxia on memory function.

Although hypoxia may affect any region in the brain, certain structures appear to be more frequently damaged than others; these include medial temporal structures and 'watershed' areas of the cortex, i.e. areas which lie at the junction between distinct cerebrovascular systems and which may be dependent for their blood supply on the most distant radiations of the cerebral arteries. Patients who have suffered from carbon monoxide poisoning have been found to show sequelae which include everyday memory symptoms, and this has been found to correlate with performance on formal memory tests (Smith and Brandon, 1973). Smith and Brandon also reported a correlation between residual memory difficulties and level of consciousness of patients at the time of hospital admission. Although they did not indicate whether any of their patients were amnesic, a few such cases have been reported (Pillon, Signoret and Lhermitte, 1977; Spinnler, Sterzi and Vallar, 1980; Della Sala and Spinnler, 1986). Unlike the more transient amnesia and generalized cognitive deficits found in the case reported by Spinnler, Sterzi and Vallar (1980), the study by Della Sala and Spinnler (1986) was particularly detailed in its documentation of the patient's amnesia, which persisted for several years as a relatively isolated deficit. A notable feature of the patient's condition was a striking indifference towards his memory deficits, although he retained some awareness of his memory difficulties. He displayed marked memory impairment over a range of memory tasks, an extensive retrograde amnesia, and evidence of intact ability to learn a simple mathematical rule.

Brierley and Cooper (1962) described a patient who developed hypoxia following anaesthesia. Seven and a half months after the operation in question, there was clinical evidence of a marked retrograde amnesia, together with confabulation and memory impairment for everyday events. Her full scale Wechsler Adult Intelligence Scale IQ of 61 suggested significant dementia in addition to her amnesia. At post-mortem, there was evidence of both cortical damage and bithalamic lesions, but the hippocampus was reported to be normal. The mamillary bodies were not available for assessment. A purer case of recent memory impairment due to a similar aetiology was described by Muramoto et al. (1979). Their amnesic patient, who was reported as showing minimal retrograde amnesia and intact perceptual-motor learning, had pneumoencephalographic evidence of bilateral hippocampal damage.

Berlyne and Strachan (1968) reviewed a number of case studies of memory deficits associated with attempted hanging, and suggested that where memory impairment was evident one month after the attempted hanging, persistent memory deficits were likely to remain. They also reported a patient who showed amnesia as a residual sequel one year after attempted hanging. This patient displayed confabulation in the acute stages, both in general conversation and recall of verbal memory test material. He appeared to have retrograde amnesia for around 9 years, although no formal assessment was carried out, and no evidence was presented as to the extent to which this retrograde amnesia showed any recovery. Berlyne and Strachan suggested that the pathophysiological basis of amnesia in this condition was arterial occlusion resulting in stagnant hypoxia and consequent bilateral hippocampal damage.

The possibility that significant memory disorders may accompany hypoxia associated with cardiac/cardiopulmonary arrest has been raised by a number of case studies, although group studies of such patients have shown that, in some patients, memory deficits show partial recovery (Finklestein and Caronna, 1978; Kotila and Kajaste, 1984), or may be restricted to older patients (Bengtsson, Holmberg and Jansson, 1969). McNeill, Tidmarsh and Rastall (1965) described a case of marked memory impairment in a patient approximately 3 years after a cardiac arrest and associated hypoxia. The patient was reported to be disorientated for time and place, and he performed poorly on story recall and recall of designs, in the context of normal IQ scores. Cummings *et al.* (1984) reported a case of amnesia, in the absence of gross dementia, where hippocampal lesions resulted from hypoxia secondary to cardiopulmonary arrest. Autopsy examination was available 2 months after this initial assessment (his condition appears to have remained the same over that time). At post-mortem, there was marked atrophy of both hippocampi with significant loss of neurons and moderate glial proliferation. Two small areas of infarction were also noted in the left thalamus and right frontoparietal cortex, although the authors argued that these were unlikely to have made a significant contribution to the patient's memory deficits. Volpe and Petito (1985) also reported hippocampal pathology in two anoxic patients, although in this study neuropsychological testing was more limited, and there was evidence of significant dementia in addition to the profound memory loss.

In one of the few studies of hypoxia where detailed neuropsychological testing was reported, Volpe and Hirst (1983b) reported three patients who showed marked memory deficits following a period of hypoxia. In all three patients, there was some degree of amnesia for events immediately preceding the hypoxic episode. Retrograde amnesia was not formally assessed but did not appear to be extensive at the clinical level. A subsequent study (Kovner, Mattis and Pass, 1985) carried out formal assessment of retrograde amnesia in one of the patients and found little in the way of significant impairment. Detailed assessment of anterograde memory in this patient yielded normal short-term memory, better recognition than recall performance and susceptibility to interference on memory tasks. There was no evidence of confabulation in any of the three patients. Two of the patients showed cued recall performance which was at the same level as that of control subjects. Further evidence for a dissociation between impaired recall and normal recognition memory for verbal material was provided by Volpe, Holtzman and Hirst (1986) in a study of six patients with amnesia following cardiac arrest. Rate of forgetting in recall tasks was significantly faster for amnesic than for control patients, while no such difference emerged in the case of recognition testing. The patients studied by Volpe, Holtzman and Hirst also showed significant retrograde amnesia, which was worse for the years immediately preceding the hypoxic episode, and marked retrograde amnesia was also evident in a hypoxic patient, reported by Parkin, Miller and Vincent (1987), who had significant cognitive dysfunction in addition to her memory deficits.

Graf, Squire and Mandler (1984) examined various aspects of memory performance in two amnesic patients where hypoxia was presumed to have occurred (one suffered a cardiac arrest and the other experienced a hypotensive episode related to open heart surgery). While free recall, cued recall and recognition memory were all impaired, the patients showed normal learning on word-completion tasks, although this contrast in performance was mainly restricted to words encoded semantically at time of presentation. One of these patients subsequently died of a non-neurological condition, and post-mortem investigations were able to offer quite unique insights into the neural mechanisms underlying his memory disorder (Zola-Morgan, Squire and Amaral, 1986). The latter authors were able to implicate field CA1 of the hippocampus as the primary site of pathology underlying their patient's amnesia (*Figure 7.2*). In this paper, they also reported normal performance by their patient on tests of retrograde amnesia. Few researchers have speculated on the nature of the memory deficit in cerebral hypoxia, although on the basis of their observations Corkin *et al.* (1985) hypothesized that attentional factors may play an important role in the memory impairment.

It has been suggested that milder forms of hypoxia might underlie memory impairment in other medical conditions which have a pulmonary or cardiac basis. However, the evidence for this derives from a limited number of studies. Krop, Block and Cohen (1973) assessed a series of patients with chronic obstructive pulmonary disease before and after continuous ambulatory oxygen therapy. These patients were presumed to have been suffering from mild hypoxia. A control group of patients was also assessed before and after a similar re-test interval. Krop, Block

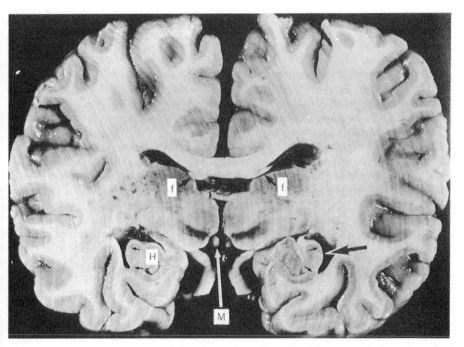

Figure 7.2 Bilateral hippocampal pathology in a patient who suffered from amnesia due to hypoxia. Photograph of 1.5 cm thick unstained coronal section of brain at a level through the anterior hippocampal formation. The hippocampus (H on left, large arrow on right) has a relatively normal appearance except for a region of thinning (between the smaller arrows) in the CA1 region. The mamillary nuclei (M) and the two fornices (f) are also indicated. (From Zola-Morgan, Squire and Amaral, 1986. Reproduced by permission of the Society of Neuroscience)

and Cohen found that although their patients' memory deficits prior to treatment were relatively mild, there was some improvement before and after therapy, with control subjects showing no significant practice-effects on the memory tasks. Huppert (1982) found impaired performance on a series of memory tasks including memory for words, memory for pictures (complex photographs) and memory for line drawings, in patients with chronic hypoxia related to obstructive lung disease. For some of the memory tasks (memory for incidentally-learned material) there was a correlation between degree of hypoxia, as indicated by blood gas measurements, and both recall and recognition performance. Unfortunately, detailed comparisons with data from control subjects were not presented, and on two tests where control data were available, the differences between control and hypoxic subjects appeared to be relatively minimal.

A study of hypoxia associated with sleep-disordered breathing (Berry et al., 1986) also found some relationship between measures of hypoxia and impaired memory performance, but in this study matched control subjects were not tested, and the authors reported their patients' test scores as falling within the normal range. In an investigation where detailed control data were gathered, Grant et al. (1982) found that their patients with chronic obstructive pulmonary disease were impaired on tests of delayed recall of drawings (although not on delayed recall of story material) and on a tactile memory task. A study by Fix et al. (1982) also reported only slightly lower-than-normal scores by patients with chronic obstructive pulmonary disease on the Benton Visual Retention Test, although matched control patients were not specifically tested for the study. In a follow-up investigation of the patients with chronic obstructive pulmonary disease, Fix et al. (1985) found that survival status 3 years after the initial assessment was related to performance on this test, with patients who had lower scores displaying a higher mortality rate at follow-up. Prigatano et al. (1983) found impaired memory in tients with chronic obstructive pulmonary disease, and argued that this could not be explained by factors such as motivation, fatigue and depression. Memory for stories, visual reproduction (geometric figures) and paired-associate learning were significantly impaired compared to controls.

A few studies have tested for possible memory deficits arising from cardiac disorders or as a side-effect of surgery to treat such disease, although, in general, the available evidence is somewhat inconclusive. Lagergren (1974) showed that at low heart rates, patients with complete heart block had poorer memory performance on tests assessing recall of figures and paired-associate learning than when heart rates were normal. However, no control data were reported to indicate the significance of the low test scores. Transient episodes of amnesia have been associated with cardiac arrhythmia (Greenlee, Crampton and Miller, 1975), and Dugan, Nordgren and O'Leary (1981) reported a case of transient global amnesia associated with bradycardia and temporal lobe spikes on EEG testing. Episodes of transient global amnesia recurred even after a pacemaker had been inserted. In open-heart surgery, transient 'confusional' states, including evidence of disorientation, have been reported in the early postoperative period, although these have usually resolved within a week after surgery (Tufo, Ostfeld and Shekelle, 1970).

The main focus of researchers in this field of study has been on longer-term residual neuropsychological sequelae. Memory deficits after open heart surgery may be present in certain patients, such as those with high blood loss during operation (Savageau et al., 1982a,b). Frank, Heller and Malm (1972) reported pre- to postoperative improvement in performance on the Benton Visual Retention

Test in patients who had undergone open heart surgery 6 months earlier. However, interpretation of these findings is limited by the absence of test–retest control data. Juolasmaa *et al.* (1981) found that some patients (between 11% and 31% of patients, depending on the test in question) improved and others (between 10% and 22%) deteriorated on memory tests administered 5 months pre-and 5 months post-open heart surgery. No clear-cut indicators as to the factors which might differentiate the two subgroups of patients were reported, apart from some general observations that preoperative mitral valve disease was more likely to be associated with deterioration in cognitive functioning after surgery. Here again, the absence of test–retest data from control subjects in this study limits the significance of the improvements which the authors found. Aberg (1974) observed that memory was less affected than other functions in open-heart surgery patients with or without cerebral complications, but the use of only one memory task in this study (a short-term picture recognition memory test) restricts the importance of this observation.

Other metabolic diseases

Metabolic disorders related to general medical conditions may sometimes result in transient or persistent memory deficits. In such cases it is important to exclude the contribution of any coexisting abnormalities, e.g. cerebrovascular disease in the case of diabetic patients.

In liver disease, hepatic encephalopathy is a well-established possible complication of this illness. Since cirrhosis of the liver is often associated with chronic alcohol abuse, it is important to screen for alcohol abuse in the assessment of the neuropsychological effects of liver dysfunction. Transient retrograde amnesia accompanied by more permanent anterograde deficits has been reported in patients recovering from hepatic coma (Summerskill *et al.*, 1956). One study has reported impaired memory functioning in non-alcoholic patients with cirrhosis of the liver (Rehnstrom *et al.*, 1977), but this report did not include testing of matched control subjects. A study which did employ control subjects (Tarter *et al.*, 1984) did not find any evidence of impaired memory in patients with non-alcoholic cirrhosis of the liver who did not have any overt clinical signs of cerebral dysfunction. Some patients with cirrhosis of the liver may require vascular surgery ('portacaval anastomosis') to halt recurrent internal bleeding, although this surgery results in a diminution of the liver's capacity to filter out toxic materials. Elsass, Lund and Ranek (1978) assessed memory functioning in a group of patients who underwent such surgery, and found deterioration in memory performance after surgery. However, it is important to note that their group of patients comprised both those with alcoholic and those with non-alcoholic cirrhosis of the liver.

Kidney disease, and the effects of treatment of such disease, have also been associated with impaired memory functioning. Heilman *et al.* (1975) showed that patients with uraemia (a biochemical disturbance associated with renal failure) were impaired on memory tasks compared to control patients. This impairment was evident on tests of digit span and both immediate and delayed story recall, although normal performance was evident on a faces–recognition memory task. The authors thought that attentional factors might underlie the memory deficits they found. They thought that uraemia affected cerebral function in a manner similar to anaesthesia, by causing dysfunction in the reticular activating system, and thereby disturbing arousal and rehearsal processes. Hart *et al.* (1983) reported impaired performance by patients with renal dysfunction on a number of memory tasks, such as story recall, memory for designs and memory for faces. Furthermore, performance on the latter task correlated with degree of renal failure, as indicated by serum creatinine levels.

In addition to the deleterious effects of uraemia, long-term complications may arise from the administration of a large number of dialysis treatments, resulting in so-called 'dialysis dementia'. Although this condition has been reported widely at the clinical level (*see* Chui and Damasio, 1980 for a review of such cases), few objective studies of memory functioning have been carried out, and where memory testing is reported this has tended to be in selected cases rather than in groups of patients (e.g. Madison *et al.*, 1977). English *et al.* (1978) did not find impaired memory performance in their group of patients undergoing home dialysis for chronic renal failure, but did note a positive correlation between impairment in block-design learning and duration of dialysis. Similarly, Ziesat, Logue and McCarty (1980) found a correlation between memory performance, in particular long-term memory for visual figures, and the number of dialysis treatments. Since the correlation with memory functioning occurred with the number of dialysis treatments, Ziesat, Logue and McCarty did not consider that uraemia as such was underlying the memory deficit, as one might have expected this to improve as the dialysis treatments increased. Hart *et al.* (1983), however, did not find any correlation between memory performance and years of dialysis treatment, and the memory impairments of their dialysis patients were generally in the mild to moderate range. Brancaccio *et al.* (1981) failed to discover any evidence of overall memory impairment in their group of patients with chronic kidney failure, or of specific memory deficits related to a history of dialysis treatments. In most of these studies, therefore, only a relatively small subgroup of patients appeared to show impaired memory performance.

The possibility of a neurologically-based memory deficit in some patients suffering from diabetes has been the subject of a number of investigations, dating back to the observations of memory impairment made by Miles and Root in the 1920s (Miles and Root, 1922). In the assessment of memory functioning in diabetic patients, it is important to be aware of possible transient, reversible forms of memory impairment which may accompany a period of hypoglycaemia, and which may compound any more persistent memory impairment. The evidence with regard to such transient memory impairment is, however, relatively limited, and existing data suggest that this impairment may be relatively mild and only evident on certain memory tasks (Holmes *et al.*, 1983; Pramming *et al.*, 1986). During the investigation of persistent memory deficits, it may nevertheless be prudent to measure a patient's blood glucose concentration, and to repeat this measurement at the time of any follow-up memory assessment. Bale (1973) found that almost 20% of his insulin-dependent diabetic patients (type 1 diabetes) were impaired on a verbal learning task, and he also reported a relationship between poor test performance and severity of previous hypoglycaemic episodes. Using the Benton Visual Retention Test and the Wechsler Memory Scale, Mattlar *et al.* (1985) failed to find any difference in memory performance between patients with type 2 diabetes (non-insulin-dependent) and control subjects. Lawson *et al.* (1984) also failed to find any significant evidence of memory impairment in diabetic patients with neuropathy. A wide range of memory tests were administered including the Wechsler Memory Scale, a recurrent recognition test for figures and a recurring recognition test for words. No correlation was found between memory performance and clinical ratings of peripheral or autonomic neuropathy. Only one of the tests, a recurring figures recognition memory test, showed a correlation with the duration of illness. Franceschi *et al.* (1984) did find a significantly lower overall Wechsler memory quotient in patients with insulin-dependent diabetes, but on individual subtests of the scale there were no statistically significant differences with control subjects. Using a large number of verbal and non-verbal memory tests, Ryan, Vega and Drash (1985) were able to detect significant memory deficits in insulin-dependent diabetic patients with an early onset of their illness (diagnosis before 5 years of age). These patients performed less well than controls on immediate and delayed recall of visual patterns. Dealing with an older age group, Meuter *et al.* (1980), however, found that patients with later onset (mean age of 49.7 years), compared to earlier onset (mean age of 27.7 years) diabetes showed more marked impairment on memory testing.

Diabetes insipidus may result directly from cerebral dysfunction, and this form of diabetes has also been associated with memory deficits (Laczi *et al.*, 1982). In such cases, there is the obvious difficulty of distinguishing the role of metabolic abnormality *per se* from the predisposing neurological condition. Laczi *et al.*. also found that administration of vasopressin improved the memory performance of their patient sample. In a later study (Laczi *et al.*, 1983b), further evidence of improvement in memory after treatment with vasopressin was gathered, but pre-treatment differences in memory performance between diabetic and control patients were not significant in this investigation.

Although memory difficulties have been reported in association with endocrine disorders such as myxoedema (e.g. Jellinek, 1962), there has been a dearth of studies using objective memory test procedures. Exceptions to this include the report by Whelan *et al.* (1980) who found that out of a group of 35 patients with Cushing's syndrome, approximately one-third showed impairment in the retention of simple designs or memory for unrelated sentences. Starkman and Schteingart (1981) reported a clinical study of patients with Cushing's syndrome. Detailed memory assessment was not carried out, although they did note that impairment of memory was a frequent symptom of their patients, and reported that in their mental status examination, a difficulty with recall of three cities after 15 minutes was seen in 31% of patients. Two patients of the 35 studied showed evidence of disorientation and of having difficulty in recalling the day of the week. The authors reported a significant correlation between overall neuropsychiatric disability rating and both cortisol and adrenocorticotrophic hormone levels.

Wilson's disease, in which there is an inborn error of copper metabolism, has seldom been associated with the occurrence of marked memory disorder. Patients with this disease may show CT scan features which include ventricular dilatation, cerebral atrophy and, in some cases, hypodense lesions in the region of the basal ganglia (Williams and Walshe, 1981). Goldstein *et al.* (1968) found improved Wechsler Memory Scale performance from an initial level which was mildly to moderately below average in a few such patients after they had received long-term treatment with penicillamine and a low-copper diet. However, repeated assessment consisted of multiple retesting over a 5–6 year period, and no allowance appears to have been made for possible practice-effects. In a single case study of a patient with Wilson's disease, Bornstein, McLean and Ho (1985) reported memory impairment to be limited to more non-verbal memory tasks, although in this study only one verbal memory test (immediate prose recall) was administered.

Distinctive features of memory disorders in patients with infectious and metabolic diseases

Infectious diseases

Patients with encephalitis, especially herpes simplex encephalitis, are similar to patients with alcoholic Korsakoff's syndrome in the high incidence of memory disorder as a long-term residual sequel to their illness. Indeed, in relation to the figures quoted by Victor, Adams and Collins (1971), namely that 21% of patients with alcoholic Korsakoff's syndrome recover completely from their initial amnesic–confusional state, then the incidence of residual memory deficits in a comparable group of patients with herpes encephalitis might in fact be higher. At both the clinical and neuropsychological levels, some distinctive features of memory disorder in encephalitic patients are evident in the literature. However, it should be borne in mind that most of these comparisons are based on small numbers of encephalitic patients, and any firm conclusions on comparisons with other types of cerebral pathology must be based on data from subjects who are matched on age, intellectual level and severity of memory impairment. Parkin (1984) has observed that clinical reports of encephalitic patients and those with Korsakoff's syndrome have pointed to a higher incidence of confabulation and lack of insight in the latter patients. Confabulation, in the form of florid, conversational confabulation, is seldom seen in the chronic phases of the alcoholic Korsakoff's syndrome. Its occurrence in the acute phases is well documented, but in my experience it may also be present in the acute phases of some patients with herpes encephalitis (see Hall, 1963, 1965), and so it may be premature to draw firm conclusions on the distinctiveness of this feature.

Turning to differences in memory test performance, Lhermitte and Signoret (1972) found that patients with alcoholic Korsakoff's syndrome performed somewhat differently from encephalitic patients in that they showed relatively intact cued recall on a spatial learning task, but impaired performance on rule learning and word-list learning tests. By comparison, encephalitic patients showed poor cued recall with evidence of a rapid rate of forgetting on the spatial learning task, but performed close to normal on the rule learning tasks. The patient reported by Cermak (1976) differed from most of those with alcoholic Korsakoff's syndrome in that he performed normally on a Brown–Peterson verbal short-term memory task, although on a visual non-verbal short-term memory task his performance was similar to that of patients with alcoholic Korsakoff's syndrome. He seemed to profit more from mediating and visual imagery cues than did the other patients. Brooks and Baddeley (1976), in a study of preserved learning in amnesia, found that while on some tasks, such as pursuit rotor learning, both oups performed at a similar, unimpaired level, on a jig-saw puzzle learning task, patients with alcoholic Korsakcff's syndrome performed at a lower level than encephalitic patients, and were markedly impaired relative to control subjects. Mattis, Kovner and Goldmeier (1978) noted differences between encephalitic and alcoholic Korsakoff's syndrome patients on tests of verbal recall and recognition memory. In general, encephalitic patients had poorer memory test scores than patients with alcoholic Korsakoff's syndrome, and performed at around chance levels on most measures. Patients with alcoholic Korsakoff's syndrome were principally impaired at retaining verbal material such as words of varying frequency levels taken from semantic categories, and in certain conditions performed close to control subjects where 'nonsense', verbal material had to be learned. Encephalitic patients, on the other hand, showed similar levels of poor memory performance over all types of test material. Butters and Cermak (1980) and Albert, Butters and Levin (1980) also presented evidence comparing encephalitic and patients with alcoholic Korsakoff's syndrome, and pointed to normal verbal short-term memory in the former patients, compared to the impaired performance of the latter subjects. In contrast, performance on a non-verbal (faces) retrograde amnesia test was more impaired in encephalitic than in patients with alcoholic Korsakoff's syndrome (*Figures 7.3* and *7.4*).

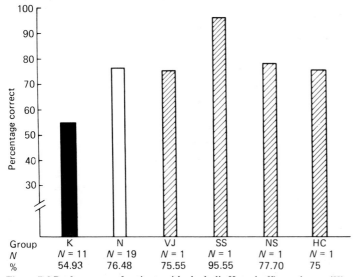

Group	K	N	VJ	SS	NS	HC
N	*N* = 11	*N* = 19	*N* = 1	*N* = 1	*N* = 1	*N* = 1
%	54.93	76.48	75.55	95.55	77.70	75

Figure 7.3 Performance of patients with alcoholic Korsakoff's syndrome (K), normal control subjects (N) and of patients who incurred herpes encephalitis (VJ, SS, NS, HC), on a verbal short-term memory task (from Butters and Cermak, 1976. Reproduced by permission of Ballinger Publishing Company)

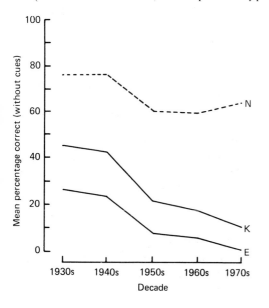

Figure 7.4 Performance of patients with alcoholic Korsakoff's syndrome (K), normal control subjects (N) and post-encephalitic patients (E) on a faces retrograde amnesia test (from Albert, Butters and Levin, 1980. Reproduced by permission of Plenum Press)

Significant, residual memory difficulties after meningitis are the exception rather than the rule, and the relative infrequency and mildness of the deficits are in themselves distinguishing features of such patients. In the case of patients who have incurred meningitis, little in the way of formal comparisons have been made with memory disorders of other aetiologies. The major study of tuberculous meningitis by Williams and Smith (1954), which was reviewed earlier (*see* p. 146), did yield some observations which seem to be relatively characteristic, although the fact that this appears to be the only detailed neuropsychological study of tuberculous meningitis suggests some caution in making generalizations from the authors' conclusions. They offered four sets of observations. First, they noted that some patients with tuberculous meningitis may have as their only sequel a relatively isolated period of retrograde amnesia, together with amnesia for the early period of the illness; this contrasts with the more usual state of affairs in other aetiologies, e.g. Teuber's claim (1975) that in patients with penetrating head injury persistent anterograde memory difficulties usually follow from the presence of some degree of pre- and post-traumatic amnesia. Second, in patients with blunt or penetrating head injury, the duration of pre-traumatic amnesia is usually a matter of minutes or hours, or in a few cases, a matter of days. In the patients with tuberculous meningitis studied by Williams and Smith, however, pre-ictal/retrograde amnesia extended for more than a year in almost one-fifth of a group of patients who were assessed up to 4 years after the onset of illness. Third, while in patients with blunt head injury, duration of post-traumatic amnesia is usually closely related to degree of neuropsychological recovery, this appears not to be the case in tuberculous meningitis, with a long post-ictal amnesia being compatible with good recovery of cognitive functions. Fourth, during the post-ictal confusional state some patients with tuberculous meningitis were observed by Williams and Smith to retain problem-solving abilities (e.g. arithmetic, playing draughts) while displaying poor memory; this is in contrast to the picture usually seen after severe blunt head injury, where some degree of generalized cognitive dysfunction often accompanies marked memory difficulties in the early stages of recovery.

Metabolic diseases

In patients who have incurred hypoxia, few comparative studies of memory functioning have been carried out to enable conclusions to be reached on distinctive features of memory deficits. Some authors (Della Sala and Spinnler, 1986) have pointed to a lack of concern, shown by some patients with carbon monoxide poisoning towards their memory impairment. Other authors (Volpe, Holtzman and Hirst, 1986) remarked on the normal recognition memory performance of hypoxic patients who otherwise had marked memory difficulties. Shimamura and Squire (1986b) reported findings on three patients whose amnesia was related, at least in part, to some degree of hypoxia. Unlike patients with alcoholic Korsakoff's syndrome, they did not show any impairment in their ability to predict whether they would be able to recognize correctly items which they were unable to recall. In the study by Zola-Morgan, Squire and Amaral (1986), the memory performance of their hypoxic patient was compared with that of patients with alcoholic Korsakoff's syndrome and with that of a patient who incurred a focal left hemisphere penetrating missile wound. The hypoxic patient performed at a similar level to patients with alcoholic Korsakoff's syndrome on the anterograde memory tasks, and his memory deficits were more generalized than those shown by the patient with penetrating head injury. In the case of retrograde amnesia, no formal comparisons were reported by Zola-Morgan, Squire and Amaral, but the absence of any such deficits in their hypoxic patient contrasts with the marked retrograde amnesia which has generally been reported in patients with alcoholic Korsakoff's syndrome. Corkin *et al.* (1985) have suggested that attentional factors may play a greater part in the memory disorder resulting from hypoxia than in other aetiologies. Heilman *et al.* (1975) made similar observations in the case of their patients who had memory difficulties secondary to uraemia.

Summary

Of the infectious diseases for which significant published data are available, herpes simplex encephalitis and tuberculous meningitis have been most commonly shown to result in significant memory impairment. It is difficult to draw definitive conclusions about the effects of such diseases on memory functioning, partly because of the small number of studies (and the small numbers of patients in such studies), and partly because many of the patients studied have been selected for the presence of a pure, global amnesic syndrome. The evidence which is available suggests that patients with herpes encephalitis may show marked anterograde memory impairment which can occur in the presence of normal performance on most short-term memory tasks. Extensive retrograde amnesia has also been noted to occur in such patients. Patients with tuberculous meningitis may show both retrograde and anterograde amnesia in the early stages of the illness; a few patients may be left with a relatively isolated retrograde amnesia but in general there is a high level of recovery of memory functioning after this type of illness.

Hypoxia, and transient reduction of blood supply to the brain with resultant cerebral ischaemia, may also lead to significant memory impairment with a variable degree of additional cognitive impairment. Here again, the amount of published evidence is relatively limited, but a few trends appear to emerge from the data. These include a lack of concern for memory impairment following carbon monoxide poisoning, absence of significant retrograde amnesia in hypoxic patients, and intact recognition memory in patients with hypoxic following cardiac arrest. More subtle forms of hypoxia and abnormalities of cerebral metabolism may also result in memory impairment, and clinicians need to be aware of the possibility of memory disorder in medical conditions such as cardiac and pulmonary disease, liver disease, kidney disease and diabetes. In the case of diabetes, the type of diabetes and the age of onset appear to be important factors in determining the severity of memory impairment which is displayed.

Comparisons between patients with encephalitis and those with alcoholic Korsakoff's syndrome have been made by some researchers, and some of these have been summarized by Parkin (1984). While features such as absence of insight to memory disorder and confabulation in the acute stages of the illness may be less common in patients with encephalitis rather than in those with alcoholic Korsakoff's syndrome, and while other features, such as rapid rate of forgetting, may be more frequent in encephalitic patients, there is a need for further, well-documented evidence from matched groups of patients before definitive conclusions can be drawn.

Chapter 8

Toxic and deficiency states

While memory dysfunction can occur after both acute and chronic toxic or deficiency states, the present chapter will focus on chronic conditions, mainly because it is these rather than acute conditions which form recognized cerebral disease states and which are more likely to present in neurological settings. The effects of alcohol on the central nervous system make up the largest single body of knowledge on the influence of toxic conditions on memory, and such studies have contributed not only to our knowledge about memory disorders, but also towards an understanding of normal memory functioning. Toxic states may often be accompanied by a variable degree of vitamin deficiency, and some conditions such as alcoholic Korsakoff's syndrome usually represent the sequelae of both chronic alcohol consumption and prolonged thiamine deficiency. In this chapter, I will review the evidence on memory functioning in alcoholic Korsakoff's syndrome, and then examine findings regarding the memory performance of subjects with a history of chronic alcoholism, but who have not developed an alcoholic Korsakoff's syndrome. Finally, I will consider evidence relating to other toxic and deficiency states.

Alcoholic Korsakoff's syndrome

Alcoholic Korsakoff's syndrome has been extensively reviewed in a number of books and articles (e.g. Talland, 1965a; Victor, Adams and Collins, 1971; Butters and Cermak, 1980; Cutting, 1985a), and the reader is referred to these sources for more detailed exposition of earlier work in this field. In this section, I will summarize the main findings relating to anterograde and retrograde memory functioning of patients with alcoholic Korsakoff's syndrome, i.e. learning of new information and retention of information acquired prior to the onset of the condition. I will also review findings on the relationship between memory disorder and neurobiological aspects in patients with this condition, and will consider studies which have attempted to improve memory functioning in patients with alcoholic Korsakoff's syndrome.

Alcoholic Korsakoff's syndrome represents the end state of two distinct conditions – a history of both chronic alcohol consumption and thiamine deficiency. It is the latter condition which appears to be critical in producing the Wernicke's encephalopathy which is characteristic of the initial stages of the Korsakoff syndrome, since thiamine deficiency alone can result in the neurological features (e.g. ataxia, ophthalmoplegia, nystagmus) and neuropsychological features (initial confusional state) associated with Wernicke's encephalopathy (Perkin and Handler, 1983). The amnesic state associated with the term 'Korsakoff's psychosis' represents the end state for a proportion of patients who initially presented with Wernicke's encephalopathy. In the study by Victor, Adams and Collins (1971) 54% of such patients showed little or no improvement in their memory functioning. Thus, the condition is often referred to as the 'Wernicke–Korsakoff' syndrome. Since most of the studies to be reviewed in this section have included Wernicke–Korsakoff patients with a history of chronic alcohol abuse, the term alcoholic Korsakoff's syndrome will be used here. The majority of the neuropsychological investigations of patients with alcoholic Korsakoff's syndrome have attempted to include subjects with a pure, global amnesic syndrome, that is those with a marked memory disorder, but without evidence of other cognitive deficits of any significance. It should be borne in mind that such patients represent a subset of patients with alcoholic Korsakoff's syndrome as a whole, and that a number of these patients may show generalized cognitive deficits in addition to their amnesia (Cutting, 1978a). It should also be borne in mind that these patients vary in the severity of their residual memory disorder, and that these two factors (extent of generalized cognitive dysfunction and severity of amnesia) may account for some of the discrepancies between studies of alcoholic Korsakoff's syndrome.

Anterograde memory deficits

Everyday memory symptoms

Everyday memory difficulties of patients with alcoholic Korsakoff's syndrome have been documented by several researchers (e.g. Gardner, 1974; Zola-Morgan and Oberg, 1980). Patients with this condition are typically disorientated for time, and sometimes also for place. They may not know the name of the current head of state, and may be unable to recount current news events. They will usually be unable to state with accuracy what they did the previous day or even several hours earlier, and will seldom be able to provide the names of people, such as medical staff, with whom they are in frequent contact. Many patients tend to show the distinctive feature of lacking insight into their memory difficulties (Zangwill, 1977), and some patients will deny any memory symptoms whatsoever. In part, this denial may simply reflect forgetting of instances of memory loss, although it may also be related to apathy secondary to frontal lobe dysfunction. More formal assessment of awareness of their memory disorder has indicated an impaired ability to predict whether or not they would be able to recognize correctly items which they are unable to recall (Shimamura and Squire, 1986b).

Confabulation

Confabulation usually refers to a fabricated representation of past experience, and may sometimes include a distorted account of the patients current state and future intentions. As indicated in Chapter 1, the term itself is somewhat imprecise, partly due to a lack of standardized means for assessing confabulation; partly because the phenomenon may vary in severity and type (Berlyne, 1972), and partly because it may also be used to refer to erroneous recall in formal memory testing situations. Early studies of patients with alcoholic Korsakoff's syndrome alluded to limitations of the concept in the assessment of memory functioning. Victor, Herman and White (1959) noted that 'the symptom of confabulation has only a limited usefulness in the diagnosis of Korsakoff's psychosis, since it lacks precise definition and is not present in all cases or at all times in any given patient'. Confabulation offered by the patient in general conversation may vary from prompted recall of a real event, but which the patient places in the wrong temporal and spatial context, to a spontaneous, florid account of a quite implausible event. It has traditionally been held that confabulation is an invariable feature of alcoholic Korsakoff's syndrome, but this is not the case. As Butters (1985) has pointed out, confabulation in its florid form is generally restricted to the acute stages of the condition. Although a few patients may confabulate in the chronic stages of alcoholic Korsakoff's syndrome, this tends to be more of a 'filling in' of memory loss rather than confabulation in its florid form. Experimental investigation of confabulation has been somewhat limited. Talland (1965a) has given examples of some of the types of confabulation which he observed in his sample of patients. Confabulation during memory testing has also been noted, as in the distorted recall of story material (Talland and Ekdahl, 1959; Butters *et al.*, 1986), and in the attempted reproduction from memory of ambiguous figures (Wyke and Warrington, 1960).

Sensory memory and short-term subspan memory

The ability of patients with alcoholic Korsakoff's syndrome to process and store information in the first few seconds after presentation has been examined in a few studies. Using a Sternberg (1966) paradigm, Naus, Cermak and DeLuca (1977) found a decrease in speed of search in a short-term memory task where lists of two to six consonants were serially presented, followed 6 seconds later by a target consonant which subjects had to identify as present or absent in the presentation list. Korsakoff and alcoholic control subjects appeared to use similar information processing strategies to perform the task, but patients with Korsakoff's syndrome were slower at searching and making comparative judgements on information stored in short-term memory. Butters and Cermak (1980) reported impaired 'sensory memory' for verbal material presented tachistoscopically for around one second, but noted methodological difficulties in probing recall of material from part of the array. Using a paradigm similar to that used in animal studies, Oscar-Berman and Bonner (1985) have reported impaired memory performance by subjects with alcoholic Korsakoff's syndrome in delayed (3–30 seconds) matching-to-sample tasks, where stimulus exposures varied between 200 and 500 ms.

The most common paradigm used by researchers to examine subspan delayed memory is that developed by Brown (1958) and by Peterson and Peterson (1959). The prototypical task involves presentation of stimuli within the patient's immediate span, followed by a variable interval (usually not more than 30 seconds) filled by some distracting activity, which is subsequently followed by a retention test for the stimuli. A number of such presentation and test trials are administered, and performance can be analysed in terms of the delay between presentation and test, types of errors over trials, etc. A large number of investigations using this paradigm have been carried out on patients with alcoholic Korsakoff's syndrome. In a series of studies (e.g. Cermak, Butters and Goodglass, 1971; Butters *et al.*, 1973; DeLuca, Cermak and Butters, 1976; Cermak, Reale and DeLuca, 1977), Butters, Cermak and their colleagues found evidence of impaired short-term memory performance using a range of verbal and non-verbal stimuli and distractor activities. As might be expected, non-verbal stimuli were poorly retained by patients with alcoholic Korsakoff's syndrome regardless of the presence or type of distractor activity, whereas subspan verbal items could be rehearsed and retained in memory if the distracting activity did not prevent such rehearsal (DeLuca, Cermak and Butters, 1975; Cermak and Uhly, 1975; Cermak and Tarlow, 1978). Strauss and Butler (1978) have extended these findings to tasks involving haptic stimuli. Kopelman (1985) has, however, reported normal performance by patients on short-term memory for verbal material (common words) using a paradigm similar to that used by Butters and Cermak. No ready explanation for this discrepancy was offered by Kopelman. It is possible, as in the differences between the Butters and Cermak findings and those obtained by Baddeley and Warrington (1970) using a mixed groups of patients, that a combination of subtle methodological differences and patient selection procedures underlie the discrepant findings. For example, the performance of patients with alcoholic Korsakoff's syndrome in Kopelman's study may have been enhanced by the apparent absence of paced distractor activity and by the possibility of some rehearsal taking place during the slide change-over interval after the presentation slide (*see* Butters and Cermak, 1974 and Piercy, 1977 for further discussion of factors which may account for the discrepancy in findings). If, as Parkin and Leng (1987) have suggested, the presence of frontal lobe dysfunction in patients with alcoholic Korsakoff's syndrome may contribute to impaired performance on the Brown–Peterson memory task, then it is possible that individual differences in severity of such dysfunction may also in part explain discrepancies in findings from different studies.

Patients with alcoholic Korsakoff's syndrome tend to make a significant number of intrusion errors in such short-term memory tasks (Samuels *et al.*, 1971; Meudell, Butters and Montgomery, 1978; Kopelman, 1985), and they seem to be particularly susceptible to the spacing of trials, producing more errors under 'massed' learning conditions, where trials follow closely on one another (Cermak and Butters, 1972). While control subjects can show 'release' from the build-up of such proactive interference if a change in category of items takes place, patients with alcoholic Korsakoff's syndrome seldom show such an improvement in memory (Cermak, Butters and Moreines, 1974), although such a shift may occur over repeated test sessions using the same paradigm (Freedman and Cermak, 1986). Freedman and Cermak suggested that these patients may learn to anticipate that shifts will occur and that this expectation facilitates encoding and retention. Patients with alcoholic Korsakoff's syndrome are also helped if there is a delay between presentation and onset of distractor activity, presumably allowing for rehearsal to aid retention (Butters and Grady, 1977).

List memory

I will use the term 'list memory' to refer to memory testing paradigms where the number of stimuli to be remembered is greater than the patient's immediate memory span, and where item retention is later tested by free recall, cued recall or recognition formats. I will also include paired-associated learning tasks, since the total number of items which is presented usually exceeds the patient's immediate memory span. A large number of studies have been carried out using memory tests of this type, and so they will be subdivided according to whether studies have focused on the role of task or retention test variables in the memory performance of patients with alcoholic Korsakoff's syndrome.

Presentation parameters

One of the features of the poor memory of patients with alcoholic Korsakoff's syndrome which distinguishes it from that of patients with focal cerebral lesions is the generality of the memory impairment across a variety of stimulus materials. Thus, patients with alcoholic Korsakoff's syndrome have been shown to have poor memory for word lists (Fuld, 1976), faces stimuli (Dricker *et al.*, 1978), complex patterns (Riege, 1977; Cutting, 1981) and tactile learning of four- or six-choice mazes (Cermak *et al.*, 1973). A number of investigators have probed the effects of particular presentation variables on patients' memory performance. Cermak and Reale (1978) and McDowall (1981) examined the effects of encoding instructions designed to focus patients' attention on particular features of verbal stimuli, e.g. phonemic, semantic features, etc. They did not find any disproportionate effects of such instructions on the memory performance of patients with alcoholic Korsakoff's syndrome compared to control patients, although the former were helped to some extent by 'semantic' encoding instructions. Similar findings were noted by Biber *et al.* (1981) in a study of memory for faces. In a series of studies, Meudell, Mayes and their colleagues (Mayes, Meudell and Neary, 1978, 1980; Meudell *et al.*, 1980) found similar patterns of memory performance in patients with alcoholic Korsakoff's syndrome and control subjects over a range of stimulus materials and types of encoding instructions. On the basis of these studies, therefore, there appears to be little support for the hypothesis that patients' memory deficits were due to a failure in semantic encoding (Cermak and Butters, 1976).

Particular factors occurring at the time of list presentation have been implicated in the poor memory performance of patients with alcoholic Korsakoff's syndrome, including inadequate rehearsal strategies (Cermak, Naus and Reale, 1976; Brown *et al.*, 1980) and reluctance to use semantic or organizational features of the word-list material spontaneously (e.g. Cermak, Butters and Gerrein, 1973; Cermak and Moreines, 1976; Rubin and Butters, 1981). Slowing the presentation rate of items does not in itself improve performance for verbal material (Cermak and Moreines, 1976), although increasing the amount of exposure time to pictorial stimuli does make the memory performance of patients with alcoholic Korsakoff's syndrome close to that of normal subjects (Huppert and Piercy, 1977, 1978b). Where the stimulus material has 'affective value' for patients with Korsakoff's syndrome, e.g. by the introduction of a sexual theme in a short story (Davidoff *et al.*, 1984) or by the use of pictures of alcoholic beverages (Markowitsch, Kessler and Bast-Kessler, 1984), memory performance of these patients is enhanced compared to 'neutral' stimuli. However, in the study by Davidoff *et al.* (1984) this difference was only evident on immediate recall and was absent on delayed retention testing.

Paired-associate learning has proved to be particularly difficult for patients with alcoholic Korsakoff's syndrome, and this difficulty has been evident on tasks with a verbal or visuospatial content (Kapur and Butters, 1977; Butters, 1984a), and in situations where subjects have to learn to discriminate two objects on the basis of a reinforcing stimulus associated with one of them (Kessler, Irle and Markowitsch, 1986). In the case of the paired-associate learning subtest of the Wechsler Memory Scale, patients may often offer familiar associations to 'hard' items in the test (Victor, Herman and White, 1959). A number of researchers have examined the effects of varying stimulus parameters on paired-associate learning. Choosing paired-associate items which are semantically related results in near normal performance by patients with alcoholic Korsakoff's syndrome, and conversely performance can be adversely affected by giving a second paired-associate task where stimulus-response associations overlap with those of the first task (Winocur and Weiskrantz, 1976). Encouraging the use of verbal mediators or visual images to link verbal paired-associates can result in some improvement in memory performance of patients with alcoholic Korsakoff's syndrome, but this is relatively limited (Cermak, 1975; Howes, 1983).

Retention test parameters

The type of response which patients are asked to make at the time of retention testing has been claimed to affect significantly the presence and extent of memory deficit in amnesic patients. Some researchers have reported that patients with alcoholic Korsakoff's syndrome, especially those with less severe amnesia, show disproportionately greater impairment on recall compared to recognition testing (Hirst *et al.*, 1986), and in the case of one study (Johnson and Kim, 1985), short-term and long-term recognition memory for abstract pictures were at similar levels in both patients and control subjects. The main body of evidence on response factors has, however, been concerned with the effects of providing cues at the time of recall testing. Since the original demonstrations (Warrington and Weiskrantz, 1970, 1974) using a group of amnesic patients of mixed aetiology (but *see* Mair, Warrington and Weiskrantz, 1979 where only data on patients with alcoholic Korsakoff's syndrome are reported), that such patients can show normal memory performance when this is tested by cued recall, a number of studies have attempted to replicate the phenomenon with patients, and to examine cued recall in greater detail. Cermak and Butters (1972) and Cermak, Butters and Gerrein (1973) did not find that amnesic patients benefited from cues any more than control subjects. Kapur (unpublished data) also could not demonstrate normal cued learning by patients nor differential facilitation by the provision of cues (*Figure 8.1*).

In several studies, the cued recall scores of patients with alcoholic Korsakoff's syndrome have been lower than those of controls, and in one of the studies (Cermak and Butters, 1972) patients actually recalled more items in free recall than in cued recall. Mayes, Meudell and Neary (1978) initially failed to replicate the cued recall effect, but later did find some evidence for normal cued retention, especially if patients were encouraged to guess at the time of cued recall (Mayes and Meudell, 1981). Mayes and Meudell noted that their patients with alcoholic Korsakoff's syndrome appeared not to know if the word they were guessing was a previous list item. This observation seems to reinforce the impression, also evident in other studies of cued recall (Gardner *et al.*, 1973), that normal memory scores in cued retention testing paradigms are more likely to occur the less the paradigm actually resembles a formal memory test and the closer it approximates to a guessing task. Graf, Squire and Mandler (1984) carried out a formal test of this hypothesis and found normal performance by patients with alcoholic Korsakoff's syndrome where the retention test was presented as a word-completion task, but found impaired scores on a comparable test where memory was tested in the usual way, with explicit reference to the stimuli presented earlier.

In addition to showing impaired ability to indicate whether an item has occurred in the recent past, patients with alcoholic Korsakoff's syndrome appear to be equally, or even more markedly impaired when they have to retrieve information about the context in which the items were presented. For example, they are impaired in making judgements about the temporal occurrence of items (Squire, 1982), tending to confuse this information with how many times items have been presented (Huppert and Piercy, 1976, 1978a; Meudell *et al.*, 1985). From their performance in cued recall situations, it also appears that patients with alcoholic Korsakoff's syndrome tend to confuse associative strength of an item in their 'semantic memory' with how recently the item has been presented (Cermak and

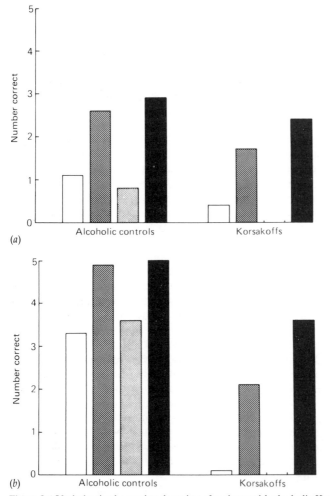

Figure 8.1 Verbal paired-associate learning of patients with alcoholic Korsakoff's syndrome and chronic alcoholics. Ten trials were administered. First letter cues (for five items) or semantic cues (for five items) were given for associates which could not be recalled in the free recall condition. Performance is shown for (*a*) trial 1 and (*b*) trial 10. Patients with Korsakoff's syndrome were impaired under cued learning conditions (scoring at zero level on the semantic uncued condition), and their memory performance was not differentially aided by the provision of cues. While their performance improved with either alphabetic or semantic cues, that of control subjects also improved (although a ceiling effect for performance on trial 10 limited the range of this improvement). There was no evidence that the memory performance of patients with alcoholic Korsakoff's syndrome was differentially aided by the provision of cues. □ Alphabetic–uncued; ▨ alphabetic–cued; ▤ semantic–uncued; ■ semantic–cued

Stiassny, 1982). The deficit in retention of contextual information in patients with alcoholic Korsakoff's syndrome seems to be particularly marked under 'incidental' learning conditions, where subjects are not specifically told to remember items for a subsequent retention test (Kohl and Brandt, 1985). Other studies (e.g. Winocur and Kinsbourne, 1978; Winocur, Kinsbourne and Moscovitch, 1981) have shown that these patients are sensitive to changes in the context (e.g. sound and lighting conditions, features of the printed stimuli) in which learning takes place, and may show reduced effects of proactive interference if they are prewarned of a change in category of the word-list material.

The inference of storage processes from memory test data is a matter of some debate (Loftus, 1985a,b; Slamecka, 1985) but, nevertheless, some useful evidence has been collected on changes in memory performance of patients with alcoholic Korsakoff's syndrome over specific time periods. At intervals of less than 30 seconds, as in the case of the Brown–Peterson paradigm, there appears to be a rapid rate of forgetting by these patients compared to control subjects, especially for non-verbal memory items (DeLuca, Cermak and Butters, 1975), perhaps due to the availability of a rehearsal mechanism for verbal stimuli (Haxby, Lundgren and Morley, 1983). In the case of a short-term recall of verbal material, patients with alcoholic Korsakoff's syndrome appear to show relatively little loss of information over a period of 1–2 minutes (Moss et al., 1986). Huppert and Piercy (1977, 1978b), Squire (1981), Kopelman (1985), and Martone, Butters and Trauner (1986) have all found evidence for normal rates of forgetting for pictorial material by patients whose initial acquisition was made equivalent to that of normal subjects by increasing the amount of exposure to the original stimuli.

Retrograde memory deficits

In addition to their marked everyday memory difficulties, patients with alcoholic Korsakoff's syndrome also suffer from memory loss for events which preceded the onset of their anterograde amnesia. The two forms of memory loss have been found to be relatively independent of each other in these patients, except for more recent time periods preceding the illness onset, where severity of retrograde amnesia has been shown to correlate significantly with the ability to learn new information (Shimamura and Squire, 1986a). The separation in time of anterograde and retrograde amnesia, or 'remote memory loss', may sometimes be difficult to determine accurately, especially since most patients will have been drinking heavily before developing a full-blown Korsakoff's syndrome, and so a proportion of the period of apparent retrograde amnesia may reflect some degree of impaired anterograde memory functioning. Retrograde memory impairment will seldom be clinically obvious in the everyday behaviour of the patient, and will rarely be within the patient's level of awareness.

Neuropsychological testing of retrograde memory functioning needs to take into account a number of possible confounding factors, such as variability in item difficulty within tests, assumptions as to how well and in what form the original material was acquired, and type of response which is required from patients. Variables such as these, together with differences in patient population, may underlie some of the discrepant findings which have appeared in the literature. Talland (1965a) drew attention to the presence of retrograde amnesia, particularly for more recent events, in his population with alcoholic Korsakoff's syndrome but did not carry out detailed investigations of remote memory loss. Seltzer and

Benson (1974) reported a temporal gradient in the retrograde amnesia of patients using a questionnaire test with multiple choice responses. Patients with Korsakoff's syndrome were impaired for recent items (covering the previous 15–20 years) and unimpaired for earlier items. Marslen-Wilson and Teuber (1975), using famous faces as stimuli, also found that patients had greater difficulty in identifying items from recent years (faces from the 1960s), although this deficit disappeared when cues were given to assist identification.

In their clinical-neuropathological report of two subjects with alcoholic Korsakoff's syndrome, Mair, Warrington and Weiskrantz (1979) reported a flat temporal gradient using questionnaire and faces test materials. It is possible that the difficulty level of items might underlie some of the differences between the above studies and the report by Sanders and Warrington (1971), (whose patients included those reported by Mair, Warrington and Weiskrantz, but also amnesic patients of other aetiologies). Sanders and Warrington found no temporal gradient in the retrograde memory loss shown by their patients, who performed at very low levels throughout the various tasks which were administered. Albert and her colleagues carried out a series of investigations of retrograde memory functioning in patients with alcoholic Korsakoff's syndrome, using test procedures which were carefully balanced for variables such as item difficulty level. They showed (Albert, Butters and Levin, 1979) that these patients had a remote memory loss which was characterized by a significant temporal gradient, with memory for items relating to the distant past being more accurate than that for events in the years prior to the illness. This memory loss was evident on tests using faces or questionnaire items as stimuli, on free recall, cued recall and recognition testing formats, and occurred for items of varying difficulty level. Similar patterns of retrograde amnesia in patients with alcoholic Korsakoff's syndrome were reported by Cohen and Squire (1981), and these sets of findings were confirmed and extended in a notable single-case study (Butters, 1984a; Butters and Cermak, 1986) of an eminent academic who developed alcoholic Korsakoff's syndrome. This patient demonstrated memory deficits for autobiographical material and other items related to his past academic activities, and his memory loss also showed a temporal gradient, with greater sparing of items from earlier years.

Preserved memory functioning

While the most distinctive feature of patients with alcoholic Korsakoff's syndrome is their severe memory loss, considerable evidence has been gathered in recent years to show that they are capable of some form of learning. This is usually evident in tasks where evidence of learning is 'implicit' in task performance rather than 'explicitly' requested in the form of, for example, a free recall or forced-choice recognition memory test. Much of the evidence in relation to preserved learning in these patients has been reviewed by Parkin (1982), although a number of studies have been published since that review. One of the most frequently quoted examples of residual memory function in patients with alcoholic Korsakoff's syndrome is that demonstrated by Claparede (1911). With a pin hidden between his fingers, he shook hands with a patient. Some time later, the patient refused to shake hands with him, although he could not provide a rational explanation for his refusal, and appeared to be unaware of the specific episode which had occurred. (However, see Barbizet (1970) for a description of similar, although more equivocal, observations relating to everyday aversive conditioning in patients with alcoholic Korsakoff's syndrome.) In a detailed investigation, Talland (1965a) was able to show eye-blink conditioning, where a buzzer preceded a puff of air, in his group of patients. Talland's main observations were replicated by Weiskrantz and Warrington (1979) in two patients, one of whom suffered alcoholic Korsakoff's syndrome, although the authors did not find extinction of the conditioned response which was noted by Talland. Warrington and Weiskrantz remarked on the dissociation, which was evident in Claparede's original demonstration, between evidence of learning and failure to recall the context in which the learning took place.

The possibility that some level of physiological arousal may be present during the production of responses to certain stimuli, in the absence of conscious awareness that the stimuli in question were previously presented, was formally tested by Markowitsch, Kessler and Denzler (1986). They assessed galvanic skin responses during picture memory performance, but did not find physiological evidence of memory without awareness. However, it is possible that monitoring of biological activity more directly related to cerebral functioning may yield data to support the presence of physiological awareness in the absence of conscious recollection of the experience in question.

Perceptual and perceptual-motor learning tasks have also proved a reliable source of evidence to show memory capabilities in patients with alcoholic Korsakoff's syndrome. Schneider (1912, quoted in Parkin, 1982) showed that patients could learn to identify pictures from fragmented representations, and could show retention of this learning up to 4 months later. Talland (1965a) observed that in learning simple manual skills (such as transferring beads from one receptacle to another) which involved the use of 'immediate proprioceptive cues', patients with alcoholic Korsakoff's syndrome 'seemed to improve with practice at much the same rate as the control group'. Cermak *et al.* (1973) and Martone *et al.* (1984) have noted the ability of patients with alcoholic Korsakoff's syndrome to learn pursuit rotor and mirror reading skills. Using a purely perceptual task, where patients had to find hidden figures in cartoon drawings, Meudell and Mayes (1981) found similar retention over a 7-week period in patients and in control subjects, in spite of the patients' impaired ability to recognize the drawings they had analysed previously. Subsequent studies of mixed aetiology amnesic groups, which have included patients with alcoholic Korsakoff's syndrome, have confirmed the ability of patients to learn tasks such as pursuit rotor and jig-saw puzzles (Brooks and Baddeley, 1976), to display object/word recognition on the basis of partial information, and to learn to detect anomalies in pictures (Warrington and Weiskrantz, 1968, 1970, 1978).

Other evidence with regard to normal cued learning in patients with alcoholic Korsakoff's syndrome has been discussed above (*see* Retention test parameters). Simple two-choice discrimination learning where, for example, the subject has to learn which of two objects contains a coin, has also been found to be within the repertoire of patients with alcoholic Korsakoff's syndrome, but where the choices are subsequently reversed, or where they have to learn a number of choices on a single trial, their performance deteriorates compared to that of control subjects (Oscar-Berman and Zola-Morgan, 1980a,b). Patients with alcoholic Korsakoff's syndrome have also been shown to be able to acquire preference and affective reactions to stimuli such as musical tunes or peoples' faces, and to retain some of this learning over periods of up to 20 days (Johnson, Kim and Risse, 1985). When considering the various studies reviewed above, it should be noted that in some instances (e.g. jig-saw puzzle learning in the Brooks and Baddeley (1976) study) patients consistently performed lower than control subjects, and in a study where the patients had to learn a simple mathematical rule (Wood, Ebert and Kinsbourne, 1982), they did show evidence of learning and long-term retention, but the authors indicated that their performance 'did not match what would be expected from normals'.

Other experimental designs have highlighted the dissociation between impaired recognition and normal or near normal perceptual identification of stimuli. For example, in 'perceptual priming' paradigms, patients with alcoholic Korsakoff's syndrome have been found to show facilitation in the tachistoscopic identification of recently-presented words, even though they cannot recognize them as having occurred previously (Cermak et al., 1985). A similar dissociation has been reported for spelling and recognition memory for a set of homophones, where one form of the homophone was 'primed' by inclusion in an earlier naming task (Jacoby and Witherspoon, 1982). However, this study only obtained control data from student subjects, and a later investigation (Cermak, O'Connor and Talbot, 1986), using a similar paradigm, found significantly less facilitation effects in patients with alcoholic Korsakoff's syndrome compared to matched alcoholic control subjects.

Relationship between memory deficits and neurobiological variables

The study by Victor, Adams and Collins (1971) was one of the first to provide detailed evidence on the relationship between the amnesia associated with the Wernicke–Korsakoff syndrome and specific areas of pathology in the brain. The medial dorsal nuclei of the thalamus and the mamillary bodies contained lesions in all 23 cases who had an initial Wernicke's encephalopathy and were left with a Korsakoff amnesic state. In the case of the thalamic nuclei, these lesions were minimal, moderate and severe in degree in 47.4%, 36.8% and 15.8% of cases respectively. In the case of the mamillary bodies, the corresponding values were 30%, 50% and 20% respectively for minimal, moderate and severe degrees of pathology. As support for their hypothesis that the dorsomedial thalamic nuclei might be the critical lesion underlying the memory disorder shown by their patients, Victor, Adams and Collins pointed to five cases who had an initial Wernicke's encephalopathy but did not develop an amnesic syndrome; these patients were the only five, out of 43 cases, where relevant data were available, whose medial dorsal thalamic nuclei were free of pathology, and in all five cases the mamillary bodies were damaged. A major limitation, however, of this study was that much of the evidence was based on retrospective analysis of case note material, and no specific memory test findings were reported to clarify further the relationship between cerebral pathology and severity of memory disorder. Further, as Mair, Warrington and Weiskrantz (1979) have pointed out, many of the studies of patients with alcoholic Korsakoff's syndrome which have gathered biological data, such as evidence relating to post-mortem neuropathological lesions, have failed to gather or report up-to-date memory test data relating to the particular patient population.

Mair, Warrington and Weiskrantz reported neuropathological data on two patients with alcoholic Korsakoff's syndrome who had been described in earlier studies by Warrington and Weiskrantz. These patients showed marked anterograde amnesia, extensive retrograde amnesia for the previous 25 years, intact short-term memory, and unimpaired performance (in fact, rather better than control subjects) on long-term memory tested by cued retention tasks. The principal lesions noted at post-mortem included gliosis, shrinkage, and discoloration of the medial nuclei of the mamillary bodies bilaterally. In addition, there was a thin band of gliosis bilaterally between the wall of the third ventricle and the medial dorsal nucleus of the thalamus. Mair, Warrington and Weiskrantz speculated that the mamillary body lesions may have been the more critical of the two sets of changes they found, and this is partly borne out by the series of patients studied by Brion and Mikol (1978), who reported the absence of any significant relationship between severity of retrograde amnesia and thalamic involvement of lesions which were verified at post-mortem. A more recent post-mortem investigation of three patients with alcoholic Korsakoff's syndrome has proposed that a further structure, the nucleus basalis of Mynert (NBM) may show selective pathology in these patients (Arendt *et al.*, 1983). This subcortical structure is a major source of cholinergic input to the cortex, and Arendt *et al.* studied the three subdivisions of the NBM – at the junction of the caudate and lenticular nuclei, in the anterior commisure and in the substantia innominata. Although some researchers (Butters, 1985) have supported the significance of this observation, others (Crosson, 1986) have voiced caution in interpretation of the findings. It is worth pointing out that not only was the finding by Arendt *et al.* found only in three patients, but also that only one of these appeared to show the severity of NBM pathology which was found in other neurological patients who were studied. In addition, no detailed memory testing was reported, nor did the authors report data on the integrity or otherwise of neighbouring limbic system structures such as the thalamus. A recent study (Hata *et al.*, 1987) of local cerebral blood flow in patients with alcoholic Korsakoff's syndrome, which showed flow reduction in the NBM, also pointed to significant disturbance in neighbouring regions.

Correlations between CT parameters and memory performance of patients with alcoholic Korsakoff's syndrome have tended to be relatively slight and inconclusive. Wilkinson and Carlen (1980) studied the relationship between measures of sulcal and ventricular atrophy, and performance on subtests of the Wechsler Memory Scale, but only found a correlation between these measures and performance on the paired-associate learning subtest. Similarly, a study by Harbinson (1984) found only one significant correlation between memory performance and CT scan measures of ventricular dilatation or cortical atrophy, namely between performance on this paired-associate learning test and dilatation of the frontal horns. It is important to note that the patients in this study appeared to suffer from a degree of generalized cognitive dysfunction in addition to their amnesia. Kopelman (1985) has reported a weak correlation between short-term memory performance and CT estimates of sulcal atrophy in his group of patients with alcoholic Korsakoff's syndrome. In my experience, CT scans of patients will tend to show a variable degree of ventricular dilatation and cortical atrophy, as reported by Harbinson. This ventricular dilatation may reduce slightly from the acute to the recovery phase of the syndrome, although this may be disproportionately small compared with changes at the level of memory functioning (*Figure 8.2*).

At the biochemical level, the evidence is also somewhat equivocal. McEntee and Mair (1978) reported a reduced concentration of a metabolite of norepinephrine in the lumbar cerebrospinal fluid of patients with alcoholic Korsakoff's syndrome, and observed a correlation between such reduction and severity of memory impairment. However, Martin *et al.* (1984) were unable to replicate the main biochemical abnormality noted by McEntee and Mair, although they did not report correlative data in respect of degree of memory impairment. It is possible that differences in methodology, and in the patient and control populations, may in part explain the discrepancy in the two sets of findings (*see* McEntee and Mair, 1984).

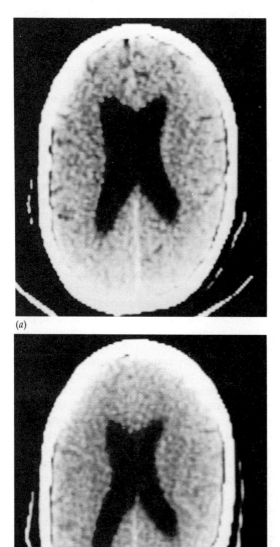

(a)

(b)

Figure 8.2 CT scans of a patient in the first few weeks of Korsakoff's psychosis and 7 months later, when he had made a good recovery from his amnesic state and showed little in the way of significant memory impairment. (a) The ventricular dilatation evident on the first scan is less marked on the second scan (b), although this change is disproportionately small compared with the improvement in his memory functioning. On the first examination, his marked memory impairment was characterized by disorientation for time and place, and by a significant degree of confabulation. These were absent on the follow-up testing at the time of the repeat scan, and at that time he showed little evidence of any significant memory impairment

Management of memory deficits

In the early stages of their illness, a number of patients with alcoholic Korsakoff's syndrome will show some degree of 'spontaneous' recovery from their confusional state, and thiamine replacement therapy has become a routine form of treatment in this early stage of the illness. Victor, Adams and Collins (1971) noted that 21% of patients made a complete recovery from their amnesia, and this was usually evident within one year of the onset of illness. A further 25% made significant recovery, 28% made slight recovery and 26% showed no recovery in their amnesia. Victor, Herman and White (1959) have documented the improvement in memory test scores which may take place in the first 6–9 months of the recovery period. Most studies concerned with specific therapeutic measures to improve memory functioning of patients with alcoholic Korsakoff's syndrome have concentrated on the chronic phase of the condition. In general, attempts to improve patients' memory functioning have tended to be unsuccessful (Cermak, 1980), and this pessimistic outlook has generally carried over into patients' everyday memory difficulties. Jaffe and Katz (1975) have presented a brief report of a successful attempt to use cueing procedures to enable a patient with alcoholic Korsakoff's syndrome to learn information such as people's names and the location of a locker. Providing patients with external memory aids such as note pads has had some limited benefit (Davies and Binks, 1983), although using such aids does in itself require some degree of intact memory. Using a relatively heterogeneous group of memory-impaired alcoholic patients, Godfrey and Knight (1985) assigned subjects to an experimental or control treatment programme. The experimental programme consisted of training in memory, orientation and attention tasks and the control programme involved participation in general activities such as social skills exercises, card games, etc. Although both groups showed improved memory functioning, which appeared to be greater than that of a group of four matched amnesic patients who did not undergo any form of therapy, there were no significant differences in memory test scores or rated memory functioning between the two groups, apart from a greater improvement in orientation in the experimental group. In addition, there was little evidence of transfer of learning over time or across situations.

Pharmacological therapies have also had a variable degree of success in improving memory in patients with alcoholic Korsakoff's syndrome. Talland, Hagen and James (1967) did not find any beneficial effects using Cylert (presumed to stimulate synthesis of RNA in the brain) on the memory performance of patients. LeBoeuf, Lodge and Eames (1978) found that vasopressin improved memory in a patient with alcoholic Korsakoff's syndrome who was administered a series of memory tests after a initial period on placebo medication. Subsequent attempts to replicate this finding using similar compounds have been somewhat disappointing (e.g. Jenkins, Mather and Coughlan, 1982; Laczi et al., 1983a). McEntee and Mair (1979) reported improved performance on some memory tests after administration of clonidine in a double-blind trial which compared it with d-amphetamine and methysergide. Digit span, memory for prose and for simple designs, together with recall of consonant trigrams, all showed an improvement but paired-associate learning, which tends to be particularly difficult for patients with alcoholic Korsakoff's syndrome, did not show any significant change. In addition, at the clinical level the improvements in memory were somewhat limited, and the authors themselves noted that none of the patients approached normal levels of memory functioning.

Chronic alcoholic subjects

While the most dramatic memory deficits associated with chronic alcoholism are found in patients with alcoholic Korsakoff's syndrome, a significant body of evidence has been gathered on the memory performance of chronic alcoholic patients who have not yet developed a full-blown syndrome (Birnbaum and Parker, 1977; Ryan and Butters, 1983). In these subjects, it is important to be aware of other factors, such as previous head injury, coexisting liver disease, vitamin deficiencies, etc., which may contribute towards any memory impairment. It is possible that these factors may only be important if present to a significant degree. For example, preliminary evidence suggests that a previous mild head injury (Alterman et al., 1985) or slightly reduced vitamin levels (Albert et al., 1982) do not have a significant effect on memory functioning in chronic alcoholics. Recent drinking history should also be carefully documented, since alcoholic subjects may show 'acute' effects of alcohol on memory performance, some of which may recover in the first few weeks or months of abstinence (Cermak and Ryback, 1976; Carlen, 1981). The pattern and degree of chronic alcohol consumptions may also be usefully documented since this has sometimes been found to be related to memory performance (Eckardt et al., 1978), although it is important to be aware of intentional and unintentional inaccuracies in reports of drinking history given by alcoholic subjects.

The present section will deal mainly with levels of memory impairment in the clinically impaired range, and will not give detailed consideration to possible memory deficits in social drinkers since these appear to be relatively mild and somewhat variable (Noble, 1983; Robertson, 1984). Transient amnesic states, which may take the form of 'alcoholic blackouts', will not be reviewed as they seldom present in a neurological setting and rarely reflect underlying cerebral disease as such.

Anterograde memory deficits

Memory deficits in chronic alcoholics have usually been evident over a range of tasks, including immediate and delayed recall of prose material (Acker et al., 1984), associating a symbol with a number, or a number with a particular location on a horizontal line (Kapur and Butters, 1977), and tests of sensory/tactile memory (Blusewicz et al., 1977). Some researchers have raised the possibility of material-specific deficits in chronic alcoholics. Thus, Cutting (1978b) noted deficits on a picture memory task (stimuli consisted both of patterns and of simple objects) but not on a verbal paired-associate learning task. Becker et al. (1983b) reported that faces memory was more significantly impaired than memory tasks involving verbal stimuli. Butters et al. (1977) failed to find significant verbal memory deficits in a group of chronic alcoholic subjects, although in a later study, Ryan and Butters (1980) did find impaired performance on a 10-item verbal paired-associate learning test. Brandt et al. (1983) reported normal subspan delayed verbal memory performance, but impaired verbal and non-verbal paired-associate learning scores in chronic alcoholic subjects who had been sober for a number of years. De Renzi et al. (1984) noted more marked impairment in chronic alcoholic patients on a test of spatial memory, which involved tapping a sequence of blocks two greater than the immediate span, than on a word-list learning test. They considered the possibility that the right cerebral hemisphere may be more susceptible to the effects of alcohol. However, while there is some neuropsychological evidence to support such an explanation (e.g. Jenkins and Parsons, 1981), most of the neuroradiological evidence (Cala et al., 1980; Lishman, Ron and Acker, 1980) suggests the presence of bilateral rather than unilateral cerebral dysfunction in chronic alcoholics. In addition, as Ryan and Butters (1983) have pointed out, differences in difficulty level between visuoperceptual and verbal memory tasks may underlie the discrepancies which have been found. Finally, one study has reported normal performance on a faces-recognition memory task in a group of chronic alcoholics who were nevertheless impaired on the Wechsler Memory Scale, which is heavily loaded on short-term verbal memory tasks (Gudeman et al., 1977).

Some studies have focused on differences within groups of chronic alcoholic subjects. For example, Ryan and Butters (1980) found that alcoholics who complained of everyday memory symptoms performed worse on a similar set of memory tasks than alcoholic subjects without everyday memory symptoms. Fabian, Parsons and Sheldon (1984) noted impaired visuospatial learning in male but not female chronic alcoholic subjects. Guthrie and Elliott (1980) found a relationship between duration of alcohol abuse and degree of impairment on verbal memory tasks. Cutting (1978b) reported that the performance of his subgroups of moderate and heavy drinkers was significantly different on a picture memory task, and Kessler, Irle and Markowitsch (1986) noted impaired performance on an object discrimination learning task in chronic alcoholics with a 15-year history of alcohol abuse, but not in those with a 10-year history. However, Ron (1983) failed to find any relationship between duration of alcohol abuse and memory performance in her study of cognitive functioning in alcoholic subjects.

A number of researchers have pointed out the importance of duration of sobriety on severity of memory impairment. Becker and Jaffe (1984) found that the severity of impaired memory of information in an alcohol education film correlated with the duration of abstinence, but Lishman, Ron and Acker (1980) only found a relationship with degree of abstinence in one of their series of memory tests. Yohman, Parsons and Leber (1985) observed that those chronic alcoholic subjects who showed persistent memory deficits on long-term follow-up, 13 months after initial assessment, tended to be ones who resumed even moderate amounts of drinking in the intervening period.

One of the issues which has pervaded much of the research on memory deficits in chronic alcoholic subjects is whether their memory impairment represents part of a continuum with the memory disorders of patients with alcoholic Korsakoff's syndrome, or whether the two types of memory loss are qualitatively different. Ryan et al. (1980) found evidence of significant deficits on a range of verbal and non-verbal memory tasks when the tests were administered to long-term alcoholics who were detoxified. Their performance fell midway between that of normal controls and patients with alcoholic Korsakoff's syndrome (see Kapur and Butters, 1977). In a larger series of patients, Brandt et al. (1983) found significant impairment on a symbol-digit learning task in chronic alcoholic patients, although their deficit was not as severe as that which had been found in those with alcoholic Korsakoff's syndrome. Becker et al. (1983a) found impaired face-name learning in chronic alcoholic patients, but here again the deficit was not as severe as that of subjects with Korsakoff's syndrome. There were no significant differences between alcoholic patients and control patients in the types of errors, and no specific evidence to relate the deficits of alcoholic patients to increased sensitivity to proactive interference, as has been found in subjects with Korsakoff's syndrome.

Butters (1985) has analysed the types of errors made by alcoholic patients and those with Korsakoff's syndrome on a verbal short-term memory task and found infrequent occurrence of errors related to proactive interference (intralist intrusions) in alcoholic patients, compared to the frequency of these errors in subjects with Korsakoff's syndrome. In a similar vein, Markowitsch, Kessler and Denzler (1986) remarked on the high level of false positive responses given by patients with Korsakoff's syndrome compared to chronic (abstinent) alcoholics.

Recent years have witnessed the availability of imaging procedures which can provide direct evidence of the presence of cerebral lesions in chronic alcoholic subjects. Several investigators (e.g. Lishman, Ron and Acker, 1980; Cala, 1983) have noted the presence of cortical atrophy and ventricular dilatation in chronic alcoholic subjects. Bergman et al. (1980) found a correlation between memory performance and measures of ventricular dilatation in chronic alcoholics. Width of the frontal horns and width of the third ventricle, but not estimates of cortical atrophy, were significantly associated with scores on a verbal-learning task and a memory-for-designs test. It is worth noting, however, that almost 20% of their sample had a previous hospital admission for head injury and a similar percentage had a past history of epilepsy. In a paper referred to earlier, Wilkinson and Carlen (1980) found a strong correlation between memory performance (subtest scores of the Wechsler Memory Scale) and measures of cortical and ventricular atrophy, but this relationship disappeared when age was partialled out of the correlation. Both Ron (1983) and Acker et al. (1984) reported the absence of any clear relationship between the degree of memory impairment and extent of cerebral pathology as indicated by CT measures. Indeed, for some memory test scores (e.g. immediate prose recall) Ron (1983) found a positive correlation between performance and aspects of ventricular or cortical widening! Using more sophisticated CT scan measurements, Gebhardt, Naeser and Butters (1984) found that in chronic alcoholic subjects long-term memory (assessed by paired-associate learning) but not short-term memory (assessed by a Brown–Peterson task) correlated with CT density numbers in the thalamic region, presumably reflecting atrophy of thalamic nuclei, and with third ventricle enlargement. More specifically, verbal and non-verbal paired-associate learning correlated with CT density measures relating to both left and right dorsomedial thalamic nuclei, and verbal paired-associate learning correlated with width of the third ventricle. There were no significant hemispheric asymmetries in the sets of correlations, although there was a higher correlation between non-verbal paired-associate learning and right thalamic rather than left thalamic CT measures.

Retrograde memory deficits

Few detailed investigations have been carried on the retrograde memory deficits of chronic alcoholic subjects. One study which did examine this topic was that of Albert, Butters and Levin (1980), who administered retrograde memory tests which assessed both memory for famous faces and memory for public events. They found that chronic alcoholic subjects performed slightly lower than normal subjects for items relating to the 1960s and 1970s, but none of the differences between alcoholic and control subjects reached statistical significance. However, Cohen and Squire (1981), using a famous faces retrograde amnesia test, did report significantly lower scores by chronic alcoholic subjects for items relating to the 1970s.

Other toxic conditions

While considerable clinical evidence exists on the presence of psychological symptoms in chronic toxic states other than prolonged alcohol abuse (Lishman, 1987), much of the evidence with regard to neuropsychological test performance is somewhat inconclusive and hampered by methodological difficulties. These include controlling for possible pre-existing low intellectual status in the population under study (Parsons and Farr, 1981) and, in the case of some studies (e.g. Tsushima and Towne, 1977), distinguishing chronic versus acute effects of drug usage. In addition, relatively few investigations have reported detailed memory testing of subjects.

Marijuana and heroin

Considerable research has been carried out on the acute effects of marijuana on memory (Darley and Tinkleberg, 1974), but relatively less attention has been paid to persistent effects of long-term marijuana use on memory functioning. Satz, Fletcher and Sutker (1976) administered a large series of memory tests to long-term marijuana users, and found no significant differences between their performance and that of control subjects. However, Gianutsos and Litwack (1976) did find impaired performance on the more difficult portions of a short-term verbal memory task in a group of chronic marijuana smokers. Although subjects had been specifically asked not to smoke before the experiment, they were all regular users of the drug (twice a week and more in the previous 3 months). It remains possible that some residual acute effects of drug intake might have contributed towards some of the impairment. Intact memory functioning has been noted in subjects with a history of marijuana use (Schaeffer, Andrysiak and Ungerleider, 1981) and those who have included marijuana within a setting of polydrug abuse (Bruhn and Maage, 1975). Normal performance on most memory tests was also reported by Stern and Langston (1985) in a group of heroin addicts with MPTP (1-methyl-phenyl-1,2,3,6-tetrahydropyridine)-induced parkinsonism, although some impairment was found on tests which assessed orientation and naming of past presidents.

Organic solvents

Studies of other toxic substances, in particular organic solvents, have provided a large body of evidence on memory dysfunction as part of a 'toxic encephalopathy' syndrome (Lindstrom, 1982). However, it is seldom clear whether memory deficits refer solely to chronic sequelae, or reflect a combination of chronic and acute effects related to recent exposure to the toxin in question. In addition, while groups such as solvent inhalers have shown some evidence of memory impairment, this may be in the context of polydrug abuse (e.g. Berry, Heaton and Kirby, 1977), and so any deficits could be due to the interactive effects of substances rather than the single compound in question. Memory deficits have been reported in painters or those exposed to solvents used in the paint industry (Iregren, 1982; Olson, 1982). Hanninen et al. (1976) noted such deficits to be mainly evident on verbal memory tasks, although in a study where memory tests were more non-verbal in content, impairment was also found (Elofsson et al., 1980). Arlien-Soborg et al. (1979) reported memory impairment in approximately 50% of house painters, but it is important to note that this was a selected sample, since patients in the study were referred 'because organic solvent intoxication or dementia was suspected'. No test data from matched control subjects were reported. A follow-up study of patients from this group (Bruhn *et al.*, 1981) did not ascertain any significant progression or recovery of the deficits initially observed, although in a single-case study of a patient exposed to trichloroethylene, Stracciari *et al.* (1985) did observe some improvement in tests of immediate memory over a 10 month follow-up period.

Mercury

A number of studies have indicated that a relationship may be found between memory performance and amount of exposure to mercury, as indicated for example by mercury levels in urine (Smith, Langolf and Goldberg, 1983), but for much of this evidence it is not possible to distinguish chronic from more acute effects of mercury exposure. Vroom and Greer (1972) reported impaired performance both on the Wechsler Memory Scale and on a test of faces memory in subjects with mercury vapour intoxication, and in most of these subjects such deficits persisted 20 months after exposure to mercury was terminated. They pointed to the focal nature of the memory impairment, with other cognitive functions relatively preserved, and also remarked on the temporal lobe EEG abnormality which was found in some of their patients. Subjects with long-term exposure to mercury have also been found to be impaired on tests of verbal paired-associate learning (Williamson, Teo and Sanderson, 1982), although the fact that this study found a correlation between active contact with mercury and memory test performance suggests that the authors may have detected acute as well as chronic effects of mercury exposure. Hanninen (1982) has reviewed evidence indicating that a relationship exists between amount of exposure to mercury and memory impairment, especially in the case of visual, non-verbal memory tasks. A recent study (Uzzell and Oler, 1986) found evidence for impairment on a visual non-verbal memory task (recurrent recognition of nonsense figures) in a group of dental workers with elevated mercury levels, while on a verbal learning task their performance was unimpaired. However, it is worth noting that the reported raw data indicated considerable overlap between the scores of the mercury-exposed and control subjects, and that the statistical test applied to the test scores was one-tailed rather than two-tailed.

Lead

Evidence relating memory deficits to exposure to lead is somewhat more inconclusive, with some studies (e.g. Baloh *et al.*, 1975; Hanninen *et al.*, 1978) failing to find significant memory deficits in subjects with chronic exposure to lead, and other investigations (e.g. Grandjean, Arnvig and Beckmann, 1978) reporting evidence of such impairment on certain tests (long-term retention of visual designs). In the case of other possible industrial toxins, Knave *et al.* (1978) examined workers exposed to jet fuel but did not find any evidence of specific memory deficits.

Other drugs

A number of drugs used in the routine treatment of medical conditions, especially neurological disorders, have been implicated in memory disturbance. The possible side-effects of anticonvulsant medication, and antiparkinsonian drugs, have been reviewed in the chapters dealing with the relevant disease. A relationship has been noted between memory impairment and concentrations of digoxin, used to treat certain cardiac diseases. For example, Tucker and Ng (1983) found a correlation between plasma digoxin levels and performance on a word-list learning task in cardiac patients. A condition resembling transient global amnesia has been noted in association with intake of clioquinol, usually after ingestion of antidiarrhoea medication which contains this substance (Ferrier and Eadie, 1973; Mumenthaler *et al.*, 1979). Some of the distinctive features of this transient amnesia, compared to the more usual descriptions of transient global amnesia, include the delay in onset (usually 12–24 hours) of the memory disturbance from the time of clioquinol intake, the relatively long period of impaired memory functioning (sometimes lasting for several days), and the frequency with which a significant degree of retrograde amnesia (ranging from a few days to several months) remained as a residual deficit.

The possibility that high aluminium levels may contribute to 'dialysis dementia' in certain patients was examined from the point of view of specific memory test performance (Rosati *et al.*, 1980), but they found no difference between the scores of dialysis patients with high serum-aluminium levels and those with normal levels. They did, however, point out that the levels in their study may have been slightly lower than the toxic range necessary for memory test deficits to be evident.

Other deficiency states

Few studies have reported systematic memory testing of deficiency conditions other than the thiamine deficiency state associated with the Wernicke-Korsakoff syndrome. Jollife *et al.* (1940) noted the presence of confabulation and disorientation in patients with nicotinic acid deficiency, although this was usually associated with chronic alcohol abuse, and the authors did not report specific memory test scores. Shulman (1967) administered a verbal memory test in his investigation of patients receiving vitamin B_{12} for the treatment of pernicious anaemia. Compared to a control group, composed mainly of patients with iron-deficiency anaemia, the former group was significantly impaired on the memory task. On retesting after vitamin replacement therapy, nine out of 12 patients available for retesting showed improved memory performance. This improvement occurred, on average, 16 days after the first vitamin injection, and in two patients it was evident 20 hours after the onset of treatment. Treatment of folic acid deficiency states has also been shown to lead to improvement in memory function (Botez *et al.*, 1979), although it is of note that in the study by Albert *et al.* (1982) referred to earlier, no significant correlation was found between folic acid levels and memory performance in alcoholic subjects assessed during the early withdrawal phase. Finally, intestinal malabsorption due to coeliac disease has also been associated with folate deficiency, but no memory test impairment was found by Hallert and Astrom (1983) in their study of such patients.

Distinctive features of memory disorders in patients with toxic and deficiency states

Most comparisons between the memory disorders associated with toxic and deficiency states, and those of other aetiologies, have centred on patients with alcoholic Korsakoff's syndrome. A number of the studies which have compared the memory disorders of these patients with those found in other forms of cerebral pathology have been reviewed by Parkin (1984). He pointed to a number of features which appeared to distinguish the memory performance of patients with alcoholic Korsakoff's syndrome. These included more frequent instances of confabulation; lack of insight and lack of concern into memory difficulties, perhaps related to more marked frontal lobe pathology in patients with alcoholic Korsakoff's syndrome compared to most other conditions; a greater likelihood of short-term memory deficits in patients with alcoholic Korsakoff's syndrome and a slower rate of forgetting compared to some other amnesic conditions. Most of these observations were, however, made on the basis of comparisons across separate studies rather than formal comparisons in a single study. In addition, in the comparisons with other aetiologies, a number of other conditions (e.g. third ventricle tumours) were grouped along with patients with alcoholic Korsakoff's syndrome (and subsumed under the term 'diencephalic' amnesia). Few studies have systematically compared the memory performance of these patients with that of patients of other aetiologies who have been matched for severity of amnesia, additional cognitive deficits, age, and premorbid intellectual level.

Turning to studies which have made direct comparisons between memory functioning of patients with alcoholic Korsakoff's syndrome and those of other aetiologies, a number of these studies have already been reviewed in earlier chapters. The reader is therefore referred to Chapter 4 for comparisons with memory deficits in patients with penetrating head injury, to Chapter 6 for comparisons of memory functioning in patients with alcoholic Korsakoff's syndrome and in the dementias, and to Chapter 7 for comparisons with memory disorders in infectious and metabolic diseases. Most of these comparisons, as well as those considered below, have assessed the memory performance of patients with alcoholic Korsakoff's syndrome in relation to other neurological conditions. As might be expected, comparisons between the memory performance of patients with Korsakoff's syndrome and subjects suffering from psychiatric conditions such as depression have demonstrated markedly inferior performance of the former subjects (Kopelman, 1986b). However, it is worth noting that this study found similar levels of performance in the two groups on a few tests of short-term verbal memory – forward digit span, repetition of semantically anomalous sentences, and learning of easily associated paired-associate items.

Samuels et al. (1971) compared the short-term memory performance of patients with cortical lesions with that of patients with alcoholic Korsakoff's syndrome, and found that while there were similar levels of impairment in the two patient groups, two differences did emerge: first, some patients with cortical lesions, in particular those with left frontal and left parietal lesions, performed less well than patients with alcoholic Korsakoff's syndrome in certain verbal memory conditions when there was no delay between presentation and retention testing; second, the performance of patients with Korsakoff's syndrome was characterized by higher levels of perseverative errors than that of cortically lesioned and control patients. A limitation of this study was the fact that the patients with cortical lesions represented a variety of aetiologies, including cerebrovascular disease, penetrating head injury and post-tumour removal, and so it is not possible to reach specific conclusions regarding the unique contribution of a specific cortical pathology on memory performance. In a later study, where the aetiology was restricted to subjects with temporal lobe ablation, Samuels et al. (1980) found that these patients were not affected by interference effects in their verbal short-term memory performance, as has often been reported to be the case for patients with alcoholic Korsakoff's syndrome.

Moscovitch (1982b), in a frequently quoted study, also assessed memory functioning in patients with cortical ablation, in this case patients with excision of frontal lobe tissue. Although he did not make a direct comparison with the performance of patients with alcoholic Korsakoff's syndrome, he did note similar patterns of performance in some of his patients, namely a build-up of proactive interference which persisted following a change in the category of material to be learned. The memory functioning of a patient (H.M.), who underwent bilateral excision of temporal lobe, hippocampus and amygdala (see p. 205) has also been compared with that of patients with alcoholic Korsakoff's syndrome. Huppert and Piercy (1979) reported normal rates of forgetting of pictorial material by the latter, but abnormally fast rates by H.M. However, as Weiskrantz (1985) has pointed out, the initial retention values for H.M. and the patients with alcoholic Korsakoff's syndrome differed somewhat, and may have contributed to the differences in rates of forgetting; in addition, a normal rate of forgetting by H.M. was reported by Freed, Corkin and Cohen (1984) when a slightly different recognition testing procedure was employed.

Huppert (1981) has also compared forgetting rates for pictorial material by 'split-brain' patients and by patients with alcoholic Korsakoff's syndrome. Two of the three split-brain patients performed similarly to the alcoholic patients in showing impaired acquisition and normal rates of forgetting; the remaining patient performed much better than the alcoholic patients, and his scores were not significantly different from those of control subjects. Marslen-Wilson and Teuber (1975) compared the retrograde memory performance of H.M. with that of patients with alcoholic Korsakoff's syndrome on a test requiring identification of famous faces. They noted that the latter patients' retrograde amnesia showed a temporal gradient with marked impairment relating to items from the 1960s, to normal scores for items dated to the 1920s. However, H.M. performed similarly to control subjects for items which were dated prior to his surgery in 1953, whereas for personalities who became famous in the 1950s and 1960s, he in fact performed somewhat worse than patients with alcoholic Korsakoff's syndrome. When H.M. and patients with alcoholic Korsakoff's syndrome were given cues to aid identification of the faces, their performance approached that of control subjects, although H.M. was still impaired for items relating to the 1960s. However, since control subjects showed ceiling effects on the cued recall portion of the task, no firm conclusions can be reached on the relative performance of H.M. and patients with alcoholic Korsakoff's syndrome under this condition.

Few studies have compared memory functioning in remaining toxic or deficiency states with that found in other neurological conditions. However, one investigation, (Eskelinen et al., 1986), has pointed to somewhat lower performance on memory tests, especially digit span and design reproduction, by patients with a history of solvent intoxication, compared to patients suffering from vertebrobasilar insufficiency or patients who incurred a mild to moderate blunt head injury.

Summary

A large number of studies have attested to the deleterious effects of chronic alcohol consumption on memory performance. In the case of patients with alcoholic Korsakoff's syndrome, memory impairment is usually evident on tasks which exceed a patient's immediate memory span or where retention for subspan information is tested after an interval filled with distracting activity. The latter deficit has not been reported by all research workers, and it possible that methodological and patient variables account for part of this discrepancy. Retention deficits in longer-term memory situations occur both for the information itself and contextual features of the information (e.g. frequency, recency of presentation). Rates of forgetting of some types of material appear to be normal in patients with alcoholic Korsakoff's syndrome, although conceptual and methodological issues remain to be clarified in respect of such data. Retrograde amnesia is an invariable feature of the memory function of patients with alcoholic Korsakoff's syndrome, and some studies have reported greater memory loss for recent compared to more distant events. In contrast to these sets of deficits shown by these alcoholic patients, performance on perceptual learning tasks, where memory testing is usually secondary to the task itself, has been much less impaired, and in some instances approaches that of control subjects. No satisfactory explanation for such selectivity of preserved learning has yet been hypothesized, but one possibility is that impaired and intact memory functioning in patients with alcoholic Korsakoff's syndrome reflect the operation of limbic system structures and areas of the association cortex respectively. Evidence to confirm or refute this type of hypothesis may emerge from online studies of cerebral metabolic activity of patients with alcoholic Korsakoff's syndrome during 'explicit' and 'implicit' tests of retention. The relationship in patients with alcoholic Korsakoff's syndrome between memory functioning and brain damage to particular anatomical structures or neurochemical pathways remains a matter of some debate. Post-mortem evidence exists to support both the mamillary bodies and the dorsomedial nuclei of the thalamus as being critical to the presence of the memory disorder shown by these patients. No firm relationship has yet been established between CT scan measures of cerebral structure and memory performance of these patients. Some researchers have suggested the importance of a disturbance in the cholinergic system for the occurrence of alcoholic Korsakoff patients' memory deficits, although some conflicting evidence has also been reported.

Long-term alcohol abuse, without the occurrence of a Wernicke's encephalopathy, may itself lead to some degree of memory impairment. Significant issues remain unresolved, such as the exact quantification of 'long-term alcohol abuse', the characterization of the memory impairment and its underlying pathology, and an explanation of individual differences in degree of memory impairment. It is possible that individual differences in brain metabolic reactivity to the toxic effects of alcohol may play an important role, and that in some subjects such effects as this may be accelerated by the normal effects of ageing. While the presence of memory impairment and cerebral atrophy in chronic alcoholics is fairly well established, no satisfactory explanation has been offered to account for the presence of these deficits and the relationship, causal or otherwise, that exists between them (see Parsons and Leber, 1981). It is possible that subjects who become chronic abusers of alcohol have a pre-existing cognitive impairment, which includes some degree of memory difficulty, and that this helps to accelerate the development of an addiction to alcohol. Non-verbal visuospatial memory and learning tasks appear to be more sensitive in detecting memory deficits in chronic alchoholics than more verbal tasks, although it is as yet unclear if this is secondary to task variables or whether it reflects susceptibility of specific brain regions to the toxic effects of alcohol.

Memory deficits have also been reported in other toxic conditions, such as chronic marijuana abuse and toxic encephalopathies related to long-term solvent exposure. However, the relatively small number of studies and the somewhat variable findings suggest that such findings should be interpreted with caution. Similarly, other deficiency states, such as nicotinic acid deficiency, have been found to lead to impaired memory functioning, but here again the relevant studies are small in number.

Chapter 9

Epilepsy

Among the range of neurological diseases discussed in this book, epilepsy is unique in that it represents a set of clinical phenomena rather than a specific cerebral pathology. Thus, epilepsy may arise from a number of neurological disease processes, ranging from cerebral tumours to penetrating head injury. Ideally, therefore, any discussion of epilepsy should be categorized on the basis of the original pathology. However, in many cases of epilepsy a definitive pathology cannot be ascertained, and more general descriptions, such as 'birth injury', may mask a range of discrete pathologies. It is possible that with advances in diagnostic and imaging procedures, a neuropathological classification of the epilepsies may be feasible, but for the present we are left with a somewhat broad-ranging term which obviously is in need of refinement. It is not surprising, therefore, that there is no definitive classification of the various types of epilepsy. The classification indicated in *Table 9.1* is taken in part from that provided by Marsden and Reynolds (1982).

Patients suffering from epilepsy may show a variable degree of cognitive impairment, ranging from severe mental handicap to the absence of any significant impairment (Brown and Reynolds, 1981). In mentally handicapped patients, the presence of memory impairment will often be clouded by general intellectual deficits. In patients where the epilepsy is a manifestation of a more focal cerebral disease, memory impairment may be the only evidence of cognitive impairment. Memory deficits in epilepsy may be due to a variety of factors: the disease process underlying the occurrence of epileptic fits; damage to the brain which occurs as a result of fits (e.g. hypoxia during the fit, concussion if the patient incurs a head injury, etc.); and any adverse side-effects of anticonvulsant medication the patient may be taking. In addition to persistent memory impairment which some epileptic patients may show between fits, more transient memory deficits can occur during clinical or subclinical epileptiform discharges (Woodruff, 1974). While these may occur spontaneously in the form of phenomena such as transient global amnesia (Deisenhammer, 1981), they have been more commonly studied in situations where electrical activity in the brain has been specifically induced. In some studies, such activity has been initiated by external sensory stimulation. In other studies, electrical stimulation of cortical tissue at the time of surgery has been used as a means of evaluating the integrity and role of certain areas of the brain in various aspects of memory functioning. The following sections will consider persistent memory impairments which have been found in epileptic patients, review the chronic effects of anticonvulsant medication on memory performance in epileptic patients, and consider the effects of brain stimulation in epileptic subjects.

Table 9.1 Classification of epilepsy

(1) Generalized

    (a) tonic-clonic (grand mal)
    (b) tonic
    (c) atonic
    (d) absence (petit mal)
    (e) atypical absence
    (f) myoclonic

(2) Partial (focal)

    (a) without impairment of consciousness (simple partial epilepsy)
    (b) with impairment of consciousness (complex partial epilepsy)
        (i)   with motor signs (e.g. Jacksonian)
        (ii)   with somato- or special sensory symptoms (e.g. olfactory, visual)
        (iii) with autonomic features (e.g. epigastric sensations)
        (iv)   with psychic symptoms (e.g. fear, déjà vu)
        (v)   with automatisms (complex partial epilepsy alone)

(3) Partial epilepsy secondarily generalized

    Clinical or electrical evidence of focal discharge during or after the generalized seizure

(4) Unclassifiable

    Seizures which cannot be classified because of incomplete data

Inter-ictal studies

In this section, I will deal with studies of memory functioning in epileptic patients who were assessed when free from any epileptic attacks. This 'inter-ictal' assessment of memory performance is to be contrasted with 'ictal' studies, to be reviewed later, which have assessed memory functioning during an episode of epileptiform activity. Large-scale studies of relatively heterogeneous groups of epileptic patients have invariably found some degree of memory impairment. Loiseau *et al.* (1980) assessed 100 epileptics who were leading relatively normal lives, and who did not show any evidence of specific cerebral pathology. He reported that on the Wechsler Adult Intelligence Scale digit span test, visual reproduction subtest of the Wechsler Memory Scale, and the Rey list learning test (Lezak, 1983), epileptic patients performed at a lower level than controls. In a subsequent study of 200 patients with similar characteristics, Loiseau *et al.* (1983) also found significant memory impairment using similar memory tests. Some studies have reported memory test deficits to be particularly evident on certain tasks, e.g. delayed recall of designs (Deutsch, 1953), and to be absent on tasks with a greater perceptual learning component (Scott *et al.*, 1967). Loiseau *et al.* (1982) argued that memory deficits were more apparent at the acquisition rather than retention stage on the basis of their particular memory test battery.

    The importance of controlling for general intellectual level when considering memory performance of epileptic patients is indicated by a study by Tomlinson *et al.* (1981) who found a difference in verbal recognition performance for visually presented material between control subjects and a mixed group of patients of varying types of epilepsy. However, when verbal IQ differences between the two groups were partialled out, no memory deficit remained. Significant recognition memory impairment for words and for faces stimuli was reported by Brittain (1980) in a relatively unselected group of 157 epileptics, although the actual raw scores for verbal items suggest that the deficit was quite mild for this material. Loiseau *et al.* (1983) found that the most marked memory impairment was found in patients whose epilepsy began during adolescence, compared to earlier or later onset times. In contrast, neither Glowinski (1973) nor Delaney *et al.* (1980) found age of onset of epilepsy to have an effect on memory performance.

While investigations such as these have confirmed the presence of memory impairment in epileptic populations, more valuable information has come from an analysis of the extent to which the presence and severity of memory impairment is related to features of the epileptic focus.

Features of the epileptic focus

While some epileptic patients have a structural lesion underlying their condition, a large proportion of patients show no evidence of specific pathology, and no abnormality may be detectable on CT scanning. In the study by Brittain (1980) referred to earlier, she observed that those epileptic patients with a known aetiology performed worse on some memory tests than those whose aetiology could not be established. Quadfasel and Pruyser (1955) found a higher incidence of memory impairment, especially on verbal memory tasks, in patients with epilepsy associated with anterior or temporal lobe spike focus (the 'psychomotor group), compared to patients with more generalized EEG abnormality ('grand mal group'), even though both groups were matched for IQ level. Using a visual memory task (recall of designs), Schwartz and Dennerll (1969) found that in their epileptic patients, the lowest scores emanated from patients with combined 'grand mal' and 'psychomotor' epilepsy, with the psychomotor component appearing to contribute most to the memory deficit. Classifications of epileptic patients using such terminology may sometimes be somewhat arbitrary, and may often lead to differences in patient populations between studies. More recent investigations have usually avoided such terminology and employed more specific EEG criteria for describing particular patient subgroups.

Patients with epilepsy originating in the temporal lobes have been found to be particularly impaired on memory tasks, compared to patients with more generalized epileptic disturbance, and to patients whose foci which have been localized to other regions of the brain. Considering the first type of comparison, Fedio and Mirsky (1969) found that while children with left temporal lobe epilepsy performed poorly on word-list recall, children with right temporal lobe epilepsy performed poorly on recall of the Rey-Osterreith figure, and those with centrencephalic epilepsy did not perform poorly on memory tasks. Centrencephalic epilepsy was defined as the presence of bilateral synchronous and symmetrical spike-wave activity, although the actual focus of the discharge may be in subcortical structures such as the thalamic nuclei or reticular activating system. On a test of sustained attention, these patients performed lower than either temporal lobe group. Using an older population of epileptic patients, Glowinski (1973) reached a similar set of conclusions, noting that patients with chronic unilateral temporal lobe epilepsy had more marked memory deficits than patients with centrencephalic epilepsy. Although there was a tendency towards material-specific memory deficits in patients with right and temporal lobe lesions, this did not reach statistical significance, probably due to the relative insensitivity of the tests used (subtests of the Wechsler Memory Scale).

Epileptic patients with bilateral EEG abnormality were noted by Mirsky *et al.* (1960) to perform less well on memory tests than those with unilateral temporal lobe abnormality, although the differences were relatively small, and the memory test scores of the bitemporal abnormality group did not indicate the presence of an amnesic syndrome. In this study, patients with centrencephalic epilepsy performed at a similar level to those with unilateral temporal lobe EEG abnormality. Mayeux *et al.* (1980) did not find any significant differences in memory test performance between patients with generalized epilepsy and those with right- or left-sided temporal lobe epilepsy, defined in terms of EEG focus (all patients had normal CT scans). They used a variety of tests, including consonant trigram retention, recall of the Rey-Osterreith figure, the Benton Visual Retention Test, or prose recall and paired-associate learning subtests of the Wechsler Memory Scale. All three groups performed at similar levels on the various memory tests, although the group with a lesion in the right temporal lobe was slightly better than the two remaining groups, both on overall Wechsler memory quotient and on the consonant trigram recall task. However, they did find a significantly lower score in the group with a lesion in the left temporal lobe on the picture naming test, and found that impairment on this task correlated with memory test scores. They suggested that some form of anomia may have contributed to memory symptoms of the left temporal lobe epileptic patients. A limitation of this study was the absence of memory test data from matched control subjects.

Loiseau *et al.* (1983) found that epileptic patients with bilateral spike-wave EEG abnormality showed more marked memory impairment than those with anterior or temporal abnormalities in either hemisphere. A similar pattern of results was reported by Rausch, Lieb and Crandall (1978), who assessed laterality of inter-ictal discharges from stereotactically placed electrodes in the region of the hippocampus and amygdala in patients with intractable temporal lobe epilepsy. Bilateral mesial temporal EEG abnormality, as indicated by recordings from the implanted electrodes, was associated with lower memory performance than was more unilateral abnormality. The degree of spike activity from each mesial temporal side did not correlate with specific memory test scores, although this absence of any correlation may have been due in part to the disproportionate number of patients with greater right hemisphere spike activity (eight out of 12 patients) and to the limited number of non-verbal memory tests used.

The assessment of memory functioning in epileptic patients at the time of an epileptic discharge is limited by the relative unpredictability of such events. However, some studies have attempted to correlate the two sets of observations, and have yielded some important findings. Symptoms offered by the patient, such as enforced recollection of images from the past, have long been associated with temporal lobe epilepsy (Hill and Mitchell, 1953). Using technology by which EEG activity can be monitored both inside and outside the laboratory by remote sensing devices, Gloor *et al.* (1982) were able to document the onset of abnormal memory events (e.g. feelings resembling déjà vu) and to show that they were contiguous with the onset of abnormal discharges from medial temporal structures such as the hippocampus. Kapur *et al.* (unpublished data) have recently examined a patient who reported experiential phenomena which included being in a dream-like state, often characterized by a particular image of someone in green, and on a few occasions she also experienced enforced recall of scenes from the distant past. Her CT scan (*Figure 9.1*) showed bilateral hippocampal calcification; her neuropsychological test profile indicated normal functioning on most cognitive tasks, with the exception of marked impairment on a visual design learning task.

Geller and Geller (1970) presented material to patients during continuous EEG monitoring. Test material consisted of pictures, letters or numbers, and a 10-second interval occurred between presentation and recall. Where a burst of paroxysmal activity occurred during this interval, memory was impaired for the material in question. A temporal gradient in the amnesic effects was observed, such that bursts which occurred immediately after presentation produced the greatest impairment, whereas those which began 4 seconds or more after presentation had no effect. Direct monitoring of EEG responses from medial temporal structures during memory testing has established the importance of the hippocampal formation, especially the hippocampal gyrus, in memory functioning (Halgren, Babb and Crandall, 1978). Aarts *et al.* (1984) showed that transient cognitive impairment, in the form of impaired performance on verbal or non-verbal short-term memory tasks which assessed memory for sequence, could be obtained in epileptic patients with subclinical EEG discharges. In 50% of patients who showed such discharges without any overt clinical changes, transient memory impairment was evident. Discharges during stimulus presentation were most disruptive of performance, whereas those confined to the period when the patient was offering a response did not have any significant effect. A relationship was found between laterality of discharge and impairment on verbal or non-verbal tasks; left-sided discharges being associated with errors on the verbal memory task, and right-sided discharges with errors on the non-verbal memory test.

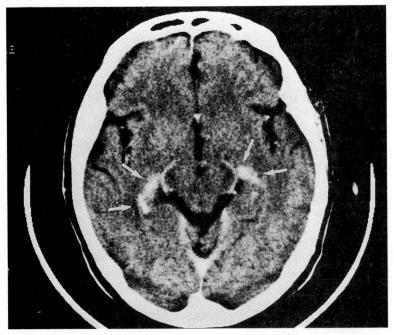

Figure 9.1 CT scan of a patient with temporal lobe epilepsy. Bilateral calcification (arrowed) can be seen in both right and left hippocampi.

In the case of comparisons of epileptogenic lesions specific to particular cortical regions, Milner (1962) found that patients with left temporal lobe epileptogenic lesions performed worse on delayed verbal recall than patients with corresponding right temporal pathology, and worse than patients with parietal or frontal pathology (the laterality of these lesions was not indicated). Patients with epileptic foci in the frontal lobes performed normally on a test of delayed story recall (Milner, 1958). Delaney et al. (1980) administered verbal and non-verbal memory tests to patients with unilateral seizure foci in the left temporal lobe, right temporal lobe or either frontal lobe. Patients with left temporal lobe lesions were impaired on verbal memory tasks, those with right temporal lobe lesions on non-verbal memory tasks, while patients with unilateral frontal lobe foci did not differ from control subjects. The difference between patients with right and left temporal lobe lesions was more evident on delayed than immediate recall of verbal or non-verbal material, and was also evident on a recurring-figures recognition memory task.

A later study by Delaney, Prevey and Mattson (1986), using a Brown–Peterson paradigm, shed further light on the possible role of short-term versus longer-term memory functioning in epileptic patients. They found impaired short-term recall of verbal material in epileptic patients with left or right temporal lobe foci, but an absence of deficits on a non-verbal short-term memory task. It is possible, however, that different retention testing procedures in the two tests (free recall for the verbal memory task and free-choice recognition for the non-verbal memory task) may have contributed towards the differing difficulty levels in the two tests. Lavadas, Umilta and Provinciali (1979) examined epileptic patients with foci in the right temporal, left temporal, right frontal or left frontal lobe. They found significant material-specific differences between patients with right and left temporal lobe lesions on tests of verbal and non-verbal long-term memory (learning of items greater than immediate span, recall of items after a delay). Analogous material-specific differences on verbal and non-verbal tests of memory for recency information were evident in patients with left and right frontal foci. This study, however, failed to test control subjects on the various memory tasks, and it is difficult to gauge the severity of the apparent memory deficits which were found. A further demonstration of a specific pattern of memory deficits in patients with unilateral temporal lesions was provided by Masui et al. (1984) who assessed memory performance using tachistoscopically-presented verbal material. The groups with right or left temporal lobe lesions both showed impaired retention, but the group with a left temporal lobe lesion was consistently worse with material presented to the right visual field. In contrast, patients with right temporal lobe lesions and normal controls tended to show higher right visual field than left visual field retention scores. Specific impairment on the recency portion of the serial position curve (i.e. items from the end of the list) was found in a study of temporal lobe epileptics (Powell, Sutherland and Agu, 1984), although no information on the role of the laterality of the lesion was provided. It is possible that this finding may have reflected some degree of 'conduction dysphasia' in those with left temporal lobe lesions.

A different aspect of memory functioning, recall of pleasant or unpleasant past experiences, has been studied by Master et al. (1986) in patients with right- and left-sided temporal lobe epilepsy. While patients with left temporal lobe epilepsy showed the normal preference for recalling pleasant as compared to unpleasant experiences, no such significant difference was evident in the performance of the group with left temporal lobe epilepsy.

Other parameters, in addition to the anatomical ones listed above, have been highlighted in studies of memory functioning in epileptic patients. Delaney *et al.* (1980), in the study discussed earlier, found that fit frequency was unrelated to memory performance, although duration of epileptic illness showed a positive correlation with degree of memory impairment. In contrast, Loiseau *et al.* (1983) found that patients with a shorter duration of epilepsy had more memory deficits than other patients. It is possible that differences in the epileptic populations may underlie the discrepancy in the two studies. Finally, Dodrill (1986) noted that epileptic patients with a history of status epilepticus associated with generalized tonic-clonic seizures performed particularly poorly on non-verbal memory items compared to those with such seizures but without a history of status epilepticus.

The effects of anticonvulsant medication on memory performance in epileptic patients

Any pharmacological agents which have an effect on the central nervous system can potentially influence performance in memory tasks. Research workers in the field of epilepsy have documented this influence at some length, and have provided data both on epileptic and normal subjects (*see* Hirtz and Nelson (1985) for a review of such effects on memory and other cognitive functions). This section will focus on the effects of anticonvulsant drugs on memory performance in adult epileptic patients. When considering such studies, it is important to bear in mind the fact that the type and severity of epilepsy may often be related to specific drugs and dose levels; for example, patients with more severe epilepsy may receive higher doses of anticonvulsant drugs. In addition, any deleterious or beneficial effects on memory performance may be specific to the particular clinical paradigm adopted in the study.

It is also important to bear in mind whether toxic or high-versus-low dose levels of drugs are considered, how long a criterion dose of drug has been administered before possible side-effects are assessed, and whether or not patients remain on their previous medication when the effects of a new drug are considered. Thompson and Trimble (1981) reported an improvement in memory of epileptic patients for verbal and pictorial stimuli, most evident on delayed retention, following the introduction of carbamazepine therapy, either as a replacement for a single-drug regimen or as a substitute for one of the drugs in a polytherapy regimen. They also noted a tendency for improvement on one memory test (delayed recall of pictures) following reduced drug intake, with no alternative medication prescribed. These results could have been due to a decrease in the deleterious effects of the drugs which had been reduced, to improvement in seizure control, or to a beneficial effect of carbamazepine on memory. Andrewes *et al.* (1984) found differences between epileptic patients on phenytoin and patients on carbamazepine on a short-term memory scanning paradigm, where recognition memory for digits was assessed after brief tachistoscopic presentation of stimuli. Patients on carbamazepine showed superior performance. Other memory tasks, such as immediate and delayed word-list learning, immediate and delayed prose recall, and recognition of shapes after 90 seconds, did not show any significant differences, although the phenytoin patients generally scored below the carbamazepine patients. Using a short-term memory scanning paradigm, Macleod, De Kaban and Hunt (1978) found that blood levels of concentration of phenobarbitol affected reaction time in epileptic patients. However, Delaney *et al.* (1980), in the study referred to earlier, did not find any correlation between serum levels of phenobarbitol or phenytoin and memory performance.

Using a variety of verbal and picture memory tasks, and different retention intervals, Trimble and Thompson (1983) compared the effects of four drugs – phenytoin, carbamazepine, sodium valproate and clobazam – on cognitive function in healthy volunteers and patients with epilepsy. They found that the most significant adverse effects on performance came from phenytoin, with the other drugs not having any significant effects on memory functions. In a further report relating to the epileptic patients tested in this study, Thompson and Trimble (1983) observed that epileptic patients with high serum levels of anticonvulsant drugs showed greater memory impairment than those with low levels, with such differences being particularly evident on immediate and delayed story recall. They showed that when anticonvulsant medication was reduced, patients who were receiving polytherapy improved their memory performance. Further, when carbamazepine was substituted for another drug, cognitive function improved. In patients who changed to carbamazepine, there was a marked improvement in memory peformance, which became apparent 3 months after the change. In a similar type of study, Butlin, Danta and Cook (1984a) found impaired faces-recognition memory test performance to be associated with phenytoin administration in a group of epileptic patients, but not with carbamazepine or sodium valproate administration. In a later report (Butlin, Danta and Cook, 1984b), a correlation was reported between level of folate deficiency and memory performance, regardless of the type of drug being administered. Serum levels of the anticonvulsant drugs did show a correlation with memory performance, but this was no longer evident when age, IQ and folate levels were partialled out.

A few studies have focused specifically on the effects of sodium valproate. In epileptic patients who were prescribed this drug as monotherapy for their epilepsy, Trimble and Thompson (1984) reported that patients on higher doses showed greater impairment on immediate recall of pictures. In a different type of investigation, Sommerbeck, Theilgaard and Rasmussen (1977) compared the effects of placebo and sodium valproate in epileptic patients, most of whom continued with their previous medication (usually more than one anticonvulsant drug). Few significant differences were evident between the effects of sodium valproate and placebo on a verbal paired-associate learning task.

Ictal studies

Psychological stimulation

Hutt, Lee and Ounsted (1963) assessed four epileptic children, two of whom showed impaired digit recall when paroxysmal activity was evoked by stroboscopy (a form of flashing light stimulation). None of the children showed impaired recall when the digits were followed by stroboscopy at a frequency which did not evoke paroxysmal activity. In a further study of five epileptic children aged between 9 and 15 years, Hutt and Gilbert (1980) used photic stimulation to generate spike wave activity and found that recall of digits was impaired if a paroxysm of spike wave activity was generated between the end of presentation and the beginning of recall, and also observed that the last two digits of the digit span were more vulnerable to recall failure than the first two. Hutt, Lee and Ounsted (1963), in a discussion of similar observations, suggested that it was the hippocampal–mamillary system which played a part in some of the effects they found. Hutt and Lee (1968) presented a single case study of a child with photosensitive epilepsy. Digits were presented and 2 seconds afterwards a 4-second spike was evoked. Recall of digit sequences of five to seven numbers during the discharge was poorer than when recall was attempted after the discharge, and recall was at its highest level when it was initiated shortly before the onset of the spike wave.

Direct electrical stimulation of the brain

The ability of the human brain to cooperate with psychological testing, under conditions where electrodes are implanted for variable periods of time into certain structures, has afforded researchers the unique opportunity to observe changes in psychological function following stimulation of specific anatomical structures. It should be pointed out that the responses to such stimulation are subject to considerable individual differences (Halgren et al., 1978). It also needs to be borne in mind that patients who undergo stimulation have, of necessity, some abnormality of brain function. Although stimulation of non-diseased tissue in epileptic patients (Halgren et al., 1978) has also been found to result in distorted memory functioning, it remains possible that, in some cases, the findings may not necessarily represent normal brain behaviour relationships. Finally, parameters such as the intensity of electrical stimulation and extent of after-discharge to neighbouring or anatomically-connected regions, need to be taken into account when considering possible variability in observations between different studies.

Cortical regions

The evocation of memory phenomena, such as feelings of déjà vu, hallucinations which include memories from the recent and distant past, and the induction of transient amnesic episodes, have been well documented after stimulation of areas of the temporal lobe and adjacent structures (Baldwin, 1960; Penfield and Perot, 1963; Penfield, 1968; Gloor et al., 1982; Halgren et al., 1983). These 'experimental' phenomena were noted by Penfield to be relatively more common after stimulation of the right temporal lobe, and there was also a tendency for the evocation of visual images to be more closely associated with stimulation of right rather than left temporal regions. However, it should be pointed out that the occurrence of 'experiential' phenomena after brain stimulation is relatively infrequent in an unselected series of epileptic patients, and mainly occurs in some patients with temporal lobe epilepsy; the reliability of patients' reports of specific records of past experience is also open to question (Loftus and Loftus, 1980). In addition, auditory and visual hallucinations, without any significant element of past experience, have been reported after stimulation of the right temporal cortex and deeper regions of the temporal lobe (Ishibashi et al., 1964).

Stimulation of the hippocampus was reported by Penfield (1968) to result in no observable response, although a brief clinical report by Chapman et al. (1967) indicated that bilateral stimulation of the hippocampus resulted in significant memory disturbance, including some retrograde amnesia in one patient, whereas unilateral stimulation produced milder effects, mostly the evocation of fragmentary memories or visual images. In a larger-scale study, Weingarten, Cherlow and Halgren (1976) also reported memory-like hallucinations with stimulation of areas of the hippocampus, and Serafetinides and Walter (1978) reported that stimulation of the hippocampus, especially on the left side, resulted in episodes resembling transient global amnesia. In a detailed investigation of similar phenomena to those originally described by Penfield and others, Gloor *et al*. (1982) confirmed Penfield's basic observations, although some of their specific findings were different. They did not find any hemispheric asymmetry for experiential responses after right and left temporal lobe stimulation. Further, their findings tended to accord greater importance to limbic structures, such as the amygdala and hippocampus, rather than to neocortical temporal regions, as being critical to the occurrence of such responses after brain stimulation. It remains possible, however, that neocortical areas, especially areas of the association cortex, play a role in mediating experiential responses as a result of their connections with the limbic system (Halgren, 1984).

In more recent years, researchers have adopted experimental paradigms in which memory testing is carried out in conjunction with stimulation of cerebral regions. Retrograde amnesia for material which has been learned 1–2 hours previously has been reported after stimulation of medial temporal and hippocampal regions (Shandurina and Kalyagina, 1979; Shandurina, Kambarova and Kalyagina, 1982). This was found to occur in the absence of any post-stimulation anterograde memory difficulties. Ommaya and Fedio (1972) reported verbal and non-verbal short-term memory deficits after stimulation of the left and right caudate regions respectively, and an absence of any such deficits after stimulation of the left or right hippocampus. Stimulation of medial temporal structures at the time of stimulus presentation, or at the time of retention testing, has also been found to impair memory performance, with memory impairment being particularly marked when stimulation occurred both at presentation and at recognition testing (Halgren, Wilson and Stapelton, 1985). Relatively few studies have been carried out of other cortical regions, although one such study has implicated left anterior and left posterior temporal neocortex in anterograde and retrograde memory processes respectively (Fedio and Van Buren, 1974). However, a later investigation by Ojemann (1978) indicated the importance of posterior left-hemisphere cortical regions in storage of verbal material in short-term memory, and more anterior regions in retrieval processes.

Subcortical and related structures
Thalamic regions have been the main focus of studies which have examined the effects of stimulation of subcortical structures on memory functioning. Ojemann, Blick and Ward (1969) noted improved short-term verbal memory scores in patients who received left lateral thalamic stimulation during stimulus presentation, but this effect was restricted to those patients who did not show any evidence of confusion after left thalamotomy. Stimulation during the recall period, or between presentation and recall led to more impaired performance than stimulation at other periods. Corresponding right-thalamic stimulation did not produce any such changes. Ojemann, Blick and Ward (1971) studied the effects of thalamic stimulation on short-term memory of patients with Parkinson's disease. Significantly more recall errors occurred with stimulation of the left ventrolateral thalamus at the time of recall than under non-stimulation conditions. Stimulation both at the time of presentation and at the time of recall produced no change in error rates from non-stimulation levels, but fewer errors occurred than when stimulation was given during recall alone. Stimulation during presentation tended to decrease subsequent recall errors. Right ventrolateral thalamic stimulation did

not produce any change in recall errors under any test situation. The authors hypothesized that stimulation of the dominant ventrolateral thalamus directed attention to specific verbal features of the environment, and that this same process interfered with search in short-term memory.

Ojemann (1971) reported a case of intractable epilepsy, where a chronic depth electrode was stereotactically placed in the right thalamus. Short-term memory testing took place 7 days later. He reported findings relating to stimulation of the right mamillothalamic tract and stimulation of the medial zona incerta. When these structures were stimulated during presentation of a random shape, the patient could not recognize the shape 8 seconds later. Verbal memory was not affected by stimulation. Stimulation during retention testing did not have any effect on non-verbal memory performance. In a later study (Ojemann, 1975), similar facilitation effects were observed. It was also noted that more posterior stimulation of the lateral thalamus was more likely to result in retrieval deficits.

Stimulation of the amygdala was reported to result in hallucinations incorporating some element of past experience (*déjà vu*) (Weingarten, Cherlow and Halgren, 1976; Gloor *et al.*, 1982). Similarly, Fernandez-Guardiola (1977) noted that reminiscence phenomena, especially those relating to distant childhood memories rather than more recent memories, could be elicited by stimulation of the amygdala and neighbouring structures in the temporal lobe. Penfield (1968) reported that stimulation in or around the amygdala strong enough to produce an ictal discharge, resulted in a seizure characterized by automatic behaviour and amnesia. With regard to specific memory test performance, verbal and non-verbal short-term memory peformance was found to be unaffected by stimulation of the left and right amygdala (Ommaya and Fedio, 1972). Fedio and Van Buren (1975) did, however, report verbal and non-verbal memory deficits after left and right pulvinar stimulation respectively. Bechtereva *et al.* (1967) noted that incorrect responses on memory tasks could occur after stimulation of the caudate nucleus. Chronic stimulation of the cerebellum in patients with epilepsy or spasticity has, by contrast, been found to result in a slight improvement in memory performance (Riklan *et al.*, 1976).

Distinctive features of memory disorders in patients with epilepsy

As indicated at the beginning of the chapter, epileptic patients form a rather heterogeneous and poorly-defined group of patients from the point of view of neuropathological classification. This may, in part, account for the limited number of reports which have compared memory disorders in epilepsy with those found in other neurological conditions. At the level of persistent memory difficulties, no such comparisons appear to have been reported. A few observations have, however, been made on the differentiation of transient memory loss found in epilepsy with that found in other cerebral pathologies. Gallassi *et al.* (1986) described an epileptic patient with episodes of memory loss and considered that epileptic amnesic attacks differed from transient global amnesia in that they were of shorter duration (10–60 minutes in their case), of more frequent occurrence (their patient had 20 episodes in a single year), and showed a favourable response to anticonvulsant medication. Pritchard *et al.* (1984) also remarked on the shorter duration of epileptic amnesic attacks, and their reduction with anticonvulsant medication; in addition, they reported an absence of pre-ictal amnesia in such attacks, compared to its frequent occurrence in transient global amnesia. It is also worth noting that while some epileptic patients may experience hallucinations, sometimes with an element of past experience, these are generally distinguishable from illusions offered by psychotic patients in that epileptic patients usually retain some awareness of the incongruity of their experience and its separation from everyday reality.

Summary

Epileptic patients form a heterogeneous population of patients and the presence, pattern and severity of memory disturbance in patients examined inter-ictally will depend on several variables. The variable most consistently evident in the research reviewed in this chapter is the extent to which temporal lobe tissue appears to be the site of pathology underlying the epilepsy. The left- and right-sided focus of the epileptic discharges has also been frequently reported to be related to the presence of verbal/non-verbal memory deficits. There seem to be less data, and less agreement where ample data are available, with regard to other variables such as frequency or duration of fits, presence of an underlying structural lesion, etc. Anticonvulsant medication has been reported to have significant effects on memory function in epileptic patients, although a number of conceptual and methodological issues remain and need to be considered in the interpretation of such data. Phenytoin has been reported by a number of research workers to be associated with memory impairment. It also appears that monotherapy is associated with less memory impairment than is the administration of several anticonvulsant drugs.

Memory functioning has also been assessed at the time of epileptic discharge, either when this occurs spontaneously at a minor, subclinical level, or is induced by psychological stimulation or by direct electrical stimulation of cerebral tissue. Relatively few studies have been carried out of memory impairment associated with spontaneous, subclinical discharges, but the available evidence does suggest a close relationship between such discharges and the presence of memory impairment, with discharges occurring during or shortly after stimulus presentation being the most disruptive. Where paroxysmal activity is induced by psychological stimulation, memory performance appears to be more critically disturbed the closer the activity occurs in relation to attempted recall. Direct electrical stimulation of the brain has yielded a large variety of findings relating to memory functioning in some epileptic patients. Stimulation of structures in or adjacent to the temporal lobe, especially the amygdala and hippocampus, has been reported to evoke experiences ranging from familiar images from the past to transient amnesic episodes. Stimulation of such tissue during memory testing has been shown to have disruptive effects, either when it occurs at the time of stimulus presentation or at recall. Such effects have also been noted after stimulation of subcortical structures such as the thalamus, although in the case of thalamic stimulation this has been found to facilitate memory functioning if it occurs during stimulus presentation. Some clues have emerged from direct stimulation studies as to the relationship between anatomical structures and memory processes, with some evidence to suggest that more posterior regions of the limbic system are implicated in recall processes and more anterior regions involved in encoding functions. It remains to be seen whether subsequent research supports and clarifies this relationship, since this may offer clues to the neurological mechanisms underlying more persistent and more marked anterograde and retrograde memory disorders.

Chapter 10

Ablation/disconnection of cerebral tissue

One of the inherent limitations of studies of clinically based memory disorders, compared to corresponding animal studies, is that lesions caused by nature are seldom discrete and restricted to single anatomical structures. In addition, pre-lesion assessment is rarely possible, and so inferences about the significance of individual memory deficits must be made with reference to a separate normative population. There are, however, a number of clinical conditions where management of the patient may entail planned destruction of specific cerebral structures, and so some of these limitations will not apply. However, a number of qualifications about studies of memory functioning in such situations need to be borne in mind. First, all of the patients who have been subject to surgical destruction of brain tissue have suffered from a significant neurological or psychiatric illness, which has usually been intractable to other therapeutic measures; therefore, the preoperative level of cognitive functioning may often be impaired, and this impairment can be due both to the condition under treatment, and to any specific measures (drugs, electroconvulsive therapy, etc.) which have been used to alleviate it. Second, some of these factors may continue to operate to a variable degree after surgery, and in some cases a pre-existing lesion may interact with the effects of neurosurgical intervention. Third, the level and type of drug therapy may change after surgery, and this may also contribute to any changes in memory performance. Fourth, surgery may result in clinical improvement (e.g. reduction in fit frequency/fit severity) which indirectly results in changes over and above those occurring as a result of surgery. Finally, to allow for possible practice-effects, memory test scores before and after surgery need to be compared with test–retest data from control subjects before the significance of any changes in memory functioning can be ascertained.

In cases such as surgery for temporal lobe epilepsy, neurosurgical destruction of tissue has usually involved removal of physiologically abnormal brain tissue. In other conditions, such as those which necessitate leucotomy or commissurotomy, the tissue has been presumed to be free of any significant pathology, and some operations have consisted of sectioning of fibre connections rather than removal of tissue. In some instances, the boundary between normal and abnormal tissue, and between tissue removal on the one hand and fibre sectioning on the other, has been blurred. A final point of note is that unlike animal studies, human investigations of memory disorders after neurosurgical lesions have seldom had the benefit of post-mortem verification of variables such as extent of tissue destruction, or extent of collateral neural degeneration.

For the purposes of this chapter, studies of memory disorder after neurosurgical destruction of tissue have been grouped into four types: (1) the effects of frontal leucotomy on memory function; (2) the effects of sectioning of interhemispheric commissural fibres (commissurotomy); (3) the effects of frontal, temporal and hippocampal resection for treatment of conditions such as epilepsy; and (4) the effects of ablation of other cortical and subcortical areas in the brain.

Leucotomy

Few systematic studies of memory function after frontal leucotomy have been undertaken. As Stuss *et al.* (1981) have pointed out, most investigations in this field have concentrated on psychiatric sequelae rather than cognitive functioning. Although some degree of transient disorientation may be present in the immediate post-surgical period, the majority of studies have commented on the absence of marked memory deficits either in patients who have undergone more extensive frontal surgery, referred to in earlier studies as 'prefrontal lobotomy' (Struckett, 1953), or in those who received more limited lesions, as described in later frontal leucotomy studies (e.g. Mirsky and Orzack, 1980). The type of frontal lesion which may remain in patients who have undergone frontal leucotomy is illustrated in *Figure 10.1.* Walsh (1977) reported impaired performance on a maze-learning task

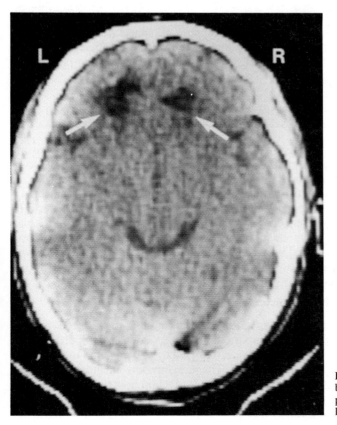

Figure 10.1 CT scan showing bilateral frontal lesion in a patient who underwent frontal leucotomy 16 years earlier

in frontal leucotomy patients, although this appeared to be related to a failure in complying with instructions rather than marked memory deficit *per se*. Some authors have even found evidence for improvement in memory functioning of leucotomy patients from preoperative to postoperative testing (Smith, Kiloh and Boots, 1977; Cochrane and Kljajic, 1979), although in these studies retest data from control subjects were not reported.

The most detailed investigation of memory function in frontal leucotomy patients was carried out by Stuss *et al.* (1982). They found that patients who had undergone prefrontal leucotomy for schizophrenia 23–30 years previously were not amnesic, but did show evidence of proactive interference on short-term verbal memory tasks, despite normal performance on a range of other verbal and non-verbal memory tasks, including a test of retrograde amnesia. Leucotomy patients were classified according to whether they had made good, moderate or no recovery (in terms of residual psychiatric disability) some 20–30 years after surgery, and their performance was compared to both a normal control group and a group of chronic schizophrenic patients who did not undergo leucotomy. On most memory tests, leucotomy patients performed better than non-leucotomized schizophrenic patients. The latter patients appeared to have marked memory impairment and their low scores may in part have reflected a degree of dementia, as indicated by their low Wechsler Adult Intelligence Scale IQ score (Stuss *et al.*, 1981), or may have been due to the effects of active schizophrenic symptoms on cognitive functioning. On some memory tests, such as the Wechsler Memory Scale or word-list recall, leucotomy patients who made a good recovery actually performed slightly better than normal control subjects. Stuss *et al.* speculated that the basic deficit underlying the short-term memory impairment in their patients may have been 'an inability to maintain consistent, directed attention over time because of vulnerability to interfering stimuli'.

Commissurotomy

Sectioning of the cerebral commissures is usually performed for one of two reasons – to alleviate uncontrollable epilepsy, or as a means of gaining access to a deep-seated cerebral lesion. As one might expect, there is considerable scope in both these types of conditions for variability in preoperative memory impairment, and the extent to which this persists postoperatively, and this must be borne in mind when considering differences between studies. In addition, the particular commissural fibres which have been transected, and the extent of transection within a set of fibres, have varied between studies and may account for some of the discrepancies between investigations.

Commissurotomy for relief of epilepsy

In their series of 'split-brain' patients, i.e. those who had undergone sectioning of the corpus callosum and the hippocampal commissure, Zaidel and Sperry (1974) noted that everyday memory symptoms were reported by patients, and in particular by relatives and friends of the patients. These symptoms included repeating anecdotes, and forgetting things they were told. Zaidel and Sperry found evidence of memory impairment in 10 patients with callosal section, eight of whom had complete section and two of whom had partial section. Memory impairment was evident on both verbal and non-verbal tasks regardless of the sensory modalities involved. Zaidel and Sperry admitted that extracommissural damage (presumably that which underlay the original epileptic condition) might have played a role in some of the impairment, although the authors did consider that performance was impaired in comparison with other published data on test scores of epileptic subjects. The two patients who had partial sectioning, i.e. involving the anterior two-thirds of the corpus callosum, showed degrees of deficits comparable with that displayed by patients who had complete sectioning.

Milner and Taylor (1972) reported hemispheric asymmetry in delayed matching of tactile patterns in patients with callosal section. Patients performed better when stimuli were processed by the right hemisphere (with stimuli presented to the left hand), although this performance was still lower than the virtually error-free scores of control subjects. Using a tactile form of the memory-for-designs test (Graham and Kendall, 1960), Kumar (1977) also found better performance by the right hemisphere (i.e. material presented to the left-hand) than the left hemisphere (i.e. material presented to the right-hand) in patients with callosal section. In this task, patients felt the design with one hand and then, immediately following stimulus presentation, drew the design with the same hand. Goldstein and Joynt (1969) reported impaired transfer of learning between hands on a task where shapes had to be identified and sorted on the basis of tactile cues alone. However, normal transfer of learning between hands was found by Gordon, Bogen and Sperry (1971) in cases where the posterior third of the corpus callosum was spared in the commissurotomy procedure. Vilkki (1981) found preoperative to postoperative improvement in memory for visual patterns in a group of patients after sectioning of the anterior portion of the corpus callosum. This improvement was evident both in the immediate postoperative period and several months later. Vilkki speculated that the improvement in memory scores may have been due to alleviation of emotional disturbance and its interfering effect on cognitive functions. No control group was included in this study, and so it is difficult to ascertain the significance of the postoperative changes.

Gazzaniga et al. (1975) found that three patients with partial callosal transection benefited from the use of imagery in the recall of paired-associates, but that a patient who had a complete transection did not benefit from imagery instruction, although here again, the absence of data from control subjects limits the significance of these findings. Dimond et al. (1977) reported the case of a patient in whom the middle third (trunk) of the corpus callosum had been removed at operation, but the hippocampal commissure remained intact. They reported the main memory disorder in their patient as being one of 'autopragmatic memory', whereby there was impaired memory for a sequence of actions the patient himself had performed. They also described instances where the patient would repeat stories which he had told before, or show newspaper advertisements to the examiner which he had shown before. On formal testing, there was some transient deficit on word-list recall tasks from pre- to immediately postoperative testing, but a return to preoperative levels occurred within 20 days after surgery.

Ledoux et al. (1977) reported a 15-year-old patient who suffered herpes encephalitis at the age of 10 years, with resultant decompression of the right temporal lobe and subsequent left hemiparesis, and who showed intractable epilepsy prior to commissurotomy. Wechsler Memory Scale scores and visual sequential memory both improved significantly after surgery. Indeed, on specific subtests of the Wechsler Memory Scale (visual reproduction and paired-associate learning) the patient performed at above the mean value of normal adults. Although no detailed normative data were gathered, Ledoux *et al.* pointed out that the published adult norms they used may have underestimated the degree of improvement shown by their patient. They also noted postoperative improvements in his recall of tachistoscopically-presented material, and on a word-list learning task. In general, Ledoux *et al.* did not find any evidence of significant memory deficits and, comparing their findings with those of Zaidel and Sperry (1974), they pointed out that the latter authors did not have preoperative baseline test scores. Ledoux *et al.* noted that the improvement shown by their patient may have been due to the improved health he showed following operation (reduction in fits) and hypothesized that the callosal sectioning may have freed the normal left hemisphere from the deleterious effects of the abnormal right hemisphere. Since their patient's anterior commissure remained intact, the complete absence of any inter-hemispheric interference may not fully account for the changes in their patient. Ledoux *et al.* offered the interesting hypothesis that after the initial encephalitic illness, some anomalous connections from their patient's right hemisphere may have crossed the midline and led to some reorganization of function in the left hemisphere, and that it was the sectioning of these connections which improved performance. In support of this hypothesis, they alluded to animal studies (Schneider, 1976) where an initial lesion may result in abnormal synaptic reorganization, and a second 'disconnection' lesion may improve test performance. Huppert (1981) assessed memory performance in three split-brain patients and found that two patients whose surgery involved sectioning of the corpus callosum required eight times longer than normal controls for acquisition of pictorial material, behaving in this respect like patients with alcoholic Korsakoff's syndrome. Their rate of forgetting over a one-week period was normal, and it seemed therefore that they had some form of acquisition defect. The remaining split-brain patient performed within normal limits both on acquisition and retention.

Commissurotomy for midline surgery

The reservations described earlier in respect of the preoperative status of patients undergoing surgical ablation are particularly relevant in those with deep-seated cerebral lesions such as tumours, since these may lead both to specific damage to subcortical structures and generalized dysfunction as a result of factors such as ventricular dilatation. Jeeves, Simpson and Geffen (1979) reported a series of patients who had small incisions made in the body of the corpus callosum in order to expose colloid cysts and other benign tumours. One of their patients showed failure to transfer learning of a tactile maze task from one hand to the other. Detailed memory testing was carried out with another patient, and this indicated a mild impairment on learning of verbal and spatial sequences greater than the immediate span, and impaired performance on story recall and paired-associate learning. The level of memory impairment appeared to be somewhat less than that reported by Zaidel and Sperry (1974) in their series of split-brain patients, and it is of note that the patient studied by Jeeves, Simpson and Geffen had, at the time of testing, been able to complete 2 years of a teacher training course. Geffen *et al.* (1980) compared the memory performance of two patients with cerebral tumours who underwent partial sectioning of the corpus callosum, and two patients in whom a transcortical approach to the tumours was adopted. On a range of verbal and non-verbal memory tests, some memory impairment was evident in most patients, but there was no marked difference between the two subgroups of patients. Of the two patients who had callosal sectioning, the patient without significant damage to the fornix performed better on memory tests than the other patient, who did have fornix transection, with the performance of the latter patient approximating that of 'split-brain' subjects of Zaidel and Sperry (1974). Bentin, Sahar and Moscovitch (1984) also found memory impairment, in the form of impaired intermanual transfer of haptic information, to be restricted to certain commissurotomy patients – namely, those who had callosal sectioning in the anterior portion of the trunk of the corpus callosum, posterior to the foramen of Monro.

Selective cortical resection

One of the main sources of our knowledge relating to memory disorders derives from observations on patients who have undergone removal of brain tissue for the relief of epilepsy. Chapter 9 deals with memory functioning in epileptic patients who had not received surgery, and the present chapter includes those patients who were studied pre- and postoperatively, and also those who were only assessed postoperatively. Earlier studies on the effects of cortical resection on memory functioning have been reviewed in a number of articles (e.g. Milner, 1975; Iversen, 1977; Taylor, 1979), and this chapter attempts to summarize the main findings, and also refers to more recent research. This section is divided into two parts: removal of frontal lobe tissue, and removal of temporal lobe cortex with or without additional removal of medial structures such as the hippocampus.

Frontal lobe tissue resection

The effects of ablation of frontal lobe tissue on memory functioning may, at least for some frontal regions, not be evident on standard tests of memory functioning (e.g. Eslinger and Damasio, 1985), and in any consideration of the effects of such ablation it is important to bear in mind both the site and amount of frontal lobe tissue resected and the types of memory tests which have been administered. Impaired performance on a number of short-term memory tasks, ranging from maze learning, recognition of single stimuli (in particular auditory clicks, flashes or colours) after a 60-second filled interval, and recognition of recurring nonsense figures, was noted to be present in patients after frontal lobectomy (Milner, 1964), this ablation being mainly restricted to the dorsolateral frontal cortex. On the maze-learning task, one of the distinctive features of the performance of patients with frontal lesions was failure to comply with test instructions, and an apparent inability to inhibit a preferred mode of response. Milner suggested that these patients may also have been unduly sensitive to interference effects from earlier trials, and this type of explanation was also invoked in earlier studies of impaired list learning by patients with bifrontal ablation (Malmo and Amsel, 1948). In a later paper, Milner (1965) reported more detailed evidence on the memory impairment of patients with lesions in frontal and other regions. On a visually-guided stylus maze, there was a tendency for patients with right frontal ablation to show more marked impairment than patients with left frontal resection, although this may have been partly due to the larger area of resection in the former patients. Corkin (1965) reported impaired performance by patients with frontal lesions on an analogous tactile maze-learning task, with the most severe deficit shown after right frontal ablation.

The presence of proactive interference in a verbal list learning task was assessed by Moscovitch (1982b) in a group of patients with ablation of frontal tissue. He observed that frontal-lesioned patients with impaired performance on the Wisconsin card sorting task were similar to patients with alcoholic Korsakoff's syndrome in that they failed to show improved recall ('release from proactive interference') when a change took place in the category of the verbal material presented for learning. Further studies by Milner and her colleagues (e.g. Milner, 1971, 1982; Petrides and Milner, 1982; Milner, Petrides and Smith 1985; Petrides, 1985) have confirmed the presence of subtle memory deficits in patients with excisions in the frontal lobe, and these often have the form of impairment in the temporal organization of memory. These tasks have included spatial and non-spatial conditional associative learning (associating the location of one stimulus with the position of another, or the colour of a stimulus with a particular hand posture); memory for self-ordered pointing responses (pointing on successive trials to stimuli in an array, with the proviso that no stimuli are touched twice); indicating the frequency of occurrence of recently presented items; and recency judgements for a variety of stimuli (indicating which of two stimuli occurred more recently). In some studies, a lack of hemispheric-specificity of memory deficits was noted (Milner, 1971).

For recency memory judgements, patients with right frontal excisions tended to show more marked and more generalized memory impairment than those with left frontal ablation (Milner, 1982). On self-ordered pointing tasks patients with left frontal ablation were impaired on both verbal and non-verbal versions of the test, whereas those with right frontal resection were only impaired in respect of non-verbal materials (Petrides and Milner, 1982), while in the case of memory for frequency of occurrence of items both left and right frontal ablation groups were impaired, although more marked impairments for verbal and non-verbal material were found after left and right frontal ablation respectively (Milner, Petrides and Smith, 1985). In addition, left but not right frontal lobe ablation has been found to result in impaired learning of a sequence of hand positions (Jason, 1985). In a further study which included patients with frontal lobe resection, Smith and Milner (1984) found evidence of impairment in delayed but not immediate recall of items in a spatial memory task. Subjects had to estimate the price of an array of 16 toys and were then asked for recall of the toys and also to indicate their location using the original toys, with repeat resting 24 hours later. In common with the other groups studied (patients with combined temporal lobe and hippocampal removal), patients with frontal ablation were impaired in delayed recall of pictures, but unlike other patients, they did not show any significant deficits on the remaining components of the task (e.g. recalling the location of stimuli). Similar types of impairment by patients with right or left frontal lobe ablation were reported by Rocchetta (1986) for immediate and delayed recall of individual pictures. These patients were also impaired at sorting the pictures into meaningful categories at time of presentation. Immediate recall of these categories was impaired in both groups, although only patients with left frontal excision showed impaired recall of categories on delayed (2 hours) testing, and only in the right frontal ablation group was there a relationship between initial sorting ability and recall performance.

Temporal lobe and adjacent tissue resection

A number of research workers have examined the effects on memory function of the removal of parts of the temporal lobe, with or without removal of adjacent cortical tissue. The pioneering studies in this respect have been by Milner and her colleagues. Earlier studies have been reviewed in a number of publications (e.g. Milner, 1971; Milner, 1975; Taylor, 1979), and readers are referred to sources such as these for more detailed coverage of these investigations. The principal contribution of studies of temporal lobe and adjacent cortical resection has been to highlight the material-specificity of memory loss after left and right temporal lobe removal; to indicate the importance of medial structures such as the hippocampus in determining the severity of memory impairment; and to establish the significance of bilateral (as opposed to unilateral) pathology in the aetiology of the amnesic syndrome. Thus, in patients with left temporal lobectomy, impairments have been noted on verbal tasks such as story recall, list learning, and verbal paired-associate learning (Milner, 1962, 1975; Blakemore and Falconer, 1967; Weingartner, 1968; Powell, Polkey and McMillan, 1985); after right temporal lobectomy, deficits have been reported on non-verbal memory tasks such as reproduction of complex drawings following a delay (Taylor, 1979), recognition memory for visual patterns (Kimura, 1963), non-verbal paired-associate learning (Ommaya and Fedio, 1972); recognition of faces stimuli (Milner, 1968; Samuels *et al.*, 1980) and recall of spatial location of stimuli (Smith and Milner, 1981).

Impaired immediate and delayed recall of pictures has been found in patients with left temporal lobectomy, but not in patients with right temporal lobectomy (Rocchetta, 1986). Zaidel and Rausch (1981) noted that patients with left anterior temporal lobectomy recognized details taken from disorganized pictures significantly better than those taken from organized pictures, but that no such dissociation was evident in patients with corresponding right temporal ablation or in the performance of control subjects. In addition, the learning of sequences of hand positions has been shown to be impaired after left but not right temporal lobectomy (Jason, 1985). Cherlow and Serafetinides (1976) also found hemispheric asymmetry in auditory verbal memory deficits after temporal lobe lesions. In addition, they assessed more remote memory by asking patients questions about past events, such as the year the Second World War ended or the date of their last follow-up at the hospital. Left temporal lobectomy patients also performed worse on this task than right temporal lobectomy patients. Distinctive patterns of errors have also been reported in patients with right- and left-sided temporal ablation. Rausch (1981) found that on recognition memory testing, left temporal lobectomy patients produced more false-positive responses than control subjects, for material presented visually or aurally. However, right temporal lobectomy patients made fewer such errors than control subjects for visually presented material, and performed at a level comparable with that of control subjects for aurally presented material. At the level of hedonic memory functioning, Master *et al.* (1986) found that patients with right temporal lobe ablation, unlike those with left temporal lobe ablation, did not show any selective preference to recall pleasant rather than unpleasant past experiences on the basis of verbal prompts.

A number of studies have reported equivalent memory deficits after right and left temporal lobectomy. In a series of studies by Samuels *et al.* (Samuels, Butters and Fedio, 1972; Samuels *et al.*, 1980), they reported that short-term memory for auditory consonant trigrams was impaired in both left and right temporal lobectomy patients. It is difficult to explain this particular finding, especially as several types of verbal stimuli and delay intervals were used in the second study (Samuels *et al.*, 1980). It is worth noting, however, that patients with right temporal ablation in this study were only marginally impaired on non-verbal memory tasks (e.g. memory for tonal patterns or faces), whereas patients in the Milner studies referred to earlier have tended to show pronounced deficits on such tasks. It is, therefore, possible that differences in patient population may in part explain the discrepant findings of Samuels *et al.*

Symmetrical memory deficits after left and right temporal lobectomy have been reported to occur in the case of delayed (24 hours) recall of pictures (Milner, 1980), although in a later study (Smith and Milner, 1984) this deficit was absent in cases of right temporal lobectomy where there was minimal hippocampal removal. Zatorre (1985) found impaired short-term recognition memory for melodies in patients who had undergone right or left temporal lobectomy. Tucker *et al.* (1986) also reported equivalent memory deficits in patients with right or left temporal lobectomy, this being accompanied by a significant degree of hippocampal ablation. Both groups with unilateral lesions were impaired on a visuospatial memory task which involved remembering the location of coloured circles in a spatial array. However, patients with right temporal lobectomy were more impaired when the array was built up through sequential presentations of the array, with one position shown at a time, rather than when the entire stimulus array was exposed at a single presentation.

Few studies have focused on the remediation of memory deficits after temporal lobectomy. One investigation by Jones (1974) did find that patients with left temporal lobectomy, with varying degrees of hippocampal ablation, could use visual imagery to improve their verbal paired-associate learning.

Pre- to postoperative changes in memory functioning after temporal lobectomy

As indicated earlier, a number of research workers (e.g. Meyer and Yates, 1955; Blakemore and Falconer, 1967; Taylor, 1979) have noted a drop in memory performance from pre- to postsurgical assessment, with some patients showing partial recovery of this deficit on long-term follow-up. However, in some cases, improvement in memory function after temporal lobectomy may occur where surgery leads to cessation of abnormal electrical activity in the hemisphere contralateral to the epileptogenic focus (Stepien and Sierpinski, 1964). Several studies have pointed to a further pattern of change, namely an improvement in some aspects of memory performance which parallels the decline evident on other aspects of memory functioning. Novelly *et al.* (1984) assessed 23 patients before and after anterior temporal lobectomy. Neuropsychological testing was carried out preoperatively, 2 weeks postoperatively and one year postoperatively. Control subjects were also studied and tested at the same intervals. Patients with a significant reduction in fits after surgery were the primary source of observations on neuropsychological performance. Preoperatively, impaired verbal memory deficits for items in the Wechsler Memory Scale were found in both left and right temporal lobe epilepsy patients. Postoperatively, there was an initial marked decline in verbal memory performance, then a slight improvement in the left temporal lobectomy group, and a slight improvement followed by a marked improvement in the right temporal lobectomy group. In the case of non-verbal memory, both groups were impaired prior to surgery, especially on delayed recall of non-verbal material. After surgery, the group who had undergone left temporal lobectomy showed a slight decline, then a marked improvement; and the right temporal lobe group showed a decline on both occasions (2 weeks and one year postoperatively). Nilsson *et al.* (1984) presented word-list material in memory tasks to epileptic patients before and after surgery. The presentation procedure involved dichotic presentations with masking in one ear to ensure the presentation of stimuli to a single hemisphere. They found evidence for improvement after surgery in memory for stimuli presented to the non-operated hemisphere, with a slight impairment in performance with regard to the hemisphere which was operated on. Unfortunately, only five patients were included, three with right temporal epilepsy, one with temporal and frontal epilepsy, and one patient with left frontal epilepsy, and control patients were not repeat tested.

Rausch and Crandall (1982) administered a series of memory and other cognitive tasks to patients preoperatively, one month, and one year postoperatively, and also carried out repeat testing of control subjects. They found that in left temporal lobectomy patients there was a drop in verbal memory performance postoperatively, especially in those patients whose fits were not controlled by surgery. Right temporal lobectomy patients tended to show improved verbal memory scores after surgery; performance on non-verbal memory tests did not show any significant pattern of change after surgery. A similar pattern of findings, i.e. improvement in non-verbal memory in left temporal lobectomy patients and verbal memory in right temporal lobectomy patients has also been noted by Powell, Polkey and McMillan (1985), although these changes were relatively slight, as were postoperative memory deficits, and interpretation was made difficult by the absence of control subjects in the study.

Ojemann and Dodrill (1985) assessed verbal memory functioning in patients who received left temporal lobectomy. Assessment was carried out preoperatively, and one month and one year postoperatively. Verbal memory scores decreased an average of 22% at one month and 11% at one year postoperatively. Memory decline was greater in patients who were not free of fits and correlated with the lateral, but not the medial, extent of the temporal lobe resection. The response of particular sites of the brain to electrical stimulation with regard to various aspects of memory functioning could predict the outcome of memory deficit in 80% of cases, and in two additional patients, where this information was applied prospectively in the selection of sites for resection, verbal memory score increased one month postoperatively. Intraoperative testing consisted of presentation of an object on a slide for 4 seconds, followed by a sentence presented for 8 seconds, which the patient had to read, followed by recall of the sentence. Stimulation of the cortical site was carried out either at time of input, during the interpolated period, or at time of recall. Patients were divided into those with or without sites related to naming or memory that were within 2 cm of the resection margin. Most cases of postoperative memory impairment occurred when 'memory' or 'naming' sites, as determined by stimulation, were within the resection zone. Ojemann and Dodrill emphasized the importance of the lateral temporal cortex, in addition to the hippocampus and structures around the third ventricle, in underlying memory function. They also pointed out some of the problems in therapeutic implementation of their findings, for example the need to have a large number of test trials for assessing intraoperative stimulation and memory functioning, and the importance of balancing the probability of freedom from fits with the probability of memory deficit if certain areas of brain tissue are resected. A limitation of the study was the lack of control subjects who had repeat testing.

The role of hippocampal ablation

The extent of hippocampal resection additional to temporal lobe ablation, in either hemisphere, has usually determined the severity of the specific memory deficit in question. However, some exceptions to this general rule have been evident. Kimura (1963) did not find greater impairment on recognition of recurring nonsense figures in patients where resection of temporal lobe and hippocampal tissue was particularly extensive. Similarly, Jones-Gotman and Milner (1978) found impairment in delayed recall of the Rey-Osterreith figure after right temporal lobectomy, but this was unrelated to the extent of hippocampal resection. Immediate and delayed recall of this figure, and also immediate and delayed recall of verbal material, was noted by McMillan *et al*. (1987) to be unrelated to the extent of hippocampal ablation. Jones-Gotman (1986a) reported that incidental delayed recall of discrete drawings was impaired in patients with right temporal lobectomy, and that this impairment was no greater in patients with more extensive hippocampal ablation. Similarly, Rocchetta (1986) found that recall of pictures after left temporal lobectomy was not affected by the amount of hippocampal removal.

In contrast to these findings, several studies have reported a close correlation between the severity of memory impairment and extent of hippocampal resection. Thus, the visual maze-learning deficit reported by Milner (1965) in patients after right temporal lobectomy was most notable in those patients where the hippocampus was also removed, although in patients with right temporal lobectomy alone, memory test scores were also well below those of control subjects. Similar observations were made by Corkin (1965) in the case of tactile maze learning, but in this study patients in whom ablation was restricted to the right temporal lobe, with sparing of the hippocampus, performed at a comparable level to control subjects. Verbal memory performance after left temporal lobectomy has been shown by Milner to be related to the amount of left hippocampal resection, this being evident both on the Brown–Peterson short-term memory task (Milner, 1970) and for recall of items from the early portions of a long word-list (Milner, 1978). Moscovitch (1982b) reported similar findings in a study of word-list recall after left temporal lobectomy. The extent of impaired learning of a supraspan series of digits, or sequence of taps on an array of blocks, was also shown by Corsi (reported by Milner, 1971) to be related to the degree of left and right hippocampal ablation in patients with left and right temporal lobectomy respectively.

A further learning task, one which required the learning of a set of visual designs over a maximum of 10 trials and included 24-hour assessment of such learning, was found to be impaired after right temporal lobectomy only if a major portion of the hippocampus was also ablated (Jones-Gotman, 1986b); right temporal lobectomy patients with minimal hippocampal excision performed at a similar level to control subjects. Smith and Milner (1981) found impaired delayed (24 hours) recall of objects after left temporal lobectomy, regardless of the extent of hippocampal removal, whereas this impairment was only evident after right temporal lobectomy if radical hippocampal resection also occurred. In the case of recall of the location of the objects, impaired performance was only found in patients with right temporal lobectomy who also had significant hippocampal ablation. Similarly, on a task involving memory for pointing responses to non-verbal stimuli, Petrides and Milner (1982) only found impaired performance after right temporal lobectomy with additional hippocampal ablation, and noted a similar, although less marked, pattern of findings when patients with left temporal lobectomy were assessed on an analogous task using low imagery words. Impaired recall of verbal material, where the use of visual imagery was encouraged as a mnemonic aid, was also found by Jones-Gotman and Milner (1978) and Jones-Gotman (1979) to be related to the extent of hippocampal resection in patients with right temporal lobectomy, but not in patients with left temporal lobectomy, the latter patients performing poorly regardless of the amount of hippocampal ablation.

Where medial temporal lobe removal is extensive and bilateral, the patient is invariably left with marked amnesia in contrast to the limited memory impairment found after bilateral temporal lobectomy where medial structures such as the hippocampus are spared (Petit-Dutaillis *et al.*, 1954). The most notable example of such a condition is the patient H.M. who was first reported by Scoville and Milner (1957) and who has been the subject of numerous subsequent studies (e.g. Milner *et al.*, 1968), most of which have been comprehensively reviewed by Corkin (1984). The reader is referred to her paper for detailed documentation of H.M.'s performance on memory and other tasks. Scoville (1968) described the site and extent of H.M.'s ablation: 'The removal of medial temporal structures extended posteriorly from the midpoint of the medial tip of the temporal lobe for a distance of roughly eight centimetres. In this fashion, the prepyrifom gyrus, uncus, amygdala, hippocampus and hippocampal gyrus were resected bilaterally. The removal was limited superiorly and laterally by the temporal horns, and extended approximately three centimetres posterior to the medial portion of the petrous ridge'. A CT scan taken in 1984 (*Figure 10.2*) shows the extent of H.M.'s lesion.

The main features of H.M.'s memory functioning are his intact immediate memory span; impaired performance on short-term and long-term memory tasks where rehearsal is prevented, or where the material exceeds his immediate memory span; a retrograde amnesia which was at first thought to be limited to one or 2 years, but which now appears on some tests to extend for up to 11 years prior to his operation; and unimpaired learning ability for tasks such as naming incomplete pictures over repeated test trials, or learning skills such as a pursuit rotor task, although for some of the findings relating to his 'intact' memory, there is evidence of lower than normal scores, or ceiling effects in normal subjects (e.g. Milner, 1970). Encouraging the use of visual imagery codes as a mnemonic aid has not been found to have any beneficial effect on H.M.'s verbal memory performance (Jones, 1974).

Several points need to be borne in mind when considering H.M.'s memory functioning. His continued need for anticonvulsant medication suggests that some epileptogenic lesion, in addition to well-documented lesions resulting from his surgery, may still be active and affecting test performance, and the medication itself may contribute to impaired cognitive functioning. Corkin (1984) reported that H.M. shows patchy evidence of generalized cognitive dysfunction, although this appears to be relatively limited and of recent occurrence, and would certainly not have any bearing on past studies of his memory functioning – it is possible that if all amnesic patients received the degree of extensive neuropsychological testing which H.M. has received, most would show some evidence of cognitive dysfunction additional to their memory impairment. The surgical procedure used in the case of H.M., and also most of the temporal lobectomy patients in the studies referred to above, included removal of the uncus and amygdala in addition to the hippocampus, hippocampal gyrus and anterior medial temporal cortex. It remains possible, although unlikely, that this combined removal, rather than just the

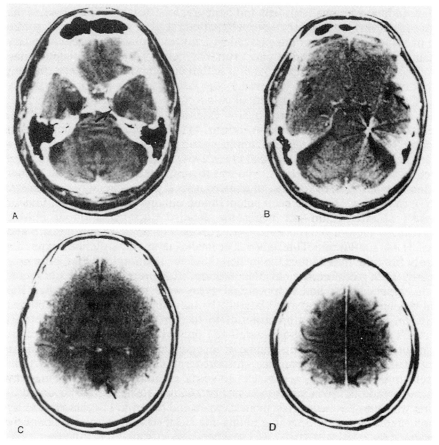

Figure 10.2 CT scan of patient H.M. (*a*) Areas of lower absorption are observed bilaterally in the region of the medial aspects of the temporal lobes anteriorly. The changes are more prominent on the left side (arrow). These areas of low absorption value are consistent with partial volume averaging of tissue loss due to the surgical resection. (*b*) Mild to moderate tissue loss is seen in the sylvian cisterns anteriorly. An arrow denotes the enlarged sylvian cistern on the left. These changes could be secondary to the surgical removal of tissue in the medial temporal lobes. The linear streaking more posteriorly is due to artefact from a surgical clip. (*c*) The sylvian cistern (arrow) is not well filled out by the superior cerebellar vermis, indicating atrophy of this structure. The cerebellum shows marked, diffuse atrophy. The ventricles are enlarged, consistent with the patient's age. (*d*) The changes laterally, over the convexity, are consistent with the patient's age. The cortical sulci are prominent bilaterally, especially medially, in the interhemispheric fissure. Whether these changes reflect some secondary alteration in the region of the cingulate gyrus cannot be determined. (From Corkin, 1984. Reproduced by permission of Thieme-Stratton Inc)

hippocampal lesion, underlies his severe amnesia (*see* Mishkin, 1978). Finally, while invaluable insights and ideas for subsequent research have emanated from the study of H.M., he remains an individual patient who might conceivably differ in memory test performance from other patients with identical lesions.

Amnesia following unilateral ablation of temporal or adjacent cortex has seldom been reported, and in a few such cases (Penfield and Milner, 1958) subsequent post-mortem findings have usually yielded evidence of a long-standing lesion in the contralateral hippocampus (Penfield and Mathieson, 1974). A further case of this type has been described in some detail by Dimsdale, Logue and Piercy (1964). This patient underwent removal of the right temporal lobe, including the amygdala and hippocampus on the right side, and suffered persistent memory difficulties. Although she showed evidence of retrograde amnesia (from general questioning about public events rather than formal testing), other aspects of her performance were somewhat atypical of a classical amnesic syndrome – her normal Wechsler memory quotient 3 weeks after surgery (this was 101 – an increase from the preoperative score of 80), her variable orientation for time (relatively good 3 weeks postoperatively, poor 10 weeks postoperatively and normal 14 months postoperatively), and some degree of asymmetry in her memory deficits, with greater impairment on visual–non-verbal than verbal learning tests. Nonetheless, in view of the absence of evidence for any left temporal lesion, her case is quite a notable one, and she has in fact been included in subsequent studies of the amnesic syndrome (e.g. Warrington and Weiskrantz, 1968).

Gol and Faibish (1967) reported an absence of marked memory deficits in patients who underwent unilateral or bilateral ablation of the hippocampus for relief of pain. Even in those patients where bilateral ablation of the hippocampus was attempted, a global amnesic syndrome did not appear to follow the operation, and the one patient who did display marked memory impairment after surgery had previously undergone frontal lobe ablation. Gol and Faibish concluded from their investigation that bilateral hippocampal ablation did not produce an amnesic syndrome as one might have expected on the basis of earlier studies, and that the extent of memory impairment depended in part on the extent of additional neocortical damage. However, the significance of this study is limited by the paucity of detailed memory testing, by the lack of preoperative and long-term postoperative assessment, and by the fact that the surgical procedure adopted by Gol and Faibish for some of their cases was sometimes characterized by 'incomplete resection and fairly marked damage to the overlying neocortex of the temporal lobe'.

Ablation of other limbic system and subcortical structures

Although there is no unanimous view as to what constitutes the 'limbic system', there is some agreement as to the principal structures which make up this region of the brain, and these are outlined in *Figure 10.3*.

Fornix

A few studies have found significant memory deficits in patients with surgical lesions of the fornix (e.g. Sweet, Talland and Ervin, 1959; Cameron and Archibald, 1981; Carmel, 1985). However, these have usually been relatively mild, and other studies have either found memory deficits to be relatively transient, or have failed to show marked persistent memory impairment following sectioning or destruction of either or both fornices (Cairns and Mosberg, 1951; Amacher, 1976; Apuzzo et al., 1982). It should be noted, however, that in most of these studies, apart from the investigation by Apuzzo et al. (1982), where patients had Wechsler memory quotients similar to their full scale IQ scores, detailed memory testing was not reported. In addition, in some instances where memory impairment has been noted

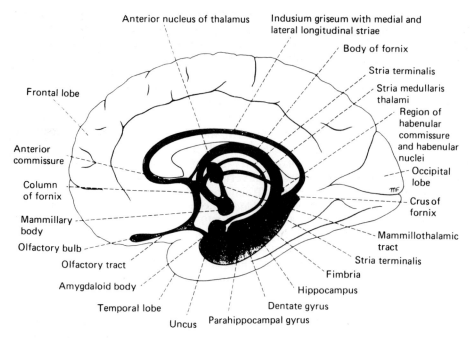

Figure 10.3 Structures which make up the limbic system. (From Snell, 1987. Published by permission of Little, Brown and Company)

(Sweet, Talland and Ervin, 1959; Cameron and Archibald, 1981), the tumours which were present prior to fornix sectioning may have resulted in indirect damage to adjacent limbic system structures.

Amygdala

Halgren (1981) and Sarter and Markowitsch (1985) have systematically reviewed evidence on the effects of lesions in the amygdaloid region on memory function. Sarter and Markowitsch hypothesized that the amygdala 'is responsible for activating or reactivating those mnemonic events which are of emotional significance for the subject's life history'. While a few authors (Kim, 1971; Siegfried and Ben-Shmuel, 1973; Andy, Jurko and Hughes, 1975) have reported memory impairment after surgical destruction of the amygdala, most studies have failed to provide convincing evidence for the presence of significant, permanent memory disorder (Balasubramaniam and Ramamurthi, 1970; Narabayashi, 1979). It is also of note that one of the patients in the Scoville and Milner (1957) series, who did not show persistent memory impairment, had bilateral removal of uncus and amygdala, in addition to ablation of medial temporal cortex, but was spared removal of the hippocampus region. Indeed, in the cases studied by Luczywek and Mempel (1980), most of whom had left-sided amygdalectomy, there was an improvement in memory performance following surgery. A further study which found some evidence for improvement in memory after amygdalectomy was that of Anderson (1978). Anderson examined memory performance after amygdalectomy in patients who suffered from temporal lobe epilepsy. Unilateral amygdalectomy was carried out, and patients were assessed preoperatively and one year after surgery. Memory tests included paired-associate learning, story recall, picture recognition, memory for designs, and the digit span subtest of the Wechsler Adult Intelligence Scale. Nine patients received coagulation of the right amygdala and six underwent coagulation of the left amygdala. Preoperatively, the performance of both amygdalectomy groups was described as being below that of normal control subjects on most of the memory tasks. There was no evidence of material-specificity in memory impairment preoperatively, and in general, memory test changes from pre- to postoperative assessment were relatively small. Anderson did, however, find that after right amygdalectomy there was improvement in delayed recall for a story, but that picture recognition memory performance declined (delayed recall being one hour after the immediate recall). No control data were presented with regard to repeat testing. In the group with right amygalectomy, digit span (mainly backward span) declined, and this was evident to a similar but lesser extent in the group with left amygdalectomy. The author pointed out that any changes found may not be directly related to the amygdala lesions, since there may have been non-specific changes due to reduction of seizures, and also indicated that there was no direct anatomical evidence that target regions had been destroyed by surgery, nor that other structures were not damaged by the operation. Wieser *et al.* (1985) reported several cases of patients with limbic epilepsy, and pointed to one case in this paper (and similar findings in earlier papers (Wieser and Yasargil, 1982)) where unilateral left amygdalo-hippocampectomy seemed to have only a mild effect on memory performance, with patients showing a mild verbal memory deficit preoperatively, which remained postoperatively. They did not, however, specify in detail the memory tasks they used. Jacobson (1986) has reported impaired memory for faces in a patient who underwent bilateral amygdalectomy, but since the patient had previously incurred bifrontal lesions following stereotactic tractotomy, it is difficult to relate this memory deficit specifically to functioning of the amygdala. In a recent study by McMillan *et al.* (1987) no differences in memory performance prior to temporal lobe surgery were found between patients with temporal lobe epilepsy who did or did not have pathology of the amygdala. Those patients with normal amygdala showed impaired memory performance after this was removed as part of the temporal lobectomy.

Thalamus

Markowitsch (1982) has summarized most of the published data with respect to the effects of surgically-induced lesions of the medial-dorsal nucleus of the thalamus (MD), and concluded that 'even bilateral coagulations of MD and of the surrounding internal medullary lamina are not a sufficient precondition to establish long-lasting memory defects in man'. In general where memory deficits have been found after ablation of thalamic nuclei (e.g. Orchinik, 1960; Watkins and Oppenheimer, 1962; Hassler and Dieckmann, 1973; Blumetti and Modesti, 1980), these have either been mild or transient, with evidence of considerable variability between patients. In addition, long-term follow-up data on the permanence of any memory impairment have usually been lacking. Riklan and Cooper (1975), in reviewing their own studies of thalamotomy, made similar observations, and noted that any effects on memory were slight. Vilkki and Laitinen (1976) and Vilkki (1978) found material-specific memory deficits after right and left ventrolateral thalamotomy, with pattern recognition and verbal retrieval components being affected by right- and left-sided lesions respectively. Similar observations were made by Perret and Eggenberger (1973), although they did not specify which thalamic nuclei were the target for surgical ablation. Jurko and Andy (1973) observed that impairment in memory test scores tended to occur in patients where the thalamic lesion was within the limits of the centrum medianum nucleus, and that deterioration in scores was more likely to follow lesions in other nuclei such as the pulvinar, ventralis posterior and ventralis oralis.

Other cortical and subcortical structures

The cingulate region has been implicated in memory disorders by a number of researchers. Whitty and Lewin (1960) were among the first to note transient confusional states after cingulotomy for the treatment of conditions such as obsessional neurosis. Their patients showed confabulation, in which they placed past experiences in the wrong temporal context. Subsequent studies, which have focused on formal memory testing somewhat later in the recovery period, have noted different effects. In the study by Vilkki (1981) described earlier, the investigation also focused on patients who underwent rostral cingulotomy. There was a slight decrease in recognition memory performance, in both the early and late postoperative periods, but no other findings of note. Corkin (1980) reported on a series of more anterior cingulotomies. A range of memory tests administered during the first few weeks after surgery failed to show any significant deficit in memory. Vasko and Kullberg (1979) did find some evidence for impairment of spatial memory after bilateral anterior cingulotomy, but this was relatively transient, and restricted to the first few weeks after surgery. Fallaice et al. (1971) also assessed patients in the first few days after bilateral cingulotomy and found deterioration in memory performance, from preoperative to postoperative testing, on a spatial memory task where subjects had to learn a relatively long tapping sequence. However, no long-term follow-up data were reported on the permanence or otherwise of this deficit, and no normal control data for the task were reported.

A slight depression in memory performance was noted by Levin et al. (1977) in some patients undergoing bilateral cingulotomy, but there were considerable individual differences between patients (with one patient showing an improvement in memory function), and their observations related to the immediate postoperative period rather than to long-term effects. Fedio and Ommaya (1970) pointed to a dissociation between the effects of lesioning and stimulation of the cingulate region, with lesioning leading to slight improvement in memory functioning (perhaps secondary to reduction in the presenting symptoms of pain), and stimulation of the left cingulum resulting in impaired memory for verbal stimuli.

Turning to subcortical nuclei other than those discussed earlier, verbal memory deficits in the early postoperative period have been reported for some patients with bilateral anterior internal capsulotomy (Vasko and Kullberg, 1979), but in most patients these recovered on long-term follow-up, and Vilkki (1981) in fact found that anterior capsulotomy patients showed some long-term improvement in memory scores, although this did not reach statistical significance. Vilkki and Laitinen (1976) and Vilkki (1978) have examined the effects of left and right pulvinotomy on memory. Some verbal retrieval deficit was noted after left-sided lesions, but otherwise no marked impairments were found.

Distinctive features of memory disorders after ablation/disconnection of cerebral tissue

Memory deficits after ablation of cortical or subcortical tissue appear, in general, to be less severe than those associated with other pathologies. For example, focal destruction of thalamic nuclei has tended not to result in the severity of memory impairment associated with infarction of thalamic arteries. In addition, global amnesic syndromes or disorders resembling dementia are relatively uncommon in ablation/disconnection patients. This may reflect the limited, usually unilateral, nature of the surgical lesion, and is consistent with the hypothesis that more than one critical lesion may be necessary for amnesia/dementia to occur. Most of the comparative studies which have included reference to patients with ablation/disconnection of cerebral tissue have been reviewed in earlier chapters, and the reader is referred to the appropriate sections of these chapters.

Summary

Surgical ablation or disconnection of brain tissue has been shown to have significant effects on memory functioning. The effects of frontal leucotomy on memory are relatively slight, with the only significant findings relating to increased interference effects in short-term memory. Sectioning of the cerebral commissures, either to relieve epilepsy or to gain access to deep-seated lesions, has been found to have a somewhat variable effect on memory functioning. While some patients undergoing commissurotomy have shown memory impairment, there is considerable individual variation in performance, possibly related in part as to whether the hippocampal commissure or fornix has been sectioned. Some commissurotomy patients have shown improved memory performance from their preoperative levels, and this may in part be secondary to improvement in the original medical/neurological condition. In those patients with impaired performance, there is seldom a global amnesic syndrome and discrete forms of memory loss have been documented, often in experimental tasks where the stimulus material is presented to either isolated hemisphere. Ablation of frontal tissue for the relief of epilepsy has resulted in a range of memory deficits, such as on tasks relating to recency judgements and memory for self-ordered responses. No single explanation appears to account for such deficits, although it is possible that increased susceptibility to interference and some impairment in the temporal organization of memory may characterize most of the memory deficits of such patients. It may, however, be the case that distinct subgroups of memory disorder arise after frontal ablation, perhaps related to the locus and size of the resection. Material-specific memory deficits, related to the side of frontal ablation, have been noted, although the picture appears somewhat complex, with more generalized memory deficits sometimes following right or left frontal ablation, depending on the type of memory task.

Removal of temporal lobe tissue, with or without adjacent hippocampal resection, has been shown to result in significant memory impairment. In the case of temporal lobectomy, there is usually a deficit in performance from pre- to postoperative testing, although this sometimes occurs in conjunction with improved performance on memory tasks related to the unoperated hemisphere. Verbal and visuospatial memory deficits have been consistently found after left and right temporal lobectomy respectively and, for most memory tasks, the greater the degree of additional hippocampal resection, the greater the severity of the memory deficit in question. Where tissue from both temporal lobes and hippocampi has been removed, a severe amnesia has ensued. However, in such operations the amygdala and uncus have also been removed, and there appear to be few well-documented cases of bitemporal lobectomy without additional hippocampal or amygdala removal. The effects of ablation of other areas of the limbic system, such as the fornix, cingulate gyrus, amygdala and thalamus have been somewhat variable, with a number of studies reporting only clinical observations of memory functioning, and some studies failing to take account of the primary lesion preceding the ablation. No firm evidence of amnesia after ablation restricted to any of these four structures has been reported, and memory deficits which have been found appear to be relatively focal, sometimes related to the left or right side of the ablation. It would seem therefore, as Markowitsch (1984) has argued, that no single structure is critical to the occurrence of amnesia.

Appendix 1

Sources for materials which may be of use in designing memory tests for the assessment of neurological patients

(1) Verbal items

(*see* Brown (1976) for a more detailed listing of sources up to 1976).

Listings of attributes of single words (e.g. frequency of occurrence, concreteness, age of acquisition, etc.)

Carroll, J. B., Davies, P. and Richman, B. (1971) *The American Heritage Word Frequency Book*. Boston: Houghton Mifflin.

Friendly, M. *et al.* (1982) The Toronto word pool: norms for imagery, concreteness, orthographic variables, and grammatical usage for 1080 words. *Behav. Res. Meth. and Instrum.,* **14,** 375–399.

Gilhooly, K. J. and Logie, R. H. (1980a) Age-of-acquisition, imagery, concreteness, familiarity, and ambiguity measures for 1944 words. *Behav. Res. Meth. and Instrum.,* **12,** 395–427.

Kucera, H. and Francis, W. N. (1967) *Computational Analysis of Present-day American English*. Providence, RI: Brown University Press.

Nickerson, C. A. and Cartwright, D. S. (1984) The University of Colorado meaning norms. *Behav. Res. Meth. Instrum. and Comp.,* **16,** 355–382.

Oxford Text Archives, Oxford University Computing Service, 13 Banbury Road, Oxford OX2 6NN (word listings similar to other listings in terms of measured attributes, but also available in a number of languages).

Palermo, D. S. and Jenkins, J. J. (1964) *Word-Association Norms: Grade School through College*. Minneapolis: University of Minnesota Press.

Pavio, A., Yuille, J. C. and Madigan, S. (1968) Concreteness, imagery, and meaningfulness values of 925 nouns. *Journal of Experimental Psychology,* **76** (Suppl.), 1–25.

Stratton, R. P., Jacobus, K. A. and Brinely, B. (1975) Age-of-acquisition, imagery, familiarity, and meaningfulness norms for 543 words. *Behav. Res. Meth. and Instrum.,* **7,** 1–6.

Thorndike, E. L. and Lorge, I. (1944) *The Teachers's Word Book of 30 000 Words*. New York: Teachers College Press, Columbia University.

Toglia, M. P. *et al.* (1978) *Handbook of Semantic Word Norms*. Hillsdale, NJ: Erlbaum.

Category items (e.g. names of animals) and related norms

Battig, W. F. and Montague, W. E. (1969) Category norms for verbal items in 56 categories: a replication and extension of the Connecticut category norms. *J. Exp. Psychol. Monog.*, **80**, 1–46

Brown W. P. (1972) Studies in word listing: some norms and their reliability. *Irish Journal of Psychology*, **1**, 117–159.

Horton, K. D. (1983) Phonemic and semantic generation norms. *Behav. Res. Meth. and Instrum.*, **15**, 109–110.

Uyeda, K. M. and Mandler, G. (1980) Prototypicality norms for 28 semantic categories. *Behav. Res. Meth. and Instrum.*, **12**, 587–595.

Words with special features (e.g. homographs)

Galbraith G. G. and Taschman, G. S. (1969) Homphone units: a normative and methodological investigation of the strength of component elements. *J. Verb. Learn. Verb. Behav.*, **8**, 737–744

Geis, M. F. and Winograd, E. (1974) Norms of semantic encoding variability for fifty homographs. *Bull. Psychonomic. Soc.*, **3**, 429–431

Gilhooly, K. J. and Hay, D. (1977) Imagery, concreteness, age-of-acquisition, familiarity, and meaningfulness values for 205 five-letter words having single solution anagrams. *Behav. Res. Meth. and Instrum.*, **9**, 12–17.

Gilhooly, K. J. and Logie, R. H. (1980b) Meaning-dependent ratings of imagery, age of acquisition, familiarity, and concreteness for 387 ambiguous words. *Behav. Res. Meth. and Instrum.*, **12**, 428–450

Nelson, D. L. *et al.* (1980) The University of South Florida homograph norms. *Behav. Res. Meth. and Instrum.* **12**, 16–37.

Whitford, H. C. (1966) *A dictionary of American homophones and homographs.* New York: Teachers college

Wollen, K. A. *et al.* (1980) Frequency of occurrence and concreteness ratings of homograph meanings. *Behav. Res. Meth. and Instrum.*, **12**, 8–15.

Other verbal items

Bloom, P. A. and Fischler, I. (1980) Completion norms for 329 sentence contexts. *Memory and Cognition*, **8**, 631–642.

Nelson, T. O. and Narens, L. (1980) Norms of 300 general-information questions: accuracy of recall, latency of recall, and feeling-of-knowing ratings. *J. Verb. Learn. Verb. Behav.*, **19**, 338–368.

Schwanenflugel, P. J. (1986) Completion norms for final words in sentences using a multiple production measure. *Behav. Res. Meth. Instrum. and Comp.*, **18**, 363–371.

Wilkinson, T. S. and Nelson, T. O. (1984) Computer-based version of data described in Nelson and Narens (1980). *J. Verb. Learn. Verb. Behav.*, **19**, 338–368

(2) Visual patterns

Computer-generated complex figures: Vanderplas, J. M. and Garvin, E. A. (1959) The association value of random shapes. *Journal of Experimental Psychology*, **57**, 147–154.

Other possible sources include symbols, foreign alphabets, etc. which are available in 'Letraset' form.

(3) Pictures

Snodgrass, J. G. and Vanderwart, M. (1980) A standardized set of 260 pictures: norms for name agreement, image agreement, familiarity and visual complexity. *J. Exp. Psychol. Learn. Mem. Cogn.*, **6**, 174–215. A computer-based version of these figures (for the Apple Macintosh Computer) has been described by Brooks (1985) *Behav. Res. Meth. Instrum. and Comp.*, **17**, 409–410.

Photographs of famous personalities are available from Camera Press, Russell Court, Coram Street, London WC1H OHB.

(4) Other materials

D-prime tables for use in interpreting recognition memory test responses are available in a number of articles – e.g. Hacker, M. J. and Ratcliff, R. (1979) A revised table of d' for M-alternative forced choice. *Perception and Psycho-physics,* **26**, 168–170.

Sources for information/materials relating to the remediation of memory disorders

Books and articles

(1) Cermak, L. S. (1976) *Improving your Memory*. New York: McGraw Hill.
This is a general description of the various techniques which may be used to improve everyday memory activities. It is mainly directed towards the normal population, but some of the ideas discussed in the book can easily be applied to patients with memory disorders.

(2) Wilson, B. and Moffatt, N. (1984) Editors. *The Clinical Management of Memory Problems*. London: Croom Helm.
This book has a number of articles relating to the management of memory disorders, mainly concentrating on psychological techniques. It includes a discussion of memory aids, group therapy to help improve memory functioning, etc.

(3) Wilson, B. (1987) *Rehabilitation of Memory*. New York: Guilford Press.
This book contains a number of single-case studies, and several group studies relating to the use of psychological techniques for improving memory deficits (some of the studies described in the book have been reported in other publications). It gives a balanced appraisal of the benefits and limitations of the techniques which were used. Many of the patients described in the book have suffered severe head injuries, although a number of patients with other aetiologies are also reported.

(4) Baddeley, A. D. (1982) *Your Memory: a User's Guide.* (1982) London: Sidgwick & Jackson.
This is a readable and well illustrated account of human memory, and includes sections on amnesia and on improving memory.

Booklets/materials

(1) Kapur, N. *The Wessex Memory Manual*. The Wessex Neurological Centre, Southampton.
This manual lists some of the techniques which may be used to ameliorate six memory symptoms commonly reported by neurological patients – remembering people's names, remembering where something has been put, remembering to do something, remembering spoken messages, remembering something which has

been read, and remembering the directions of how to get somewhere. It is intended for use by patients with mild or moderate memory difficulties.

(2) *Working with the elderly* – a series of publications by Winslow Press, 23 Horn Street, Winslow, Buckingham, MK18 3AP, UK. The main booklets within this series which may be of benefit to those working with memory disordered patients are those dealing with reality orientation and several booklets which include 'nostalgia' materials dating from the past – these include famous faces, banner headlines, royalty, objects and vehicles. The intention of using such material is to try to stimulate past memories and encourage the patient to discuss items which are both within his repertoire of memories and which he enjoys relating to.

Organizations (in the UK) which may provide advice and information relating to the management of memory disorders in neurological patients.

(1) The Amnesia Association, 25 Prebend Gardens, Chiswick, London W4 1TN.

(2) Headway, National Head Injuries Association, 17 Clumber Avenue, Sherwood Rise, Nottingham, NG5 1AG.

(3) Alzheimer's Disease Society, 3rd Floor, Bank Buildings, Fulham Broadway, London SW6 1EP.

References

AARTS, J. H. P., BINNIE, C. D., SMIT, A. M. and WILKINS, A. J. (1984) Selective cognitive impairment during focal and generalized epileptiform EEG activity. *Brain,* **107,** 293–308

ABBRUZZESE, G., ARATA, L., BINO, G., DALL'AGATA, D. and LEONARDI, A. (1986) Thalamic dementia: a report of a case with unusual lesion location. *Italian Journal of Neurological Science,* **7,** 55–59

ABERG, T. (1974) Effect of open heart surgery on intellectual function. *Scandinavian Journal of Thoracic and Cardiovascular Surgery,* Suppl. 15, 1–63

ACKER, W. and ACKER, C. (1982) *Bexley Maudsley Automated Psychological Screening and Bexley Maudsley Category Sorting Test.* Windsor: NFER-Nelson

ACKER, W., RON, M. A., LISHMAN, W. A., and SHAW, G. K. (1984) A multivariate analysis of psychological, clinical and CT scanning measures in detoxified chronic alcoholics. *British Journal of Addiction,* **79,** 293–302

ADOLFSSON, R., BRANE, G., BUCHT, G., KARLSSON, I., GOTTFRIES, C. G., PERSSON, S. *et al.* (1982) A double-blind study with levodopa in dementia of Alzheimer type. *Alzheimer's Disease: a Report of Progress in Research,* edited by S. Corkin, K. L. Davis, J. H. Growdon, E. Usdin and R. J. Wurtman, pp. 469–473. New York: Raven Press

AGNOLI, A., RUGGIERE, S., MECO, G., CASACCHIA, M., DENARO, A., CONTI, L. et al. (1984) An appraisal of the problem of dementia in Parkinson's disease. In *Advances in Neurology,* edited by R. G. Hassler and J. F. Christ, pp. 299–306. New York: Raven Press

AHMED, I. (1978) Transient global amnesia. Report of a case secondary to bilateral middle cerebral artery involvement. *Journal of the Kansas Medical Society,* **79,** 670–672

AIMARD, G., BOISSON, P., TROUILLAS, P. and DEVIC, M. (1979) Encephalites et encephalopathies aigues amnesiantes. *Rev Neurol,* **135,** 679–692

AIMARD, G., TRILLET, M., PERROUDON, C., TOMMASI, M. and CARRIER, H. (1971) Symptomatic amnesic attack in glioblastoma involving the trigone. *Rev Neurol,* **124,** 392–396

AIMARD, G., VIGHETTO, A., CONFAVREUX, C. and DEVIC, M. (1981) La desorientation spatiale. *Rev Neurol,* **137,** 97–111

ALBERT, M. S., BUTTERS, N. and BRANDT, J. (1981a) Patterns of remote memory loss in amnesic and demented patients. *Archives of Neurology,* **38,** 495–500

ALBERT, M. S., BUTTERS, N. and BRANDT, J. (1981b) Development of remote memory loss in patients with Huntington's disease. *Journal of Clinical Neuropsychology,* **3,** 1–12

ALBERT, M. S., BUTTERS, N. and LEVIN, J. (1979) Temporal gradients in the retrograde amnesia of patients with alcoholic Korsakoff's disease. *Archives of Neurology,* **36,** 211–216

ALBERT, M. S., BUTTERS, N. and LEVIN, J. (1980) Memory for remote events in chronic alcoholics and alcoholic Korsakoff patients. *Advances in Experimental and Medical Biology,* **126,** 719–730

ALBERT, M. S., BUTTERS, N., ROGERS, S., PRESSMAN, J. and GELLER, A. (1982) A preliminary report: nutritional levels and cognitive performance in chronic alcohol abusers. *Drug and Alcohol Dependence,* **9,** 131–142

ALBERT, M. L., FELDMAN, R. G. and WILLIS, A. L. (1974) The 'subcortical dementia' of progressive supranuclear palsy. *Journal of Neurology, Neurosurgery and Psychiatry,* **37,** 121–130

ALBERT, M. S. and MOSS, M. (1984) The assessment of memory disorders in patients with Alzheimer disease. In *Neuropsychology of Memory*, edited by L. S. Squire and N. Butters, pp. 236–246. New York: Guildford Press

ALEXANDER M. P. (1982) Episodic behaviours due to neurological disorders other than epilepsy. In *Pseudoseizures*, edited by T. L. Riley and A. Roy, pp. 83–109. Baltimore: Williams and Wilkins

ALEXANDER, M. P. and FREEDMAN, M. (1984) Amnesia after anterior communicating artery aneurysm rupture. *Neurology*, **34**, 752–757

ALEXANDER, M. P., STUSS, D. T. and BENSON, D. Z. (1979) Capgras syndrome: a reduplicative phenomenon. *Neurology*, **29**, 334–339

ALLEN, I. V., SCOTT, R. and TANNER, J. A. (1982) Experimental high-velocity missile head injury. *Injury*, **14**, 183–193

ALLPORT, D. A. (1985) Distributed memory, modular subsystems and dysphasia. In *Current Perspectives in Dysphasia*, edited by S. Newman and R. Epstein, pp. 32–60. Edinburgh: Churchill Livingstone

ALTERMAN, A. I., GOLDSTEIN, G., SHELLY, C., BOBER, B. and TARTER, R. E. (1985) The impact of mild head injury on neuropsychological capacity in chronic alcoholics. *International Journal of Neuroscience*, **28**, 155–162

AMACHER, A. L. (1976) Transient loss of recent memory following deep midline cerebral operations. *Childs Brain*, **2**, 81–84

ANDERSON, R. (1978) Cognitive changes after amygdalectomy. *Neuropsychologia*, **16**, 439–451

ANDREWES, D. G., TOMLINSON, L., ELWES, R. D. and REYNOLDS, E. H. (1984) The influence of carbamazepine and phenytoin on memory and other aspects of cognitive function in new referrals with epilepsy. *Acta Neurologica Scandinavica*, **99**, (Suppl.) 23–30

ANDY, O. J., JURKO, M. F. and HUGHES, J. R. (1975) Amygdalectomy for bilateral temporal lobe seizures. *Southern Medical Journal*, **68**, 743–748

ANGELERGUES, R. (1969) Memory disorders in neurological disease. In *Handbook of Clinical Neurology*, edited by P. J. Vinker and G. W. Bruyn. Amsterdam: North-Holland

APUZZO, M. L., CHIKOVANI, O. K., GOTT, P. S., TENG E. L., ZEE, C. S., GIANNOTTA, S. L. *et al.* (1982) Transcallosal, interfornicial approaches for lesions affecting the third ventricle: surgical considerations and consequences. *Neurosurgery*, **10**, 547–554

ARENDT, T., BIGL, V., ARENDT, A. and TENNSTEDT, A. (1983) Loss of neurons in the nucleus basalis of Mynert in Alzheimer's disease, paralysis agitans and Korsakoff's disease. *Acta Neuropath (Berl.)*, **61**, 101–108

ARLIEN-SOBORG, P., BRUHN, P., GLYNDENSTEAD, C. and MELGAARD, B. (1979) Chronic painters' syndrome. *Acta Neurologica Scandinavica*, **60**, 149–156

ASKEN, M. J. and HOBSON, R. W. (1977) Current research review: intellectual change and carotid endarterectomy, subjective speculation or objective reality: a review. *Journal of Surgical Research*, **23**, 3367–3375

ASSAL, G. (1969) Regression des troubles de la reconnaissance des physionomies et de la memoire topographique chex un malade opere d'un hematome intracerebral parieto-temporal droit. *Rev Neurol*, **121**, 184–185

ASSAL, G., PROBST, A., ZANDER, E. and RABINOWICZ, T. (1976) Syndrome amnesique per infiltration tumorale. *Schweiz Arch Neurol Neurochir Psychiatr*, **119**, 317–324

ASSO, D., CROWN, S., RUSSELL, J. A. and LOGUE, V. (1969) Psychological aspects of the stereo-taxic treatment of parkinsonism. *British Journal of Psychiatry*, **115**, 541–553

BABCOCK, H. (1930) An experiment in the measurement of mental deterioration. *Archives of Psychology*, **117**, 93–105

BADDELEY, A. D. and WARRINGTON, E. K. (1970) Amnesia and the distinction between long- and short-term memory. *J Verb Learn Verb Behav*, **9**, 176–189

BADDELEY, A. D. and WILSON, B. (1986) Amnesia, autobiographical memory, and confabulation. In *Autobiographical Memory*, edited by D. C. Rubin, pp. 225–252. Cambridge: Cambridge University Press

BAHRICK, H. P. and KARIS, D. (1982) Long-term ecological memory. In *Handbook of Research Methods in Human Memory and Cognition*, edited by R. C. Puff, pp. 427–465. New York: Academic Press

BAIRD, A. D., ADAMS, K. M., SHATZ, M. W., BROWN, G. G., DIAZ, F. and AUSMAN, J. J. (1984) Can neuropsychological tests detect the sites of cerebrovascular stenoses and occlusions? *Neurosurgery*, **14**, 416–423

BAIRD, A. D., BOULOS, R., MEHTA, B., ADAMS, K. M., SHATZ, M. W., AUSMAN, J. I. *et al.* (1985) Cerebral angiography and neuropsychological measurement. The twain may meet. *Surg Neurol,* **23,** 641–650

BAKARE, C. G. M. and ADELOYE, A. (1972) Intellectual deficits in Nigerians after missile wounds of the brain. *Brain,* **95,** 79–86

BALASUBRAMANIAM, V. and RAMAMURTHI, B. (1970) Stereotaxic amygdalectomy in behaviour disorders. *Confina Neurologica,* **32,** 367–373

BALDWIN, M. (1960) Electrical stimulation of the medial temporal region. In *Electrical stimulation of the Unanesthetized Brain,* edited by E. R. Ramey and D. S. O'Doherty, pp. 159–176. New York: Paul B. Hoeber

BALE, R. N. (1973) Brain damage in diabetes mellitus. *British Journal of Psychiatry,* **122,** 337–341

BALL, J. A. C. and TAYLOR, A. R. (1967) Effects of cyclandelate on mental function and cerebral blood flow in elderly patients. *British Medical Journal,* **3,** 525–528

BALOH, R., STURM, R., GREEN, B. and GLESER, G. (1975) Neuropsychological effects of chronic asymptomatic increased lead absorption. *Archives of Neurology,* **32,** 326–330

BANDERA, R., CAPITANI, E., DELLA SALA, S. and SPINNLER, H. (1985) Discrimination between senile dementia Alzheimer type patients and education-matched normal controls by means of a 6-test set. *Italian Journal of Neurological Science,* **6,** 339–344

BANNA, M. (1973) Craniopharyngioma in adults. *Surg Neurol,* **1,** 202–204

BARBIZET, J. (1970) *Human Memory and its Pathology.* San Francisco: W. H. Freeman & Co.

BARBIZET, J. and CANY, R. (1968) Clinical and psychometrical study of a patient with memory disturbances. *Int. J. Neurol,* **7,** 44–54

BARBIZET, J., DEGOS, J. D., LOUARN, F., NGUYEN, J. P. and MAS, J. L. (1981) Amnesie par lesion ischemique bi-thalamique. *Rev Neurol,* **137,** 415–424

BARBIZET, J., DUIZABO, P. and POIRIER, J. (1978) Etude anatomo-clinique d'un cas d'encepahlite amnesiante d'origine herpetique. *Rev Neurol,* **134,** 241–253

BARTH, J. T., MACCIOCHI, S N., GIORDANI, B., RIMEL, R., JANE, J. A. and BOLL, T. J. (1983) Neuropsychological sequelae of minor head injury, *Neurosurgery,* **13,** 529–533

BASSO, A., SPINNLER, H., VALLAR, G. and ZANOBIA, M. E., (1982) Left-hemisphere damage and selective impairment of auditory verbal short-term memory. A case study. *Neuropsychologia,* **20,** 263–274

BATTIG, W. F. and MONTAGUE, W. E. (1969) Category norms for verbal items in 56 categories: a replication and extension of the Connecticut category norms. *J Exp Psychol Monog* **80,** 1–46

BAUER, R. M. (1982) Visual hypoemotionality as a symptom of a visual-limbic disconnection in man. *Archives of Neurology,* **39,** 702–708

BEAL, M. F., KLEINMAN, G. M., OJEMANN, R. G. and HOCHBERG, F. H. (1981) Gangliocytoma of third ventricle: hyperphagia, somnolence and dementia. *Neurology,* **31,** 1224–1228

BEANEY, R. P., BROOKS, D. J., LEENDERS, K. L., THOMAS, D. G. T., JONES T. and HALNAN, K. E. (1985) Blood flow and oxygen utilisation in the contralateral cerebral cortex of patients with untreated intracranial tumours studied by positron emission tomography, with observations on the effect of decompressive surgery. *Journal of Neurology, Neurosurgery and Psychiatry,* **48,** 310–319

BEATTY, W. W. and BUTTERS, N. (1986) Further analysis of encoding in patients with Huntington's disease. *Brain and Cognition,* **5,** 387–398

BEATTY, P. A. and GANGE, J. J. (1977) Neuropsychological aspects of multiple sclerosis. *Journal of Nervous and Mental Disease,* **164,** 42–50

BECHTEREVA, N. P., GENKIN, A. A., MOISEEVA, N. I. and SMIRNOV, V. M. (1967) Electrographic evidence of participation of deep structures of the human brain in certain mental processes. *Electroencephalogr Clin Neurophysiol,* Suppl. **25,** 153–166

BECKER, J., BUTTERS, N., HERMANN, A. and D'ANGELO, N. (1983a) Learning to associate names and faces: impaired acquisition on an ecologically relevant memory task. *Journal of Nervous and Mental Disease,* **171,** 617–623

BECKER, J. T., BUTTERS, N., HERMANN, A. AND D'ANGELO, N. (1983b) A comparison of the effects of long-term alcohol abuse and aging on the performance of verbal and nonverbal divided attention tasks. *Alcoholism,* **7,** 213–219

BECKER, J. T. and JAFFE, J. H. (1984) Impaired memory for treatment-relevant information in inpatient men alcoholics. *J Stud Alcohol,* **45,** 339–343

BEDOU, G., CARUEL, N. and PERTUISET, B. (1972) Tumeurs de septum lucidum. *Rev Neurol,* **127,** 341–353

BELLER, S. A., OVERALL, J. E. and SWANN, A. C. (1985) Efficacy of oral physostigmine in primary degenerative dementia. *Psychopharmacology,* **87,** 147–151

BENDER, M. B., FURLOW, L. T. and TEUBER, H. L. (1949) Alterations in behaviour after massive trauma (intraventricular foreign body). *Confina. Neurologica,* **9,** 140–157

BENGTSSON, M., HOLMBERG, S. and JANSSON, B. (1969) A psychiatric-psychological investigation of patients who had survived circulatory arrest. *Acta Psychiatrica Scandinavica,* **45,** 327–346

BENNET-LEVY, J. (1984) Determinants of performance on the Rey-Osterreith complex figure test: an analysis, and a new technique for single-case assessment. *British Journal of Clinical Psychology,* **23,** 109–119

BENNET-LEVY, J., POLKEY, C. E. and POWELL, G. E. (1980) Self-report of memory skills after temporal lobectomy: the effect of clinical variables. *Cortex,* **16,** 543–557

BENSON, D. F. (1982) Amnesia: a clinical approach to memory. In *Psychiatric Aspects of Neurological Disease II,* edited by D. F. Benson and D. Blumer. New York: Grune and Stratton

BENSON, D. F., GARDNER, H. and MEADOWS, J. C. (1976) Reduplicative paramnesia. *Neurology,* **26,** 147–151

BENSON, D. F. and GESCHWIND, N. (1967) Shrinking retrograde amnesia. *Journal of Neurology, Neurosurgery and Psychiatry,* **30,** 539–544

BENSON, D. F., MARSDEN, C. D. and MEADOWS, J. C. (1974) The amnesic syndrome of posterior cerebral artery occlusion. *Acta Neurologica Scandinavica,* **50,** 133–145

BENTIN, S., SAHAR, A. and MOSCOVITCH, M. (1984) Intermanual information transfer in patients with lesions in the trunk of the corpus callosum. *Neuropsychologia,* **22,** 601–611

BENTON, A. L. (1974) *The Revised Visual Retention Test,* 4th edn. New York: Psychological Corporation

BENTON, A. L. and HAMSHER, K. (1978) *Multilingual Aphasia Examination.* Iowa City: University of Iowa

BENTON, A. L., HAMSHER, K., VARNEY, N. R. and SPREEN, O. (1983) *Contributions to Neuropsychological Assessment. A Clinical Manual.* New York: Oxford University Press

BENTON, A. L. and SPREEN, O. (1961) Visual memory test: the simulation of mental incompetence. *Archives of General Psychiatry,* **4,** 79–83

BENTON, A. L., VAN ALLEN, M. W. and FOGEL, M. L. (1964) Temporal orientation in cerebral disease. *Journal of Nervous and Mental Diseases,* **139,** 110–119

BERGLUND, M., GUSTAFSON, L. and HAGBERG, B. (1979) Amnestic-confabulatory syndrome in hydrocephalic dementia and Korsakoff's psychosis in alcoholism. *Acta Psychiatrica Scandinavica,* **60,** 323–333

BERGMAN, H., BORG, S., HINDMARSH, T., IDESTROM, C. M. and MUTZELL, S. (1980) Computed tomography of the brain and neuropsychological assessment of male alcoholic patients. In *Addiction and Brain Damage,* edited by D. Richter, pp. 201–226. Baltimore: University Park Press

BERLYNE, N. (1972) Confabulation. *British Journal of Psychiatry,* **120,** 31–39

BERLYNE, N. and STRACHAN, M. (1968) Neurospsychiatric sequelae of attempted hanging. *British Journal of Psychiatry,* **114,** 411–422

BERMAN, S. A., HAYMAN, L. A. and HINCK, V. C. (1980) Correlation of CT cerebral vascular territories with function. *American Journal of Radiology,* **135,** 253–257

BERMAN, S. A., HAYMAN, L. A. and HINCK, V. C. (1984) Correlation of CT cerebral vascular territories with function: 3. Middle cerebral artery. *American Journal of Radiology,* **142,** 1035–1040

BERRY, D. T. R., WEBB, W. B., BLOCK, A. J., BAUER, R. M. and SWITZER, D. A. (1986) Nocturnal hypoxia and neuropsychological variables. *Journal of Clinical and Experimental Neuropsychology,* **8,** 229–238

BERRY, G. J., HEATON, R. K. and KIRBY, M. W. (1977) Neuropsychological deficits in chronic inhalant abusers. In *Management of the Poisoned Patient,* edited by B. H. Rumack and A. R. Temple, pp. 9–31. Princeton: Science Press

BERTRANDO, P., MAFFEI, C. and GHEZZI, A. (1983) A study of neuropsychological alterations in multiple sclerosis. *Acta Psychiatrica Belgica,* **83,** 13–21

BIBER, C., BUTTERS, N., ROSEN, J., GERSTMANN, L. and MATTIS, S. (1981) Encoding strategies and recognition of faces by alcoholic Korsakoff and other brain-damaged patients. *Journal of Clinical Neuropsychology,* **3,** 315–330

BIELIAUSKAS, L. A., TOPEL, J. L. and HUCKMAN, M. S. (1980) Cognitive, neurologic and radiologic test data in a changing lesion pattern. *Journal of Clinical Neuropsychology,* **2,** 217–230

BIGLER, E. D., HUBLER, D. W., CULLUM, C. M., and TURKHEIMER, E. (1985) Intellectual and memory impairment in dementia. Computerized axial tomography volume correlations. *Journal of Nervous and Mental Disease*, **173**, 347–352

BIGLER, E. D., PAVER, S., CULLUM, C. M., TURKHEIMER, E., HUBLER, D. and YEO, R. (1984) Ventricular enlargement, cortical atrophy and neuropsychological performance following head injury. *International Journal of Neuroscience*, **24**, 295–298

BINDER, L., TANABE, E., WALLER, F. and WORSTER, E. (1982) Behavioural effects of superficial temporal artery to middle cerebral artery bypass surgery; Preliminary report. *Neurology*, **32**, 422–424

BINDER, L. M. and PANKRANTZ, L. (1987) Neuropsychological evidence of a factitious memory complaint. *Journal of Clinical and Experimental Neuropsychology*, **9**, 167–171

BIRNBAUM, I. M. and PARKER, E. S. (1977) *Alcohol and Human Memory*. Hillsdale, NJ: Lawrence Erlbaum Associates

BLACK, F. W. (1973) Cognitive and memory performance in subjects with brain damage secondary to penetrating missile wounds and closed head injury. *Journal of Clinical Psychology*, **29**, 441–442

BLAKEMORE, C. B. and FALCONER, M. A. (1967) Long-term effects of anterior temporal lobectomy on certain cognitive functions. *Journal of Neurology, Neurosurgery and Psychiatry*, **30**, 364–367

BLESSED, G., TOMLINSON, B. E. and ROTH, M. (1968) The association between quantitative measures of dementia and of senile change in the cerebral grey matter of elderly subjects. *British Journal of Psychiatry*, **114**, 797–811

BLOMERT, D. M. and SISLER, G. C. (1974) The measurement of retrograde post-traumatic amnesia. *Canadian Psychiatric Association Journal*, **19**, 185–192

BLOOM, B. L. (1959) Comparison of the alternate Wechsler Memory Scale forms. *Journal of Clinical Psychology*, **15**, 72–74

BLOOM, P. A. and FISCHLER, I. (1980) Completion norms for 329 sentence contexts. *Memory and Cognition*, **8**, 631–642

BLUMETTI, A. E. and MODESTI, L. M. (1980) Long term cognitive effects of stereotactic thalamotomy on non-parkinsonian dyskinetic patients. *Applied Neurophysiology*, **43**, 259–262

BLUSEWICZ, M. J., DUSTMAN, R. E., SCHENKENBERG, T. and BECK, E. C. (1977) Neuropsychological correlates of chronic alcoholics and aging. *Journal of Nervous and Mental Disease*, **165**, 348–355

BOLLER, F. (1980) Mental status of patients with parkinson disease. *Journal of Clinical Neuropsychology*, **2**, 157–172

BORNSTEIN, R. A. (1985) Neuropsychological performance in Moya Moya disease: a case study. *International Journal of Neuroscience*, **26**, 39–46

BORNSTEIN, R. A., MCLEAN, D. R. and HO, K. (1985) Neuropsychological and electrophysiological examination of a patient with Wilson's disease. *International Journal of Neuroscience*, **26**, 239–247

BOTEZ, M. I., BOTEZ, T., LEVEILLE, J., BIELMANN, P. and CADOTTE, M. (1979) Neuropsychological correlates of folic acid deficiency: facts and hypotheses. In *Folic Acid Deficiency in Neurology, Psychiatry and Internal Medicine*, edited by M. I. Botez and E. H. Reynolds, pp. 435–461. New York: Raven Press

BOUCKOMS, A. MARTUZA, R. and HENDERSON, M. (1986) Capgras syndrome with subarachnoid haemorrhage. *Journal of Nervous and Mental Disease*, **174**, 484–488

BOUDIN, G., PEPIN, B., MIKOL, J., HAGUEMAAU, M. and VERNANT, J. (1975) Gliome du systeme limbique posterieur, revele pour une amnesia globale transitoire. *Rev Neurol (Paris)*, **131**, 157–163

BOUVIER, J. B. PASSERON, O. and CHUPIN, M. P. (1974) Psychometric study of praxilene. *J Int Med Res*, **2**, 59–65

BOWEN, F. P., BRADY, E. M. and YAHR, M. D. (1973) Short and long range studies of memory, intelligence, and perception in Parkinson patients treated with levodopa. In *Parkinson's Disease, Volume 2*, edited by J. Siegfried, pp. 315–324. Bern: Hans Huber

BOYSEN, G., HEMMINGSEN, R., MEJSHOLM, B., VORSTRUP, S., LASSEN, N. A., LESTER, J. *et al.* (1985) Improvement of intellectual function following carotid endarterectomy. In *Cerebral Vascular Disease 5*, edited by J. S. Meyer, H. Lechner, M. Reivich and E. O. Ott, pp. 278–281. Amsterdam: Excerpta Medica

BRADBURN, N. M., RIPS, L. J. and SHEVELL, S. K. (1987) Answering autobiographical questions: the impact of memory and inference on surveys. *Science*, **236**, 157–161

BRANCACCIO, D., DAMASSO, R., SPINNLER, H., STERZI, R. and VALLAR, G. (1981) Does chronic kidney failure lead to mental failure? *Archives of Neurology*, **38**, 757–758

BRANCONNIER, R. J., COLE, J. O., SPERA, K. F. and DEVITT, D. R. (1982) Recall and recognition as diagnostic indices of malignant memory loss in senile dementia: a bayesian analysis. *Exp Aging Res,* **8,** 189–193

BRANDT, J., BUTTERS, N., RYAN, C. and BAYOG, R. (1983) Cognitive loss and recovery in long-term alcohol abusers. *Archives of General Psychiatry,* **40,** 435–442

BRANDT, J., RUBINSKY, E. and LASSEN, G. (1985) Uncovering malingered amnesia. *Annals of the New York Academy of Sciences,* **444,** 502–503

BRIERLEY, J. B. and COOPER, J. E. (1962) Cerebral complications of hypotensive anaesthesia in a healthy adult. *Journal of Neurology, Neurosurgery and Psychiatry,* **25,** 24–30

BRINDLEY, G. S. and JANOTA, I. (1975) Observations on cortical blindness and on vascular lesions that cause loss of recent memory. *Journal of Neurology, Neurosurgery and Psychiatry,* **38,** 459–464

BRINKMAN, S. D., BRAUN, P., GANJI, S., MORRELL, R. M. and JACOBS L. A. (1984) Neuropsychological performance one week after carotid endarterectomy reflects intraoperative ischaemia. *Stroke,* **15,** 497–503

BRINKMAN, S. D. and GERSHON, S. (1983) Measurement of cholinergic drug effects on memory in Alzheimer's disease. *Neurobiol Aging,* **4,** 139–145

BRINKMAN, S. D., LARGEN, J. W., GERGANOFF, S. and POMARA, N. (1983) Russell's revision of the Wechsler Memory Scale in the evaluation of dementia. *Journal of Clinical Psychology,* **39,** 989–993

BRINKMAN, S. D., POMARA, N., GOODNICK, P. J., BARNETT, N. and DOMINO, E. F. (1982) A dose-ranging study of lecithin in the treatment of primary degenerative dementia (Alzheimer disease). *Journal of Clinical Psychopharmacology,* **2,** 281–285

BRION, S., DEROME, P., GUIOT, G. and TEITGEN, M. (1968) Syndrome de Korsakoff par aneurysme de l'artere communicante anteriere: le probleme des syndromes Korsakoff par hemorragie meningée. *Rev Neurol (Paris),* **118,** 293–299

BRION, S. and MIKOL, J. (1978) Atteinte du noyau lateral dorsal du thalamus et syndrome de Korsakoff alcoolique. *Journal of Neurological Science,* **38,** 249–261

BRION, S., PRAGIER, G., GUERIN, R. and TEITGEN, M. (1969) Syndrome de Korsakoff par ramollissement bilateral du fornix. *Rev. Neurol.,* **120,** 255–262

BRITTAIN, H. (1980) Epilepsy and intellectual functions. In *Epilepsy and Behaviour,* edited by B. M. Kulig, H. Meinardi and G. Stores, pp. 2–13. Lisse: Swets and Zeitlinger

BROOKS, D. J., LEENDERS, K. C., HEAD, G., MARSHALL, J., LEGG, N. J. and JONES, T. (1984) Memory in early and middle phases of multiple sclerosis. *Journal of Neurology, Neurosurgery and Psychiatry,* **47,** 1182–1191

BROOKS, D. N. (1972) Memory and head injury. *Journal of Nervous and Mental Disease,* **155,** 350–355

BROOKS, D. N. (1974a) Recognition memory and head injury. *Journal of Neurology, Neurosurgery and Psychiatry,* **37,** 794–801

BROOKS, D. N. (1974b) Recognition memory after head injury: a signal detection analysis. *Cortex,* **10,** 224–230

BROOKS, D. N. (1975) Long and short term memory in head injured patients. *Cortex,* **11,** 329–340

BROOKS, D. N. (1976) Wechsler Memory Scale performance and its relationship to brain damage after severe closed head injury. *Journal of Neurology, Neurosurgery and Psychiatry,* **39,** 593–601

BROOKS, D. N. (1984) Editor. Cognitive deficits after head injury. In *Closed Head Injury,* pp. 44–73. Oxford: Oxford University Press

BROOKS, D. N. and AUGHTON, M. E. (1979) Cognitive recovery during the first year after severe blunt head injury. *Int Rehabil Med,* **1,** 166–172

BROOKS, D. N., AUGHTON, M. E., BOND M. R., JONES, P. and RIZVI, S. (1980) Cognitive sequelae in relationship to early indices of severity of brain damage after severe blunt head injury. *Journal of Neurology, Neurosurgery and Psychiatry,* **43,** 529–534

BROOKS, D. N. and BADDELEY, A. D. (1976) What can amnesic patients learn? *Neuropsychologia,* **14,** 111–122

BROOKS, D. N., HOSIE, J., BOND, M. R., JENNETT, B. and AUGHTON, M. (1986) Cognitive sequelae of severe head injury in relation to the Glasgow Outcome Scale. *Journal of Neurology, Neurosurgery and Psychiatry,* **49,** 549–553

BROOKS, J. O. (1985) Pictorial stimuli for the Apple Macintosh computer. *Behav. Res. Meth. Instrum. and Comp.,* **17,** 409–410

BROWN, A. S. (1976) Catalog of scaled verbal material. *Memory and Cognition*, **4**, (Suppl), 1S–45S

BROWN, G. G., ROSENBAUM, G., LEWIS, R. and ROURKE, D. (1980) The effects of rehearsal rate on serial recall in Korsakoff amnesia. *Neuropsychologia*, **18**, 185–191

BROWN, J. (1958) Some tests of the decay theory of memory. *Quarterly Journal of Experimental Psychology*, **10**, 12–21

BROWN, S. W. and REYNOLDS, E. H. (1981) Cognitive impairment in epileptic patients. In *Epilepsy and Psychiatry*, edited by E. H. Reynolds and M. R. Trimble, pp. 147–164. London: Churchill Livingstone

BROWN, W. P. (1972) Studies in word listing: some norms and their reliability. *Irish Journal of Psychology*, **1**, 117–159

BRUHN, P., ARLIEN-SOBORG, P., GYLDENSTEAD, C. and CHRISTENSEN, E. L. (1981) Prognosis in chronic toxic encephalopathy. *Acta Neurologica Scandinavica*, **64**, 259–272

BRUHN, P. and MAAGE, N. (1975) Intellectual and neuropsychological functions in young men with heavy and long-term patterns of drug abuse. *American Journal of Psychiatry*, **132**, 397–401

BRUST, J. C. (1983a) Vascular dementia – still overdiagnosed. *Stroke*, **14**, 298–300

BRUST, J. C. M. (1983b) Dementia and cerebrovascular disease. In *The Dementias*, edited by R. Mayeux and W. G. Rosen. New York: Raven Press

BUSCHKE, H. (1973) Selective reminding for analysis of memory and learning. *J Verb Learn Verb Behav*, **12**, 543–550

BUSCHKE, H. and FULD, P. A. (1974) Evaluating storage, retention, and retrieval in disordered memory and learning. *Neurology*, **24**, 1019–1025

BUTLIN, A. T., DANTA, G. and COOK, M. L. (1984a) Anticonvulsant effects on the memory performance of epileptics. In *Clinical and Experimental Neurology*, Volume 20, edited by J. H. Tyrer and M. J. Eadie, pp. 27–35. Sydney: ADS Health Science Press

BUTLIN, A. T., DANTA, G. and COOK, M. L. (1984b) Anticonvulsants, folic acid and memory dysfunction in epileptics. In *Clinical and Experimental Neurology*, Volume 20, edited by J. H. Tyrer and M. J. Eadie, pp. 58–62. Sydney: ADS Health Science Press

BUTTERS, N. (1984a) Alcoholic Korsakoff's syndrome: an update. *Seminars in Neurology*, **4**, 226–244

BUTTERS, N. (1984b) The clinical aspects of memory disorders: contributions from experimental studies of amnesia and dementia. *Journal of Clinical Neuropsychology*, **6**, 17–36

BUTTERS, N. (1985) Alcoholic Korsakoff's syndrome: some unresolved issues concerning etiology, neuropathology and cognitive deficits. *Journal of Clinical Neuropsychology*, **7**, 181–210

BUTTERS, N. and ALBERT, M. S. (1982) Processes underlying failure to recall remote events. In *Human Memory and Amnesia*, edited by L. S. Cermak, pp. 257–274. Hillsdale, New Jersey: Laurence Erblaum Associates

BUTTERS, N., ALBERT, M. S., MILIOTIS, P., PHILLIPS, J., STERSTE, A. and SAX, D. S. (1983) The effect of verbal mediators on the pictorial memory of brain-damaged patients. *Neuropsychologia*, **21**, 307–323

BUTTERS, N. and CERMAK, L. S. (1974) Some comments on Warrington and Baddeley's report of normal short-term memory in amnesic patients. *Neuropsychologia*, **12**, 283–285

BUTTERS, N. and CERMAK, L. S. (1976) Neuropsychological studies of alcoholic Korsakoff patients. In *Empirical Studies of Alcoholism*, edited by G. Goldstein and C. Neuringer. Cambridge: Ballinger

BUTTERS, N. and CERMAK, L. S. (1980) *Alcoholic Korsakoff's syndrome: an Information Processing Approach to Amnesia*. New York: Academic Press

BUTTERS, N. and CERMAK, L. S. (1986) A case study of the forgetting of autobiographical knowledge: implications for the study of retrograde amnesia. In *Autobiographical Memory*, edited by D. C. Rubin, pp. 253–272. Cambridge: Cambridge University Press

BUTTERS, N., CERMAK, L. S., MONTGOMERY, K. and ADINOLFI, A. (1977) Some comparisons of the memory and visuoperceptive deficits of chronic alcoholics and patients with Korsakoff's disease. *Alcoholism*, **1**, 73–80

BUTTERS, N. and GRADY, M. (1977) Effect of predistractor delays on short-term memory performance of patients with Korsakoff's and Huntington's disease. *Neuropsychologia*, **15**, 701–705

BUTTERS, N., LEWIS, R., CERMAK, L. S. and GOODGLASS, H. (1973) Material-specific memory deficits in alcoholic Korsakoff patients. *Neuropsychologia*, **11**, 291–299

BUTTERS, N. and MILIOTIS, P. (1985) Amnesic disorders. In *Clinical Neuropsychology*, edited by K. M. Heilman and E. Valenstein, pp. 403–451. New York: Oxford University Press

BUTTERS, N., MILOTIS, P., ALBERT, M. S. and SAX, D. S. (1984) Memory assessment: evidence of the heterogeneity of amnesic symptoms. In *Advances in Clinical Neuropsychology, Volume 1*, edited by G. Goldstein. New York: Plenum Press

BUTTERS, N., SAX, D., MONTGOMERY, K. and TARLOW, S. (1978) Comparison of the neuropsychological deficits associated with early and advanced Huntington's disease. *Archives of Neurology*, **35**, 585–589

BUTTERS, N. TARLOW, S. and CERMAK, L. S. (1976) A comparison of the information processing deficits of patients with Huntington's chorea and Korsakoff's syndrome. *Cortex*, **12**, 134–144

BUTTERS, N., WOLFE, J., GRANHOLM, E. and MARTONE, M. (1986) An assessment of verbal recall, recognition and fluency abilities in patients with Huntington's disease. *Cortex*, **22**, 11–32

BUTTERS, N., WOLFE, J., MARTONE, M., GRANHOLM, E. and CERMAK, L. S. (1985) Memory disorders associated with Huntington's disease. Verbal recall, verbal recognition and procedural memory. *Neuropsychologia*, **23**, 729–743

CAFFARRA, P., MORETTI, G., MAZZUCCHI, A. and PARMA, M. (1981) Neuropsychological testing during a transient global amnesia episode and its follow up. *Acta Neurologica Scandinavica*, **63**, 44–50

CAINE, E. D., BAMFORD, K. A., SCHIFFER, R. B., SHOULSON, I. and LEVY, S. (1986) A controlled neuropsychological comparison of Huntington's disease and multiple sclerosis. *Archives of Neurology*, **43**, 249–254

CAINE, E. D., EBERT, M. H. and WEINGARTNER, H. (1977) An outline for the analysis of dementia. *Neurology*, **27**, 1087–1092

CAINE, E. D., HUNT, R. D., WEINGARTNER, H. and EBERT, M. H. (1978) Huntington's dementia: clinical and neuropsychological features. *Archives of General Psychiatry*, **35**, 377–384

CAIRNS, H. and MOSBERG, W. H. (1951) Colloid cyst of the third ventricle. *Surgery, Gynecology and Obstetrics*, **92**, 545–570

CALA, L. A. (1983) CT demonstrations of the early effects of alcohol on the brain. *Recent Developments in Alcoholism*, Volume 3, edited by M. Galanter, pp. 253–264. New York: Plenum Press

CALA, L. A., JONES, R., WILEY, B. and MASTAGLIA, F. L. (1980) A computerised axial tomography (CAT) study of alcohol induced cerebral atrophy in conjunction with other correlates. *Acta Psychiatrica Scandinavica*, **62** (Suppl 286), 31–40

CALTAGIRONE, C., ALBANESE, A., GAINOTTI, G. and MASULLO, C. (1983) Acute administration of individual optimal dose of physostigmine fails to improve mnemonic performances in Alzheimer's presenile dementia. *International Journal of Neuroscience*, **18**, 143–148

CALTAGIRONE, C., GAINOTTI, G. and MASULLO, C. (1982) Oral administration of chronic physostigmine does not improve cognitive or mnemonic performances in Alzheimer's presenile dementia. *International Journal of Neuroscience*, **16**, 247–249

CALTAGIRONE, C., GAINOTTI, G., MASULLO, C. and VILLA, G. (1982) Neuropsychological study of normal pressure hydrocephalus. *Acta Psychiatrica Scandinavica*, **65**, 93–100

CAMERON, A. S. and ARCHIBALD, Y. M. (1981) Verbal memory deficit after left fornix removal: a case report. *International Journal of Neuroscience*, **12**, 201

CANAVAN, A. G. M., JANOTA, I. and SCHURR, P. H. (1985) Luria's frontal lobe syndrome: psychological and anatomical considerations. *Journal of Neurology, Neurosurgery and Psychiatry*, **48**, 1049–1053

CAPITANI, E., SPINNLER, H., STERZI, R. and VALLAR, G. (1980) The hemispheric side of neocortical damage does not affect memory for undimensional position. An experiment with Posner and Konick's test. *Cortex*, **16**, 295–304

CAPLAN, L. R. (1980) Top of the basilar syndrome. *Neurology*, **30**, 72–79

CAPLAN, L. R. (1985) Transient global amnesia. In *Handbook of Clinical Neurology*, Volume 1, edited by J. A. M. Fredriks, p. 45. Amsterdam: Elsevier Science

CAPLAN, L., CHEDRU, F., LHERMITTE, F. and MAYMAN, C. (1981) Transient global amnesia and migraine. *Neurology*, **31**, 1167–1170

CAPLAN, L. R. and HEDLEY-WHYTE, T. (1974) Cuing and memory dysfunction in alexia without agraphia. *Brain*, **97**, 251–262

CARAMAZZA, A., ZURIF, E. B. and GARDNER, H. (1978) Sentence memory in aphasia. *Neuropsychologia*, **16**, 661–669

CARLEN, P. L. (1981) Reversible effects of chronic alcoholism on the human central nervous system: possible biological mechanisms. In *Cerebral Deficits in Alcoholism*, edited by D. A. Wilkinson, pp. 107–127. Toronto: Addiction Research Foundation

CARMEL, P. W. (1985) Tumours of the third ventricle. *Acta Neurochirurgica,* **75,** 136–146

CARR, I. (1982) The Ophelia syndrome: memory loss in Hodgkin's disease. *Lancet,* **i,** 844–845

CARROLL, J. B., DAVIES, P. and RICHMAN, B. (1971) *The American Heritage Word Frequency Book.* Boston: Houghton Mifflin

CARROLL, M., GATES, R. and ROLDEN, F. (1984) Memory impairment in multiple sclerosis. *Neuropsychologia,* **22,** 297–302

CASTAIGNE, P., LHERMITTE, F., BUGE, A., ESCOUROLLE, R., HAUW, J. J. and LYON-CAEN, O. (1981) Paramedian thalamic and midbrain infarct: clinical and neuropathological study. *Annals of Neurology,* **10,** 127–148

CATSMAN-BERROVOETS, C. E., VAN HARSKAMP, F. and APPELHOF, A. (1986) Beneficial effect of physostigmine on clinical amnesic behaviour and neuropsychological test results in a patient with a post-encephalitic syndrome. *Journal of Neurology, Neurosurgery and Psychiatry,* **49,** 1088–1089

CATTAINO, G., QUERIN, F., POSNER, A. and PIAZZA, P. (1984) Transient global amnesia. *Acta Neurologica Scandinavica,* **70,** 385–390

CAVAZZUTI, V., WINSTON, K., BAKER, R. and WELCH, K. (1980) Psychological changes following surgery for tumors in the temporal lobe. *Journal of Neurosurgery,* **53,** 618–626

CAVAZZUTI, V., FISCHER, E. G., WELCH, K., BELLI, J. A. and WINSTON, K. R. (1983) Neurological and psychophysiological sequelae following different treatments of craniopharyngioma in children. *Journal of Neurosurgery,* **59,** 409–417

CERMAK, L. S. (1975) Imagery as an aid to retrieval for Korsakoff patients. *Cortex,* **11,** 163–169

CERMAK, L. S. (1976) The encoding capacity of a patient with amnesia due to encephalitis. *Neuropsychologia,* **14,** 311–326

CERMAK, L. S. (1980) Improving retention in alcoholic Korsakoff patients. *J Stud Alcohol,* **41,** 159–169

CERMAK, L. S., BLACKFORD, S. P., O'CONNOR, M. and BLEICH, R. P. (1987) The implicit memory of a patient with amnesia due to encephalitis. *Brain and Cognition,* (in press)

CERMAK, L. S. and BUTTERS, N. (1972) The role of interference and encoding in the short-term memory deficits of Korsakoff patients. *Neuropsychologia,* **10,** 89–95

CERMAK, L. S. and BUTTERS, N. (1976) The role of language in the memory disorders of brain damaged patients. *Annals of the New York Academy of Sciences,* **280,** 857–867

CERMAK, L. S., BUTTERS, N. and GERREIN, J. (1973) The extent of the verbal encoding ability of Korsakoff patients. *Neuropsychologia,* **11,** 85–94

CERMAK, L. S., BUTTERS, N. and GOODGLASS, H. (1971) The extent of memory loss in Korsakoff patients. *Neuropsychologia,* **9,** 307–315

CERMAK, L. S., BUTTERS, N. and MOREINES, J. (1974) Some analyses of the verbal encoding deficit of alcoholic Korsakoff patients. *Brain Lang,* **1,** 141–150

CERMAK, L. S., LEWIS, R., BUTTERS, N. and GOODGLASS, H. (1973) Role of verbal mediation in performance of motor tasks by Korsakoff patients. *Percept Mot Skills,* **37,** 259–262

CERMAK, L. S. and MOREINES, J. (1976) Verbal retention deficits in aphasic and amnesic patients. *Brain Lang,* **3,** 16–27

CERMAK, L. S., NAUS, M. J. and REALE, L. (1976) Rehearsal strategies of alcoholic Korsakoff patients. *Brain Lang,* **3,** 375–385

CERMAK, L. S. and O'CONNOR, M. (1983) The anterograde and retrograde retrieval ability of a patient with amnesia due to encephalitis. *Neuropsychologia,* **21,** 213–234

CERMAK, L. S., O'CONNOR, M. and TALBOT, N. (1986) Biasing of alcoholic Korsakoff patients' semantic memory. *Journal of Clinical and Experimental Neuropsychology,* **8,** 543–555

CERMAK, L. S. and REALE, L. (1978) Depth of processing and retention of words by alcoholic Korsakoff patients. *J Exp Psychol: Learn Mem Cogn,* **4,** 165–174

CERMAK, L. S., REALE, L. and DELUCA, D. (1977) Korsakoff patients' nonverbal vs verbal memory: effects of interference and mediation on rate of information loss. *Neuropsychologia,* **15,** 303–310

CERMAK, L. S. and RYBACK, R. S. (1976) Recovery of verbal short-term memory in alcoholics. *J Stud Alcohol,* **37,** 46–52

CERMAK, L. S. and STIASSNY, D. (1982) Recall failure following successful generation and recognition of responses by alcoholic Korsakoff patients. *Brain and Cognition,* **1,** 165–176

CERMAK, L. S., TALBOT, N., CHANDLER, K. and WOLBARST, L. R. (1985) The perceptual priming phenomenon in amnesia. *Neuropsychologia,* **23,** 615–622

CERMAK, L. S. and TARLOW, S. (1978) Aphasic and amnesic patients' verbal versus nonverbal retentive abilities. *Cortex,* **14,** 32–40

CERMAK, L. S. and UHLY, B. (1975) Short-term motor memory in Korsakoff patients. *Percept Mot Skills,* **40,** 275–281

CHADWICK, O., RUTTER, M., BROWN, G., SHAFFER, D. and TRAUB, M. (1981a) A prospective study of children with head injuries: II cognitive sequelae. *Psychological Medicine,* **11,** 49–62

CHADWICK, O., RUTTER, M., THOMPSON, J. and SHAFFER, D. (1981b) Intellectual performance and reading skills after localized head injury in childhood. *Journal of Child Psychology and Psychiatry,* **22,** 117–139

CHAPMAN, L. F., WALTER, R. D., RAND, R. W., MARKHAM, C. H. and CRANDALL, P. H. (1967) Memory changes induced by stimulation of hippocampus or amygdala in epilepsy patients with implanted electrodes. *Transactions of the American Neurological Association,* **92,** 50–56

CHASE, T. N., DURSO, R., FEDIO, P. and TAMMINGA, C. A. (1982) Vasopressin treatment of cognitive deficits in Alzheimer's disease. In *Alzheimer's Disease: A Report of Progress* (Aging, Volume 19), edited by S. Corkin *et al.*, pp. 457–461. New York: Raven Press

CHEE, P. C., DAVID, A., GALBRAITH, S. and GILLHHAM, R. (1985) Dementia due to meningioma: outcome after surgical removal. *Surg Neurol,* **23,** 414–416

CHERLOW, D. G. and SERAFETINIDES, E. A. (1976) Speech and memory assessment in psychomotor epileptics. *Cortex,* **12,** 21–26

CHOI, D., SUDARSKY, L., SCHACHTER, S., BIBER, M. and BURKE, P. (1983) Medical thalamic haemorrhage with amnesia. *Archives of Neurology,* **40,** 611–613

CHOUZA, C., ROMERO, S., LAGUARDIA, G., POU, G., LORENZO, J., FLORES, M. *et al.* (1984) Hemi-parkinsonism: clinical, neuropsychological, and tomographical studies. *Advances in Neurology,* **40,** 415–425

CHRISTIE, J. E. (1982) Physostigmine and arecoline infusions in Alzheimer's disease. In *Alzheimer's Disease: A Report of Progress* (Aging, Volume, 19), edited by S. Corkin *et al.* pp. 413–419. New York: Raven Press

CHUI, H. C. and DAMASIO, A. R. (1980) Progressive dialysis encephalopathy ('dialysis dementia'). *Journal of Neurology,* **222,** 145–157

CHUI, H. C., MORTIMOR, J. A., SLAGER, U., ZAROW, C., BONDAROFF, W. and WEBSTER, D. D. (1986) Pathologic correlates of dementia in Parkinson's disease. *Archives of Neuroloyg,* **43,** 991–995

CLAPAREDE, E. (1911) Recognition et moiite. *Archives de Psychologie,* **11,** 79–90

COCHRAN, J. W., MORRELL, F., HUCKMAN, M. S. and COCHRAN, E. J. (1982) Transient global amnesia after cerebral angiography. *Archives of Neurology,* **39,** 593–594

COCHRANE, N. and KLJAJIC, I. (1979) The effects on intellectual functioning of open prefrontal leucotomy. *Medical Journal of Australia,* **1,** 258–260

COHEN, N. J. and SQUIRE, L. R. (1980) Preserved learning and retention of pattern analyzing skill in amnesia: dissociation of knowing how and knowing that. *Science,* **210,** 207–209

COHEN, N. J. and SQUIRE, L. R. (1981) Retrograde amnesia and remote memory impairment. *Neuropsychologia,* **119,** 337–356

CONKEY, R. C. (1938) Psychological changes associated with head injuries. *Archives of Psychology,* **232,** 1–62

CONLEY, F. K., MOSES, J. A. and HELLE, T. L. (1980) Deficits of higher cortical functioning in two patients with posterior parietal arteriovenous malformations. *Neurosurgery,* **7,** 230–237

COOK, G. C. (1985) Write a single-author book. In *How To Do It,* edited by S. Lock, pp. 241–244. London: British Medical Association

CORKIN, S. (1965) Tactually guided maze learning in man: effects of unilateral cortical excisions and bilateral hippocampal lesions. *Neuropsychologia,* **3,** 339–351

CORKIN, S. (1968) Acquisition of motor skill after bilateral medial temporal lobe excision. *Neuropsychologia,* **6,** 255–264

CORKIN, S. (1980) A prospective study of cingulotomy. In *The Psychosurgery Debate. Scientific, Legal and Ethical Perspectives,* edited by E. S. Valenstein, pp. 164–204. San Francisco: W. H. Freeman & Co

CORKIN, S. (1982) Some relationships between global amnesias and the memory impairments in Alzheimer's disease. In *Alzheimer's Disease,* edited by S. Corkin, K. Davies, J. Growdon and E. Usdin, pp. 149–164. New York: Raven Press

CORKIN, S. (1984) Lasting consequences of bilateral medial temporal lobectomy: clinical course and experimental findings in H.M. *Seminars in Neurology*, **4**, 249–259

CORKIN, S. (1985) Neuropsychological studies in Alzheimer's disease. In *Normal Aging, Alzheimer's Disease and Senile Dementia*, edited by C. G. Gottfries, pp. 219–224. Brussels: University of Brussels

CORKIN, S., COHEN N. J., SULLIVAN, E. V., CLEGG, R. A., ROSEN, J. and ACKERMAN, R. H. (1985) Analysis of global memory impairments of different aetiologies. *Annals of the New York Academy of Sciences*, **444**, 10–40

CORKIN, S., DAVIS, K., GROWDON, J., USDIN, E. and WURTMAN, R. (1982) *Alzheimer's disease: a Report of Progress in Research*. New York: Raven Press

CORKIN, S., GROWDON, J. H., NISSEN, M. J., HUFF, F. J., FREED, D. M. and SAGAR, H. J. (1984) Recent advances in the neuropsychological study of Alzheimer's disease. In *Alzheimer's Disease: Advances in Basic Research and Therapies*, edited by R. J. Wurtman, S. H., Corkin and J. H. Growdon, pp. 75–93. Cambridge: Center for Brain Sciences and Metabolism Charitable Trust

CORSELLIS, J. A. N., GOLDBERG, G. J. and NORTON, A. R. (1968) 'Limbic encephalitis' and its association with carcinoma. *Brain*, **91**, 481–496

COUGHLAN, A. K. (1979) Effects of localised cerebral lesions and dysphasia on verbal memory. *Journal of Neurology, Neurosurgery and Psychiatry*, **42**, 914–923

COUGHLAN, A. K. and HOLLOWS, S. E. (1984) The use of memory tests in differentiating organic disorder from depression. *British Journal of Psychiatry*, **145**, 164–167

COUGHLAN, A. K. and HOLLOWS, S. E. (1985) *The Adult Memory and Information Processing Battery*. St James's University Hospital, Leeds: A. K. Coughlan

COURVILLE, C. B. (1945) *Pathology of the Central Nervous System*, 2nd edn. Mountain View: Pacific Press Publishers Association

CRITCHLEY, M. (1930) The anterior cerebral artery, and its syndromes. *Brain*, **53**, 120–165

CROFT, P. B., HEATHFIELD, K. W. G. and SWASH, M. (1973) Differential diagnosis of transient amnesia. *British Medical Journal*, **4**, 593–596

CRONHOLM, B. and JONSSON, I. (1957) Memory functions after cerebral concussion. *Acta Chirurgica Scandinavica*, **113**, 263–271

CROOK, T., FERRIS, S. and MCCARTHY, M. (1979) The misplaced objects test: a brief test for memory dysfunction in the aged. *Journal of the American Geriatric Society*, **27**, 284–287

CROOK, T. (1985) Clinical drug trials in Alzheimer's disease. *Annals of the New York Academy of Sciences*, **444**, 528–536

CROOKES, T. G. and MCDONALD, K. G. (1972) Benton's Visual Retention Test in the differentiation of depression and early dementia. *Br J Soc Clin Psychol*, **11**, 66–69

CROSSON, B. (1986) On localization versus systemic effects in alcoholic Korsakoff syndrome. A comment on Butters (1985). *Journal of Clinical and Experimental Neuropsychology*, **8**, 744–748

CROSSON, B. and BUENNING, W. (1984) An individualized memory retraining program after closed head injury: a single case study. *Journal of Clinical Neuropsychology*, **6**, 287–301

CROVITZ, H. F. (1979) Memory retraining in brain-damaged patients: the airplane list. *Cortex*, **15**, 131–134

CROVITZ, H. F. (1986) Loss and recovery of autobiographical memory after head injury. In *Autobiographical Memory*, edited by D. C. Rubin, pp. 273–290. Cambridge: Cambridge University Press

CROVITZ, H. F., HARVEY, M. T. and HORN, R. W. (1979) Problems in the acquisition of imagery mnemonics: three brain-damaged cases. *Cortex*, **15**, 225–234

CROVITZ, H. F., HORN, R. W. and DANIEL, W. F. (1983) Inter-relationships among retrograde amnesia, post-traumatic amnesia, and time since head injury: a retrospective study. *Cortex*, **19**, 407–412

CROWELL, G. F., STUMP, D. A., BILLER, J., MCHENRY, L. C. and TOOLE, J. F. (1984) The transient global amnesia-migraine connection. *Archives of Neurology*, **41**, 75–79

CROWELL, R. M. and MORAWETZ, R. B. (1977) The anterior communicating artery has significant branches. *Stroke*, **8**, 272–273

CULLUM, C. M. and BIGLER, E. D. (1985) Late effects of haematoma on brain morphology and memory in closed head injury. *International Journal of Neuroscience*, **28**, 279–283

CULLUM, C. M. and BIGLER, E. D. (1986) Ventricular size, cortical atrophy and the relationship with neuropsychological status in closed head injury: a quantitative analysis. *Journal of Clinical and Experimental Neuropsychology*, **8**, 437–452

CUMMINGS, J. L. (1985) Organic delusions: phenomenology, anatomical correlations and review. *British Journal of Psychiatry*, **46**, 184–197

CUMMINGS, J. L. and DUCHEN, L. W. (1981) Kluver-Bucy syndrome in Pick's disease: clinical and pathological correlations. *Neurology*, **31**, 1415–1422

CUMMINGS, J. L., LANDIS, T. and BENSON, D. F. (1983) Environmental disorientation: clinical and radiological findings. *Neurology*, **33** (Suppl. 2), 103–104

CUMMINGS, J. L., TOMIYASU, U., READ, S. and BENSON, D. F. (1984) Amnesia with hippocampal lesions after cardiopulmonary arrest. *Neurology*, **34**, 679–681

CUTLER, N. R., HAXBY, J. V., DUARA, R., GRADY, C. L., KAY, A. D., KESSLER, R. M. *et al.* (1985) Clinical history, brain metabolism and neuropsychological function in Alzheimer's disease. *Annals of Neurology*, **18**, 298–309

CUTTING, J. (1978a) The relationship between Korsakov's syndrome and 'alcoholic dementia'. *British Journal of Psychiatry*, **132**, 240–251

CUTTING, J. (1978b) Specific psychological deficits in alcoholism. *British Journal of Psychiatry*, **133**, 119–122

CUTTING, J. (1979) Memory in functional psychosis. *Journal of Neurology, Neurosurgery and Psychiatry*, **42**, 1031–1037

CUTTING, J. (1981) Response bias in Korsakoff's syndrome. *Cortex*, **17**, 107–112

CUTTING, J. (1985a) Korsakoff's syndrome. In *Handbook of Clinical Neurology, Volume 1(45): Clinical Neuropsychology*, edited by J. A. M. Frederiks. Amsterdam: Elsevier Science Publishers

CUTTING, J. (1985b) *The Psychology of Schizophrenia*. Edinburgh: Churchill Livingstone

DAMASIO, A. R. and GRAFF-RADFORD, N. R. (1983) Transient partial amnesia. *Archives of Neurology*, **40**, 656–657

DAMASIO, A. R., GRAFF-RADFORD, N. R., ESLINGER, P. J., DAMASIO, H. and KASSELL, N. (1985a) Amnesia following basal forebrain lesions. *Archives of Neurology*, **42**, 263–271

DAMASIO, A. R., ESLINGER, P. J., DAMASIO, H., VAN HOESEN, G. W. and CORNELL, S. (1985b) Multimodal amnesic syndrome following bilateral temporal and basal forebrain damage. *Archives of Neurology*, **42**, 252–259

DARLEY, C. F. and MURDOCK, B. B. (1971) Effects of prior free-recall testing on final recall and recognition. *Journal of Experimental Psychology*, **91**, 66–73

DARLEY, C. F. and TINKLENBERG, J. R. (1974) Marijuana and memory. In *Marijuana. Effects on Human Behaviour*, edited by L. L. Miller, pp. 73–102. New York: Academic Press

DAVIDOFF, D. A., BUTTERS, N., GESTMAN, L. J., ZURIF, E., PAUL, I. H. and MATTIS, S. (1984) Affective/motivational factors in the recall of prose passages by alcoholic Korsakoff patients. *Alcohol*, **1**, 63–69

DAVIDOFF, J. B. and OSTERGAARD, A. L. (1984) Colour anomia resulting from weakened short-term colour memory. *Brain*, **107**, 415–431

DAVIES, A. D. M. and BINKS, M. G. (1983) Supporting the residual memory of a Korsakoff patient. *Behavioural Psychotherapy*, **11**, 62–74

DAVIS, K. L. and MOHS, R. C. (1982) Enhancement of memory processes in Alzheimer's disease with multiple dose intravenous physostigmine. *American Journal of Psychiatry*, **139**, 1421–1424

DAVIS, K. L., MOHS, R. C., DAVIS, R. M., LEVY, M. I., HORVATH, T. B., ROSENBERG, G. S., *et al.* (1982) Cholingeric treatment in Alzheimer's disease. In *Alzhemier's Disease: A Report of Progress*, edited by S. Corkin, *et al.*, pp. 483–494. New York: Raven Press

DAVIS, P. E. and MUMFORD, S. J. (1984) Cued recall and the nature of the memory disorder in dementia. *British Journal of Psychiatry*, **144**, 383–386

DEARY, I. J., WESSELY, S. and FARRELL, M. (1985) Dementia and Mrs Thatcher. *British Medical Journal*, **291**, 1768

DEISENHAMMER, E. (1981) Transient global amnesia as an epileptic manifestation. *Journal of Neurology*, **225**, 289–292

DE JONG, R. N., ITABASHI, H. H. and OLSON, J. R. (1969) Memory loss due to hippocampal lesions. Report of a case. *Archives of Neurology*, **20**, 339–348

DELANEY, R. C., PREVEY, M. L. and MATTSON, R. H. (1986) Short-term retention with lateralized temporal lobe epilepsy. *Cortex*, **22**, 591–600

DELANEY, R. C., ROSEN, A. J., MATTSON, R. H. and NOVELLY, R. A. (1980) Memory function in focal epilepsy. *Cortex*, **16**, 103–117

DELANEY, R., WALLACE, J. and EGELKO, S. (1980) Neuropsychological aspects of transient ischemic attacks. *Journal of Clinical Neuropsychology*, **2**, 107–114

DELAY, J., BRION, S. and DEROUESNE, C. (1964) Syndrome de Korsakoff et etiologie tumorale: etude anatomo-clinque de trois observations. *Rev Neurol*, **111**, 97–133

DE LEON, M. J., FERRIS, S. H., GEORGE, A. E., REISBERG, B., KRICHEFF, I. I. and GERSHON, S. (1980) Computed tomography evaluations of brain-behaviour relationships in senile dementia of the Alzheimer's type. *Neurobiological Aging*, **1**, 69–79

DE LEON, M. J. and GEORGE, A. E., (1983) Computed tomography in aging and senile dementia. In *Advances in Neurology, Volume 38: The Dementias*, edited by R. Mayeux and W. G. Rosea. New York: Raven Press

DELIS, D., DIRENFIELD, L., ALEXANDER, M. P. and KAPLAN, E. (1982) Cognitive fluctuations associated with on-off phenomenon in Parkinson disease. *Neurology*, **32**, 1049–1052

DELLA SALA, S. and SPINNLER, H. (1986) 'Indifference amnesique' in a case of global amnesia following acute hypoxia. *European Neurology*, **25**, 98–109

DELUCA, D., CERMAK, L. S. and BUTTERS, N. (1975) An analysis of Korsakoff patients' recall following varying types of distractor activity. *Neuropsychologia*, **13**, 271–279

DELUCA, D., CERMAK, L. S. and BUTTERS, N. (1976) The differential effects of semantic, acoustic and nonverbal distraction on Korsakoff patients' verbal retention performance. *International Journal of Neuroscience*, **6**, 279–284

DE RENZI, E. (1986) Prosopagnosia in two patients with CT evidence of damage confined to the right hemisphere. *Neuropsychologia*, **24**, 385–389

DE RENZI, E., FAGLIONI, P., NICHELLI, P. and PIGNATTARI, L. (1984) Intellectual and memory impairment in moderate and heavy drinkers. *Cortex*, **20**, 525–534

DE RENZI, E., FAGLIONI, P. and VILLA, P. (1977) Topographical amnesia. *Journal of Neurology, Neurosurgery and Psychiatry*, **40**, 498–505

DESROSIERS, G. and IVISON, D. (1986) Paired associate learning: normative data for differences between high and low associate word pairs. *Journal of Clinical and Experimental Neuropsychology*, **8**, 637–642

DESTEE, A., BLOND, S., LESOIN, F., SZILKA, G., WAROT, P. and LAINE, E. (1985) Syndrome de Korsakoff aigu et transitoire par hematome du plancher de 3 ventricule. *Rev Neurol*, **141**, 305–310

DEUTSCH, C. P. (1953) Differences among epileptics and non-epileptics in terms of some memory and learning variables. *Archives of Neurology and Psychiatry*, **70**, 474–482

DEWHURST, K. (1969) The neurosyphilitic psychoses today: a survey of 91 cases. *British Journal of Psychiatry*, **115**, 31–38

DIESFELDT, H. F. A. (1978) The distinction between long-term and short-term memory in senile dementia: an anlysis of free recall and delayed recognition. *Neuropsychologia*, **16**, 115–119

DIKMEN, S., TEMKIN, N., WEILER, M. and WYLER, A. R. (1984) Behavioural effects of anticonvulsant prophylaxis: no effect or artifact? *Epilepsia*, **25**, 741–746

DIMOND, S. J., SCAMMELL, R. E., BROUWERS, E. Y. and WEEKS, R. (1977) Functions of the centre section (trunk) of the corpus callosum in man. *Brain*, **100**, 543–562

DIMSDALE, H., LOGUE, V. and PIERCY, M. (1964) A case of persisting memory impairment following right temporal lobectomy. *Neuropsychologia*, **1**, 287–298

DODRILL, C. B. (1986) Correlates of generalized tonic-clonic seizures with intellectual, neuropsychological, emotional, and social functioning in patients with epilepsy. *Epilepsia*, **27**, 399–411

DONALDSON, I. M. (1985) 'Psychometric' assessment during transient global amnesia. *Cortex*, **21**, 149–152

DONNAN, G. A., WALSH, K. W. and BLADIN, P. F. (1978) Memory disorder in vertebrobasilar disease. *Clinical and Experimental Neurology*, **15**, 215–220

DONNELLY, E. F. and CHASE, T. N. (1973) Intellectual and memory function in Parkinsonian and non-Parkinsonian patients treated with L-dopa. *Diseases of the Nervous System*, **34**, 119–123

DRACHMAN, D. A. and ADAMS, R. D. (1962) Herpes simplex and acute inclusion-body encephalitis. *Archives of Neurology*, **7**, 45–63

DRACHMAN, D. A. and ARBIT, J. (1966) Memory and the hippocampal complex. *Archives of Neurology*, **15**, 52–61

DRACHMAN, D. A. and HUGHES, J. R. (1971) Memory and the hippocampal complexes. *Neurology*, **21**, 1–14

DRICKER, J., BUTTERS, N., BERMAN, G., SAMUELS, I. and CAREY, S. (1978) The recognition and encoding of faces by alcoholic Korsakoff and right hemisphere patients. *Neuropsychologia*, **16**, 683–695

DUARA, R., GRADY, C., HAXBY, J., SUNDARAM, M., CUTLER, N. R., HESTON, L., *et al.* (1986) Positron emission tomography in Alzheimer's disease. *Neurology*, **36**, 879–887

DUFFNER, P. K., COHEN, M. E. and THOMAS, P. (1983) Late effects of treatment on the intelligence of children with posterior fossa tumours. *Cancer*, **51**, 233–237

DUGAN, T. M., NORDGREN, R. E. and O'LEARY, P. (1981) Transient global amnesia associated with bradycardia and temporal lobe spikes. *Cortex*, **17**, 633–637

DUNN, J. and BROOKS, D. N. (1974) Memory and post traumatic amnesia. *Journal of International Research Communications*, **2**, 1947

DUYCKAERTS, C., DEROUESNE, C., SIGNORET, J. L. and GRAY, F. (1985) Bilateral and limited amygdalohippocampal lesions causing a pure amnesic syndrome. *Annals of Neurology*, **18**, 314–319

DYE, O. A., MILBY, J. B. and SAXON, S. A. (1979) Effects of early neurological problems following head trauma on subsequent neuropsychological performance. *Acta Neurologica Scandinavica*, **59**, 10–14

DYSKEN, M. W., FOVALL, P., HARRIS, C. M., NORONHA, A., BERGEN, D., HOEPPNER, T. *et al.* (1982) Lecithin administration in patients with primary degenerative dementia and in normal volunteers. In *Alzheimer's Disease: a Report of Progress in Research*, edited by S. Corkin, K. L. Davis, J. H. Growdon, E. Usdun and R. J. Wurlman, pp. 385–392. New York: Raven Press

ECKARDT, M. J., PARKER, E. S., NOBLE, E. P., FELDMAN, D. J. and GOTTSCHALK, L. A. (1978) Relationship between neuropsychological performance and alcohol consumption in alcoholics. *Biol Psychiat*, **13**, 551–565

EDEN, K. and TURNER, J. W. A. (1941) Loss of consciousness in different types of head injury. *Proceedings of the Royal Society of Medicine*, **34**, 685–692

EISER, C. (1978) Intellectual abilities among survivors of childhood leukaemia as a function of CNS irradiation. *Archives of Diseases in Childhood*, **53**, 391–395

ELLIOT, C. D., MURRAY, D. J. and PEARSON, L. S. (1983) *British Ability Scales*. Windsor: NFER-Nelson

ELOFSSON, S-A., GAMBERALE, F., HINDMARSH, T., IREGREN, A., ISAKSSON, A., JOHNSSON, I., *et al.* (1980) Exposure to organic solvents. *Scandinavian Journal of Work and Environmental Health*, **6**, 239–273

ELSASS, P., LUND, Y. and RANEK, L. (1978) Encephalopathy in patients with cirrhosis of the liver: a neuropsychological study. *Scandinavian Journal of Gastroenterology*, **13**, 241–247

ENGLISH, A., SAVAGE, R. D., BRITTON, P. G., WARD, M. K. and KERR, D. N. (1978) Intellectual impairment in chronic renal failure. *British Medical Journal*, **1**, 888–890

ERICKSON, R. C. and SCOTT, M. L. (1977) Clinical memory testing: a review. *Psychology Bulletin*, **84**, 1130–1149

ESKELINEN, L., LUISTO, M., TENKANEN, L. and OSVALDO, M. (1986) Neuropsychological methods in the differentiation of organic solvent intoxication from certain neurological conditions. *Journal of Clinical and Experimental Neuropsychology*, **8**, 239–256

ESLINGER, P. J. and DAMASIO, A. R. (1985) Severe disturbance of higher cognition after bilateral frontal lobe ablation: patient EVR. *Neurology*, **35**, 1731–1741

ESLINGER, O. J., DAMASIO, H., GRAFF-RADFORD, N. and DAMASIO, A. R., (1984) Examining the relationship between computed tomography and neuropsychological measures in normal and demented elderly. *Journal of Neurology, Neurosurgery and Psychiatry*, **47**, 1319–1325

FABIAN, M. S., PARSONS, O. A. and SHELDON, M. D. (1984) The effects of gender and alcoholism on verbal and visuospatial learning. *Journal of Nervous and Mental Disease*, **172**, 16–20

FALLAICE, L. A., ALLEN, R. P., MCQUEEN, J. D. and NORTHROP, B. (1971) Cognitive deficits from bilateral cingulotomy for intractable pain in man. *Diseases of the Nervous System*, **32**, 171–175

FAMUYIWA, O. O., ECCLESTON, D., DONALDSON, A. A. and GARSIDE, R. F. (1979) Tardive dyskinesia and dementia. *British Journal of Psychiatry*, **135**, 500–504

FAULSTICH, M. E. (1986) Acquired immune deficiency syndrome: an overview of central nervous system complications and neuropsychological sequelae. *International Journal of Neuroscience*, **30**, 249–254

FEDIO, P., COX, C. S., NEOPHYTIDES, A., CANAL-FREDERICK, G. and CHASE, T. N. (1979) Neuropsychological profile of Huntington's disease: patients and those at risk. In *Advances in Neurology*, Volume 23, edited by T. N. Chase, N. S. Wexler and A. Barbeau. New York: Raven Press

FEDIO, P. and MIRSKY, A. F. (1969) Selective intellectual deficits in children with temporal lobe or centrencephalic epilepsy. *Neuropsychologia*, **7**, 287–300

FEDIO, P. and OMMAYA, A. K. (1970) Bilateral cingulum lesions and stimulation in man with lateralized impairment in short-term verbal memory. *Expl Neurol*, **29**, 84–91

FEDIO, P. and VAN BUREN, J. M. (1974) Memory deficits during electrical stimulation of the speech centre in conscious man. *Brain Lang*, **1**, 29–42

FEDIO, P. and VAN BUREN, J. M. (1975) Memory and perceptual deficits during electrical stimulation in the left and right thalamus and parietal subcortex. *Brain Lang*, **2**, 78–100

FERNANDEZ-GUARDIOLA, A. (1977) Reminiscences elicited by electrical stimulation of the temporal lobes in humans. In *Neurobiology of Sleep and Memory*, edited by R. R. Drucker-Colin and J. L. McGaugh, pp. 273–280. New York: Academic Press

FERRIER, T. M. and EADIE, M. J. (1973) Clioquinol encephalopathy. *Medical Journal of Australia*, **2**, 1008–1009

FERRIS, S. H., CROOK, T. and CLARK, E. (1980) Facial recognition memory deficits in normal aging and senile dementia. *Journal of Gerontology*, **35**, 707–714

FERRIS, S. H., REISBERG, B., CROOK, T., FRIEDMAN, E., SCHNECK, M. K., MIR, P., *et al.* (1982) Pharmacologic treatment of senile dementia: choline, L-dopa, piracetam, and choline plus piracetam. In *Alzheimer's Disease: a Report of Progress in Research*, edited by S. Corkin, K. L. Davis, J. Growdon, E. Usdin and R. Wurrman, pp. 475–484. New York: Raven Press

FERRIS, S. H., SATHANANTHAN G., REISBERG, B. and GERSHON, S. (1979) Long-term choline treatment of memory impaired elderly patients. *Science*, **205**, 1039–1040

FINDLER, G., FEINSOD, M., LIJOVETZKY, G. and HADANI, M. (1983) Transient global amnesia associated with a single metastasis in the non-dominant hemisphere. *Journal of Neurosurgery*, **58**, 303–305

FINE, E. W., LEWIS, D., VILLA-LANDA, I. and BLAKEMORE, C. B. (1970) The effect of cyclandelate on mental function in patients with arteriosclerotic brain disease. *British Journal of Psychiatry*, **117**, 157–161

FINKELSTEIN, S. and CARONNA, J. J. (1978) Amnestic syndrome following cardiac arrest. *Neurology*, **28**, 389

FISHER, C. M. (1966) Concussion amnesia. *Neurology*, **16**, 826–830

FISHER, C. M. (1982a) Transient global amnesia. *Archives of Neurology*, **39**, 605–608

FISHER, C. M. (1982b) Disorientation for place. *Archives of Neurology*, **39**, 33–36

FISHER, J. M., KENNEDY, J. L., CAINE, E. D. and SHOULSON, I. (1983) Dementia in Huntington's disease: a cross-section analysis of intellectual decline. In *The Dementias*, edited by R. Mayeux and W. G. Rosen. New York: Raven Press

FIX, A. J., DAUGHTON, D., KASS, I., BELL, C. W. and GOLDEN, C. J. (1985) Cognitive functioning and survival among patients with chronic obstructive pulmonary disease. *International Journal of Neuroscience*, **27**, 13–17

FIX, A. J., GOLDEN, C. J., DAUGHTON, D., KASS, I. and BELL, C. W. (1982) Neuropsychological deficits among patients with chronic obstructive pulmonary disease. *International Journal of Neuroscience*, **16**, 99–105

FLICKER, C., BARTUS, R., CROOK, T. H. and FERRIS, S. H. (1984) Effects of aging and dementia upon recent visuospatial memory. *Neurobiol Aging*, **5**, 275–283

FLOWERS, K. A., PEARCE, I. and PEARCE, J. M. S. (1984) Recognition memory in Parkinson's disease. *Journal of Neurology, Neurosurgery and Psychiatry*, **47**, 1174–1181

FODOR, I. E. (1972) Impairment of memory functions after acute head injury. *Journal of Neurology, Neurosurgery and Psychiatry*, **35**, 818–824

FOGELHOLM, R., KIVALO, E. and BERGSTROM, L. (1975) The transient global amnesia syndrome. *European Neurology*, **13**, 72–84

FOLETTI, G., REGLI, F. and ASSAL, G. (1980) Syndrome amnesique d'origine encephalitique. *Rev Med Suisse Romande*, **100**, 179–185

FOLSTEIN, M. F., FOLSTEIN, S. E. and MCHUGH, P. R. (1975) Mini-mental state: a practical method for grading the cognitive state of patients for clinicians. *Journal of Psychiatric Research*, **12**, 189–198

FORTUNY, A I. L., BRIGGS, M., NEWCOMBE, F., RATCLIFF, G. and THOMAS, C. (1980) Measuring the duration of post traumatic amnesia. *Journal of Neurology, Neurosurgery and Psychiatry*, **43**, 377–379

FOSTER, N. L., CHASE, T. N., FEDIO, P., PATRONAS, M. J., BROOKS, R. A. and DI CHIRO, G. (1983) Alzheimer's disease: focal cortical changes shown by positron emission tomography. *Neurology*, **33**, 961–965

FOWLER, R. S., JR (1969) A simple non-language test of new learning. *Percept. Mot. Skills*, **29**, 895–901

FRANCESCHI, M., CECCHETTO, R., MINICUCCI, F., SMIZNE, S., BAIO, G. and CANAL, N. (1984) Cognitive processes in insulin-dependent diabetes. *Diabetes Care*, **7**, 228–231

FRANK, K. A., HELLER, S. S. and MALM, J. R. (1972) Long-term effects of open-heart surgery on intellectual functioning. *Journal of Thoracic and Cardiovascular Surgery*, **64**, 811–815

FREED, D. M., CORKIN, S. and COHEN, N. J. (1984) Rate of forgetting in H.M.: a reanalysis. *Society of Neuroscience Abstracts*, **10**, 383

FREEDMAN, M. and CERMAK, L. S. (1986) Semantic encoding deficits in frontal lobe disease and amnesia. *Brain and Cognition*, **5**, 108–114

FREEDMAN, M., KNOEFEL, J., NAESER, M. and LEVINE, H. (1984a) Computerized axial tomography and aging. In *Clinical Neurology of Aging*, edited by M. L. Albert. New York: Oxford University Press

FREEDMAN, M. and OSCAR-BERMAN, M. (1986) Selective delayed response deficits in Parkinson's and Alzheimer disease. *Archives of Neurology*, **43**, 886–890

FREEDMAN, M., RIVOIRA, P., BUTTERS, N., SAX, D. S. and FELDMAN, R. G. (1984b) Retrograde amnesia in Parkinson's disease. *Canadian Journal of Neurological Science*, **11**, 297–301

FRIENDLY, M., FRANKLIN, P. E., HOFFMAN, D. and RUBIN, D. C. (1982) The Toronto word pool: norms for imagery, concreteness, orthographic variables, and grammatical usage for 1080 words. *Behav Res Meth & Instrum*, **14**, 375–399

FRITH, C., BLOXHAM, C. A. and CARPENTER, K. N. (1986) Impairments in the learning and performance of a new manual skill in patients with Parkinson's disease. *Journal of Neurology, Neurosurgery and Psychiatry*, **49**, 661–668

FULD, P. A. (1976) Storage, retention, and retrieval in Korsakoff's syndrome. *Neuropsychologia*, **14**, 225–236

FULD, P. A. (1980) Guaranteed stimulus-processing in the evaluation of memory and learning. *Cortex*, **16**, 255–271

FULD, P. A. (1982) Behavioural signs of cholinergic deficiency in Alzheimer dementia. In *Alzheimer's Disease: A Report of Progress*, edited by S. Corkin *et al.*, pp. 193–196. New York: Raven Press

FULD, P., KATZMAN, R., DAVIES, P. and TERRY, R. (1982) Intrusions as a sign of Alzheimer dementia. Chemical and pathological verification. *Annals of Neurology*, **11**, 155–159

GADE, A. (1982) Amnesia after operations on aneurysms of the anterior communicating artery. *Surg Neurol*, **18**, 46–49

GALBRAITH, G. G. and TASCHMAN, C. S. (1969) Homphone units: a normative and methodological investigation of the strength of component elements. *J. Verb. Learn. Verb. Behav.*, **8**, 737–744

GALLASSI, R., PAZZAGLIA, P., LORUSSO, S. and MORREALE, A. (1986) Neuropsychological findings in epileptic amnesic attacks. *European Neurology*, **25**, 299–303

GALLASSI, R., LORUSSO, S. and STRACCIARI, A. (1986) Neuropsychological findings during a transient global amnesia attack and its follow-up. *Italian Journal of Neurological Science*, **7**, 45–49

GARCIA C. A., TWEEDY, J. R., BLASS, J. P. and MCDOWELL, F. H. (1982) Lecithin and parkinsonian dementia. In *Alzheimer's Disease: A Report of Progress*, edited by S. Corkin *et al.*, pp. 443–449. New York: Raven Press

GARDNER, H. (1974) *The Shattered Mind*. New York: Random House

GARDNER, H., BOLLER, F., MOREINES, J. and BUTTERS, N. (1973) Retrieving information from Korsakoff patients: effects of categorical cues and reference to the task. *Cortex*, **9**, 165–75

GASPARRINI, B. and SATZ, P. (1979) A treatment for memory problems in left hemisphere CVA patients. *Journal of Clinical Neuropsychology*, **1**, 137–150

GAZZANIGA, M. S., RISSE G. L., SPRINGER, S. P., CLARK D. E. and WILSON, D. H. (1975) Psychologic and neurologic consequences of partial and complete cerebral commissurotomy. *Neurology*, **25**, 10–15

GEBHARDT, C. A., NAESER, M. A. and BUTTERS, N. (1984) Computerized measures of CT scans of alcoholics: thalamic region related to memory. *Alcohol*, **1**, 133–140

GEFFEN, G., WALSH, A., SIMPSON, D. and JEEVES, M. (1980) Comparison of the effects of transcortical and transcallosal removal of intraventricular tumours. *Brain*, **103**, 773–788

GEIS, M. F. and WINOGRAD, E. (1974) Norms of semantic encoding variability for fifty homographs. *Bull Psychonomic Soc,* **3,** 429–431

GELLER, M. R. and GELLER, A. (1970) Brief amnestic effects of spike wave discharges. *Neurology (Minneapolis),* **20,** 380–381

GENTILINI, M., NICHELLI, P., SCHOENHUBER, R., BORTOLOTTI, P., TONELLI, L., FALASCA, A. *et al.* (1985) Neuropsychological evaluation of mild head injury. *Journal of Neurology, Neurosurgery and Psychiatry,* **48,** 137–140

GEORGE, A. E., DE LEON, M. J., ROSENBLOOM, S., FERRIS, S. H., GENTES, C., EMMERICH, M. *et al.* (1983) Ventricular volume and cognitive deficit: a computed tomographic study. *Radiology,* **149,** 493–498

GESCHWIND, N. and FUSILLO, M. (1966) Color naming defects in association with alexia. *Archives of Neurology,* **15,** 137–146

GHENT, L., MISHKIN, M. and TEUBER, H. L. (1962) Short-term memory after frontal-lobe injury in man. *J. Comp Physiol Psychol,* **55,** 705–709

GIANUTSOS, R. (1981) Training the long- and short-term verbal recall of a post-encephalitic amnesic. *Journal of Clinical Neuropsychology,* **3,** 143–153

GIANUTSOS, R. and GIANUTSOS, J. (1979) Rehabilitating the verbal recall of brain injured patients by mnemonic training: an experimental demonstration using single case methodology. *Journal of Clinical Neuropsychology,* **1,** 117–135

GIANUTSOS, R. and GRYNBAUM, B. B. (1983) Helping brain-injured people contend with hidden cognitive deficits. *Int Rehab Med,* **5,** 37–40

GIANUTSOS, R. and LITWACK, A. R. (1976) Chronic marijuana smokers show reduced coding into long-term storage. *Bull Psychonomic Soc,* **7,** 277–279

GIBSON, A. J. (1981) A further analysis of memory loss in dementia and depression in the elderly. *British Journal of Clinical Psychology,* **20,** 179–185

GILHOOLY, K. J. and HAY, D. (1977) Imagery, concreteness, age-of-acquisition, familiarity, and meaningfulness values for 205 five-letter words having single solution anagrams. *Behav Res Meth & Instrum,* **9,** 12–17

GILHOOLY, K. J. and LOGIE, R. H. (1980a) Age-of-acquisition, imagery, concreteness, familiarity, and ambiguity measures for 1944 words. *Behav Res Meth & Instrum,* **12,** 395–427

GILHOOLY, K. J. and LOGIE, R. H. (1980b) Meaning-dependent ratings of imagery, age of acquisition, familiarity, and concreteness for 387 ambiguous words. *Behav Res Meth & Instrum,* **12,** 428–450

GIROTTI, F., CARELLA, F., GRASSI, M. P., SOLIVERI, P., MARANO, R. and CARACENI, T. (1986) Motor and cognitive performances of Parkinsonian patients in the one and off phases of the disease. *Journal of Neurology, Neurosurgery and Psychiatry,* **49,** 657–660

GLASGOW, R. E., ZEISS, R. A., BARRERA, M. and LEWINSON, P. M. (1977) Case studies on remediating memory deficits in brain-damaged individuals. *Journal of Clinical Psychology,* **33,** 1049–1054

GLEES, P. and GRIFFITH, H. B. (1952) Bilateral destruction of the hippocampus (cornu Ammonis) in a case of dementia. *Monat fur Psychiatr Neurol,* **123,** 193–204

GLISKY, E. L., SCHACTER, D. L. and TULVING, E. (1986a) Computer learning by memory-impaired patients: acquisition and retention of complex knowledge. *Neuropsychologia,* **24,** 313–328

GLISKY, E. L., SCHACTER, D. L. and TULVING, E. (1986b) Learning and retention of computer-related vocabulary in memory-impaired patients: method of vanishing cues. *Journal of Clinical and Experimental Neuropsychology,* **8,** 292–312

GLOBUS, M., MILDWORF, B. and MELAMED, E. (1985) Cerebral blood flow and cognitive impairment in Parkinson's disease. *Neurology,* **35,** 1135–1139

GLOOR, P., OLIVIER, A., QUESNEY, L. F., ANDERMANN, F. and HOROWITZ, S. (1982) The role of the limbic system in experiential phenomena of temporal lobe epilepsy. *Annals of Neurology,* **12,** 129–144

GLOWINSKI, H. (1973) Cognitive deficits in temporal lobe epilepsy. An investigation of memory functioning. *Journal of Nervous and Mental Disease,* **157,** 129–137

GODFREY, H. P. D. and KNIGHT, R. G. (1985) Cognitive rehabilitation of memory functioning in amnesic alcoholics. *J Consult Clin Psychol,* **53,** 555–557

GOFF, J. R., ANDERSON, H. R. and COOPER, P. F. (1981) Distractability and memory deficits in long-term survivors of acute lymphoblastic leukemia. *J Dev Behav Pediatr,* **2,** 29–34

GOL, A. and FAIBISH, G. M. (1967) Effects of human hippocampal ablation. *Journal of Neurosurgery,* **26,** 390–398

236   References

GOLDBERG, E., AUSTIN, S. P., BILDER, R. M., GERSTMAN, L. J., HUGHES, J. E. O. and MATTIS, S. (1981) Retrograde amnesia: possible role of mesencephalic reticular formation in long-term memory. *Science,* **213,** 1392–1394

GOLDBERG, E., GERSTMAN, L. J., MATTIS, S., HUGHES, J. E. O., BILDER, R. M. and SIRIO, C. A. (1982a) Effects of cholinergic treatment on posttraumatic anterograde amnesia. *Archives of Neurology,* **39,** 581

GOLDBERG, E., GERSTMAN, L. J., MATTIS, S., HUGHES J. E. O. SIRIO, C. A. and BILDER, R. M. (1982b) Selective effects of cholinergic treatment of verbal memory in posttraumatic amnesia. *Journal of Clinical Neuropsychology,* **4,** 219–234

GOLDEN, C. J., HAMMEKE, T. A. and PURISCH, A. D. (1980) *The Luria-Nebraska Neuropsychological Battery.* Los Angeles: Western Psychological Services

GOLDENBERG, G., WIMMER, A. and MALY, J. (1983) Amnesic syndrome with a unilateral thalamic lesion: a case report. *Journal of Neurology,* **229,** 79–86

GOLDFARB, A. I., HOCHSTADT, N. J., JACOBSON, J. H. and WEINSTEIN, E. A. (1972) Hyperbaric oxygen treatment of organic mental syndrome in aged persons. *Journal of Gerontology,* **27,** 212–217

GOLDSTEIN, M. N. and JOYNT, R. J. (1969) Long-term follow-up of a callosal-sectioned patient. *Archives of Neurology,* **20,** 96–102

GOLDSTEIN, N. P., EWERT, J. C., RANDALL, R. V. and GROSS, J. B. (1968) Psychiatric aspects of Wilson's disease: results of psychometric tests during long-term therapy. *Birth Defects,* **4,** 77–84

GOODGLASS, H., GLEASON, J. B. and HYDE, M. R. (1970) Some dimensions of language comprehension in aphasia. *Journal of Speech and Hearing Research,* **13,** 595–606

GOODGLASS, H. and KAPLAN, E. (1983) *The Assessment of Aphasia and Related Disorders,* 2nd edn. Philadelphia: Lea and Febiger

GORDON, B. and MARIN, O. S. M. (1979) Transient global amnesia: an extensive case report. *Journal of Neurology, Neurosurgery and Psychiatry,* **42,** 572–575

GORDON, H. W., BOGEN, J. E. and SPERRY, R. W. (1971) Absence of deconnexion syndrome in two patients with partial section of the neocommisures. *Brain,* **94,** 327–336

GRAF, P., SQUIRE, L. R. and MANDLER, G. (1984) The information that amnesic patients do not forget. *J Exp Psychol: Learn Mem Cogn,* **10,** 164–178

GRAFF-RADFORD, N. R., DAMASIO, H., YAMADA, T., ESLINGER, P. J. and DAMASIO, A. R. (1985) Nonhaemorrhagic thalamic infarction: clinical, neuropsychological and electrophysiological findings in four anatomical groups defined by computerized tomography. *Brain,* **108,** 485–516

GRAFF-RADFORD, N. R., ESLINGER, P. J., DAMASIO, A. R. and YAMADA, T. (1984) Nonhaemorrhagic infarction of the thalamus: behavioral, anatomic and physiological correlates. *Neurology,* **34,** 14–23

GRAFMAN, J., SALAZAR, A., WEINGARTNER, H. and AMIN, D. (1986) Face memory and discrimination: an analysis of the persistent effects of penetrating brain wounds. *International Journal of Neuroscience,* **29,** 125–139

GRAFMAN, J., SALAZAR, A. M., WEINGARTNER, H., VANCE, S. C. and LUDLOW, C. (1985) Isolated impairment of memory following a penetrating lesion of the fornix. *Archives of Neurology,* **42,** 1162–1168

GRAHAM, F. K. and KENDALL, B. S. (1960) Memory-for-designs: revised general manual. *Percept Mot Skills, Monog,* Suppl. **11,** 147–188

GRANDJEAN, P., ARNVIG, E. and BECKMANN, J. (1978) Psychological dysfunctions in lead-exposed workers. *Scandinavian Journal of Work and Environmental Health,* **4,** 295–303

GRANHOLM, L. (1976) An explanation of the reversible memory defect in hydrocephalus. In *Intracranial Pressure,* edited by J. W. J. Becks, D. A. Bosch and M. Brock, pp. 173–176. Berlin: Springer Verlag

GRANT, I., HEATON, R. K., MCSWEENY, J., ADAMS, K. M. and TIMMS, R. M. (1982) Neuropsychological functioning in hypoxemic chronic obstructive pulmonary disease. *Archives of Internal Medicine,* **142,** 1470–1476

GRANT, I., MCDONALD, W. I., TRIMBLE, M. R., SMITH, E. and REED, R. (1984) Deficient learning in early and middle phases of multiple sclerosis. *Journal of Neurology, Neurosurgery and Psychiatry,* **47,** 250–255

GREENLEE, J. E., CRAMPTON, R. S. and MILLER, J. Q. (1975) Transient global amnesia associated with cardiac arrhythmia and digitalis intoxication. *Stroke,* **6,** 513–516

GROBER, E. (1984) Nonlinguistic memory in aphasia. *Cortex,* **20,** 67–74

GROHER, M. (1977) Language and memory disorders following closed head trauma. *Journal of Speech and Hearing Research*, **20**, 212–223

GRONWALL, D. and WRIGHTSON, P. (1980) Duration of post-traumatic amnesia after mild head injury. *Journal of Clinical Neuropsychology*, **2**, 51–60

GRONWALL, D. and WRIGHTSON, P. (1981) Memory and information processing capacity after closed head injury. *Journal of Neurology, Neurosurgery, and Psychiatry*, **44**, 889–895

GROWDON, J. H., CORKIN, S. and HUFF, F. J. (1985) Clinical evaluation of compounds for treatment of memory dysfunction. *Annals of the New York Academy of Sciences*, **444**, 437–449

GUBERMAN, A. and STUSS, D. (1983) The syndrome of bilateral paramedian thalamic infarction. *Neurology*, **33**, 540–546

GUDEMAN, H. E., CRAINE, J. F., GOLDEN, C. J. and MCLAUGHLIN, D. (1977) Higher cortical dysfunction associated with long term alcoholism. *International Journal of Neurosciences*, **8**, 33–40

GUR, R. C. (1985) Imaging regional brain physiology in behavioural neurology. In *Principles of Behavioural Neurology*, edited by M. M. Mesulam, pp. 347–383. Philadelphia: FA Davis

GUSTAFSON, L. and HAGBERG, B. (1978) Recovery in hydrocephalic dementia after shunt operation. *Journal of Neurology, Neurosurgery and Psychiatry*, **41**, 940–947

GUTHRIE, A. and ELLIOTT, W. A. (1980) The nature and reversibility of cerebral impairment in alcoholism. *J Stud Alcohol*, **41**, 147–158

HAALAND, K. Y., LINN, R. T., HUNT, W. C. and GOODWIN, J. S. (1983) A normative study of Russell's variant of the Wechsler Memory Scale in a healthy elderly population. *J Cons Clin Psychol*, **51**, 878–881

HAAS, D. C. and ROSS, G. S. (1986) Transient global amnesia triggered by mild head trauma. *Brain*, **109**, 251–257

HACKER, M. J. and RATCLIFF, R. (1979) A revised table of d' for M-alternative forced choice. *Perception and Psychophysics*, **26**, 168–170

HAGBERG, B. (1978) Defects of immediate memory related to the cerebral blood flow distribution. *Brain Lang*, **5**, 366–377

HAGBERG, B. and INGVAR, D. H. (1976) Cognitive reduction in presenile dementia related to regional abnormalities of the cerebral blood flow. *British Journal of Psychiatry*, **128**, 209–222

HALGIN, R., RIKLAN, M. and MISIAK, H. (1977) Levodopa, parkinsonism and recent memory. *Journal of Nervous and Mental Disease*, **164**, 268–272

HALGREN, E. (1981) The amygdala contribution to emotion and memory: current studies in humans. In *The Amygdaloid Complex*, edited by Ben-Ariy, pp. 395–408. Amsterdam: Elsevier/North Holland

HALGREN, E. (1984) Human hippocampal and amygdala recording and stimulation: evidence for a neural model of recent memory. In *Neuropsychology of Memory*, edited by L. R. Squire and N. Butters, pp. 165–182. New York: The Guildford Press

HALGREN, E., BABB, T. L. and CRANDALL, P. H. (1978) Activity of the human hippocampal formation and amygdala neurons during memory testing. *Electroencephalogr Clin Neurophysiol*, **45**, 585–601

HALGREN, E., ENGEL, J., WILSON, C. L., WALTER R. D., SQUIRES, N. K. and CRANDALL, P. H. (1983) Dynamics of the hippocampal contribution to memory: stimulation and recording studies in humans. In *Neurobiology of the Hippocampus*, edited by W. Seifert, pp. 529–572. New York: Academic Press

HALGREN, E., WALTER, R. D., CHERLOW, D. G. and CRANDALL, P. H. (1978) Mental phenomena evoked by electrical stimulation of the human hippocampal formation and amygdala. *Brain*, **101**, 83–117

HALGREN, E., WILSON, C. L. and STAPELTON, J. M. (1985) Human medial temporal-lobe stimulation disrupts both formation and retrieval of recent memories. *Brain and Cognition*, **4**, 287–295

HALL, P. (1963) Korsakov's syndrome following-herpes zoster encephalitis. *Lancet*, **i**, 752

HALL, P. (1965) Subacute viral encephalitis amnesia. *Lancet*, **ii**, 1077

HALLERT, C. and ASTROM, J. (1983) Intellectual ability of adults after lifelong intestinal malabsorption due to coeliac disease. *Journal of Neurology, Neurosurgery and Psychiatry*, **46**, 87–89

HAMSHER, K., BENTON, A. L. and DIGRE, K. (1980) Serial digit learning: normative and clinical aspects. *Journal of Clinical Neuropsychology*, **2**, 39–50

HAMSHER, K. D. and ROBERTS, R. J. (1985) Memory for recent US presidents in patients with cerebral disease. *Journal of Clinical and Experimental Neuropsychology*, **7**, 1–13

HANLEY, I. G., MCGUIRE, R. J. and BOYD, W. D. (1981) Reality orientation and dementia: a controlled trials of two approaches. *British Journal of Psychiatry*, **138**, 10–14

HANNAY, H. J. and LEVIN, H. S. (1985) Selective reminding test: an examination of the equivalence of four forms. *Journal of Clinical and Experimental Neuropsychology*, **7**, 251–263

HANNAY, H. J., LEVIN, H. S. and GROSSMAN, R. G. (1979) Impaired recognition memory after head injury. *Cortex*, **15**, 269–283

HANNINEN, H. (1982) Behavioral effects of occupational exposure to mercury and lead. *Acta Neurologica Scandinavica*, **66** (Suppl. 92) 167–175

HANNINEN, H., ESKELINEN, K., HUSMAN, K. and NURMINEN, M. (1976) Behavioural effects of long-term exposure to a mixture of organic solvents. *Scandinavian Journal of Work and Environmental Health*, **4**, 240–255

HANNINEN, H., HERNBERG, S., MANTERE, P., VESANTO, R. and JALKANEN, M. (1978) Psychological performance of subjects with low exposure to lead. *Journal of Occupational Medicine*, **20**, 683–689

HARBINSON, H. J. (1984) Alcoholic Korsakoff's psychosis: a psychometric, neuroradiological and neurophysiological investigation of nine cases. *Ulster Medical Journal*, **53**, 103–110

HART, R. P., PEDERSON, J. A., CZERWINSKI, A. W. and ADAMS, R. L. (1983) Chronic renal failure, dialysis and neuropsychological dysfunction. *Journal of Clinical Neuropsychology*, **5**, 301–312

HART, S., SMITH, C. M. and SWASH, M. (1986) Intrusion errors in Alzheimer's disease. *British Journal of Clinical Psychology*, **25**, 149–150

HARTLEY, T., HEILMAN, K. and GARCIA-BENGOCHEA, F. (1974) A case of transient global amnesia due to a pituitary tumor. *Neurology (Minneapolis)*, **58**, 998–1000

HASSLER, R. and DIECKMANN, G. (1973) Relief of obsessive-compulsive disorders, phobias and tics by stereotactic coagulation of the rostral intralaminar and medial-thalmic nuclei. In *Surgical Approaches to Psychiatry*, edited by L. V. Laitinen and K. Livingston, pp. 206–212. Lancaster: Medical and Technical Press

HATA, T., MEYER, J. S., TANAHASHI, N., ISHIKAWA, Y., IMAI, A., SHINOHARA, T. *et al.* (1987) Three-dimensional mapping of local cerebral perfusion in alcoholic encephalopathy with and without Wernicke-Korsakoff syndrome. *J. Cereb. Blood Flow Metab.*, **7**, 35–44

HAXBY, J. V., DUARA, R., GRADY, C. L., CUTLER, N. R. and RAPAPORT, S. I. (1985) Relationships between neuropsychological and cerebral metabolic asymmetries in early Alzheimer's disease. *J Cereb Blood Flow Metab*, **5**, 193–200

HAXBY, J. V., GRADY, C. L., DUARA, R., SHLAGETER, N., BERG, G. and RAPAPORT, S. I. (1986) Neocortical metabolic abnormalities precede nonmemory deficits in early Alzhemier's-type dementia. *Archives of Neurology*, **43**, 882–885

HAXBY, J. V., LUNDGREN, S. L. and MORLEY, G. K. (1983) Short-term retention of verbal, visual shape and visuospatial location information in normal and amnesic subjects. *Neuropsychologia*, **21**, 25–33

HAYMAN, L. A., BERMAN, S. A. and HINCK, V. C. (1981) Correlation of CT cerebral vascular territories with function: II. Posterior cerebral artery. *American Journal of Radiology*, **137**, 13–19

HEATON, R. K., BAADE, L. E. and JOHNSON, K. L. (1978) Neuropsychological test results associated with psychiatric disorders in adults. *Psychol Bull.* **85**, 141–162

HEATON, R. K., NELSON, L. M., THOMPSON, D. S., BURKS, J. S. and FRANKLIN, G. M. (1985) Neuropsychological findings in relapsing-remitting and chronic-progressive multiple sclerosis. *J Consult Clin Psychol*, **53**, 103–110

HECAEN, H. and AJURIAGUERRA, J. DE (1956) *Troubles mentaux au cours des tumeurs intracraniennes*. Masson: Paris

HECAEN, H., TZORTZIS, C. and RONDOT, P. (1980) Loss of topographic memory with learning deficits. *Cortex*, **6**, 525–542

HEILMAN, K. M., MOYER, R. S., MELENDEX, F., SCHWARTZ, H. D. and MILLER, B. D. (1975) A memory defect in uremic encephalopathy. *Journal of Neurological Science*, **26**, 245–249

HEILMAN, K. M. and SYPERT, G. W. (1977) Korsakoff's syndrome resulting from bilateral fornix lesions. *Neurology*, **27**, 490–493

HEMMINGSEN, R., MEJSHOLM, B., VORSTRUP, S., HENRIKSEN, L., LESTER, J., ENGELL, H. C. *et al.* (1982) Intellectual function, regional cerebral blood flow (CBF) and CT scanning in patients with transient ischaemic attacks before and after carotid endarterectomy. *Acta Neurologica Scandinavica*, **65** (Suppl.), 160–161

HERMANN, D. J. (1982) Know thy memory: the use of questionnaires to assess and study memory. *Psych Bull*, **92**, 434–462

HETHERINGTON, R. (1967) A neologism learning test. *British Journal of Psychiatry*, **113**, 1133–1137

HEYMAN, A., LOGUE, P., WILKINSON, W., HOLLOWAY, D. and HURWITZ, (1982) Lecithin therapy of Alzheimer's disease: a preliminary report. In *Alzheimer's Disease: A Report of Progress*, edited by S. Corkin *et al.*, pp. 373–378. New York: Raven Press

HIETANEN, M. and TERAVAINEN, H. (1984) Psychomotor and cognitive performance in parkinsonism. *Acta Neurologica Scandinavica*, **69** (Suppl. 98), 61–62

HILL, D. and MITCHELL, W. (1953) Epileptic anamnesis. *Folia Psych Neurol Neurochir*, **56**, 718–725

HILLBOM, E. and JARHO, L. (1969) Post-traumatic Korsakoff syndrome. In *The Late Effects of Head Injury*, edited by A. E. Walker, W. F. Caveness and M. Critchley. Illinois: Charles C. Thomas

HIRST, W., JOHNSON, M. K., KIM, J. K., RISSE, G., PHELPS, E. A. and VOLPE, B. T. (1986) Recognition and recall in amnesics. *J Exp Psychol: Learn Mem Cogn*, **12**, 445–451

HIRST, W. and VOLPE, B. T. (1982) Temporal order judgements with amnesia. *Brain and Cognition*, **1**, 294–306

HIRTZ, D. G. and NELSON, K. B. (1985) Cognitive effective of anti-epileptic drugs. In *Recent Advances in Epilepsy*, edited by T. A. Pedley and B. S. Meldrum, pp. 161–181. Edinburgh: Churchill Livingstone

HOCHBERG, F. and SLOTNICK, B. (1980) Neuropsychologic impairment in astrocytoma survivors. *Neurology*, **30**, 172–177

HOLLISTER, L. E. (1985) Alzheimer's disease: is it worth treating. *Drugs*, **29**, 483–488

HOLMES, C. S., HAYFORD, J. T., GONZALEZ, J. L. and WEYDERT, J. A. (1983) A survey of cognitive functioning at different glucose levels in diabetic persons. *Diabetes Care*, **6**, 180–185

HOM, J. and REITAN, R. M. (1984) Neuropsychological correlates of rapidly vs. slowly growing intrinsic cerebral neoplasms. *Journal of Clinical Neuropsychology*, **6**, 309–324

HOOKER, W. D. and RASKIN, N. H. (1986) Neuropsychologic alterations in classic and common migraine. *Archives of Neurology*, **43**, 709–712

HORENSTEIN, S., CHAMBERLAIN, W. and CONOMY, J. (1967) Infarctions of the fusiform and calcarine regions with agitated delirium and hemianopsia. *Transactions of the American Neurological Association*, **92**, 85–89

HORN, S. (1974) Some psychological factors in Parkinsonism. *Journal of Neurology, Neurosurgery and Psychiatry*, **37**, 27–31

HORNE, D. J. and ROYLE, J. P. (1974) Cognitive changes after carotid endarterectomy. *Medical Journal of Australia*, **1**, 316–317

HORTON, K. D. (1983) Phonemic and semantic generation norms. *Behav Res Meth Instrum*, **15**, 109–110

HOWES, J. L. (1983) Effects of experimenter- and self-generated imagery on the Korsakoff patient's memory performance. *Neuropsychologia*, **21**, 341–349

HUBER, S. J., SHUTTLEWORTH, E. C. and PAULSON, G. W. (1986) Dementia in Parkinson's disease. *Archives of Neurology*, **43**, 987–990

HUBER, S. J., SHUTTLEWORTH, E. C., PAULSON, G. W., BELLCHAMBERS, M. J. G. and CLAPP, L. E. (1986) Cortical versus subcortical dementia. Neuropsychological differences. *Archives of Neurology*, **43**, 392–394

HUPPERT, F. A. (1981) Memory in split brain patients: a comparison with organic amnesic syndromes. *Cortex*, **17**, 303–312

HUPPERT, F. (1982) Memory impairment associated with chronic hypoxia. *Thorax*, **37**, 858–860

HUPPERT, F. A. and PIERCY, M. (1976) Recognition memory in amnesic patients: effect of temporal context and familiarity of material. *Cortex*, **12**, 3–20

HUPPERT, F. A. and PIERCY, M. (1977) Recognition memory in amnesic patients: a defect of acquisition? *Neuropsychologia*, **15**, 643–652

HUPPERT, F. A. and PIERCY, M. (1978a) The role of trace strength in recency and frequency judgements by amnesic and control subjects. *Quarterly Journal of Experimental Psychology*, **30**, 347–354

HUPPERT, F. A. and PIERCY, M. (1978b) Dissociation between learning and remembering in organic amnesia. *Nature*, **275**, 317–318

HUPPERT, F. A. and PIERCY, M. (1979) Normal and abnormal forgetting in organic amnesia: effect of locus of lesion. *Cortex*, **15**, 385–390

HUTT, S. J., LEE, D. and OUNSTED, C. (1963) Digit memory and evoked discharges in four light sensitive children. *Dev Med Child Neurol*, **5**, 559–571

HUTT, S. J. and LEE, D. (1968) Some determinants of an amnesic phenomenon in a light-sensitive epileptic child. *Journal of Neurological Science*, **6**, 155–164

HUTT, S. J. and GILBERT, S. (1980) Effects of evoked spike-wave discharges upon short-term memory in patients with epilepsy. *Cortex*, **16**, 445–457

HYMAN, B. T., ESLINGER, P. J. and DAMASIO, A. R. (1985) Effect of naltrexone on senile dementia of the Alzheimer type. *Journal of Neurology, Neurosurgery and Psychiatry*, **48**, 1169–1171

IGNELZI, R. J. and SQUIRE, L. R. (1976) Recovery from anterograde and retrograde amnesia after percutaneous drainage of a cystic craniopharyngioma. *Journal of Neurology, Neurosurgery and Psychiatry*, **39**, 1231–1235

INGLIS, J. (1958) Psychological investigations of cognitive deficit in elderly psychiatric patients. *Psychol Bull*, **55**, 197–214

INGLIS, J. (1959) A paired-associate learning test for use with elderly psychiatric patients. *Journal of Mental Science*, **105**, 440–443

IREGREN, A. (1982) Effects on psychological test performance of workers exposed to a single solvent (toluene) – a comparison with effects of exposure to a mixture of organic solvents. *Neurobehav Toxicol Teratol*, **4**, 695–701

ISAACS, B. and WALKEY, F. A. (1964) A simplified paired-associate learning test for elderly hospital patients. *British Journal of Psychiatry*, **110**, 80–83

ISHIBASHI, T., HORI, H., ENDO, K. and SATO, T. (1964) Hallucinations produced by electrical stimulation of the temporal lobes in schizophrenic patients. *Tohoku Journal of Experiemental Medicine*, **82**, 124–139

IVERSEN, S. D. (1977) Temporal lobe amnesia. In *Amnesia*, edited by C. W. M. Whitty and O. L. Zangwill, pp. 136–182. London: Butterworths

IVSON, D. (1986) Anna Thompson and the American liner New York: some normative data. *Journal of Clinical Neuropsychology*, **8**, 317–320

JACOBS, L. A., GANJI, S., SHIRLEY, J. G., MORRELL, R. M., BRINKMAN, S. D. (1983) Cognitive improvement after extracranial reconstruction for the low flow-endangered brain. *Surgery*, **93**, 683–687

JACOBSON, R. R. (1986) Disorders of facial recognition, social behaviour and affect after combined bilateral amygdalectomy and subcaudate tractotomy. *Psychol Med*, **16**, 439–450

JACOBY, L. L. and WITHERSPOON, D. (1982) Remembering without awareness. *Canadian Journal of Psychology*, **36**, 300–324

JACOBY, R. J. and LEVY, R. (1980) Computed tomography in the elderly: 2. Senile dementia: diagnosis and functional impairment. *British Journal of Psychiatry*, **136**, 256–269

JAFFE, P. G. and KATZ, A. N. (1975) Attenuating anterograde amnesia in Korsakoff's psychosis. *Journal of Abnormal Psychology*, **84**, 559–562

JAMBOR, K. L. (1969) Cognitive functioning in multiple sclerosis. *British Journal of Psychiatry*, **115**, 765–775

JARHO, L. (1973) Korsakoff-like amnesic syndrome in penetrating brain injury. *Acta Neurologica Scandinavia*. **49** (Suppl. 54), 1–156

JASON, G. W. (1985) Manual sequence learning after focal cortical lesions. *Neuropsychologia*, **23**, 483–496

JEEVES, M. A., SIMPSON, D. A. and GEFFEN, G. (1979) Functional consequences of the transcallosal removal of intraventricular tumours. *Journal of Neurology, Neurosurgery and Psychiatry*, **42**, 134–142

JEFFREYS, R. V. and WOOD, M. M. (1978) Adult non-tumourous dementia and hydrocephalus. *Acta Neurochirurgica*, **45**, 103–114

JELLINEK, E. H. (1962) Fits, faints, coma and dementia and myxoedema. *Lancet*, **ii**, 1010–1012

JENKINS, C. D., HURST, M. W. and ROSE, R. M. (1979) Life events: do people really remember? *Archives of General Psychiatry*, **36**, 779–784

JENKINS, J. S., MATHER, H. M. and COUGHLAN, A. K. (1982) Effect of desmopressin on normal and impaired memory. *Journal of Neurology, Neurosurgery and Psychiatry*, **45**, 830–831

JENKINS, R. L. and PARSONS, O. A. (1981) Neuropsychological effect of chronic alcoholism on tactual-spatial performance and memory in males. *Alcoholism*, **5**, 26–33

JENNEKENS-SCHINKEL, A. and SANDERS, E. A. C. M. (1986) Decline of cognition in multiple sclerosis: dissociable deficits. *Journal of Neurology, Neurosurgery and Psychiatry*, **49**, 1354–1360

JENNET, B. and BOND, M. (1975) Assessment of outcome after severe head injury: a practical scale. *Lancet*, **i**, 480–484

JENSEN, T. S. and OLIVARIUS, B. (1980) Transient global amnesia as a manifestation of transient cerebral ischaemia. *Acta Neurologica Scandinavica*, **61**, 115–124

JENSEN, T. S. and OLIVARIUS, B. (1981) Transient global amnesia: its clinical and pathophysiological basis and prognosis. *Acta Neurologica Scandinavica*, **63**, 220–230

JETTER, W., POSER, U., FREEMAN, R. B. and MARKOWITSCH, H. J. (1986) A verbal long term memory deficit in frontal lobe damaged patients. *Cortex*, **22**, 229–242

JOHANNESSON, G., HAGBERG, B., GUSTAFSON, L. and INGVAR, D. H. (1979) EEG and cognitive impairment in presenile dementia. *Acta Neurologica Scandinavica*, **59**, 225–240

JOHNSON, M. K. and KIM, J. K. (1985) Recognition of pictures by alcoholic Korsakoff patients. *Bull Psychonom Soc*, **23**, 456–458

JOHNSON, M. K., KIM, J. K. and RISSE, G. (1985) Do alcoholic Korsakoff's syndrome patients acquire affective reactions? *J Exp Psychol: Learn Mem Cogn*, **11**, 22–36

JOLLIFE, N., BOWMAN, K. M., ROSENBLUM, L. A. and FEIN, H. D. (1940) Nicotinic acid deficiency encephalopathy. *Journal of the American Medical Association*, **114**, 307–312

JONES, M. K. (1974) Imagery as a mnemonic after left temporal lobectomy: contrast between material-specific and generalized memory disorders. *Neuropsychologia*, **12**, 21–30

JONES-GOTMAN, M. (1979) Incidental learning of image-related or pronounced words after right temporal lobectomy. *Cortex*, **15**, 187–197

JONES-GOTMAN, M. (1986a) Memory for designs: the hippocampal contribution. *Neuropsychologia*, **24**, 193–203

JONES-GOTMAN, M. (1986b) Right hippocampal excision impairs learning and recall of a list of abstract designs. *Neuropsychologia*, **5**, 659–670

JONES-GOTMAN, M. and MILNER, B. (1978) Right temporal-lobe contribution to image-mediated verbal learning. *Neuropsychologia*, **16**, 61–71

JUOLASMAA, A., OUTAKOSKI, J., HIRVENOJA, R., TIENARI, P., SOTANIEMI, K. and TAKKUNEN, J. (1981) Effect of open heart surgery on intellectual performance. *Journal of Clinical Neuropsychology*, **3**, 181–197

JURKO, M. F. and ANDY, O. J. (1973) Psychological changes correlated with thalamotomy site. *Journal of Neurology, Neurosurgery and Psychiatry*, **36**, 846–852

KAHN, E. A. and CROSBY, E. C. (1972) Korsakoff's syndrome associated with surgical lesions involving the mammillary bodies. *Neurology*, **22**, 117–125

KAHN, R. L., ZARIT, S. H., HILBERT, N. M. and NIEDEREHE, G. (1975) Memory complaint and impairment in the aged. The effect of depression and altered brain function. *Archives of General Psychiatry*, **32**, 1569–1573

KANE, R. L. (1986) Comparison of Halstead – Reitan and Luria – Nebraska Neuropsychological Batteries. In *Clinical Applications of Neuropsychological Test Batteries*, edited by T. Incagnoli, G. Goldstein and C. J. Golden, pp. 277–301. New York: Plenum Press

KAPUR, N. (1979) Neuropsychological retraining paradigms as a tool to study human memory. In *Practical Aspects of Memory*, edited by M. M. Gruneberg, P. E. Morris and R. N. Sykes. London: Academic Press

KAPUR, N. (1985) Double dissociation between perseveration in memory and problem solving tasks. *Cortex*, **21**, 461–465

KAPUR, N. (1987a) Pattern of verbal memory deficits in patients with bifrontal pathology and patients with third ventricle lesions. *International Conference on Practical Aspects of Memory*, Swansea, August 1987.

KAPUR, N. (1987b) Selective sparing of memory functioning in a patient with amnesia following herpes encephalitis. *Brain and Cognition*, (in press)

KAPUR, N. and BUTTERS, N. (1977) Visuoperceptive deficits in long term alcoholics and alcoholics with Korsakoff's psychosis. *J Stud Alcohol*, **38**, 2025–2035

KAPUR, N. and COUGHLAN, A. K. (1980) Confabulation and frontal lobe dysfunction. *Journal of Neurology, Neurosurgery and Psychiatry*, **43**, 461–463

KAPUR, N. and DUNKLEY, B. (1984) Neuropsychological analysis of a case of crossed dysphasia verified at postmortem. *Brain Lang*, **23**, 134–147

KAPUR, N. and PEARSON, D. (1983) Memory symptoms and memory performance of neurological patients. *British Journal of Psychology*, **74**, 409–415

KARABELAS, G., KALFAKIS, N., KASUIKIS, I. and VASSILOPOULOS, D. (1985) Unusual features in a case of bilateral paramedian infarction. *Journal of Neurology, Neurosurgery and Psychiatry*, **48**, 186

KASZNIAK, A. W., GARRON, D. C. and FOX, J. (1979) Differential effects of age and cerebral atrophy upon span of immediate recall and paired-associate learning in older patients suspected of dementia. *Cortex*, **15**, 285–295

KAUSHALL, P. I., ZETIN, M. and SQUIRE, L. R. (1981) A psychosocial study of chronic, circumscribed amnesia. *Journal of Nervous and Mental Disease*, **169**, 383–389

KAYE, W. H., SITARAM, N. and WEINGARTNER, H. (1982) Modest facilitation of memory in dementia with combined lecithin and anticholinesterase treatment. *Biol Psychiat*, **17**, 275–280

KAYE, W. H., WEINGARTNER, H., GOLD, P., EBERT, M. H., GILLIN, J. C., SITARAM, N. *et al.* (1982) Cognitive effects of cholinergic and vasopressin-like agents in patients with PDD. In *Alzheimer's Disease*, edited by S. Corkin *et al.*, pp. 433–442. New York: Raven Press

KEAR-COLWELL, J. J. and HELLER, M. (1980) The Wechsler Memory Scale and closed head injury. *Journal of Clinical Psychology*, **36**, 782–787

KEESLER, T. Y., SCHULTZ, E. E., SCIARA, A. D. and FRIEDENBERG, L. (1984) Equivalence of alternate subtests for the Russell revision of the Wechsler Memory Scale. *Journal of Clinical Neuropsychology*, **6**, 215–219

KELLY, M. P., GARRON, D. C. and JAVID, H. (1980) Carotid artery disease, carotid endarterectomy and behaviour. *Archives of Neurology*, **37**, 743–748

KELLY, R. (1981) Post-traumatic syndrome. *Journal of the Royal Society of Medicine*, **74**, 243–245

KENDRICK, D. (1985) *Kendrick Cognitive Tests for the Elderly*. Windsor: NFER–Nelson

KENDRICK, D. C. (1982) Administrative and interpretative problems with the Kendrick battery for the detection of dementia in the elderly. *British Journal of Clinical Psychology*, **21**, 149–150

KENDRICK, D. C., GIBSON, A. J. and MOYES, I. C. A. (1979) The revised Kendrick battery: clinical studies. *Br J Soc Clin Psychol*, **18**, 329–340

KENDRICK, D. C., PARBOOSINGH, R. C. and POST, F. (1965) A synonym learning test for use with the elderly psychiatric subject: a validation study. *Br J Soc Clin Psychol*, **4**, 63–71

KESSLER, J., IRLE, E. and MARKOWITSCH, H. J. (1986) Korsakoff and alcoholic subjects are severely impaired in animal tasks of associative memory. *Neuropsychologia*, **24**, 671–680

KIM, Y. K. (1971) Effects of basolateral amygdalotomy. In *Special Topics and Stereotaxis*, edited by W. Unbach, pp. 69–81. Stuttgart: Hippokrates-Verlag

KIMURA, D. (1963) Right temporal-lobe damage. *Archives of Neurology*, **8**, 264–271

KIMURA, D., BARNETT, H. J. M. and BURKHART, G. (1981) The psychological test performance in progressive supranuclear palsy. *Neuropsychologia*, **19**, 301–306

KITAGAWA, Y., MEYER, J. S., TACHIBANA, H., MORTEL, K. F. and ROGERS, R. L. (1984) CT-CBF correlations of cognitive deficits in multi-infarct dementia. *Stroke*, **15**, 1000–1009

KLOVE, H. and CLEELAND, C. S. (1972) The relationship of neuropsychological impairment to other indices of severity of head injury. *Scandinavian Journal of Rehabilitative Medicine*, **4**, 55–60

KNAVE, B., OLSON, B. A., ELOFSON, S., GAMBERALE, F., ISAKKSON, A., MINDUS, P., *et al.* (1978) Long-term exposure to jet fuel II. *Scandinavian Journal of Work and Environmental Health*, **4**, 19–45

KNIGHT, R. G. and GODFERY, H. P. D. (1985) The assessment of memory impairment: the relationship between different methods of evaluating dysmnesic deficits. *British Journal of Clinical Psychology*, **24**, 25–31

KOHL, D. and BRANDT, J. (1985) An automatic encoding deficit in the amnesia of Korsakoff's syndrome. *Annals of the New York Academy of Sciences*, **444**, 460–462

KOLAKOWSKA, T., WILLIAMS, A. O., JAMBOR, K. and ARDERN, M. (1985) Schizophrenia with good and poor outcome III: neurological soft signs, cognitive impairment, and their clinical significance. *British Journal of Psychiatry*, **146**, 348–357

KOPELMAN, M. D. (1985) Rates of forgetting in Alzheimer-type dementia and Korsakoff's syndrome. *Neuropsychologia*, **23**, 623–638

KOPELMAN, M. D. (1986a) Recall of anomalous sentences in dementia and amnesia. *Brain Lang*, **29**, 154–170

KOPELMAN, M. D. (1986b) Clinical tests of memory. *British Journal of Psychiatry*, **148**, 517–525

KOTILA, M. and KAJASTE, S. (1984) Neurological and neuropsychological symptoms after cardiac arrest. *Acta Neurologica Scandinavica,* **69** (Suppl.), 337–338

KOVNER, R., MATTIS, S. and PASS, R. (1985) Some amnesic patients can freely recall large amounts of information in new contexts. *Journal of Clinical and Experimental Neuropsychology,* **7,** 395–411

KRAEMER, H. C., PEABODY, C. A., TINKLENBERG, J. R. and YESAVAGE, J. A. (1983) Mathematical and empirical development of a test of memory for clinical and research use. *Psychol Bull,* **94,** 367–380

KROP, H. D., BLOCK, A. J. and COHEN, E. (1973) Neuropsychologic effects of continuous oxygen therapy in chronic obstructive pulmonary disease. *Chest,* **64,** 317–322

KUCERA, H. and FRANCIS, W. N. (1967) *Computational Analysis of Present-day American English.* Providence, RI: Brown University Press

KUMAR, S. (1977) Short term memory for a nonverbal tactual task after cerebral commissurotomy. *Cortex,* **13,** 55–61

KUN L. E., MULHERN, R. K. and CRISCO, J. J. (1983) Quality of life in children treated for brain tumours, intellectual, emotional and academic function. *Journal of Neurosurgery,* **58,** 1–6

KUSHNER, M. J. and HAUSER, W. A. (1985) Transient global amnesia: a case-control study. *Annals of Neurology,* **18,** 684–691

LACZI, F., VALKUSZ, Z., LASZLO, F. A., WAGNER, A., JARDANHAZY, T., SZASZ, A. *et al.* (1982) Effects of LVP and DDAVP on memory in healthy individuals and diabetes insipidus patients. *Psychoneuroendocrinology,* **7,** 185–193

LACZI, F., VAN REE, J. M., BALOGH, L., SZASZ, A., JARDANHAZY, T., WAGNER, A. *et al.* (1983a) Lack of effect of DGAVP on memory in patients with Korsakoff's syndrome. *Acta Endocrinologica,* **104,** 177–182

LACZI, F., VAN REE, J. M., WAGNER, A., VALKURZ, Z., JARDANHAZY, T., KOVACS, G. L. *et al.* (1983b) Effects of DG-AVP on memory processes in diabetes insipidus patients and non-diabetic subjects. *Acta Endocrinologica,* **102,** 205–212

LADURNER, G., SKUARC, A. and SAGER, W. (1982) Computer tomography in transient global amnesia. *European Neurology,* **21,** 34–40

LAGERGREN, K. (1974) Effect of exogenous changes in heart rate upon mental performance in patients treated with artificial pacemakers for complete heart block. *British Heart Journal,* **36,** 1126–1132

LANDI, G., GIUSTI, M. C. and GUIDOTTI, M. (1982) Transient global amnesia due to left temporal haemorrhage. *Journal of Neurology, Neurosurgery and Psychiatry,* **45,** 1062–1063

LANG, W., LANG, M., KORNHUBER, A., GALLWITZ, A. and KRIEBEL, J. (1985) Neuropsychological and neuroendocrinological disturbances associated with extracerebral cysts of the anterior and middle cranial fossa. *European Archives of Psychiatry and Neurological Science,* **235,** 38–41

LARNER, S. (1977) Encoding in senile dementia and elderly depressives: a preliminary study. *Br J Soc Clin Psychol,* **16,** 379–390

LARRABEE, G. T. and KANE, R. L. (1986) Reversed digit repetition samples visual and verbal processes. *International Journal of Neuroscience,* **30,** 11–15

LARRABEE, G. T., KANE, R. L., SCHUCK, J. R. and FRANCIS, D. J. (1985) Construct validity of various memory test procedures. *Journal of Clinical and Experimental Neuropsychology,* **7,** 239–250

LA RUE, A. (1982) Memory loss and ageing. Distinguishing dementia from benign senescent forgetfulness and depressive pseudodementia. *Psychiatric Clinics of North America,* **5,** 89–103

LAVADAS, E., UMILTA, C. and PROVINCIALI, L. (1979) Hemisphere-dependent cognitive performances in epileptic patients. *Epilepsia,* **20,** 493–502

LAVY, S., MELAMED, E. and PORTINOY, Z. (1975) The effect of cerebral infarction on the regional cerebral blood flow of the contralateral hemisphere. *Stroke,* **6,** 160–163

LAWSON, J. S., WILLIAMS-ERDAHL, D. L., MONGA, T. N., BIRD, C. E., DONALD, M. W., SURRIDGE, D. H. C. *et al.* (1984) Neuropsychological function in diabetic patients with neuropathy. *British Journal of Psychiatry,* **145,** 263–268

LEBOEUF, A., LODGE, J. and EAMES, P. G. (1978) Vasopressin and memory in Korsakoff syndrome. *Lancet,* **ii,** 1370

LEDOUX, J. E., RISSE, G. L., SPRINGER, S. P., WILSON, D. H. and GAZZANIGA, M. S. (1977) Cognition and commissurotomy. *Brain,* **100,** 87–104

LEES, A. J. and SMITH, E. (1983) Cognitive deficits in the early stages of Parkinson's Disease. *Brain,* **106,** 257–270

LEFTOFF, S. (1981) Learning functions for unilaterally brain damaged patients for serially and randomly ordered stimulus material: analysis of retrieval strategies and their relationship to rehabilitation. *Journal of Clinical Neuropsychology*, **3**, 301–313

LEHTONEN, R. (1973) Learning, memory and intellectual performance in a chronic state of amnesic syndrome. *Acta Neurologica Scandinavica*, **49** (Suppl.), 107–133

LEVIN, H. S., BENTON, A. L. and GROSSMAN, R. G. (1982) *Neurobehavioural Consequences of Closed Head Injury*. New York: Oxford University Press

LEVIN, H. S. and EISENBERG, H. M. (1979a) Neuropsychological outcome of closed head injury in children and adolescents. *Childs Brain*, **5**, 281–292

LEVIN, H. S. and EISENBERG, H. M. (1979b) Neuropsychological impairment after closed head injury in children and adolescents. *Journal of Paediatric Psychology*, **4**, 389–402

LEVIN, H. S. and EISENBERG, H. M. (1979c) Verbal learning and memory in relation to focal and diffuse effects of closed head injury. Paper presented at Academy of Aphasia meeting, October 1979, San Diego

LEVIN, H. S., EISENBERG, H. M., WIGG, N. R. and KOBAYASHI, K. (1982) Memory and intellectual ability after head injury in children and adolescents. *Neurosurgery*, **11**, 668–673

LEVIN, H. S. and GOLDSTEIN, F. C. (1986) Organization of verbal memory after severe closed head injury. *Journal of Clinical and Experimental Neuropsychology*, **8**, 643–656

LEVIN, H. S., GROSSMAN, R. G. and KELLY, P. J. (1976) Short-term recognition memory in relation to severity of head injury. *Cortex*, **12**, 175–182

LEVIN, H. S., GROSSMAN, R. G. and KELLY, P. J. (1977) Assessment of long-term memory in brain damaged patients. *J Consult Clin Psychol*, **45**, 684–688

LEVIN, H. S., GROSSMAN, R., ROSE, J. E. and TEASDALE, G. (1979) Long-term neuropsychological outcome of closed head injury. *Journal of Neurosurgery*, **50**, 412–422

LEVIN, H. S., HIGH W. M., MEYERS, C. A., VON LAUFEN, A., HAYDEN, M. E. and EISENBERG, H. M. (1985) Impairment of remote memory after closed head injury. *Journal of Neurology, Neurosurgery and Psychiatry*, **48**, 556–563

LEVIN, H. S., MEYERS, C. A., GROSSMAN, R. G. and SARWAR, M. (1981) Ventricular enlargement after closed head injury. *Archives of Neurology*, **38**, 623–629

LEVIN, H. S., O'DONNELL, V. M. and GROSSMAN, R. G. (1979) The Galveston Orientation and Amnesia Test: a practical scale to assess cognition after head injury. *Journal of Nervous and Mental Disease*, **167**, 675–684

LEVIN, H. S., O'NEAL, J. T., BARRATT, E. S., ADAMS, P. M. and LEVIN, E. M. (1977) Outcome of stereotactic bilateral cingulotomy. In *Neurosurgical Treatment in Psychiatry, Pain and Epilepsy*, edited by W. H. Sweet, S. Obrador, J. G. Martin-Rodriguez, pp. 401–413. Baltimore: University Park Press

LEVIN, H. S., PAPANICOLAOU, A. and EISENBERG, H. M. (1984) Observations on amnesia after nonmissile head injury. In *Neuropsychology of Memory*, edited by L. Squire and N. Butters, pp. 247–257. New York: The Guilford Press

LEVIN, H. S. and PETERS, B. H. (1976) Neuropsychological testing following head injuries: prosopagnosia without visual field defect. *Diseases of the Nervous Systems*, **37**, 68–71

LEVIN, H. S. and PETERS, B. H. (1977) Hyperbaric oxygenation in the treatment of postencephalitic syndrome. *Aviation, Space, and Environmental Medicine*, **48**, 688–671

LEVIN, H. S. and PETERS, B. H. (1984) Long-term administration of oral physostigmine and lecithin improve memory in Alzheimer's disease. *Annals of Neurology*, **15**, 210

LEVINE, D. N. and GREK, A. (1984) The anatomic basis of delusions after right cerebral infarction. *Neurology*, **34**, 577–582

LEWIS, A. (1961) Amnesic syndromes. *Proceedings of the Royal Society of Medicine*, **54**, 955–961

LEZAK, M. (1983) *Neuropsychological Assessment*, 2nd edn. New York: Oxford University Press

LEZAK, M. D. (1979) Recovery of memory and learning functions following traumatic brain injury. *Cortex*, **15**, 63–72

LHERMITTE, F. and SIGNORET, J. L. (1972) Analyse neuropsychologique et differenciation des syndrome amnesiques. *Rev Neurol*, **126**, 161–178

LIDDLE, P. F. and CROW, T. J. (1984) Age disorientation in chronic schizophrenia is associated with global intellectual impairment. *British Journal of Psychiatry*, **144**, 193–199

LINDQUIST, G. and NORLEN, G. (1966) Korsakoff's syndrome after operation on ruptured aneurysm of the anterior communicating artery. *Acta Psychiatrica Scandinavica*, **42**, 23–34

LINDSTROM, K. (1982) Behavioural effects of long-term exposure to organic solvents. *Acta Neurologica Scandinavica*, **66** (Suppl. 92), 131–141

LINDVALL, H. V., LINDEROTH, B. and NORLIN, B. (1974) Causes of the post-concussional syndrome. *Acta Neurologica Scandinavica*, **50**, Suppl 56

LISAK, R. and ZIMMERMAN, R. (1977) Transient global amnesia due to a dominant hemisphere tumor. *Archives of Neurology*, **34**, 317–318

LISHMAN, A. W. (1978) *Organic Psychiatry*. Oxford: Blackwell Scientific Publications

LISHMAN, A. W. (1987) *Organic Psychiatry* 2nd edn. Oxford: Blackwell Scientific Publications

LISHMAN, W. A., RON, M. and ACKER, W. (1980) Computed tomography of the brain and psychometric assessment of alcoholic men – a British study. In *Addiction and Brain Damage*, edited by D. Richter. London: Croom Helm

LITTLE, A., LEVY, R., CHUAQUI-KIDD, P. and HAND, D. (1985) A double-blind, placebo controlled trial of high dose lecithin in Alzheimer's disease. *Journal of Neurology, Neurosurgery and Psychiatry*, **48**, 736–742

LJUNGGREN, B., SOWESSON, B., SAVELAND, H. and BRANDT, L. (1985) Cognitive impairment and adjustment in patients without neurological deficits after aneurysmal subarachnoid haemorrhage and early operation. *Journal of Neurosurgery*, **62**, 673–679

LOBOSKY, J. M., VANGILDER, J. C. and DAMASIO, A. R. (1984) Behavioural manifestations of third ventricular colloid cysts. *Journal of Neurology, Neurosurgery and Psychiatry*, **47**, 1075–1080

LOCKE, J. and DECK, J. (1978) Retrieval failure, rehearsal deficiency and short-term memory loss in the aphasic adult. *Brain Lang*, **5**, 227–235

LOEW, D. M. and WEIL, C. (1982) Hydergine in senile mental impairment. *Gerontology*, **28**, 54–74

LOFTUS, E. F. and BURNS, T. E. (1982) Mental shock can produce retrograde amnesia. *Mem Cog*, **10**, 318–323

LOFTUS, E. F. and LOFTUS, G. R. (1980) On the permanence of stored information in the human brain. *Am Psychol*, **35**, 409–420

LOFTUS, G. R. (1985a) Evaluating forgetting curves. *J Exp Psychol: Learn Mem Cogn.* **11**, 397–406

LOFTUS, G. R. (1985b) Consistency and confoundings: reply to Slamecka. *J Exp Psychol: Learn Mem Cogn*, **11**, 817–820

LOGUE, P. and WYRICK, L. (1979) Initial validation of Russell's revised Wechsler Memory Scale: a comparison of normal aging versus dementia. *J Consult Clin Psychol*, **47**, 176–178

LOGUE, V., DURWARD, M., PRATT, R. T. C., PIERCY, M. and NIXON, W. L. B. (1968) The quality of survival after rupture of an anterior cerebral aneurysm. *British Journal of Psychiatry*, **114**, 137–160

LOISEAU, P., SIGNORET, J. L., STRUBE E., BROUSTET, D. and DARTIGUES, J. F. (1982) Nouveaux procedes d'appreciation des troubles de la memoire chez les epileptiques. *Rev Neurol*, **138**, 387–400

LOISEAU, P., STRUBE, E., BROUSTET, D., BATTELLOCHI, S., GOMENI, C. and MORSELLI, P. L. (1980) Evaluation of memory function in a population of epileptic patients and matched controls. *Acta Neurologica Scandinavica*, **80**, (Suppl.) 58–61

LOISEAU, P., STRUBE, E., BROUSTET, D., BATTELLOCHI, S., GOMENI, C. and MORSELLI, P. L. (1983) Learning impairment in epileptic patients. *Epilepsia*, **24**, 183–192

LONGRIDGE, N. S., HACHINSKI, V. and BARBER, H. O. (1979) Brain stem dysfunction in transient global amnesia. *Stroke*, **10**, 473–474

LORING, D. W. and PAPANICOLAOU, A. C. (1987) Memory assessment in neurophysiology: theoretical considerations and practical utility. *Journal of Clinical and Experimental Neuropsychology*, **9**, 340–358

LOU, H. O. C. L. (1968) Repeated episodes of transient global amnesia. *Acta Neurologica Scandinavica*, **44**, 612–618

LUCZYWEK, E. and MEMPEL, E. (1980) Memory and learning in epileptic patients treated by amygdalotomy and anterior hippocampotomy *Acta Neurochirurgica*, **30** (Suppl.), 169–175

LUNSFORD, L.D., MAROON, J. C. and VEGA, A. (1977) Amnestic syndrome in limbic lesions: Report of three cases. *Surgical Forum*, **28**, 481–484

LURIA, A. R. (1976) *The Neuropsychology of Memory*. Washington: VH Winston & Sons

LUXENBERG, J. S., MAY, C., HAXBY, J. V., GRADY, C., MOORE, A., BERG, G., *et al.* (1987) Cerebral metabolism, anatomy and cognition in monozygotic twins discordant for dementia of the Alzheimer-type. *Journal of Neurology, Neurosurgery and Psychiatry,* **50,** 333–334

LYLE, O. E. and GOTTESMAN, I. I. (1977) Premorbid psychometric indicators of the gene for Huntington's disease. *J Consult Clin Psychol,* **45,** 1011–1022

LYNCH, S. and YARNELL, P. R. (1973) Retrograde amnesia: delayed forgetting after concussion. *Am Psychol,* **86,** 643–645

McCARTY, S. M., ZIESAT, H. A., LOGUE, P. E., POWER, D. G. and ROSENSTIEL, A. K. (1980) Alternate form reliability and age-related scores for Russell's revised Wechsler Memory Scale. *J Cons Clin Psychol,* **48,** 296–298

McDOWALL, J. (1981) Effects of encoding instructions on recall and recognition in Korsakoff patients. *Neuropsychologia,* **19,** 43–48

McENTEE, W. J., BIBER, M. P. and PERL, D. P. (1976) Diencephalic amnesia: a reappraisal. *Journal of Neurology, Neurosurgery and Psychiatry,* **39,** 436–441

McENTEE, W. J. and MAIR, R. G. (1978) Memory impairment in Korsakoff's psychosis: a correlation with brain noradrenergic activity. *Science,* **202,** 905–907

McENTEE, W. J. and MAIR, R. G. (1979) Memory enhancement in Korsakoff's psychosis by clonidine: further evidence for a noradrenergic deficit. *Annals of Neurology,* **7,** 466–470

McENTEE, W. J. and MAIR, R. G. (1984) Catecholamines and amnesia: the need for psychometric verification. *Annals of Neurology,* **16,** 16–17

McKHANN, G., DRACHMAN, D., FOLSTEIN, M., KATZMAN, R., PRICE, D. and STADLAN, E. M. (1984) Clinical diagnosis of Alzheimer's disease. *Neurology,* **34,** 939–944

McKINLAY, W. W., BROOKS, D. N. and BOND, M. R. (1983) Post-concussional symptoms, financial compensation and outcome of severe blunt head injury. *Journal of Neurology, Neurosurgery and Psychiatry,* **46,** 1084–1091

McLATCHIE, G., BROOKS, N., GALBRAITH, S. B., HUTCHISON, J. S. F., WILSON, L., MELVILLE, I. *et al.* (1987) Clinical neurological examination, neuropsychology, electroencephalography and computed tomographic head scanning in active amateur boxers. *Journal of Neurology, Neurosurgery and Psychiatry,* **50,** 96–99

McLEAN, A., TEMKIN, N. R., DIKMEN, S. and WYLER, A. R. (1983) The behavioural sequelae of head injury. *Journal of Clinical Neuropsychology,* **5,** 361–376

McLEOD, C. M., DE KABAN, A. S. and HUNT, E. (1978) Memory impairment in epileptic patients: selective effects of phenobarbitone concentration. *Science,* **202,** 1102–1104

McMILLAN, M., POWELL, G. E., JANOTA, I. and POLKEY, C. E. (1987) Relationship between neuropathology and cognitive functioning in temporal lobectomy patients. *Journal of Neurology, Neurosurgery and Psychiatry,* **50,** 167–176

McNEILL, D. L., TIDMARSH, D. and RASTALL, M. L. (1965) A case of dysmnestic syndrome following cardiac arrest. *British Journal of Psychiatry,* **111,** 697–699

MADISON, D. P., BAEHR, E. T., BAZELL, M., HARTMAN, R. W., MAHURKAR, S. D. and DUNEA, G. (1977) Communicative and cognitive deterioration in dialysis dementia: two case studies. *Journal of Speech and Hearing Research,* **42,** 238–246

MAHER, E. R., SMITH E. M. and LEES, A. J. (1985) Cognitive deficits in the Steele-Richardson-Olszewski syndrome (progressive supranuclear palsy). *Journal of Neurology, Neurosurgery and Psychiatry,* **48,** 1234–1239

MAIR, W. G., WARRINGTON, E. K. and WEISKRANTZ, L. (1979) Memory disorder in Korsakoff's psychosis: a neuropathological and neuropsychological investigation of two cases. *Brain,* **102,** 749–783

MALMO, R. B. and AMSEL, A. (1948) Anxiety-produced interference in serial rote learning with observations on rote learning after partial frontal lobectomy. *Journal of Experimental Psychology,* **28,** 440–454

MARKOWITSCH, H. J. (1982) Thalamic mediodorsal nucleus and memory: a critical evaluation of studies in animals and man. *Neurosci Biobehav Rev,* **6,** 351–380

MARKOWITSCH, H. J. (1983) Transient global amnesia. *Neurosci Biobehav Rev,* **7,** 35–43

MARKOWITSCH, H. J. (1984) Can amnesia be caused by caused by damage of a single brain structure? *Cortex,* **20,** 27–46

MARKOWITSCH, H. J., KESSLER, J. and BAST-KESSLER, C. (1984) Differential emotional tones significantly affect recognition performance in patients with Korsakoff psychosis. *International Journal of Neuroscience*, **25**, 145–159

MARKOWITSCH, H. J., KESSLER, J. and DENZLER, P. (1986) Recognition memory and psychophysiological responses to stimuli with neutral or emotional content: a study of Korsakoff patients and recently detoxified and longterm abstinent alcoholics. *International Journal of Neuroscience*, **29**, 1–35

MARSDEN, C. D. and REYNOLDS, E. H. (1982) Neurology. In *Textbook of Epilepsy*, edited by J. Laidlaw and A. Richens. Edinburgh: Churchill Livingstone

MARSH, G. G., MARKHAM C. M. and ANSEL, R. (1971) Levodopa's awakening effect on patients with parkinsonism. *Journal of Neurology, Neurosurgery and Psychiatry*, **34**, 209–218

MARSLEN-WILSON, W. D. and TEUBER, H. L. (1975) Memory for remote events in anterograde amnesia: recognition of public figures from newsphotographs. *Neuropsychologia*, **13**, 353–364

MARTIN, A. (1987) Representation of semantic and spatial knowledge in Alzheimer's patients: implications for models of preserved learning in amnesia. *Journal of Clinical and Experimental Neuropsychology*, **9**, 191–224

MARTIN, A., BROUWERS, P., COX, C. and FEDIO, P. (1985a) On the nature of the verbal memory deficit in Alzheimer's disease. *Brain Lang*, **25**, 323–341

MARTIN, A., COX, C., BROUWERS, P. and FEDIO, P. (1985b) A note on the different patterns of impaired and preserved cognitive abilities and their relation to episodic memory deficits in Alzheimer's patients. *Brain Lang*, **26**, 181–185

MARTIN, P. R., WEINGARTNER, H., GORDON, E. K., BURNS, R. S., LINNOILA, M., KOPIN, I. J., *et al.* (1984) Central nervous system catecholamine metabolism in Korsakoff's psychosis. *Annals of Neurology*, **15**, 184–187

MARTONE, M., BUTTERS, N., PAYNE, M., BECKER, J. T. and SAX, D. S. (1984) Dissociations between skill learning and verbal recognition in amnesia and dementia. *Archives of Neurology*, **41**, 965–970

MARTONE, M., BUTTERS, N. and TRAUNER, D. (1986) Some analyses of forgetting of pictorial material in amnesic and demented patients. *Journal of Clinical and Experimental Neuropsychology*, **8**, 161–178

MASSMAN, P. J., BIGLER, E. D., CULLUM, C. M. and NAUGLE, R. I. (1986) The relationship between cortical atrophy and ventricular volume. *International Journal of Neuroscience*, **30**, 87–99

MASTER, D. R., THOMPSON, C., DUNN, G. and LISHMAN, W. A. (1986) Memory selectivity and unilateral cerebral dysfunction. *Psychol Med*. **16**, 781–788

MASUI, K., NIWA, S. I., ANZAI, N., KAMEYAMA, T., SAITOH, O. and RYMAR, K. (1984) Verbal memory disturbances in left temporal lobe epileptics. *Cortex*, **20**, 361–368

MATHEW, N. T. and MEYER, J. S. (1974) Pathogenesis and natural history of transient global amnesia. *Stroke*, **5**, 303–311

MATTIS, S. (1976) Dementia rating scale. In *Geriatric Psychiatry*, edited by R. Bellack and B. Karasu. New York: Grune and Stratton

MATTIS, S., KOVNER, R. and GOLDMEIER, E. (1978) Different patterns of mnemonic deficits in two organic amnestic syndromes. *Brain Lang*, **6**, 179–191

MATTLAR, C. E., FALCK, B., RONNEMAA, T. and HYPPA, M. T. (1985) Neuropsychological cognitive performance of patients with type-2 diabetes. *Scandinavian Journal of Rehabilitative Medicine*, **17**, 101–105

MAYES, A. R. and MEUDELL, P. R. (1981) How similar is immediate memory in amnesic patients to delayed memory in normal subjects? A replication, extension and reassessment of the amnesic cueing effect. *Neuropsychologia*, **19**, 647–654

MAYES, A. R., MEUDELL, P. R. and NEARY, D. (1978) Must amnesia be caused by either encoding or retrieval disorders? In *Practical Aspects of Memory*, edited by M. M. Gruneberg, P. E. Morris and R. N. Sykes, pp. 712–719. London: Academic Press

MAYES, A. R., MEUDELL, P. and NEARY, D. (1980) Do amnesics adopt inefficient encoding strategies with faces and random shapes? *Neuropsychologia*, **18**, 527–540

MAYEUX, R., ALEXANDER, M. P., BENSON, D. F., BRANDT, J. and ROSEN, J. (1979) Poriomania. *Neurology*, **29**, 1616–1619

MAYEUX, R., BRANDT, J., ROSEN, J. and BENSON, D. F. (1980) Inter-ictal memory and language impairment in temporal lobe epilepsy. *Neurology*, **30**, 120–125

MAZZUCCHI, A., MORETTI, G., CAFFARRA, P. and PARMA, M. (1980) Neuropsychological functions in the follow-up of transient global amnesia. *Brain*, **103**, 161–178

MEADOR, K. J., ADAMS, R. J. and FLANIGAN, H. F. (1985) Transient global amnesia and meningioma. *Neurology*, **35**, 769–771

MEADOWS, A. T., MASSARI, D. J., FERGUSSON, J., GORDON, J., LITTMAN, P. and MOSS, K. (1981) Declines in IQ scores and cognitive dysfunctions in children with acute lymphocytic leukaemia treated with cranial irradiation. *Lancet*, **ii**, 1015–1018

MEDINA, J., RUBINO, F. and ROSS, E. (1974) Agitated delirium caused by infarctions of the hippocampal formation and fusiform and lingual gyri. *Neurology*, **24**, 1181–1183

MERCER, B., WAPNER, W., GARDNER, H. and BENSON, D. F. (1977) A study of confabulation. *Archives of Neurology*, **34**, 429–433

MESULAM, M. M., WAXMAN, S. G., GESCHWIND, N. and SABIN, T. D. (1976) Acute confusional states with right middle cerebral artery infarctions. *Journal of Neurology, Neurosurgery and Psychiatry*, **39**, 84–89

METTER, E. J., RIEGE, W. H., HANSON, W. R., KUHL, D. E., PHELPS, M. E., SQUIRE L. R., *et al.* (1983) Comparison of metabolic rates, language and memory in subcortical aphasias. *Brain Lang*, **19**, 33–47

MEUDELL, P., BUTTERS, N. and MONTGOMERY, K. (1978) The role of rehearsal in the short-term memory performance of patients with Korsakoff's and Huntington's disease. *Neuropsychologia*, **16**, 507–510

MEUDELL, P. R. and MAYES, A. R. (1981) The Claparede phenomenon: a further example in amnesics, a demonstration of a similar effect in normal people with attenuated memory and a reinterpretation. *Current Psychological Research*, **1**, 75–88

MEUDELL, P. R., MAYES, A. R., OSTERGAARD, A. and PICKERING, A. (1985) Recency and frequency judgements in alcoholic amnesics and normal people with poor memory. *Cortex*, **21**, 487–511

MEUDELL, P. R., NORTHERN, B., SNOWDEN, J. S. and NEARY, D. (1980) Long-term memory for famous voices in amnesic and normal subjects. *Neuropsychologia*, **18**, 133–139

MEUTER, F., THOMAS, W., GRUNEKLEE, D., GRIES, F. A. and LOHMANN, R. (1980) Psychometric evaluation of performance in diabetes mellitus. *Hormone Metab Res*, **9**, 9–17

MEYER, V. and FALCONER, M. A. (1960) Defects of learning ability with massive lesions of the temporal lobe. *Journal of Mental Science*, **106**, 472–477

MEYER, V. and YATES, H. J. (1955) Intellectual changes following temporal lobectomy for psychomotor epilepsy. *Journal of Neurology, Neurosurgery and Psychiatry*, **18**, 44–52

MICHEL, M. D., LAURENT, B., FOYATIER, N., BLANC, A. and PORTAFAIX, M. (1982) Infarctus thalamique paramedian gauche. Etude de la memoire et du language. *Rev Neurol*, **138**, 533–550

MILBERG, W. P., HEBBEN, N. and KAPLAN, E. (1986) The Boston process approach to neuropsychological assessment. In *Neuropsychological Assessment of Neuropsychiatric Disorders*, edited by I. Grant and K. M. Adams, pp. 64–86. New York: Oxford University Press

MILES, W. R. and ROOT, H. F. (1922) Psychologic tests applied to diabetic patients. *Archives of Internal Medicine*, **30**, 767–777

MILLER, E. (1971) On the nature of the memory disorder in presenile dementia. *Neuropsychologia*, **9**, 75–81

MILLER, E. (1972) Efficiency of coding and the short-term memory defect in presenile dementia. *Neuropsychologia*, **10**, 133–136

MILLER, E. (1973) Short- and long-term memory in presenile dementia (Alzheimer's disease). *Psychol Med*, **3**, 221–224

MILLER, E. (1975) Impaired recall and the memory disturbance in presenile dementia. *Br J Soc Clin Psychol*, **14**, 73–79

MILLER, E. (1977) *Abnormal Ageing*. London: Wiley

MILLER, E. (1978) Retrieval from long-term memory in presenile dementia: two tests of an hypothesis. *Br J Soc Clin Psychol*, **17**, 143–148

MILLER, E. (1979) The long-term consequences of head injury: a discussion of the evidence with special reference to the preparation of legal reports. *Br J Soc Clin Psychol*, **18**, 87–98

MILLER, E. (1980) The training characteristics of severely head-injured patients: a preliminary study. *Journal of Neurology, Neurosurgery and Psychiatry*, **43**, 525–528

MILLER, E. and LEWIS, P. (1977) Recognition memory in elderly patients with depression and dementia: a signal detection analysis. *Journal of Abnormal Psychology*, **86**, 84–86

MILLER, G. A. (1956) The magical number seven, plus or minus two. *Psychol Rev*, **63**, 81–97

MILLER, H. (1961) Accidental neurosis. *British Medical Journal*, **i**, 919–925

MILLS, R. P. and SWANSON, P. D. (1978) Vertical oculomotor apraxia and memory loss. *Annals of Neurology*, **4**, 149–153

MILNER B. (1958) Psychological defects produced by temporal lobe excision. *Res Publs Ass Res Nerv Ment Dis.* **36**, 244–257

MILNER B. (1962) Laterality effects in audition. In *Interhemispheric Relations and Cerebral Dominance*, edited by V. B. Mountcastle. Baltimore: Johns Hopkins Press

MILNER, B. (1964) Some effects of frontal lobectomy in man. In *The Frontal Granular Cortex and Behaviour*, edited by J. M. Warren and K. Akert, pp. 313–334. New York: McGraw Hill

MILNER, B. (1965) Visually-guided maze learning in man: effects of bilateral hippocampal, bilateral frontal and unilateral cerebral lesions. *Neuropsychologia*, **3**, 316–338

MILNER, B. (1968) Disorders of memory after brain lesions in man. *Neuropsychologia*, **6**, 175–179

MILNER, B. (1969) Residual intellectual and memory deficits after head injury. In *The Late Effects of Head Injury*, edited by E. A. Walker, W. Caveness and M. Critchley, pp. 84–97. Springfield, Illinois: C. Thomas

MILNER, B. (1970) Memory and the medial temporal regions of the brain. In *Biology of Memory*, edited by K. H. Pribram and D. E. Broadbent, pp. 29–50. London: Academic Press

MILNER, B. (1971) Interhemispheric differences in the localization of psychological processes in man. *British Medical Bulletin*, **27**, 272–277

MILNER, B. (1975) Psychological aspects of focal epilepsy and its neurosurgical management. In *Advances in Neurology*, Volume 8, edited by D. P. Purpura, J. K. Penry and R. D. Walter, pp. 299–321. New York: Raven Press

MILNER, B. (1978) Clues to the cerebral organization of memory. In *Cerebral Correlates of Conscious Experience*, edited by P. A. Buser and A. Rougeul-Buser, pp. 139–153. Amsterdam: North-Holland Publishing Company

MILNER, B. (1980) Complementary functional specializations of the human cerebral hemispheres. In *Nerve Cells, Transmitters and Behaviour*, edited by R. Levi-Montalcini, pp. 601–625. Amsterdam: Elsevier/North-Holland Biomedical Press

MILNER, B. (1982) Some cognitive effects of frontal lobe lesions in man. In *The Neuropsychology of Cognitive Function*, edited by D. E. Broadbent and L. Weiskrantz, pp. 211–226. London: The Royal Society

MILNER, B., CORKIN, S. and TEUBER, H. L. (1968) Further analysis of the hippocampal amnesic syndrome: 14-year follow-up study of HM. *Neuropsychologia*, **6**, 215–234

MILNER, B., PETRIDES, M. and SMITH, M. L. (1985) Frontal lobes and the temporal organization of memory. *Human Neurobiology*, **4**, 137–142

MILNER, B. and TAYLOR, L. (1972) Right-hemisphere superiority in tactile pattern-recognition after cerebral commissurotomy: evidence for nonverbal memory. *Neuropsychologia*, **10**, 1–15

MILNER, B. and TEUBER, H. L. (1968) Alteration of perception and memory in man: reflections on methods. In *Analysis of Behavioural Change*, edited by L. Weiskrantz, pp. 268–375. New York: Harper & Row

MIRSKY, A. F. and ORZACK, M. H. (1980) Two retrospective studies of psychosurgery. In *The Psychosurgery Debate. Scientific, Legal and Ethical Perspectives*, edited by E. S. Valenstein, pp. 205–244. San Francisco: W. H. Freeman & Co

MIRSKY, A. F., PRIMAC, D. W., MARSAN, C. A., ROSVOLD, H. E. and STEVENS, J. R. (1960) A comparison of the psychological test performance of patients with focal and nonfocal epilepsy. *Exp Neurol*, **2**, 75–89

MISHKIN, M. (1978) Memory in monkeys severely impaired by combined but not by separate removal of amygdala and hippocampus. *Nature*, **273**, 297–298

MITSUYAMA, Y. (1984) Presenile dementia with motor neurone disease in Japan: clinical pathological review of 26 cases. *Journal of Neurology, Neurosurgery and Psychiatry*, **47**, 953–959

MOHR, J. P., LEICESTER, J., STODDARD, L. T. and SIDMAN, M. (1971) Right hemianopia with memory and colour deficits in circumscribed left posterior cerebral artery territory infarction. *Neurology*, **21**, 1104–1113

MOHS, R. C., DAVIS, B. M., MATHE, A. A., ROSEN, W. G., JOHNS, C. A., GREENWALD, B. S., *et al.* (1985) Intravenous and oral physostigmine in Alzheimer's disease. In *Modern Approaches to the Dementias*, edited by F. C. Rose, pp. 140–152. Basel: Karger

MOORE, W. H. (1986) Hemispheric alpha asymmetries and behavioural responses of aphasic and normal subjects after recall and recognition of active, passive and negative sentences. *Brain and Language,* **29,** 286–300

MORRIS, R., WHEATLEY, J. and BRITTON, P. (1983) Retrieval from long-term memory in senile dementia; cued recall revisited. *British Journal of Psychology,* **22,** 141–142

MORRIS, R. G. (1986) Short-term forgetting in senile dementia of the Alzheimer type. *Cognitive Neuropsychology,* **3,** 77–97

MORRIS, R. G. and KOPELMAN, M. D. (1986) The memory deficits in Alzheimer-type dementia. *Quarterly Journal of Experimental Psychology,* **38A,** 575–602

MORTIMOR, J. A., PIROZZOLO, F. J., HANSCH, E. C. and WEBSTER, D. D. (1982) Relationship of motor symptoms to intellectual deficits in Parkinson's disease. *Neurology,* **32,** 133–137

MOSCOVITCH, M. (1982a) A neuropsychological approach to perception and memory in normal and pathological aging. In *Aging and Cognitive Processes,* edited by F. K. M. Craik and S. Trehub, pp. 55–78. New York: Plenum Press

MOSCOVITCH, M. (1982b) Multiple dissociations of function in amnesia. In *Amnesia,* edited by L. S. Cermak, pp. 337–370. Hillsdale, NJ: Lawrence Erlbaum Associates

MOSCOVITCH, M. (1984) The sufficient conditions for demonstrating preserved memory in amnesia: a task analysis. In *Neuropsychology of Memory,* edited by L. R. Squire and N. Butters, pp. 104–114. New York: The Guildford Press

MOSES, J. A., GOLDEN, C. J., BERGER, P. A. and WISNIEWSKI, A. M. (1981) Neuropsychological deficits in early, middle, and late stage Huntington's disease as measured by the Luria-Nebraska neuropsychological battery. *International Journal of Neuroscience,* **14,** 95–100

MOSS, M. B., ALBERT, M. S., BUTTERS, N. and PAYNE, M. (1986) Differential patterns of memory loss among patients with Alzheimer's disease, Huntington's disease and alcoholic Korsakoff's syndrome. *Archives of Neurology,* **43,** 239–248

MOSS, H. A., NANNIS, E. D. and POPLACK, D. G. (1981) The effects of prophylactic treatment of the central nervous system on the intellectual functioning of children with acute lymphocytic leukemia. *American Journal of Medicine,* **71,** 47–52

MULDER, D. W. and SWENSON, W. (1974) Psychologic and psychiatric aspects of brain tumors. In *Handbook of Clinical Neurology,* edited by P. J. Vinken and G. W. Bruyen, pp. 727–740. Amsterdam: North-Holland Publishing Company

MULLALAY, W., HUFF, K., ROWTHAL, M. and GESCHWIND, N. (1982) Chronic confusional state with right middle cerebral artery occlusion. *Neurology,* **32,** A96

MUMENTHALER, M., KAESER, H. E., MEYER, A. and HESS, T. (1979) Transient global amnesia after clioquinol. *Journal of Neurology, Neurosurgery and Psychiatry,* **42,** 1084–1090

MURAMOTO, O. (1984) Selective reminding in normal and demented aged people: auditory verbal versus visual spatial task. *Cortex,* **20,** 461–478

MURAMOTO, O., KURU, Y., SUGISHITA, M. and TOYOKURA, Y. (1979) Pure memory loss with hippocampal lesions. *Archives of Neurology,* **36,** 54–56

NARABAYASHI, H. (1979) Long-range results of medial amygdalotomy on epileptic traits in adult patients. In *Functional Neurosurgery,* edited by T. Rasmussen and R. Marino, pp. 243–252. New York: Raven Press

NAUS, M. J., CERMAK, L. S. and DELUCA, D. (1977) Retrieval processes in alcoholic Korsakoff patients. *Neuropsychologia,* **15,** 737–742

NEARY, D., SNOWDEN, J. S., BOWEN, D. M., SIMS, N. R., MANN, D. M. A., BENTON, J. S. et al. (1986) Neuropsychological syndromes in presenile dementia due to cerebral atrophy. *Journal of Neurology, Neurosurgery and Psychiatry,* **49,** 63–74

NELSON, D. L., McEVOY, C. L., WALLING, J. R. and WHEELER, J. W. (1980) The University of South Florida homograph norms. *Behav Res Meth & Instrum,* **12,** 16–37

NELSON, T. O. and NARENS, L. (1980) Norms of 300 general-information questions: accuracy of recall, latency of recall, and feeling-of-knowing ratings. *J Verb Learn Verb Behav,* **19,** 338–368

NEWCOMBE, F. (1965) Memory-for-designs test: the performance of ex-servicemen with missile wounds of the brain. *Br J Soc Clin Psychol,* **4,** 230–231

NEWCOMBE, F. (1969) *Missile Wounds of the Brain.* London: Oxford University Press

NEWCOMBE, F. (1982) The psychological consequences of closed head injury: assessment and rehabilitation. *Injury,* **14,** 111–136

NEWCOMBE, F. and MARSHALL, J. (1967) Immediate recall of sentences by subjects with unilateral cerebral lesions. *Neuropsycholgia,* **5,** 329–334

NICKERSON, C. A. and CARTWRIGHT, D. S. (1984) The University of Colorado meaning norms. *Behav Res Meth Instrum & Comp,* **16,** 355–382

NIELSEN, H., HOJER-PEDERSEN, E., GULLIKSEN, G., HAASE, J. and ENEVOLDSEN, E. (1985) A neuropsychological study of 12 patients with transient ischaemic attacks before and after EC/IC bypass surgery. *Acta Neurologica Scandinavica,* **71,** 317–320

NILSSON, L. G., CHRISTIANSON, S. A., SILFVENIUS, H. and BLOM, S. (1984) Preoperative and postoperative memory testing of epileptic patients. *Acta Neurologica Scandinavica,* **99,** (Suppl.), 43–56

NOBLE, E. P. (1983) Social drinking and cognitive function: a review. *Subst Alcohol Actions Misuse,* **4,** 205–216

NOVELLY, R. A., AUGUSTINE, F. A., MATTSON, R. H., GLASER, G. H., WILLIAMSON, P. D., SPENCER, D. D. *et al.* (1984) Selective memory improvement and impairment in temporal lobectomy for epilepsy. *Annals of Neurology,* **15,** 64–67

O'BRIEN, C. P., DIGIACOMO, J. N., FAHN, S. and SCHWARZ, G. A. (1971) Mental effects of high dose Levodopa. *Archives of General Psychiatry,* **24,** 61–64

OBER, B. A., KOSS, E., FRIEDLAND, R. P. and DELIS, D. C. (1985) Processes of verbal memory failure in Alzheimer-type dementia. *Brain and Cognition,* **4,** 90–103

OGDEN, J. A. (1986) Neuropsychological and psychological sequelae of shunt surgery in young adults with hydrocephalus. *Journal of Clinical and Experimental Neuropsychology,* **8,** 657–679

OJEMANN, G. A. (1971) Alteration in non verbal short-term memory with stimulation in the region of the mamillothalamic tract in man. *Neuropsychologia,* **9,** 195–201

OJEMANN, G. A. (1975) Language and the thalamus: object naming and recall during and after thalamic stimulation. *Brain and Language,* **2,** 101–120

OJEMANN, G. A. (1978) Organization of short-term verbal memory in language areas of human cortex: evidence from electrical stimulation. *Brain and Language,* **5,** 331–340

OJEMANN, G. A., BLICK, K. I. and WARD, A. A. (1969) Improvement and disturbance of short-term verbal memory during human ventrolateral thalamic stimulation. *Transactions of the American Neurological Association,* **94,** 72–75

OJEMANN, G. A., BLICK, K. and WARD, A. (1971) Improvement and disturbance of short-term memory with human ventrolateral thalamic stimulation. *Brain,* **94,** 225–240

OJEMANN, G. A. and DODRILL, C. B. (1985) Verbal memory deficits after left temporal lobectomy for epilepsy. Mechanism and intraoperative prediction. *Journal of Neurosurgery,* **62,** 101–107

OLSON, B. A. (1982) Effects of organic solvents on behavioural performance of workers in the paint industry. *Neurobehav Toxicol Teratol,* **4,** 703–708

OMMAYA, A. K. and FEDIO, P. (1972) The contribution of the cingulum and hippocampal structures to memory mechanisms in man. *Confina Neurologica,* **34,** 398–411

ORCHINIK, C. W. (1960) Some psychological aspects of circumscribed lesions of the diencephalon. *Confina Neurologica,* **20,** 292–310

OSBORNE, D. P., BROWN, E. R. and RANDT, C. T. (1982) Qualitative changes in memory function: aging and dementia. In *Alzheimer's Disease: A Report of Progress,* edited by S. Corkin *et al.,* pp. 165–169. New York: Raven Press

OSCAR-BERMAN, M. and BONNER, R. T. (1985) Matching- and delayed matching-to-sample as measures of visual processing, selective attention and memory in aging and alcoholic individuals. *Neuropsychologia,* **23,** 639–651

OSCAR-BERMAN, M. and ZOLA-MORGAN, S. M. (1980a) Comparative neuropsychology and Korsakoff's syndrome. I – Spatial and visual reversal learning. *Neuropsychologia,* **18,** 499–512

OSCAR-BERMAN, M. and ZOLA-MORGAN, S. M. (1980b) Comparative neuropsychology and Korsakoff's syndrome. II – Two-choice visual discrimination learning. *Neuropsychologia,* **18,** 513–525

OWENS, M., PRESSMAN, M., EDWARDS, E. E., TOURTELLOTTE, W., ROSE, J. G., STEIN, D., *et al.* (1980) The effect of small infarcts and carotid endarterectomy on postoperative psychologic test performance. *Journal of Surgical Research,* **28,** 209–216

OXBURY, J. M., CAMPBELL, D. C. and OXBURY, S. M. (1974) Unilateral spatial neglect and impairment of spatial analysis and spatial perception. *Brain, 97,* 551–564

PALERMO, D. S. and JENKINS, J. J. (1964) *Word Association Norms: Grade School through College.* Minneapolis: University of Minnesota Press

PARKER, J. C., GRANBERG, B. W., NICHOLS, W. K., JONES, J. G. and HEWETT, J. E. (1983) Mental status outcomes following carotid endarterectomy: a six month analysis. *Journal of Clinical Neuropsychology, 5,* 345–353

PARKER, S. A. and SERRATS, A. F. (1976) Memory recovery after traumatic coma. *Acta Neurochirurgica, 34,* 71–77

PARKIN, A. J. (1982) Residual learning capability in organic amnesia. *Cortex, 18,* 417–440

PARKIN, A. J. (1984) Amnesic syndrome: a lesion specific disorder? *Cortex, 20,* 479–508

PARKIN, A. J. and LENG, N. R. C. (1987) Comparative studies of human amnesia: syndrome or syndromes? In *Information Processing in the Human Brain,* edited by H. Markowitsch. Toronto: Hans Huber

PARKIN, A. J., LENG, N. R. C., STANHOPE, N. and SMITH, A. P. (1987) Memory impairment following ruptured aneurysm of the anterior communicating artery. *Brain and Cognition,* (in press)

PARKIN, A. J., MILLER, J. and VINCENT, R. (1987) Multiple neuropsychological deficits due to anoxic encephalopathy: a case study. *Cortex,* (in press)

PARSONS, O. A. and FARR, S. P. (1981) The neuropsychology of alcohol and drug abuse. In *Handbook of Clinical Neuropsychology,* edited by S. B. Filskov and T. J. Boll. New York: Wiley-Interscience

PARSONS, O. A. and LEBER, W. R. (1981) The relationship between cognitive dysfunction and brain damage in alcoholics: causal, interactive or epiphenomenal? *Alcoholism, 5,* 326–343

PATERSON, A. and ZANGWILL, O. L. (1944) Recovery of spatial disorientation in the post-traumatic confusional state. *Brain, 67,* 54–68

PATTERSON, M. B. and MACK, J. L. (1985) Neuropsychological analysis of a case of reduplicative paramnesia. *Journal of Clinical and Experimental Neuropsychology, 7,* 111–121

PAVIO, A., YUILLE, J. C. and MADIGAN, S. (1968) Concreteness, imagery, and meaningfulness values for 925 nouns. *Journal of Experimental Psychology Monograph, 76* (Suppl.), 1–25

PEARCE, J. M. S. (1983) Dementia in cerebral arterial disease. In *Vascular Disease of the Central Nervous System,* edited by R. W. Ross-Russell, pp. 356–367. London: Churchill Livingstone

PEARCE, J. M. S. (1984) Migraine: a cerebral disorder. *Lancet, ii,* 86–89

PENFIELD, W. (1968) Engrams in the human brain. *Proceedings of the Royal Society of Medicine, 61,* 831–840

PENFIELD, W. and MATHIESON, G. (1974) Memory. Autopsy findings and comments on the role of hippocampus in experiential recall. *Archives of Neurology, 31,* 145–154

PENFIELD, W. and MILNER, B. (1958) Memory deficit produced by bilateral lesions in the hippocampal zone. *Archives of Neurology and Psychiatry, 79,* 475–497

PENFIELD, W. and PEROT, P. (1963) The brain's record of auditory and visual experience. *Brain, 86,* 595–696

PEREZ, F. I., GAY, J. R. A., TAYLOR, R. L. and RIVERA, V. M. (1975) Patterns of memory performance in the neurologically impaired aged. *Canadian Journal of Neurological Science, 2,* 347–355

PEREZ, F. I., MATHEW, N. T., STUMP, D. A. and MEYER, J. S. (1977) Regional cerebral blood flow statistical patterns and psychological performance in multi-infarct dementia and Alzheimer's disease. *Canadian Journal of Neurological Science, 4,* 53–62

PERKIN, G. D. and HANDLER, C. E. (1983) Wernicke-Korsakoff syndrome. *British Journal of Hospital Medicine, 30,* 331–334

PERLMUTTER, D. and RHOTON, A. L. (1976) Microsurgical anatomy of the anterior cerebral anterior communicating recurrent artery complex. *Journal of Neurosurgery, 45,* 259–272

PERRET, E. and EGGENBERGER, E. (1973) Plasticity of learning ability in Parkinson patients before and after thalamotomy. In *Parkinson's Disease,* Volume 2, edited by J. Siegfried, p. 349. Bern: Hans Huber

PETERS, B. H. and LEVIN, H. S. (1977) Memory enhancement after physostigmine treatment in the amnesic syndrome. *Archives of Neurology, 34,* 215–219

PETERS, B. H. and LEVIN, H. S. (1982) Chronic oral physostigmine and lecithin administration in memory disorders of aging. In *Alzheimer's Disease: A Report of Progress,* edited by S. Corkin *et al.,* pp. 421–426. New York: Raven Press

PETERSON, L. R. and PETERSON, M. J. (1959) Short-term retention of individual verbal items. *Journal of Experimental Psychology*, **58**, 193–198

PETIT, H., ROUSSEAUX, M., CLARISSE, J. and DELAFOSSE, A. (1981) Troubles oculocephalomoteurs et infarctus thalamo-sous-thalamique bilateral. *Rev Neurol*, **137**, 709–722

PETIT-DUTAILLIS, D. J., CHRISTOPHE, J., PERTUISET, B., DREYFUS-BRISAC, C. and BLANC, C. (1954) Lobectomie temporale pour epilepsie: evolution des perturbations functionelles postoperatores. *Rev Neurol*, **91**, 129–133

PETRIDES, M. (1985) Deficits on conditional associative learning tasks after frontal- and temporal-lobe lesions in man. *Neuropsychologia*, **23**, 601–614

PETRIDES, M. and MILNER, B. (1982) Deficits on subject-ordered tasks after frontal and temporal lobe lesions in man. *Neuropsychologia*, **20**, 249–262

PICKARD, J. (1982) Adult communicating hydrocephalus. *British Journal of Hospital Medicine*, **27**, 35–44

PIERCY, M. (1977) Experimental studies of the amnesic syndrome. In *Amnesia*, 2nd edn, edited by C. W. M. Whitty and O. L. Zangwill. London: Butterworths

PILLON, B., DUBOIS, B., LHERMITTE, F. and ARID, Y. (1986) Heterogeneity of cognitive impairment in progressive supranuclear palsy, Parkinson's disease and Alzheimer's disease. *Neurology*, **36**, 1179–1185

PILLON, B., SIGNORET, J. L. and LHERMITTE, F. (1977) Troubles de la pensée spatiale et syndrome amnesique consecutifs à une encephalopathie anoxique. *Ann Med Interne*, **128**, 269–274

PIROZZOLO, F. J., HANSCH, E. C., MORTIMER, J. A., WEBSTER, D. D. and KUSKOWSKI, M. A. (1982) Dementia in Parkinson disease: a neuropsychological analysis. *Brain and Cognition*, **1**, 71–83

POLONI, M., CAPITANI, E., MAZZINI, L. and CERONI, M. (1986) Neuropsychological measures in amyotrophic lateral sclerosis and their relationship with CT scan-assessed cerebral atrophy. *Acta Neurologica Scandinavica*, **74**, 257–260

PONSFORD, J. L. and DONNAN, G. A. (1980) Transient global amnesia – a hippocampal phenomenon? *Journal of Neurology, Neurosurgery and Psychiatry*, **43**, 285–287

PONSFORD, J. L., DONNAN, G. A. and WALSH, K. W. (1980) Disorders of memory in vertebrobasilar disease. *Journal of Clinical Neuropsychology*, **2**, 267–276

PORTIN, R., RAININKO, R. and RINNE, U. K. (1984) Neuropsychological disturbances and cerebral atrophy determined by computerized tomography in parkinsonian patients with long-term levodopa treatment. In *Advances in Neurology*, edited by R. G. Hassler and J. F. Christ, Volume 40, pp. 219–227. New York: Raven Press

POWELL, G. E., POLKEY, C. E. and McMILLAN, T. (1985) The new Maudsley series of temporal lobectomy. I: Short-term cognitive effects. *British Journal of Clinical Psychology*, **24**, 109–124

POWELL, G. E., SUTHERLAND, G. and AGU, G. A. (1984) Serial position, rehearsal and recall in temporal lobe epilepsy. *British Journal of Clinical Psychology*, **23**, 153–154

POWELL-PROCTOR, L. and MILLER, E. (1982) Reality orientation: a critical appraisal. *British Journal of Psychiatry*, **140**, 457–463

POWERS, W. J. and RAICHLE, M. E. (1985) Positron emission tomography and its application to the study of cerebrovascular disease in man. *Stroke*, **16**, 361–376

PRAMMING, S., THORSTEINSSON, B., THEILGAARD, A., PINNER, E. M. and BINDER, C. (1986) Cognitive functioning during hypoglycaemia in type I diabetes mellitus. *British Medical Journal*, **292**, 647–650

PRATT, R. T. C. (1977) Psychogenic loss of memory. In *Amnesia*, 2nd edn, edited by C. W. M. Whitty and O. L. Zangwill, pp. 224–232. London: Butterworths

PRIEST, R. G., TARIGHATI, S. and SHARIATMADARI, M. E. (1969) A brief test of organic brain disease validation in a mental hospital population. *Acta Psychiatrica Scandinavica*, **45**, 347–354

PRIGATANO, G. P. (1978) The Wechsler Memory Scale: a selective review of the literature. *Journal of Clinical Psychology*, **34**, 816–832

PRIGATANO, G. P., PARSONS, O., WRIGHT, E., LEVIN, D. C. and HAWRYLUK, G. (1983) Neuropsychological test performance in mildly hypoxemic patients with chronic obstructive pulmonary disease. *J Consult Clin Psychol*, **51**, 108–116

PRIGATANO, G. P., FORDYCE, D. J., ZEINER, H. K., ROUECHE, J. R., PEPPING, M. and WOOD, B. C. (1984) Neuropsychological rehabilitation after closed head injury in young adults. *Journal of Neurology, Neurosurgery and Psychiatry*, **47**, 505–513

PRITCHARD, P. B., HOLSTROM, V. L., ROITZSCH, J. C. and CHARLSTON, S. C. (1984) Epileptic amnesic attacks: differentiation from transient global amnesia and benefit from anti-epileptic drugs. *Neurology,* **34** (Suppl. 1), 161

PROFESSIONAL AFFAIRS BOARD. (1980) Technical recommendations for psychological tests. *Bulletin of the British Psychological Society,* **33,** 161–164

PUFF, R. C. (1982) Editor. *Handbook of Research Methods in Human Memory and Cognition.* New York: Academic Press

QUADFASEL, A. F. and PRUYSER, P. W. (1955) Cognitive deficits in patients with psychomotor epilepsy. *Epilepsia,* **4,** 80–90

QUERY, W. T. and MEGRAN, J. (1983) Age-related norms for AVLT in a male patient population. *Journal of Clinical Psychology,* **39,** 136–138

RABINS, P. V., MERCHANT, A. and NESTADT, G. (1984) Criteria for distinguishing reversible dementia caused by depression: validation by 2-year follow up. *British Journal of Psychiatry,* **144,** 488–492

RAFAL, R. D., POSNER, M. I., WALKER, J. A. and FRIEDRICH, F. J. (1984) Cognition and the basal ganglia – separating mental and motor components of performance in Parkinson's disease. *Brain,* **107,** 1083–1094

RANDT, C. T., BROWN E. R. and OSBORNE, D. P. (1983) A memory test for longitudinal measurement of mild to moderate deficits. *Clinical Neuropsychology,* **2,** 184–194

RAO, S. M. and BIELIAUSKAS, L. A. (1983) Cognitive rehabilitation two and one-half years post right temporal lobectomy. *Journal of Clinical Neuropsychology,* **5,** 313–320

RAO, S. M., HAMMEKE, T. A., McQUILLEN, M. P., KHATRI, B. O. and LLOYD, D. (1984) Memory disturbance in chronic progressive multiple sclerosis. *Archives of Neurology,* **41,** 625–631

RATCLIFF, G. and NEWCOMBE, F. (1973) Spatial orientation in man: effects of left, right, and bilateral posterior cerebral lesions. *Journal of Neurology, Neurosurgery and Psychiatry,* **36,** 448–454

RAUSCH, R. (1981) Lateralization of temporal lobe dysfunction and verbal encoding. *Brain and Language,* **12,** 92–100

RAUSCH, R. and CRANDALL, P. H. (1982) Psychological status related to surgical control of temporal lobe seizures. *Epilepsia,* **23,** 191–202

RAUSCH, R., LIEB, J. P. and CRANDALL, P. H. (1978) Neuropsychological correlates of depth spike activity in epileptic patients. *Archives of Neurology,* **35,** 699–705

REEVES, A. G. and PLUM, L. (1969) Hyperphagia, rage and dementia accompanying a ventromedial hypothalamic neoplasm. *Archives of Neurology,* **20,** 616–624

REGARD, M. and LANDIS, T. (1984) Transient global amnesia: neuropsychological dysfunction during attack and recovery in two 'pure' cases. *Journal of Neurology, Neurosurgery and Psychiatry,* **47,** 668–672

REHNSTROM, S., SIMERT, G., HANSSON, J. A., JOHNSON, G. and VANG, J. (1977) Chronic hepatic encephalopathy. A psychometrical study. *Scandinavian Journal of Gastroenterology,* **12,** 305–311

REISBERG, B. (1983) *Alzheimer's Disease: The Standard Reference.* London: Collier Macmillan

REITAN, R. M. and DAVISON, L. A. (1974) *Clinical Neuropsychology: Current Status and Applications.* New York: Hemisphere

REITAN, R. M. and FITZHUGH, K. B. (1971) Behavioural deficits in groups with cerebral vascular lesions. *J Consult Clin Psychol,* **37,** 215–223

REY, A. (1964) *L'examen clinique en psychologie.* Paris: Presses Universitaires de France

RIBOT, T. (1885) *Diseases of Memory.* London: Kegan Paul, Trench & Co.

RICHARDSON, F. (1963) Some effects of severe head injury. *Dev Med Child Neurol,* **5,** 471–482

RICHARDSON, J. T. (1979a) Signal detection theory and the effects of severe head injury upon recognition memory. *Cortex,* **15,** 145–148

RICHARDSON, J. T. (1979b) Mental imagery, human memory, and the effects of closed head injury. *Br J Soc Clin Psychol,* **18,** 319–327

RICHARDSON, J. T. (1984) The effects of closed head injury upon intrusions and confusions in free recall. *Cortex,* **20,** 413–420

RICHARDSON, J. T. and BARRY, C. (1985) The effects of minor closed head injury upon human memory: further evidence on the role of mental imagery. *Cognitive Neuropsychology,* **2,** 149–168

RICHARDSON, J. T. and SNAPE, W. (1984) The effects of closed head injury upon human memory: an experimental analysis. *Cognitive Neuropsychology,* **1,** 217–231

RIDDELL, S. A. (1962) The performance of elderly psychiatric patients on equivalent forms of tests of memory and learning. *Br J Soc Clin Psychol*, **1,** 70–71

RIEGE, W. (1977) Inconstant nonverbal recognition memory in Korsakoff patients and controls. *Neuropsychologia*, **15,** 269–276

RIKLAN, M. and COOPER, I. S. (1975) Psychometric studies of verbal functions following thalamic lesions in humans. *Brain and Language*, **2,** 45–64

RIKLAN, M., CULLINAN, T., SHULMAN, M. and COOPER, I. S. (1976) A psychometric study of chronic cerebellar stimulation in man. *Biol Psychiat*, **11,** 543–574

RIKLAN, M., WHELIHAN, W. and CULLINAN, T. (1976) Levodopa and psychometric test performance in parkinsonism – 5 years later. *Neurology*, **26,** 173–179

RIVERA, V. M., MEYER, J. S., BAER, P. E., FAIBISH, G. M. and MATHEW, N. T. (1976) Vertebrobasilar insufficiency as a cause of dementia. Controlled therapeutic trial with betahistine-HCL. In *Cerebral Vascular Disease*, edited by J. S. Meyer, H. Lechner and M. Reivich, pp. 113–118. Stuttgart: Georg Thieme

ROBERTS, A. H. (1969) *Brain Damage in Boxers.* London: Pitman

ROBERTS, A. H. (1979) *Severe Accidental Head Injury.* London: Macmillan Press

ROBERTSON, E. E., LE ROUX, A. and BROWN, J. H. (1958) The clinical differentiation of Pick's disease. *Journal of Mental Science*, **104,** 1000–1024

ROBERTSON, G. and TAYLOR, P. J. (1985) Some cognitive correlates of schizophrenic illnesses. *Psychol Med*, **15,** 81–98

ROBERTSON, I. (1984) Does moderate drinking cause mental impairment? *British Medical Journal*, **289,** 711–712

ROBINSON, B. W. and LONG, W. D. (1972) Transient global amnesia and carotid lesions. *Neurology*, **22,** 405

ROCCHETTA, A. I. (1986) Classification and recall of pictures after unilateral frontal and temporal lobectomy. *Cortex*, **22,** 189–211

ROMAN-CAMPOS, G., POSER, C. M. and WOOD, F. (1980) Persistent retrograde memory deficit after transient global amnesia. *Cortex*, **16,** 500–519

RON, M. A. (1983) The alcoholic brain: CT and psychological findings. *Psychol Med*, Monograph Supplement 3

ROSATI, G., DE BASTIANI, P., GILLI, P. and PAOLINO, E. (1980) Oral aluminium and neuropsychological functioning. *Journal of Neurology*, **223,** 251–257

ROSE, F. C. and SYMONDS, C. P. (1960) Persistent memory defect following encephalitis. *Brain*, **83,** 195–212

ROSEN, W. G. (1983) Neuropsychological investigation of memory, visuoconstructional, visuoperceptual, and language abilities in senile dementia of the Alzheimer type. In *The Dementias*, edited by R. Mayeux and W. G. Rosen. New York: Raven Press

ROSEN, W. G. and MOHS, R. C. (1982) Evolution of cognitive decline in dementia. In *Alzheimer's Disease: A Report of Progress*, edited by S. Corkin *et al.*, pp 182–188. New York: Raven Press

ROSENBERG, S. I., RYAN, J. J. and PRIFITERA, A. (1984) Rey auditory verbal learning test performance of patients with and without memory impairment. *Journal of Clinical Psychology*, **40,** 785–787

ROSS, E. D. (1980a) Sensory-specific and fractional disorders of recent memory in man. I – Unilateral loss of visual memory. *Archives of Neurology*, **37,** 197–200

ROSS, E. D. (1980b) Sensory-specific and fractional disorders of recent memory in man. II – Unilateral loss of tactile recent memory. *Archives of Neurology*, **37,** 267–272

ROSS, R. (1983) Transient tumor attacks. *Archives of Neurology*, **40,** 633–666

ROTH, M. and IVERSEN, L. L. (1986) Editors. Alzheimer's disease and related disorders. *British Medical Bulletin*, **42,** 1–116

ROTHI, L. and HUTCHINSON, E. (1981) Retention of verbal information by rehearsal in relation to verbal output in aphasia. *Brain and Language*, **12,** 347–359

ROUSSEAUX, M., CABARET, M., LESOIN, F., DEVOS, P., DUBOIS, F. and PETIT, H. (1986) Bilan de l'amnesia des infarctus thalamiques restreints – 6 cas. *Cortex*, **22,** 213–228

ROWAN, A. J. and PROTASS, L. M. (1979) Transient global amnesia: clinical and electroencephalographic findings in 10 cases. *Neurology*, **29,** 869–872

RUBIN, D. C. (1986) Editor. *Autobiographical Memory.* Cambridge: Cambridge University Press

RUBIN, D. C. and BUTTERS, N. (1981) Clustering by alcoholic Korsakoff patients. *Neuropsychologia*, **19**, 137–140

RUFF, R. L. and VOLPE, B. T. (1981) Environmental reduplication associated with right frontal and right parietal lobe injury. *Journal of Neurology, Neurosurgery and Psychiatry* **44**, 382–386

RUSSELL, E. W. (1975) A multiple scoring method for the assessment of complex memory functions. *J Consult Clin Psychol*, **43**, 800–809

RUSSELL, E. W. (1982) Factor analysis of the revised Wechsler Memory Scale tests in a neuropsychological battery. *Percept Mot Skills*, **54**, 971–974

RUSSELL, R. W. (1983) Editor. *Vascular Disease of the Central Nervous System*, 2nd edn. Edinburgh: Churchill Livingstone

RUSSELL, W. R. (1932) Cerebral involvement in head injury. *Brain*, **35**, 549–603

RUSSELL, W. R. (1935) Amnesia following head injuries. *Lancet*, **ii**, 762–763

RUSSELL, W. R. (1948) Studies in amnesia. *Edinburgh Medical Journal*, **55**, 92–99

RUSSELL, W. R. (1971) *The Traumatic Amnesias*. New York: Oxford University Press

RUSSELL, W. R. and ESPIR, M. L. E. (1961) *Traumatic Aphasia*. Oxford: Oxford University Press

RUSSELL, W. R. and NATHAN, P. W. (1946) Traumatic amnesia. *Brain*, **69**, 183–187

RUSSELL, W. R. and SMITH, A. (1961) Post-traumatic amnesia in closed head injury. *Archives of Neurology*, **5**, 4–17

RYAN, C. and BUTTERS, N. (1980) Further evidence for a continuum-of-impairment encompassing male alcoholic Korsakoff patients and chronic alcoholic men. *Alcoholism (NY)*, **4**, 190–198

RYAN, C. and BUTTERS, N. (1983) Cognitive deficits in alcoholics. In *Biology of Alcoholism*, Volume 7, edited by B. Kissin and H. Begleiter, pp. 485–538. New York: Plenum Press

RYAN, C., BUTTERS, N., MONTGOMERY, K., ADINOLFI, A. and DIDARIO, B. (1980) Memory deficits in chronic alcoholics: continuities between the 'intact' alcoholic and the alcoholic Korsakoff patient. *Adv Exp Med Biol*, **126**, 701–718

RYAN, C., VEGA, A. and DRASH, A. (1985) Cognitive deficits in adolescents who developed diabetes early in life. *Paediatrics*, **75**, 921–927

RYAN, J. J., GEISSER, M. E., RANDALL, D. M. and GEORGEMILLER, R. J. (1986) Alternate form reliability and equivalency of the Rey auditory verbal learning test. *Journal of Clinical and Experimental Neuropsychology*, **8**, 611–616

SAGAR, H. J., COHEN, N. J., CORKIN, S. and GROWDEN, J. H. (1985) Dissociations among processes in remote memory. *Annals of the New York Academy of Sciences*, **444**, 533–535

SALAZAR, A. M., GRAFMAN, J., SCHLESSELMAN, S., VANCE, S. C., CARPENTER, M., PEVSNER, P., et al. (1986a) Penetrating war injuries to the basal forebrain: neurologic and cognitive correlates. *Neurology*, **36**, 459–465

SALAZAR, A. M., GRAFMAN, J. H., VANCE, S. C., WEINGARTNER, H., DILLON J. D. and LUDLOW, C. (1986b) Consciousness and amnesia after penetrating head injury: neurology and anatomy. *Neurology*, **36**, 178–187

SAMUELS, I., BUTTERS, N. and FEDIO, P. (1972) Short term memory disorders following temporal lobe removals in humans. *Cortex*, **8**, 283–298

SAMUELS, S. I., BUTTERS, N., FEDIO, P. and COX, C. (1980) Deficits in short-term auditory memory for verbal material following right temporal removals in humans. *International Journal of Neuroscience*, **11**, 101–107

SAMUELS, I., BUTTERS, N., GOODGLASS, H. and BRODY, B. (1971) A comparison of subcortical and cortical damage on short-term visual and auditory memory. *Neuropsychologia*, **9**, 293–306

SANDERS, H. (1972) The problems of measuring very long term memory. *International Journal of Mental Health*, **1**, 98–102

SANDERS, H. I. and WARRINGTON, E. K. (1971) Memory for remote events in amnesic patients. *Brain*, **94**, 661–668

SANDSON, J., ALBERT, M. L. and ALEXANDER, M. P. (1986) Confabulation in aphasia. *Cortex*, **22**, 621–626

SARTER, M. and MARKOWITSCH, H. J. (1985) The amygdala's role in human mnemonic processing. *Cortex*, **21**, 7–24

SATZ, P., FLETCHER, J. M. and SUTKER, L. S. (1976) Neuropsychologic, intellectual and personality correlates of chronic marijuana use in native Costa Rica. *Annals of the New York Academy of Sciences*, **282**, 266–306

SAVAGEAU, J. A., STANTON, B. A., JENKINS, C. D. and KLEIN, M. D. (1982a) Neuropsychological dysfunction following elective cardiac operation I. Early assessment. *Journal of Thoracic and Cardiovascular Surgery,* **84,** 585–594

SAVAGEAU, J. A., STANTON, B. A., JENKINS, C. D. and FRATER, R. W. (1982b) Neuropsychological dysfunction following elective cardiac operation II. A six month reassessment. *Journal of Thoracic and Cardiovascular Surgery,* **84,** 595–600

SAX, D. S., O'DONNELL, B., BUTTERS, N., MENZER, L., MONTGOMERY, K. and KAYNE, H. L. (1983) Computed tomographic, neurologic, and neuropsychological correlates of Huntington's disease. *International Journal of Neuroscience,* **18,** 21–36

SCHACTER, D. L. (1986) Feeling-of-knowing ratings distinguish between genuine and simulated forgetting. *J Exp Psychol: Learn Mem Cogn,* **12,** 30–41

SCHACTER, D. L. and CROVITZ, H. F. (1977) Memory function after closed head injury: a review of the quantitative research. *Cortex,* **13,** 150–176

SCHACTER, D. L. and GRAF, P. (1986) Preserved learning in amnesic patients: perspectives from research on direct priming. *Journal of Clinical and Experimental Neuropsychology,* **8,** 727–743

SCHACTER, D. L., RICH, S. A. and STAMPP, M. S. (1985) Remediation of memory disorders: experimental evaluation of the spaced-retrieval technique. *Journal of Clinical and Experimental Neuropsychology,* **7,** 79–96

SCHACTER, D. L., WANG, P. L., TULVING, E. and FREEDMAN, M. (1982) Functional retrograde amnesia: a quantitative case study. *Neuropsychologia,* **20,** 523–532

SCHAEFFER, J., ANDRYSIAK, T. and UNGERLEIDER, J. T. (1981) Cognition and long-term use of ganja (cannabis). *Science,* **213,** 465–466

SCHMIDLEY, J. W. and MESSING, R. O. (1984) Agitated confusional states in patients with right hemisphere infarctions. *Stroke,* **15,** 883–885

SCHNEIDER, G. E. (1976) Growth of abnormal neural connections following focal brain lesions: constraining factors and functional effects. In *Neurosurgical Treatment in Psychiatry,* edited by W. H. Swelt, S. Obrador and J. G. Martin-Rodriguez. Baltimore: University Park Press

SCHNEIDER, K. (1912) Uber einige klinisch-pathologische Untersuchungsmethoden und ihre Ergebnesse. Zugleich ein Beitrag zur Psychopathologie der Korsakowschen Psychose. *Z Neurol Psychiat,* **8,** 553–616

SCHOLZ, O. B. and SASTRY, M. (1985) Memory characteristics in Parkinson's disease. *International Journal of Neuroscience,* **27,** 229–234

SCHOTT, B., MAUGUIERE, F., LAURENT, B., SERCLERAT, O. and FISCHER, C. (1980) L'amnesie thalamique. *Rev Neurol,* **136,** 117–130

SCHWANENFLUGEL, P. J. (1986) Completion norms for final words of sentences using a multiple production measure. *Behav Res Meth Intrum & Comp,* **18,** 363–371

SCHWARTZ, M. L. and DENNERLL, R. D. (1969) Immediate visual memory as a function of epileptic seizure type. *Cortex,* **5,** 69–74

SCOTT, D. F., MOFFATT, A., MATTHEWS, A. and ETTLINGER, G. (1967) The effect of epileptic discharges on learning and memory in patients. *Epilepsia,* **8,** 188–194

SCOVILLE, W. B. (1968) Amnesia after bilateral mesial temporal-lobe excision: introduction to case H.M. *Neuropsychologia,* **6,** 211–213

SCOVILLE, W. B. and MILNER, B. (1957) Loss of recent memory after bilateral hippocampal lesions. *Journal of Neurology, Neurosurgery and Psychiatry,* **20,** 11–21

SELTZER, B. and BENSON, D. F. (1974) The temporal pattern of retrograde amnesia in Korsakoff's disease. *Neurology,* **24,** 527–530

SEMPLE, S. A., SMITH, C. M. and SWASH, M. (1982) The Alzheimer disease syndrome. In *Alzheimer's Disease: A Report of Progress,* edited by S. Corkin *et al.,* pp. 93–107. New York: Raven Press

SENGUPTA, R. P., CHIU, J. S. P. and BRIERLY, H. (1975) Quality of survival following direct surgery for anterior communicating artery aneurysms. *Journal of Neurology,* **43,** 58–64

SERAFETINIDES, E. A. and WALTER, R. D. (1978) Induced amnesic confusional phenomena. Pathology and lateralization. *Journal of Nervous and Mental Disease,* **166,** 661–662

SHANDURINA, A. N. and KALYAGINA, G. B. (1979) Dynamics of mental functions in epileptics during electrical stimulation of deep brain structures. *Human Physiology,* **5,** 764–773

SHANDURINA, A. A., KAMBAROVA, D. K. and KALYAGINA, G. V. (1982) Neuropsychological and neurophysiological analysis of different types of amnesia. *Human Physiology*, **8**, 350–366

SHAPIRO, B. E., ALEXANDER, M. P., GARDNER, H. and MERCER, B. (1981) Mechanisms of confabulation. *Neurology*, **31**, 1070–1076

SHIMAMURA, A. P. (1986) Priming effects in amnesia: evidence for a dissociable memory function. *Quarterly Journal of Experimental Psychology*, **38A**, 619–644

SHIMAMURA, A. P. and SQUIRE, L. R. (1986a) Korsakoff's syndrome: a study of the relationship between anterograde amnesia and remote memory impairment. *Behav Neurosci*, **100**, 165–170

SHIMAMURA, A. P. and SQUIRE, L. R. (1986b) Memory and metamemory: a study of the feeling-of-knowing phenomenon in amnesic patients. *J Exp Psychol: Learn Mem Cogn*, **12**, 452–460

SHINDLER, A. G., CAPLAN, L. R. and HIER, D. B. (1984) Intrusions and perseverations. *Brain and Language*, **23**, 148–158

SHULMAN, R. (1967) Psychiatric aspects of pernicious anaemia: a prospective controlled investigation. *British Medical Journal*, **3**, 266–270

SHUPING, J., TOOLE, J. and ALEXANDER, E. (1980) Transient global amnesia due to glioma in the dominant hemisphere. *Neurology*, **30**, 88–90

SHUTTLEWORTH, E. C. and WISE, G. R. (1973) Transient global amnesia due to arterial embolism. *Archives of Neurology*, **29**, 340–342

SIEGFRIED, J. and BEN-SHMUEL, A. (1973) Long-term assessment of stereotactic amygdalotomy for aggressive behaviour. In *Surgical Approaches in Psychiatry*, edited by L. V. Laitinen and K. Livingston, pp. 138–141.

SIGNORET, J. L., WHITELEY, A. and LHERMITTE, F. (1978) Influence of choline on amnesia in early Alzheimer's disease. *Lancet*, **ii**, 837

SIMPSON, B. A. and SWASH, M. (1985) Left temporal lobe abscess presenting as an acute amnesic syndrome 28 years after contralateral temporal lobe abscess. *Journal of Neurology, Neurosurgery and Psychiatry*, **48**, 90–92

SINATRA, M. G., BOERI, R., DEL TON, F., FORNARI, M., MUSICCO, M. and GIROTTI, F. (1984) Neuropsychological evaluation in transient ischaemic attack and minor stroke. *Journal of Neurology*, **231**, 194–197

SISLER, G. and PENNER, H. (1975) Amnesia following severe head injury. *Canadian Psychiatric Association Journal*, **20**, 333–336

SITARAM, N., WEINGARTNER, H., KAYE, W. H., EBERT, M. H. and EPSTEIN, R. (1983) Combination treatment of Alzheimer's dementia. In *Alzheimer's Disease*, edited by B. Reisburg, pp 355–351. New York: The Free Press

SKELTON-ROBINSON, M. and TELFORD, R. (1982) Observations on the object learning test of the Kendrick battery for the detection of dementia. *British Journal of Clinical Psychology*, **21**, 147–148

SKILBECK, C. E. and WOODS, R. T. (1980) The factorial structure of the Wechsler Memory Scale: samples of neurological and psychogeriatric patients. *Journal of Clinical Neuropsychology*, **2**, 293–300

SLAMECKA, N. J. (1985) On comparing rates of forgetting. *J Exp Psychol: Learn Mem Cogn*, **11**, 817–820

SLAMECKA, N. J. and McELREE, B. (1983) Normal forgetting of verbal lists as a function of their degree of learning. *J Exp Psychol: Learn Mem Cogn*, **9**, 384–397

SMITH, C. M., SEMPLE, S. A. and SWASH, M. (1982) Effects of physostigmine on responses in memory tests in patients with Alzheimer's disease. In *Alzheimer's Disease: A Report of Progress*, edited by S. Corkin *et al.*, pp. 405–411. New York: Raven Press

SMITH, C. M. and SWASH, M. (1979) Possible biochemical basis of memory disorder in Alzheimer's disease. *Age and Ageing*, **8**, 289–293

SMITH, E. (1974) Influence of site of impact on cognitive impairment persisting long after severe closed head injury. *Journal of Neurology, Neurosurgery and Psychiatry*, **37**, 719–726

SMITH, J. S. and BRANDON, S. (1973) Morbidity from acute carbon monoxide poisoning at three-year follow-up. *British Medical Journal*, **i**, 318–321

SMITH, J. S., KILOH, L. G. and BOOTS, J. A. (1977) Prospective evaluation of prefrontal leucotomy: results at 30 months follow-up. In *Neurosurgical Treatment in Psychiatry, Pain and Epilepsy*, edited by W. H. Sweet, *et al.*, pp. 217–224. Baltimore: University Park Press

SMITH, M. L. and MILNER, B. (1981) The role of the right hippocampus in the recall of spatial location. *Neuropsychologia*, **19**, 781–793

SMITH, M. L. and MILNER, B. (1984) Differential effects of frontal-lobe lesions on cognitive estimation and spatial memory. *Neuropsychologia*, **22**, 697–705

SMITH, P. J., LANGOLF, G. D. and GOLDBERG, J. (1983) Effects of occupational exposure to elemental mercury on short-term memory. *British Journal of Industrial Medicine*, **40**, 413–419

SMITH, R. A. and SMITH, W. A. (1966) Loss of recent memory as a sign of focal temporal lobe disorder. *Journal of Neurosurgery*, **24**, 91–95

SMITH, W. L., PHILIPPUS, M. J. and LOWREY, J. B. (1968) A comparison of psychological and psychophysical test patterns before and after receiving papaverine HCL. *Curr Ther Res*, **10**, 428–431

SNELL, R. S. (1987) *Clinical Neuroanatomy for Medical Students*. Boston: Little, Brown and Company

SNODGRASS, J. G. and VANDERWART, M. (1980) A standardized set of 260 pictures: norms for name agreement, image agreement, familiarity and visual complexity. *J Exp Psychol: Learn Mem Cogn*, **6**, 174–215

SOMMERBECK, K. W., THEILGAARD, A. and RASMUSSEN, K. E. (1977) Valproate sodium: evaluation of so-called psychotrophic effect. A controlled study. *Epilepsia*, **18**, 159–165

SPALDING, J. M. K. and ZANGWILL, O. L. (1950) Disturbance of number-form in a case of brain injury. *Journal of Neurology, Neurosurgery and Psychiatry*, **13**, 24–29

SPEEDIE, L. J. and HEILMAN, K. M. (1982) Amnesic disturbance following infarction of the left dorsomedial nucleus of the thalamus. *Neuropsychologia*, **20**, 597–604

SPEEDIE, L. J. and HEILMAN, K. M. (1983) Anterograde memory deficits for visuospatial material after infarction of the right thalamus. *Archives of Neurology*, **40**, 183–186

SPINNLER, H., STERZI, R. and VALLAR, G. (1980) Amnesic syndrome after carbon monoxide poisoning. *Schweiz Arch Neurol Neurochir Psychiatr*, **127**, 79–88

SPROFKIN, B. E. and SCIARRA, D. (1952) Korsakoff's psychosis associated with cerebral tumours. *Neurology*, **2**, 427–434

SQUIRE, L. R. (1981) Two forms of human amnesia: an analysis of forgetting. *Journal of Neuroscience*, **1**, 635–640

SQUIRE, L. R. (1982) Comparisons between forms of amnesia: some deficits are unique to Korsakoff's syndrome. *J Exp Psychol: Learn Mem Cogn*, **8**, 560–571

SQUIRE, L. and BUTTERS, N. (1984) Editors. *Neuropsychology of Memory*. New York: Guilford Press

SQUIRE, L. R. and COHEN, N. J. (1982) Remote memory, retrograde amnesia and the neuropsychology of memory. In *Human Memory and Amnesia*, edited by L. S. Cermak, pp. 275–303. Hillsdale, New Jersey: Lawrence Erlbaum Associates

SQUIRE, L. R. and MOORE, R. Y. (1979) Dorsal thalamic lesion in a noted case of chronic memory dysfunction. *Annals of Neurology*, **6**, 503–506

SQUIRE, L. R. and SHIMAMURA, A. P. (1986) Characterizing amnesic patients for neurobehavioural study. *Behav Neurosci*, **100**, 866–877

SQUIRE, L. R. and SLATER, P. C. (1977) Remote memory in chronic anterograde amnesia. *Behav Biol*, **20**, 398–403

SQUIRE, L. R. and SLATER, P. C. (1978) Anterograde and retrograde memory impairment in chronic amnesia. *Neuropsychologia*, **16**, 313–322

STANDING, L., CONEZIO, S. and HABER, R. N. (1980) Perception and memory for pictures: single trial learning of 2500 visual stimuli. *Psychon Sci*, **19**, 73–74

STAPLES, D. and LINCOLN, N. B. (1979) Intellectual impairment in multiple sclerosis and its relation to functional abilities. *Rheumatology and Rehabilitation*, **18**, 153–160

STARKMAN, M. N. and SCHTEINGART, D. E. (1981) Neuropsychiatric manifestations of patients with Cushing's syndrome. *Archives of Internal Medicine*, **141**, 215–219

STARR, A. and PHILLIPS, L. (1970) Verbal and motor memory in the amnesic syndrome. *Neuropsychologia*, **8**, 75–82

STATON, R. D., BRUMBACK, R. A. and WILSON, H. (1982) Reduplicative paramnesia: a disconnection syndrome of memory. *Cortex*, **18**, 23–36

STEPIEN, L. and SIERPINSKI, S. (1964) Impairment of recent memory after temporal lesions in man. *Neuropsychologia*, **2**, 291–303

STERN, Y. and LANGSTON, J. W. (1985) Intellectual changes in patients with MPTP-induced parkinsonism. *Neurology*, **35**, 1506–1509

STERNBERG, S. (1966) High speed scanning in human memory. *Science*, **153**, 652–654

STOREY, P. B. (1970) Brain damage and personality change after subarachnoid haemorrhage. *British Journal of Psychiatry*, **117**, 129–142

STRACCIARI, A., GALLASSI, R., CIARDULLI, C. and COCCAGNA, G. (1985) Neuropsychological and EEG evaluation in exposure to trichloroethylene. *Journal of Neurology*, **232**, 120–122

STRATTON, R. P., JACOBUS, K. A. and BRINELY, B. (1975) Age-of-acquisition, imagery, familiarity, and meaningfulness norms for 543 words. *Behav Res Meth & Instrum*, **7**, 1–6

STRAUSS, E. H. and BUTLER, R. B. (1978) The effect of varying types of interference on haptic memory in the Korsakoff patient. *Neuropsychologia*, **16**, 81–90

STRAUSS, M. E., WEINGARTNER, H. and THOMPSON, K. (1985) Remembering words and how often they occurred in memory-impaired patients. *Memory and Cognition*, **13**, 507–510

STRUB, R. L. and BLACK, F. W. (1977) *The Mental Status Examination in Neurology*. Philadelphia: FA Davis

STRUCKETT, P. B. A. (1953) Effect of prefrontal lobotomy on intellectual functioning in chronic schizophrenia. *Arch Neurol Psychiat*, **69**, 293–304

STUSS, D. T., ALEXANDER, M. P., LIEBERMAN, A. and LEVINE, H. (1978) An extraordinary form of confabulation. *Neurology*, **28**, 1166–1172

STUSS, D. T. and BENSON, D. F. (1984) Neuropsychological studies of the frontal lobes. *Psychol Bull*, **95**, 3–28

STUSS, D. T., ELY, P., HUGENHOLTZ, H., RICHARD, M. T., LAROCHELLE, S., POIRIEN, C. A. *et al.* (1985) Subtle neuropsychological deficits in patients with good recovery after closed head injury. *Neurosurgery*, **17**, 41–47

STUSS, D. T., KAPLAN, E. F., BENSON, D. F., WEIR, W. S., CHIULLI, S. and SARAZIN, F. F. (1982) Evidence for the involvement of orbitofrontal cortex in memory functions: an interference effect. *Journal of Comparative Physiology and Psychology*, **96**, 913–925

STUSS, D. T., KAPLAN, E. F., BENSON, D. F., WEIR, W. S., NAESER, M. A. and LEVINE, H. L. (1981) Long term effects of prefrontal leucotomy – an overview of the neuropsychologic residuals. *Journal of Clinical Neuropsychology*, **3**, 13–22

STUSS, D. T., KATES, M. H., POIRER, C. A., HYLTON, D., HUMPHREYS, P., KEENE, D. *et al.* (1987) Evaluation of information-processing speed and neuropsychological functioning in patients with myotonic dystrophy. *Journal of Clinical and Experimental Neuropsychology*, **9**, 131–146

SULKAVA, R. and AMBERLA, K. (1982) Alzheimer's disease and senile dementia of Alzheimer type. A neuropsychological study. *Acta Neurologica Scandinavica*, **65**, 651–660

SULLIVAN, E. V., SHEDLACK, K. J., CORKIN, S. and GROWDON, J. H. (1982) Physostigmine and lecithin in Alzheimer's disease. In *Alzheimer's Disease: A Report of Progress*, edited by S. Corkin *et al.*, pp. 361–367. New York: Raven Press

SUMMERSKILL, W. H. J., DAVIDSON, E. A., SHERLOCK, S. and STEINER, R. E. (1956) The neuropsychiatric syndrome associated with hepatic cirrhosis and an extensive portal collateral circulation. *Quarterly Journal of Medicine*, **25**, 245–266

SUNDERLAND, A., HARRIS, J. E. and BADDELEY, A. D. (1983) Do laboratory tests predict everyday memory? A neuropsychological study. *J Verb Learn Verb Behav*, **22**, 341–357

SUNDERLAND, A., HARRIS, J. E. and GLEAVE, J. (1984) Memory failures in everyday life following severe head injury. *Journal of Clinical Neuropsychology*, **6**, 127–142

SWANSON, R. A. and SCHMIDLEY, J. W. (1985) Amnestic syndrome and vertical gaze palsy: early detection of bilateral thalamic infarction by CT and NMR. *Stroke*, **16**, 823–827

SWEET, W. H., TALLAND, G. A. and BALLANTYNE, H. T. (1966) A memory and mood disorder associated with ruptured anterior communicating aneurysm. *Transactions of the American Neurological Association*, **91**, 346–348

SWEET, W. H., TALLAND, G. A. and ERVIN, F. R. (1959) Loss of recent memory following section of the fornix. *Transactions of the American Neurological Association*, **84**, 876–882

SYMONDS, C. P. and RUSSELL, W. R. (1943) Accidental head injuries: prognosis in service patients. *Lancet*, **i**, 1–10

SYMONDS, C. (1962) Concussion and its sequelae. *Lancet*, **i**, 1–5

TALLAND, G. A. (1962) Cognitive function in Parkinson's disease. *Journal of Nervous and Mental Disease*, **135**, 196–205

TALLAND, G. A. (1965a) *Deranged Memory*. New York: Academic Press

TALLAND, G. A. (1965b) An amnesic patient's disavowal of his own recall performance, and its attribution to the interviewer. *Psychiat. Neurol.* **149**, 67–76

TALLAND, G. A. and EKDAHL, M. (1959) Psychological studies of Korsakoff's psychosis: the rate and mode of forgetting of narrative material. *Journal of Nervous and Mental Disease,* **129**, 391–404

TALLAND, G. A., HAGEN, D. Q. and JAMES, M. (1967) Performance tests of amnesic patients with cylert. *Journal of Nervous and Mental Disease,* **144**, 421–429

TALLAND, G. A., SWEET, W. H. and BALLANTYNE, H. T. (1967) Amnesic syndrome with anterior communicating artery aneurysm. *Journal of Nervous and Mental Disease,* **145**, 179–192

TARTER, R. E., HEGEDUS, A. M., VAN THIEL, D. H., SCHADE, R. R., GAVALER, J. S. and STARZL, T. E. (1984) Nonalcoholic cirrhosis associated with neuropsychological deficits in the absence of overt evidence of hepatic encephalitis. *Gastroenterology,* **86**, 1421–1427

TAYLOR, A. E., SAINT-CYR, J. A. and LANG, A. E. (1986) Frontal lobe dysfunction in Parkinson's disease. *Brain,* **109**, 845–883

TAYLOR, A. E., SAINT-CYR, J. A. and LANG, A. E. (1987) Parkinson's disease. Cognitive changes in relation to treatment responses. *Brain,* **110**, 35–51

TAYLOR, A. E., SAINT-CYR, J. A., LANG, A. E. and KENNY, F. T. (1986) Parkinson's disease and depression. *Brain,* **109**, 279–292

TAYLOR, L. B. (1979) Psychological assessment of neurosurgical patients. In *Functional Neurosurgery,* edited by T. Rasmussen and R. Marino, pp. 165–180. New York: Raven Press

TAYLOR, P. J. and KOPELMAN, M. D. (1984) Amnesia for criminal offences. *Psychol Med,* **14**, 581–588

TEASDALE, G. and JENNETT, B. (1974) Assessment of coma and impaired consciousness. A practical scale. *Lancet,* **ii**, 81–84

TEISSER DU CROS, J. and LHERMITTE, F. (1984) Neuropsychological analysis of ruptured saccular aneurysm of the anterior communicating artery after radical therapy (32 cases). *Surg Neurol,* **22**, 353–359

TEUBER, H. L. (1968) Disorders of memory following penetrating missile wounds of the brain. *Neurology,* **18**, 287–288

TEUBER, H. L. (1969) Neglected aspects of the post-traumatic syndrome. In *The Late Effects of Head Injury,* edited by A. E. Walker, W. F. Caveness and M. Critchley, pp. 13–34. Springfield, Illinois: Thomas

TEUBER, H. L. (1975) Recovery of function after brain injury in man. In *Outcome of Severe Damage to the Central Nervous System,* edited R. Porter, pp. 159–190. Ciba Foundation Symposium 34. Amsterdam: Elsevier

TEUBER, H. L., MILNER, B. and VAUGHAN, H. G. (1968) Persistent anterograde amnesia after stab wound of the basal brain. *Neuropsychologia,* **6**, 267–282

TEUBER, H. L. and WEINSTEIN, S. (1954) Performance on a formboard-task after penetrating brain injury. *Journal of Psychology,* **38**, 177–190

THAL, L. J., FULD, P. A., MASUR, D. M. and SHARPLES, N. S. (1983) Oral physostigmine and lecithin improve memory in Alzheimer disease. *Annals of Neurology,* **13**, 491–496

THAL, L. J., MASUR, D. M., SHARPLESS, N. S., FULD, P. A. and DAVIES, P. (1984) Acute and chronic effects of oral physostigmine and lecithin in Alzheimer's disease. In *Alzheimer's Disease: Advances in Basic Research and Therapies,* edited by R. J. Wurtman, S. H. Corkin and J. H. Growdon, pp. 333–347. Cambridge: Centre for Brain Sciences and Metabolism Charitable Trust

THOMASSEN, A., JUUL-JENSEN, P., OLIVARIUS, B., BRAEMER, J. and CHRISTENSEN, A. L. (1979) Neurological, electroencephalographic and neuropsychological examination of 53 former amateur boxers. *Acta Neurologica Scandinavica,* **60**, 352–362

THOMPSON, C. and CHECKLY, S. (1981) Short term memory deficit in a patient with cerebral sarcoidosis. *British Journal of Psychiatry,* **139**, 160–161

THOMPSON, L. W., DAVIS, G. C., OBRIST, W. D. and HEYMAN, A. (1976) Effects of hyperbaric oxygen on behavioural and psychophysiological measures in elderly demented patients. *Journal of Gerontology,* **31**, 23–28

THOMPSON, P. J. and TRIMBLE, M. R. (1981) Further studies on anticonvulsant drugs and seizures. *Acta Neurologica Scandinavica,* **89**, (Suppl.) 51–58

THOMPSON, P. J. and TRIMBLE, M. R. (1983) Anticonvulsant serum levels: relationship to impairments of cognitive functioning. *Journal of Neurology, Neurosurgery and Psychiatry,* **46**, 227–233

THOMSEN, A. M., BORGESEN, S. E., BRUHN, P. and GJERRIS, F. (1986) Prognosis of dementia in normal-pressure hydrocephalus after a shunt operation. *Annals of Neurology*, **20**, 304–310

THOMSEN, I. V. (1977) Verbal learning in psychiatric and non-psychiatric patients with severe head injuries. *Scandinavian Journal of Rehabilitative Medicine*, **9**, 73–77

THORNDIKE, E. L. and LORGE, I. (1944) *The Teacher's Word Book of 30 000 Words*. New York: Teachers College Press, Columbia University

TIMMING, R., ORRISON, W. W. and MIKULA, J. A. (1982) Computerized tomography and rehabilitation outcome after severe head injury. *Archs Phys Med Rehab*, **63**, 154–159

TINKLENBERG, J. R., PIGACHE, R., PFEFFERBAUM, A. and BERGER, P. A. (1982) Vasopressin peptides and dementia. In *Alzheimer's Disease: A Report of Progress*, edited by S. Corkin *et al.*, pp. 463–468. New York: Raven Press

TOGLIA, M. P., BATTIG, W. F., BARROW, K., CARTWRIGHT, D. S., POSNANSKY, C. J., PELLEGRINO, J. W., *et al.* (1978) *Handbook of Semantic Word Norms*. Hillsdale, NJ: Erlbaum

TOMLINSON, L., STIRLING, N., MERRIFIELD, E. and REYNOLDS, E. H. (1981) Recognition memory in treated epileptic patients. *Acta Neurologica Scandinavica*, **89** (Suppl.), 43–50

TRIMBLE, M. R. (1981) *Post-traumatic Neurosis*. Chichester: Wiley

TRIMBLE, M. R. and THOMPSON, P. J. (1983) Anticonvulsant drugs, cognitive function, and behaviour. *Epilepsia*, **24** (Suppl. 1), S55–S63

TRIMBLE, M. R. and THOMPSON, P. J. (1984) Sodium valproate and cognitive function. *Epilepsia*, **25** (Suppl. 1), S60–S64

TSUSHIMA, W. T. and TOWNE, W. S. (1977) Effects of paint sniffing on neuropsychological performance. *Journal of Abnormal Psychology*, **86**, 402–407

TUCKER, A. R. and NG, K. T. (1983) Digoxin-related impairment of learning and memory in cardiac patients. *Psychopharmacology*, **81**, 86–88

TUCKER, D. M., NOVELLY, R. A., ISAAC, W. and SPENCER, D. (1986) Effects of simultaneous vs sequential stimulus presentation on memory performance following right temporal lobe resection in humans. *Neuropsychologia*, **24**, 277–281

TUFO, H. M., OSTFELD, A. M. and SHEKELLE, R. (1970) Central nervous system dysfunction following open-heart surgery. *Journal of the American Medical Association*, **212**, 1333–1340

TULVING, E. (1985) How many memory systems are there? *Am Psychol*, **40**, 385–398

TUNE, L. E., STRAUSS, M. E., LEW M. F., BREITLINGER, E. and COYLE, J. T. (1982) Serum levels of anticholinergic drugs and impaired recent memory in chronic schizophrenic patients. *American Journal of Psychiatry*, **139**, 1460–1462

TWEEDY, J. R., LANGER, K. G. and McDOWELL, F. H. (1982) The effect of semantic relations on the memory deficit associated with Parkinson's disease. *Journal of Clinical Neuropsychology*, **4**, 235–247

UNDERWOOD, B. J. (1983) *Attributes of Memory*. Glenview, Illinois: Scott, Foresman and Company

UYEDA, K. M. and MANDLER, G. (1980) Protypicality norms for 28 semantic categories. *Behav Res Meth & Instrum*, **12**, 587–595

UZZELL, B. P. and OLER, J. (1986) Chronic low-level mercury exposure and neuropsychological functioning. *Journal of Clinical and Experimental Neuropsychology*, **8**, 581–593

VAN BUREN, J. M. and BORKE, R. C. (1972) The mesial temporal substratum and memory. *Brain*, **95**, 599–632

VAN DEN BURG, W., SAAN, R. J., VAN ZOMEREN, A. H., BOONTJE, H., HAAXMAN, R. and WICHMANN, T. E. (1985) Carotid endarectomy: does it improve cognitive or motor functioning? *Psychol Med*, **15**, 341–346

VANDERPLAS, J. M. and GARVIN, E. A. (1959) The association value of random shapes. *Journal of Experimental Psychology*, **57**, 147–154

VAN ZOMEREN, A. H. and VAN DEN BERG, W. (1985) Residual complaints of patients two years after severe head injury. *Journal of Neurology, Neurosurgery and Psychiatry*, **48**, 21–28

VASKO, T. and KULLBERG, G. (1979) Results of psychological testing of cognitive functions in patients undergoing stereotactic psychiatric surgery. In *Modern Concepts in Psychiatric Surgery*, edited by E. R. Hitchcock, H. T. Ballantine and B. A. Meyerson, pp. 303–310. Amsterdam: Elsevier/North Holland

VICTOR, M., HERMAN, K. and WHITE, E. E. (1959) A psychological study of the Wernicke-Korsaskoff syndrome. *Q J Stud Alc*, **20**, 467–479

VICTOR, M., ANGEVINE, J. B., MANCALL, E. L. and FISHER, C. M. (1961) Memory loss with lesions of hippocampal formation. *Archives of Neurology*, **5**, 244–263

VICTOR, M., ADAMS, R. D. and COLLINS, G. H. (1971) The Wernicke-Korsakoff syndrome. Philadelphia: FA Davis

VIGHETTO, A., AIMARD, G., CONFAVREUX, C. and DEVIC, M. (1980) Une observation anatomo-clinique de fabulation (ou delire) topografique. *Cortex*, **16**, 501–507

VIGHETTO, A., CONFAVREUX, C. H., BOISSON, D., AIMARD, G. and DEVIC, M. (1986) Paralysie de l'abaissement du regard et amnesie globale durables par lesion thalamo-sous-thalamique bilaterale. *Rev Neurol*, **142**, 449–455

VIGNOLO, G. E. (1980) Closed head injuries of school-age children: neuropsychological sequelae in early adulthood. *Italian Journal of Neurological Science,*, **2**, 65–73

VILKKI, J. (1978) Effects of thalamic lesions on complex perception and memory. *Neuropsychologia*, **16**, 427–437

VILKKI, J. (1981) Changes in complex perception and memory after three different psychosurgical operations. *Neuropsychologia*, **19**, 553–563

VILKKI, J. (1985) Amnesic syndromes after surgery of anterior communicating artery aneurysms. *Cortex*, **21**, 31–44

VILKKI, J. and LAITINEN, L. V. (1976) Effects of pulvinotomy and ventrolateral thalamotomy on some cognitive functions performances. *Neuropsychologia*, **14**, 67–78

VILLARDITA, C., SMIRNI, P., LE PIRA, F., ZAPPALA, G. and NICOLETTI, F. (1982) Mental deterioration, visuoperceptive disabilities and constructional apraxia in Parkinson's disease. *Acta Neurologica Scandinavica*, **66**, 112–120

VISSER, R. S. H. (1980) *Manual of the Complex Figure Test (CFT)*, 2nd edn. Lisse: Swets & Zeitlinger

VITALIANO, P. P., BREEN, A. R., ALBERT, M. S., RUSSO, J. and PRINZ, P. N. (1984) Memory, attention, and functional status in community residing Alzheimer type dementia patients and optimally healthy aged. *Journal of Gerontology*, **39**, 58–64

VOLPE, B. T., HERSCOVITSCH, P. and RAICHLE, M. E. (1984) Positron emission tomography defines metabolic abnormality in mesial temporal lobes of two patients with amnesia after rupture and repair of anterior communicating artery aneurysm. *Neurology*, **34** (Suppl. 1), 188

VOLPE, B. T. and HIRST, W. (1983a) Amnesia following the rupture and repair of an anterior communicating artery aneurysm. *Journal of Neurology, Neurosurgery and Psychiatry*, **46**, 704–709

VOLPE, B. T. and HIRST, W. (1983b) The characterization of an amnesic syndrome following hypoxic ischemic injury. *Archives of Neurology*, **40**, 436–440

VOLPE, B. T., HOLTZMAN, J. D. and HIRST, W. (1986) Further characterization of patients with amnesia following cardiac arrest: preserved recognition memory. *Neurology*, **36**, 408–411

VOLPE, B. T. and PETITO, C. K. (1985) Dementia with bilateral medial temporal lobe ischemia. *Neurology*, **35**, 1793–1797

VON CRAMON, D. Y., HEBEL, N. and SCHURI, U. (1985) A contribution to the anatomical basis of thalamic amnesia. *Brain*, **108**, 993–1008

VON WOWERN, F. (1966) Post-traumatic amnesia and confusion as an index of severity in head injury. *Acta Neurologica Scandinavica*, **42**, 373–378

VOSS, J., TYLER, S. W. and BISANZ, G. L. (1982) Prose comprehension and memory. In *Handbook of Research Methods in Human Memory and Cognition*, edited by C. R. Puff, pp. 349–353. New York: Academic Press

VROOM, F. Q. and GREER, M. (1972) Mercury vapour intoxication. *Brain*, **95**, 305–318

WABER, D. P. and HOLMES, J. M. (1986) Assessing children's memory productions of the Rey-Osterreith complex figure. *Journal of Clinical and Experimental Neuropsychology*, **8**, 563–580

WALKER, G. L., ROSSER, R., MASTAGLIA, F. L. and WALTON, J. N. (1984) Psychometric and cranial CT study in myotonic dystrophy. In *Clinical and Experimental Neurology*, Volume 20, edited by J. H. Tyrer and M. J. Eadie, pp. 161–168. Sydney: ADIS Health Science Press

WALLESCH, C. W., KORNHUBER, H. H., KUNZ, T. and BRUNNER, R. J. (1983) Neuropsychological deficits associated with small unilateral thalamic lesions. *Brain*, **106**, 141–152

WALSH, K. W. (1977) Neuropsychological aspects of modified leucotomy. In *Neurosurgical Treatment in Psychiatry, Pain and Epilepsy*, edited by W. H. Sweet, S. Obrador and J. G. Martin-Rodriguez, pp. 163–174. Baltimore: University Park Press

WALSH, K. W. (1978) *Neuropsychology. A clinical Approach.* London: Churchill Livingstone

WALTON, D. and BLACK, D. A. (1957) The validity of a psychological test of brain damage. *British Journal of Psychiatry,* **30,** 270–279

WALTON, J. N. (1953) The Korsakoff syndrome in spontaneous subarachnoid haemorrhage. *Journal of Mental Science,* **99,** 521–530

WARBURTON, J. W. (1963) The Babcock sentence in clinical practice. *British Journal of Medical Psychology,* **36,** 351–353

WARBURTON, J. W. (1967) Memory disturbance and Parkinson syndrome. *British Journal of Medical Psychology,* **40,** 169–171

WARINGTON, E. K. (1974) Deficient recognition memory in organic amnesia. *Cortex,* **10,** 289–291

WARRINGTON, E. K. (1984) *Recognition Memory Test.* Windsor: NFER-Nelson

WARRINGTON, E. K. (1986) Memory for facts and memory for events. *British Journal of Clinical Psychology,* **25,** 1–12

WARRINGTON, E. K. and JAMES, M. (1967) Disorders of visual perception in patients with localized cerebral lesions. *Neuropsychologia,* **5,** 253–266

WARRINGTON, E. K. and SHALLICE, T. (1969) The selective impairment of auditory verbal short-term memory. *Brain,* **92,** 885–896

WARRINGTON, E. K. and WEISKRANTZ, L. (1968) New method of testing long-term retention with special reference to amnesic patients. *Nature,* **217,** 972–974

WARRINGTON, E. K. and WEISKRANTZ, L. (1970. Amnesic syndrome: consolidation or retrieval? *Nature,* **228,** 628–630

WARRINGTON, E. K. and WEISKRANTZ, L. (1974) The effect of prior learning on subsequent retention in amnesic patients. *Neuropsychologia,* **12,** 419–428

WARRINGTON, E. K. and WEISKRANTZ, L. (1978) Further analyses of the prior learning effect in amnesic patients. *Neuropsychologia,* **16,** 169–176

WASTERLAIN, C. G. (1971) Are there two types of post-traumatic retrograde amnesia? *European Neurology,* **5,** 225–228

WATKINS, E. S. and OPPENHEIMER, D. K. (1962) Mental disturbances after thalamolysis. *Journal of Neurology, Neurosurgery and Psychiatry,* **25,** 243–250

WEBSTER'S THIRD NEW INTERNATIONAL DICTIONARY. (1966) Springfield, Mass: J&C Merriam Co

WECHSLER, D. (1945) A standardized memory scale for clinical use. *Journal of Psychology,* **19,** 87–95

WECHSLER, D. (1955) *Wechsler Adult Intelligence Scale.* New York: Psychological Corporation

WECHSLER, D. (1981) *Wechsler Adult Intelligence Scale – Revised.* New York: Psychological Corporation

WECHSLER, A. F., GUISADO, R. and BENTSON, J. R. (1974) Pneumoencephalographic demonstration of the anatomical basis of a postencephalitic Korsakoff syndrome. *Mount Sinai Journal of Medicine,* **41,** 230–234

WECHSLER, A. F., VERITY, M. A., ROSENSCHWEIN, S., FRIED, I. and SCHEIBEL, A. B. (1982) Pick's disease. A clinical, computed tomographic and histological study with golgi impregnation observations. *Archives of Neurology,* **39,** 287–290

WEINGARTEN, S. M., CHERLOW, D. G. and HALGREN, E. (1976) Relationship of hallucinations to depth structures of the temporal lobe. In *Neurosurgical Treatment in Psychiatry, Pain and Epilepsy,* edited by W. H. Sweet, S. Obrador and J. G. Martin-Rodriguez, pp. 553–568. Baltimore, University Park Press

WEINGARTNER, H. (1968) Verbal learning in patients with temporal lobe lesions. *J Verb Learn Verb Behav,* **7,** 520–526

WEINGARTNER, H., CAINE, H. D. and EBERT, M. H. (1979a) Encoding processes, learning and recall in Huntington's disease. In *Advances in Neurology,* Volume 23, edited by T. N. Chase, N. S. Wexler and A. Barbeau, pp. 215–226. New York: Raven Press

WEINGARTNER, H., CAINE, E. D. and EBERT, M. H. (1979b) Imagery, encoding and the retrieval of information from memory: some specific encoding-retrieval changes in Huntington's disease. *Journal of Abnormal Psychology,* **88,** 52–58

WEINGARTNER, H., COHEN, R. M., MURPHY, D. L., MARTELLO, J. and GERDT, C. (1981b) Cognitive processes in depression. *Archives of General Psychiatry,* **38,** 42–47

WEINGARTNER, H., COHEN, R. M., BUNNEY, W. E., EBERT, M. H. and KAYE, W. (1982b) Memory learning impairments in progressive dementia and depression. *American Journal of Psychiatry,* **139,** 135–136

WEINGARTNER, H., GRAFMAN, J., BOUTELLE, W., KAYE, W. and MARTIN, P. R. (1983) Forms of memory failure. *Science,* **221,** 380–382

WEINGARTNER, H., KAYE, W., SMALLBERG, S. A., EBERT, M. H., GILLIN, J. C. and SITARAM, N. (1981a) Memory failures in progressive idiopathic dementia. *Journal of Abnormal Psychology,* **90,** 187–196

WEINGARTNER, H., KAYE, W., SMALLBERG, S., COHEN, R., EBERT, M. H., GILLIN, J. C. et al. (1982a) Determinants of memory failures in dementia. In *Alzheimer's Disease: A Report of Progress,* edited by S. Corkin *et al.*, pp. 171–176. New York: Raven Press

WEINSTEIN, E. A. (1969) Patterns of reduplication in organic brain disease. In *Handbook of Clinical Neurology,* Vol. 3, edited by P. J. Vinken, and G. W. Bruyn, pp. 251–257. Amsterdam: North Holland Publishing Company

WEINSTEIN, E. A. and LYERLY, O. G. (1968) Confabulation following brain injury. *Archives of General Psychiatry,* **18,** 348–354

WEISKRANTZ, L. (1985) On issues and theories of the human amnesic syndrome. In *Memory Systems of the Brain,* edited by N. M. Weinberger, J. L. McGaugh and G. Lynch, pp. 380–418. New York: The Guilford Press

WEISKRANTZ, L. and WARRINGTON, E. K. (1979) Conditioning in amnesic patients. *Neuropsychologia,* **17,** 187–194

WESTREICH, G., ALTER, M. and LUNDGREN, S. (1975) Effect of cyclandelate on dementia. *Stroke,* **6,** 535–538

WETTSTEIN, A. and SPIEGEL, R. (1985) Performance of patients with Alzheimer's disease treated with RS86, a direct muscarine agonist. In *Modern Approaches to the Dementias,* edited by F. C. Rose, pp. 167–178. Basel: Karger

WETZEL, D. C. and SQUIRE, L. R. (1980) Encoding in anterograde amnesia. *Neuropsychologia,* **18,** 177–184

WEXLER, N. S. (1979) Perceptual-motor, cognitive and emotional characteristics of persons at risk for Huntington's disease. In *Advances in Neurology,* Volume 23, edited by T. N. Chase, N. S. Wexler and A. Barbeau, pp. 257–271. New York: Raven Press

WHELAN, T. B., SCHTEINGART, D. E., STARKMAN, M. N. and SMITH, A. (1980) Neuropsychological deficits in Cushing's syndrome. *Journal of Nervous and Mental Disease,* **168,** 753–757

WHELIHAN, W. M., LESHER, E. L., KLEEBAN, M. H. and GRANICK, S. (1984) Mental status and memory assessment as predictors of dementia. *Journal of Gerontology,* **39,** 572–576

WHITE, J. G., MERRICK, M. and HARBISON, J. J. (1969) Williams scale for the measurement of memory: test reliability and validity in a psychiatric population. *Br J Soc Clin Psychol,* **8,** 141–151

WHITEHEAD, A. (1975) Recognition memory in dementia. *Br J Soc Clin Psychol,* **14,** 191–194

WHITEHEAD, A. (1984) Psychological intervention in dementia. In *Handbook of Studies on Psychiatry and Old Age,* edited by D. W. Kay and G. D. Burrows, pp. 182–199. Amsterdam: Elsevier Science

WHITFORD, H. C. (1966) *A Dictionary of American Homophones and Homographs.* New York: Teachers College

WHITTY, C. W. M. and LEWIN, W. (1960) A Korsakoff syndrome in the post-cingulectomy confusional state. *Brain,* **83,** 648–653

WHITTY, C. W. M. and ZANGWILL, O. (1977) Editors. Traumatic amnesia. In *Amnesia,* London: Butterworths

WIESER, H. G., HAILEMARIAM, S., REGAARD, M. and LANDIS, T. (1985) Unilateral limbic epileptic status activity: stereo EEG, behavioural, and cognitive data. *Epilepsia,* **26,** 19–29

WIESER, H. G. and YASARGIL, M. G. (1982) Selective amygdalohippocampectomy as a surgical treatment of mesiobasal limbic epilepsy. *Surg Neurol,* **17,** 445–457

WIKKELSO, C., ANDERSSON, H., BLOMSTRAND, C. and LINDQVIST, G. (1982) The clinical effect of lumbar puncture in normal pressure hydrocephalus. *Journal of Neurology, Neurosurgery and Psychiatry,* **45,** 64–69

WILKINSON, D. A. and CARLEN, P. L. (1980) Relationship between neuropsychological test performance to brain morphology in amnesic and non-amnesic patients. *Acta Psychiatrica Scandinavica,* **62** (Suppl. 286), 89–101

WILKINSON, T. S. and NELSON, T. O. (1984) Fact retrieval 2: a Pascal program for assessing someone's recall of general-information facts, confidence about recall correctness, feeling-of-knowing judgements for nonrecalled facts, and recognition of non-recalled facts. *Behav Res Meth Instrum & Comp,* **16,** 486–488

WILLIAMS, F. J. B. and WALSHE, J. M. (1981) Wilson's disease: an analysis of the cranial computerized tomographic appearances found in 60 patients and the changes in response to treatment with chelating agents. *Brain*, **104**, 735–752

WILLIAMS, M. (1965) *Memory Testing in Clinical Practice*. Oxford: Pergamon Press

WILLIAMS, M. (1968) The measurement of memory in clinical practice. *Br J. Soc Clin Psychol*, **7**, 19–34

WILLIAMS, M. (1969) Traumatic retrograde amnesia and normal forgetting. In *The Pathology of Memory*, edited by G. Talland and N. Waugh, pp. 75–80. New York: Academic Press

WILLIAMS, M. (1977) Clinical assessment of memory. In *Advances in Psychological Assessment*, Volume 4, edited by P. McReynolds, pp. 426–461. San Francisco: Jossey-Bass

WILLIAMS, M. and McGEE, T. F. (1964) Psychological study of carotid occlusion and endarterectomy. *Archives of Neurology*, **10**, 293–297

WILLIAMS, M. and OWEN, G. (1977) Word vs picture recognition in amnesic and aphasic patients. *Neuropsychologia*, **15**, 351–354

WILLIAMS, M. and PENNYBACKER, J. (1954) Memory disturbances in third ventricle tumours. *Journal of Neurology, Neurosurgery and Psychiatry*, **17**, 115–123

WILLIAMS, M. and SMITH, H. V. (1954) Mental disturbances in tuberculosis meningitis. *Journal of Neurology, Neurosurgery and Psychiatry*, **17**, 173–182

WILLIAMS, M. and ZANGWILL, O. L. (1952) Memory defects after head injury. *Journal of Neurology, Neurosurgery and Psychiatry*, **15**, 54–58

WILLIAMSON, A. M., TEO, R. K. C. and SANDERSON, J. (1982) Occupational mercury exposure and its consequences for behaviour. *Int Arch Occup Environ Health*, **50**, 273–286

WILSON, B. A. (1981) Teaching a patient to remember people's names after removal of a left temporal lobe tumour. *Behavioural Psychotherapy*, **9**, 338–344

WILSON, B. A. (1982) Success and failure in memory training following a cerebral vascular accident. *Cortex*, **18**, 581–594

WILSON, B. A. (1987) *Rehabilitation of Memory*. New York: Guilford Press

WILSON, B. A., COCKBURN, J. and BADDELEY, A. D. (1985) *The Rivermead Behavioural Memory Test*. Reading: Thames Valley Test Company

WILSON, B. A., COCKBURN, J. and BADDELEY, A. D. (1987) *Rivermead Behavioural Memory Test. Manual Supplement 2*. Reading: Thames Valley Test Company (in press)

WILSON, B. A. and MOFFAT, N. (1984) Editors. *Clinical Management of Memory Problems*. London: Croom Helm

WILSON, B. C. (1986) An approach to the neuropsychological assessment of the preschool child with developmental deficits. In *Handbook of Clinical Neuropsychology*, edited by S. B. Filskov and T. J. Boll, pp. 121–171. Volume 2. New York: Wiley

WILSON, R. S., BACON, L. D., FOX, J. H. and KASZNIAK, A. W. (1983b) Primary memory and secondary memory in dementia of the Alzheimer type. *Journal of Clinical Neuropsychology*, **5**, 337–344

WILSON, R. S., BACON, L. D., FOX, J. H., KRAMER, R. L. and KASZNIAK, A. W. (1983a) Word frequency effect and recognition memory in dementia. *Journal of Clinical Neuropsychology*, **5**, 97–104

WILSON, R. S., BACON, L. D., KASZNIAK, A. W. and FOX, J. H. (1982b) The episodic-semantic memory distinction and paired associate learning. *J Consult Clin Psychol*, **50**, 154–155

WILSON, R. S., COMO, P. G., GARRON, D. C., KLAWANS, H. L., BARR, A. and KLAWANS, D. (1987) Memory failure in Huntington's disease. *Journal of Clinical and Experimental Neuropsychology*, **9**, 147–154

WILSON, R. S., KASZNIAK, A. W., BACON, L. D., FOX, J. H. and KELLY, M. P. (1982a) Facial recognition memory in dementia. *Cortex*, **18**, 329–336

WILSON, R. S., KASZNIAK, A. W. and FOX, J. H. (1981) Remote memory in senile dementia. *Cortex*, **17**, 41–48

WILSON, R. S., KASZNIAK, A. W., KLAWANS, H. L. and GARRON, D. C. (1980) High speed memory scanning in parkinsonism. *Cortex*, **16**, 67–72

WILSON, R. S., KOLLER, W. and KELLY, M. P. (1980) The amnesia of transient global amnesia. *Journal of Clinical Neuropsychology*, **2**, 259–266

WINBLAD, B., HARDY, J., BACKMAN, L. and NILSSON, L-G. (1985) Memory function and brain biochemistry in normal aging and senile dementia. *Annals of the New York Academy of Sciences*, **444**, 255–267

WINOCUR, G. and KINSBOURNE, M. (1978) Contextual cueing as an aid to Korsakoff amnesics. *Neuropsychologia*, **16**, 671–682

WINOCUR, G., KINSBOURNE, M. and MOSCOVITCH, M. (1981) The effect of cueing on release from proactive interference in Korsakoff amnesic patients. *J Exp Psychol: Learn Mem Cogn*, **7**, 56–65

WINOCUR, G., OXBURY, S., ROBERTS, R., AGNETTI, V. and DAVIS, C. (1984) Amnesia in a patient with bilateral lesions of the thalamus. *Neuropsychologia*, **22**, 123–144

WINOCUR, G. and WEISKRANTZ, L. (1976) An investigation of paired-associate learning in amnesic patients. *Neuropsychologia*, **14**, 97–110

WOLLEN, K. A., COX S. D., COAHRAN, M. M., SHEA, D. S. and KIRBY, R. F. (1980) Frequency of occurrence and concreteness ratings of homograph meanings. *Behav Res Meth & Instrum*, **12**, 8–15

WOOD, F. B., EBERT, V. and KINSBOURNE, M. (1982) The episodic-semantic memory distinction in memory and amnesia: clinical and experimental observations. In *Human Memory and Amnesia*, edited by L. Cermak, pp. 167–193. Hillsdale, N J: Lawrence Erlbaum Associates

WOOD, R. A. (1984) Memory loss. *British Medical Journal*, **288**, 1443–1447

WOODRUFF, M. L. (1974) Subconvulsive epileptiform discharge and behavioural impairment. *Behav Biol*, **11**, 431–458

WOODS, B. T., SCHOENE, W. and KNEISLEY, L. (1982) Are hippocampal lesions sufficient to cause amnesia? *Journal of Neurology, Neurosurgery and Psychiatry*, **45**, 243–247

WOOLSEY, R. M. and NELSON, J. S. (1975) Asymptomatic destruction of the fornix in man. *Archives of Neurology*, **32**, 566–568

WURTMAN, R. J., CORKIN, S. H. and GROWDON, J. H. (1984) Editors. *Alzheimer's Disease: Advances in Basic Research and Therapies*. Cambridge: Center for Brain Sciences and Metabolism Charitable Trust

WYKE, M. and WARRINGTON, E. K. (1960) An experimental analysis of confabulation in a case of Korsakoff's syndrome using a tachistocopic method. *Journal of Neurology, Neurosurgery and Psychiatry*, **23**, 327–333

YESAVAGE, J. A., WESTPHAL, J. and RUSH, L. (1981) Senile dementia: combined pharmacological and psychologic treatment. *Journal of the American Geriatric Society*, **29**, 164–171

YIN, R. K. (1970) Face recognition by brain-injured patients: a dissociable ability? *Neuropsychologia*, **8**, 395–402

YOHMAN, J. R., PARSONS, O. A. and LEBER, W. R. (1985) Lack of recovery in male alcoholics' memory performance one year after treatment. *Alcoholism: Clinical and Experimental Research*, **9**, 114–117

YOUNG, A. C., SAUNDERS, J. and PONSFORD, J. R. (1976) Mental change as an early feature of multiple sclerosis. *Journal of Neurology, Neurosurgery and Psychiatry*, **39**, 1008–1013

YOUNG, J., HALL, P. and BLAKEMORE, C. (1974) Treatment of the cerebral manifestations of arteriosclerosis with cyclandelate. *British Journal of Psychiatry*, **124**, 177–180

YOUNG, R. I., RANDALL, C. P., KAPLAN, P. W., JAMES, A., BYDDEN, G. M. and STEINER, R. E. (1983) Nuclear magnetic resonance (NMR) imaging in white matter disease of the brain using spin-echo sequences. *J. Comp. Assist. Tomography*, **7**, 290–294

ZAIDEL, D. W. (1986) Memory for scenes in stroke patients. *Brain*, **109**, 547–560

ZAIDEL, D. W. and RAUSCH, R. (1981) Effects of semantic organization on the recognition of pictures following temporal lobectomy. *Neuropsychologia*, **19**, 813–817

ZAIDEL, D. and SPERRY, R. W. (1974) Memory impairment after commissurotomy in man. *Brain*, **97**, 263–272

ZANGWILL, O. (1943) Clinical tests of memory impairment. *Proceedings of the Royal Society of Medicine*, **36**, 576–580

ZANGWILL, O. L. (1953) Disorientation for age. *Journal of Mental Science*, **99**, 698–701

ZANGWILL, O. L. (1967) The Grunthal-Storring case of amnesic syndrome. *British Journal of Psychiatry*, **113**, 113–128

ZANGWILL, O. L. (1977) The amnesic syndrome. In *Amnesia*, edited by C. W. M. Whitty and O. L. Zangwill. London: Butterworths

ZANGWILL, O. L. (1983) Disorders of memory. In *Handbook of Psychiatry 1. General Psychopathology*, edited by H. Shepherd and O. L. Zangwill, pp. 97–113. Cambridge: Cambridge University Press

ZATORRE, R. J. (1985) Discrimination and recognition of tonal melodies after unilateral cerebral excisions. *Neuropsychologia*, **23**, 31–41

ZATORRE, R. J. and McENTEE, W. J. (1983) Semantic deficits in a case of traumatic amnesia. *Brain and Cognition*, **2**, 331–345

ZEITLIN, C. and ODDY, M. (1984) Cognitive impairment in patients with severe migraine. *British Journal of Clinical Psychology,* **23,** 27–35

ZIEGLER, D. K., KAUFMAN, A. and MARSHALL, H. E. (1977) Abrupt memory loss associated with a thalamic tumour. *Archives of Neurology,* **34,** 545–548

ZIESAT, H. A., LOGUE, P. E. and McCARTY, S. M. (1980) Psychological measurement of memory deficits in dialysis patients. *Percept Mot Skills,* **50,** 311–318

ZOLA-MORGAN, S., COHEN, N. J. and SQUIRE, L. R. (1983) Recall of remote episodic memory in amnesia. *Neuropsychologia,* **21,** 487–500

ZOLA-MORGAN, S. M. and OBERG, R. G. (1980) Recall of life experiences in an alcoholic Korsakoff patient: a naturalistic approach. *Neuropsychologia,* **18,** 549–557

ZOLA-MORGAN, S. and SQUIRE, L. R. (1985) Complementary approaches to the study of memory: human amnesia and animal models. In *Memory Systems of the Brain,* edited by N. M. Weinberger, J. L. McGaugh and G. Lynch, pp. 463–478. New York: The Guilford Press

ZOLA-MORGAN, S., SQUIRE, L. R. and AMARAL, D. G. (1986) Human amnesia and the medial temporal region: enduring memory impairment following a bilateral lesion limited to field CA1 of the hippocampus. *Journal of Neuroscience,* **6,** 2950–2967

Author index

Aarts, J. H. P., 186
Abbruzzese, G., 58
Aberg, I., 151
Acker, C., 15, 30
Acker, W., 15, 30, 172, 173, 174
Adams, R. D., 143, 154, 158, 159, 168, 171
Adams, R. J., 72
Adeloye, A., 88
Adolfsson, R., 125
Agnoli, A., 130
Agu, G. A., 187
Ahmed, I., 51, 54, 62
Aimard, G., 21, 55, 74, 143
Ajuriaguerra, J., 71
Albert, M. L., 20
Albert, M. S., 36, 115, 128, 132, 138, 155, 166, 172, 174, 177
Alexander, E., 75
Alexander, M. P., 8, 20, 21, 48
Allen, I. V., 83, 88
Allport, D. A., 1
Alter, M., 66
Alterman, A. I., 172
Amacher, A. L., 207
Amaral, D. G., 149, 156
Amberla, K., 115
Amsel, A., 199
Anderson, R., 74, 208
Andrewes, D. G., 188
Andrysiak, T., 175
Andy, O. J., 208, 210
Angelergues, R., 74
Ansel, R., 130
Appelhof, A., 146
Apuzzo, M. L., 207
Arbit, J., 22
Archibald, Y. M., 207, 208
Arendt, T., 169
Arlien-Soborg, P., 175
Arnvig, E., 176
Asken, M. J., 66
Assal, G., 55, 74, 143
Asso, D., 129
Astrom, J., 177
Aughton, M., 110

Baade, L. E., 2
Babb, T. L., 186
Babcock, H., 27, 44
Baddeley, A. D., 18, 26, 28, 41, 42, 102, 103, 154, 161, 167, 168, 216
Bahrick, H. P., 36
Baird, A. D., 45, 53, 64
Bakare, C. G. M., 88
Balasubramaniam, V., 208
Baldwin, M., 190
Bale, R. N., 152
Ball, J. A. C., 65
Ballantyne, H. T., 47, 48
Baloh, R., 176
Bandera, R., 115
Banna, M., 75
Barber, H. O., 62
Barbizet, J., 30, 33, 35, 143, 166
Barnett, H. J. M., 133, 141
Barry, C., 104
Barth, J. T., 104
Basso, A., 56
Bast-Kessler, C., 162
Battig, W. F., 214
Bauer, R. M., 108
Beal, M. F., 77
Beaney, R. P., 71
Beatty, P. A., 132
Beatty, W. W., 126
Bechtereva, M. P., 192
Becker, J., 31, 172, 173
Beckman, J., 176
Bedou, G., 77
Beller, S. A., 125
Ben-Shmuel, A., 208
Bender, M. B., 86
Bengtsson, M., 148
Bennet-Levy, J., 18, 29
Benson, D. F., 16, 21, 52, 54, 99, 100, 102, 165
Bentin, S., 199
Benton, A. L., 9, 13, 19, 22, 25, 27, 29, 38, 107, 135
Bentson, J. R., 143
Berglund, M., 135, 141
Bergman, H., 174

Index

Principal sections about a particular subject are marked in **bold**

Also of interest...

NEUROPSYCHOLOGY OF THE AMNESIC SYNDROME

ALAN J. PARKIN, NICHOLAS R.C LENG
(University of Sussex)

"Overall this book can certainly be recommended as a useful and clear introduction to the psychology of amnesic syndromes. As such it fills a definite gap and deserves to be widely read by members of the various disciplines concerned with the problem of amnesia and not just psychologists." **E. Miller** *in Journal of Neurology, Neurosurgery and Psychiatry.*

"[The authors] have succeeded in producing an eminently readable and well-organised guide to the understanding of a complex subject... I am sure it will become a valuable resource for undergraduates, researchers, and clinicians." **Janet Cockburn** *(McDonnell-Pew Centre for Cognitive Neuroscience and Rivermead Rehabilitation Centre) in Neuropsychological Rehabilitation.*

"Overall, this book manages to integrate clinical and theoretical issues in memory research in a most skilful way. In my view it is most appropriate and readable for students and as well for clinicians with a special interest in the neuropsychology of memory. Irrespective of the numerous publications in this field, it is not easy to find a well-organized, high level book with not too many confusing details for beginners. In addition, this book is an enjoyable reading experience at a more advanced level, too. **Hely Kalsksa** *(University of Helsinki) in The European Journal of Cognitive Psychology.*

Contents: Preface. Defining the Amnesic Syndrome. Assessment of Memory Disorders. Wernicke-Korsakoff Syndrome. Thalamic and other Diencephalic Amnesias. Temporal Lobe Amnesia. Herpes Simplex Encephalitis. Ruptured Aneurysms of the Anterior Communicating Artery. Some Theoretical Issues. Remediation. *Glossary. Author Index. Subject Index.*

ISBN 0-86377-200-5 1993 216pp. $46.50 £24.95 hbk
ISBN 0-86377-201-3 1993 216pp $24.95 £12.95 pbk
Brain Damage, Behaviour and Cognition Series.

Published by:
Lawrence Erlbaum Associates, Ltd.,
27 Church Road, Hove East Sussex, BN3 2FA UK.
Tel: (0273) 748427 Fax: (0273) 722180